Identifying
ANTIQUE BRITISH
SILVER

Identifying
ANTIQUE BRITISH
SILVER

~ T.R. POOLE ~

BLOOMSBURY

First published 1988

Copyright © 1988 by T.R. Poole
Bloomsbury Publishing Limited, 2 Soho Square, London W1V 5DE

British Library Cataloguing in Publication Data

Poole, T.R. (Thomas R.)
Identifying antique British silver.
1. British silver products to 1900
I. Title
739.2′3741
ISBN 0 7475 0092 4

Designed by Clare Clements
Typeset by Bookworm Typesetting, Manchester
Printed in Great Britain by Butler & Tanner Ltd, Frome and London

CONTENTS

ACKNOWLEDGEMENTS

Grateful acknowledgements and thanks for permission, help and
co-operation are extended to the following:
The Joint Committee of the Assay Offices of Great Britain, for
permission to use the date letters and Assay Office marks.
Messrs Sotheby & Co, for permission to reproduce illustrations
from their catalogues.
The Worshipful Company of Goldsmiths.
The British Museum Library.
The Cambridge University Press.

INTRODUCTION

Information necessary to establish the exact origin of a piece of antique silver, and thus its correct value, is of upmost importance both to dealers and amateurs starting a collection. It is a common mistake to believe that the whole truth about a piece of antique silver is contained in the hallmarked date letter which in fact only reveals the date and place of assay. Proper identification requires that the mark, age and design of a piece are all compatible. However, even when these facts have been established the value of a piece remains very dependent on the status of its maker. The maker's mark is thus as important as any other. *Identifying Antique British Silver* examines all these essential elements to enable the reader to correctly identify the origin and possible value of a piece of silver.

Identifying Antique British Silver is a comprehensive general guide to antique silver made in Britain over the last 300 years. It looks in detail at domestic silver made in the period 1700–1900; domestic silver made prior to 1700 is rare and beyond the pocket of most collectors. *Identifying Antique British Silver* contains information on recognizing hallmarks, includes a chart of the most common punch shapes and looks at how to date a piece of silver from date letters and the style of decoration. An additional feature is the listing of over 2,000 silver makers and their marks, organized alphabetically by both maker's name and mark.

So much important information for collectors is contained in the hallmark of a piece of silver – the year it was made, where it was made and who made it. *The development of the hallmark* looks briefly at the origins and function of each type of hallmark and comes right up to date by including the most recent commemorative marks for Elizabeth II's Silver Jubilee in 1977.

Punch shapes play an important part in the identification of the date and maker of a piece of silver. Each date letter cycle for each Assay Office is set within a particular punch shape (see pages 18 to 33) as is each maker's mark (see pages 135 to 281). A standardized method of punch shape definition has been devised and a chart of the main punch shapes used appears on page 14.

The section *How to date silver* clearly lists each date letter for the major Assay Offices to the present day and introduces a system of approximate dating for quick reference. It also gives, in chart form, a chronology of the main events in the development of the manufacture of silver, from the introduction of the Britannia Standard in 1697 to the fashion for Art Nouveau designs at the end of the nineteenth century.

How can you tell the likely period of a piece of silver if the hallmark is rubbed or badly stamped? How can you tell if a piece is a reproduction or a forgery? *Silver A-Z* is an illustrated guide to nearly 100 types of silver object, from alms dishes to wine tasters. With over 1,000 illustrations it charts the changing fashions in silver design, explains the uses of such items as biggins and vinaigrettes and gives helpful information on the location of hallmarks and warnings about where damage or replacements are most likely to occur.

The final section of the book takes a look at British *Silver makers* – a chronology is included of the most important silversmiths since the end of the seventeenth century giving the date they first registered their marks. Over 2,000 makers' marks are listed with dates of registration, town of assay, dates of earliest and latest examples of their work and additional features of their marks which may aid identification. The information is also given alphabetically by maker's name to help collectors interested in work by particular silversmiths. Only silversmiths with existing and authoritatively recorded work are included.

The quality of wrought plate (manufactured articles of silver) has been controlled since the beginning of the fourteenth century, when it was considered necessary to protect the public from fraud by regulating the standard of silver used in manufacture. Makers had to take their wares to be examined at an Assay Office, where the quality of the metal had to be checked and passed.

This was the beginning of the hallmarking system. It has been developed and refined over a period of several hundred years, with legislation introduced to control the quality of the silver and the payment of tax, as well as to register the identity of the maker and the year and place of manufacture.

The box below gives the date when each type of mark was first used and what it signifies.

Type of mark	What it signifies	Date first used
mark of origin	the Assay Office town	from 1300
maker's mark	identity of the maker	1363
date letter	year of assay	1478
sterling mark *or*	purity of the metal	1544
Britannia standard		1697
duty mark	payment of tax	1784

mark of
origin
London

maker's
mark
Paul Storr

date
letter
1801

sterling
assay mark
Lion Passant

sovereign's
head
duty mark

THE MARK OF ORIGIN. This indicates the town of the Assay Office to which the wrought plate was taken to be assayed. It is also known as the town mark.

London has been represented by a leopard's head since an Act of Parliament of 1300. The style has changed over the centuries. It was uncrowned at first and then, in 1478, when the date letter was first adopted, a crown was added. This remained until 1821. Several provincial offices used the leopard's head in addition to their own mark of origin.

Birmingham gold and silversmiths, increasing in importance by the eighteenth century, became dissatisfied with the necessity of transporting their wares to Chester for assay. Matthew Boulton, who had founded a thriving factory at Soho Hill, Handsworth, petitioned Parliament for the establishment of a Birmingham office. Sheffield manufacturers, in a similar position, joined him in his lobby of Parliament. The petition was at first opposed by the London Goldsmiths' Company, but the Royal assent was finally given in 1773, granting Birmingham and Sheffield the power to assay their own wares. The Birmingham mark of origin is an anchor. (*See also* Sheffield.)

Chester used the city arms as the mark of origin from 1779, but there is evidence of the regulation of the manufacture of silver as early as the thirteenth century. The town mark of three wheatsheaves and a sword was used continuously until 1962 when the office was closed, with the last date letter M.

Dublin began using the crowned harp, which was also the sterling mark (see page 12), as the mark of origin in 1637 when the Guild of Goldsmiths was established. Hibernia was added in 1730 as the duty mark. It replaced the harp as the mark of origin in 1806 and the king's head became the duty mark.

Edinburgh has had a mark of origin since 1457 when the Deacon, as the Assay Master, stamped his initials, together with the mark of the gold- or silversmith, on each item of plate. An emblematic mark was introduced in 1485. This is a castle with three fortified towers on a rock, taken from the city arms, and is still in use. All Scottish trade was supervised by Edinburgh until the Glasgow office was opened in 1819 by statute of George III.

 Exeter had a Guild of Goldsmiths before the reign of Elizabeth I, and the earliest town mark was the Roman numeral X. After 1701 the city arms, a three-towered castle, was adopted as the mark of origin, but between 1831 and 1837 it became three separate towers. The office was closed in 1882, with the last date letter F.

 Glasgow goldsmiths and metalworkers were protected by an Incorporation of Hammermen in 1536, but it was not until 1819 that Glasgow's Assay Office was established and the city's date letters began. The mark of origin is based on the city arms, depicting a tree, fish, bell and bird. The office closed in 1964 with the last date letter R for 1963.

 Newcastle goldsmiths were mentioned in an ordinance of 1248, and the original Charter of Incorporation of 1536 still exists. From about 1670, the mark of origin was the Newcastle coat of arms, 'The Three Castles'. This design varies considerably, possibly owing to the master goldsmiths having been allowed to have their own town mark stamp. The office closed in 1884. The last date letter was U for 1883.

 Sheffield gained the right to assay silver at the same time as Birmingham. The town mark is a crown. The crown with the date letter in a single punch was also adopted by Sheffield for use on small wares (in addition to conventional marks), from 1780 to 1865. It is interesting to note that much of the business connected with the Assay Bill for Birmingham and Sheffield was conducted at the tavern popular with politicians, the Crown and Anchor in the Strand, which may have been what suggested these emblems to Matthew Boulton and his Sheffield friends.

 York Guilds of Goldsmiths date from 1423, and an early reference mentions the 'towch and mark belonging to this cittye, called the half leopard head and half flower de luce'. After 1700 the arms of the city became the town mark: a cross charged with five lions rampant. The office was closed between 1713 and 1778, and was finally shut down in 1856, with the last date letter V.

Assay Offices and guilds have existed in many other towns. The principal ones are listed below, with dates of closure or approximate last dates. Silver bearing these marks is becoming quite rare and, correspondingly, more valuable.

Aberdeen 1880		Gateshead c.1680	

 Aberdeen 1880

 Arbroath 1840

 Banff 1855

 Bristol 1880

 Canongate 1836

 Carlisle c.1660

 Cork 1840

 Dundee 1850

 Elgin 1830

 Galway 1750

 Gateshead c.1680

 Greenock c.1830

 Hull 1710

 Inverness 1880

 King's Lynn 1700

 Leeds 1700

 Leicester 1695

 Limerick 1846

Lincoln 1710

 Montrose 1817

Norwich 1701　　 Taunton 1700

 Perth 1850　　 Truro c.1630

 Shrewsbury 1695　　 Wick c.1820

 Tain 1800　　 Youghal c.1720

THE MAKER'S MARK. This identifies the maker, and consists usually of his or her initials within a punch of varying shape. It may also identify a wholesaler or retailer, and is now called the sponsor's mark. It was first instituted in England by statute in 1363 when all master goldsmiths were directed to record and register their own marks. Early marks were often simply a symbol connected with the maker's name or the location of his or her business. Later, symbols were used in conjunction with initials (see the marks for Andrew Ravan and Joseph Bell below). The business side of gold- or silversmiths' work was often conducted at the local tavern, whose sign frequently became associated with their business and would be displayed on their trade cards and makers' marks. For example, David Hennell was described as 'Working Goldsmith at the Flower de Lis and Star in Gutter Lane, Ye Corner of Cary Lane, Cheapside.' The most common symbols are pellets or roundels (dots) mostly appearing between initials. Their precise significance is uncertain but they are often the only differentiation between two or more similar marks. Mullets (stars) also appear frequently; these may have originated from the rowel of a spur or have been part of a tavern sign.

With the introduction of the Britannia Standard in 1697, makers were required to register new marks consisting of the first two letters of their surname. From 1720, however, they were again allowed to use their initials. For a time, both styles were in use, but in 1739 makers were required to register new marks, consisting of their initials only. The only addition permitted was a pellet, a mullet, or a crown to signify Royal patronage. Women silversmiths' marks are often contained within a lozenge- or diamond-shaped punch (see Louisa Courtauld's mark below), presumably following the heraldic practice of portraying the arms of maids or widows. Hester Bateman's mark (see below) is an exception. Makers may thus each have more than one mark, and different marks when working on their own account from those used when working in partnership with other silversmiths. The following are a few examples of interesting makers' marks.

 William Grundy　　 Andrew Raven

 John Tuite　　 Richard Syng

 Francis Nelme　　 Seth Lofthouse

 David Hennell　　 Joseph Bell I

 Paul de Lamerie　　 Pierre Platel

 Humphrey Payne　　 Hester Bateman

 Ralph Leeke　　 Samuel Lee

 Peter and Jonathan Bateman　　 Louisa Courtauld

 Rebecca and William Emes　　 John, Henry and Charles Lias

THE DATE LETTER. A letter of the alphabet, changed annually indicates the year in which the plate was assayed (examined). This was originally introduced as a means of identifying the Assay Master (an annual post) in each town, so that he could be held responsible if any malpractice occurred. The system was first established in London in 1478, with a cycle of 20 letters beginning with A and omitting J, V, W, X, Y and Z. Each Assay Office adopted the date-letter system at a different time, and each town had its own style. Sheffield, for example, generally included the letters W, X, Y and Z, while Dublin introduced the letter V to its series from 1841. Each town also changed its date letter at a different time of year: London in May, Birmingham and Sheffield in July, Edinburgh in October and Dublin in January. At the end of each alphabetical cycle a new design of alphabet and a new punch shape was introduced. The 1478 London series remained unchanged until 1697, when a new series, called the court hand cycle, was started, following the introduction of the Britannia standard. This series lasted until January 1975, when the remaining four British Assay Offices agreed to use the same style of date letter. The use of the 20-letter cycle adopted by the London Assay Office has greatly facilitated the identification of dates. For example, between 1700 and 1975 (when the system was changed), the letter E is used to denote a new century and every twentieth year thereafter (1800, 1820, 1840, 1860 etc.). (See the section *How to Date Silver* and the London date letters for further information.) Unfortunately the same method of identifying dates cannot be applied in the case of other Assay Offices, because cycles were often interrupted or changed.

 THE STERLING MARK. A lion passant (i.e. walking, with one front paw raised) confirms the quality of English silver as 92.5 per cent pure. By the seventeenth century there was a growing practice among silversmiths of clipping the edges off coins and melting them down to augment their supplies of metal, and it became necessary to introduce a new standard. (Coins remained at the old standard, which meant that the substitution of clippings became difficult.) The higher, or Britannia, standard of 95.8 per cent, introduced in 1697, was indicated by a lion's head erased (i.e torn off at the neck) and the figure of Britannia, in place of the lion passant. The new metal was, however, more expensive and less durable, and the complaints of the silversmiths finally resulted in a resumption, in 1720, of the old standard of 92.5 per cent, again indicated by the lion passant. The Britannia standard was still allowed optionally and remains so today. Edinburgh gold- and silversmiths used the Deacon's or Assay Master's initials as their sterling mark, but after 1759 used the thistle. Glasgow used the lion rampant and Dublin the crowned harp.

 THE DUTY MARK. Although duty had been payable on silver for varying periods, it was not until 1784 that a mark was introduced to indicate that duty (at a rate of 6d per ounce of silver) had been paid at the time of assay. The first mark was a representation of the head of George III; subsequent marks depicted the heads of George IV, William IV and Queen Victoria. The duty mark was stamped incuse (inwards) in 1784 and 1785, and thereafter in cameo (relief). The duty varied from time to time and the stamp was often omitted from small pieces. At the Dublin office the duty mark was not stamped until 1807, and at the Glasgow office not until 1819. After 1890 the duty was abolished and the mark dropped.

COMMEMORATIVE MARKS. There are three additional marks which have been used to commemorate Royal events and are found on twentieth-century silver:

 Silver Jubilee Mark to commemorate the 25th anniversary of the accession of George V and Queen Mary in 1935. Found on silver plate in the years 1933–35.

 Coronation Mark to commemorate the accession of Elizabeth II in 1953. Found on silver plate with the date letters for 1952 and 1953.

 Silver Jubilee Mark to commemorate the 25th anniversary of the accession of Elizabeth II in 1977. Found on silver plate with the date letter for 1977.

Ellis Gamble *Ellis Gamble*
GOLDSMITH, ORFEURE,
at the Golden Angel in a L'Enseigne de l'Ange d'Or
Cranbourn-Street, dans Cranbourn-Street
LEICESTER-FIELDS. LEICESTER-FIELDS
Makes, Buys & Sells all Fait, Achete, & Vend toutes
sorts of Plate, Rings, & sortes d'Argenterie, Baques
Jewells &c. & Bijoux, &c.

PRIMARY PUNCH SHAPES

The primary shapes indicate the basic forms of punch shapes. These may, however, be more complex, with further detail added either at the top or at the bottom. Punch shapes help in dating and are also a useful aid to identification of makers; each Assay Office used one style of punch shape for each alphabetical cycle and each maker used one particular shape.

 rectangle

 bevelform

 cavetto

 square

 quadriform

 cone

 trigon

 lozenge

 rhombus

tetragon

 hexagon

 pentagon

 octagon

 polygon

 taperform

 cruciform

 circle

oval

ovoid

billet

domeform

kidney

 sinistroid

 dextroid

 heart

 baluster

 reelform

 woolsack

 cinquefoil

 bifoil

 trefoil

 quatrefoil

 sexfoil

 multifoil

invectoid

 engrailoid

waveform

spikeform

profiloid

 sexfoil

 multifoil

 invectoid

 engrailoid

 waveform

 spikeform

 profiloid

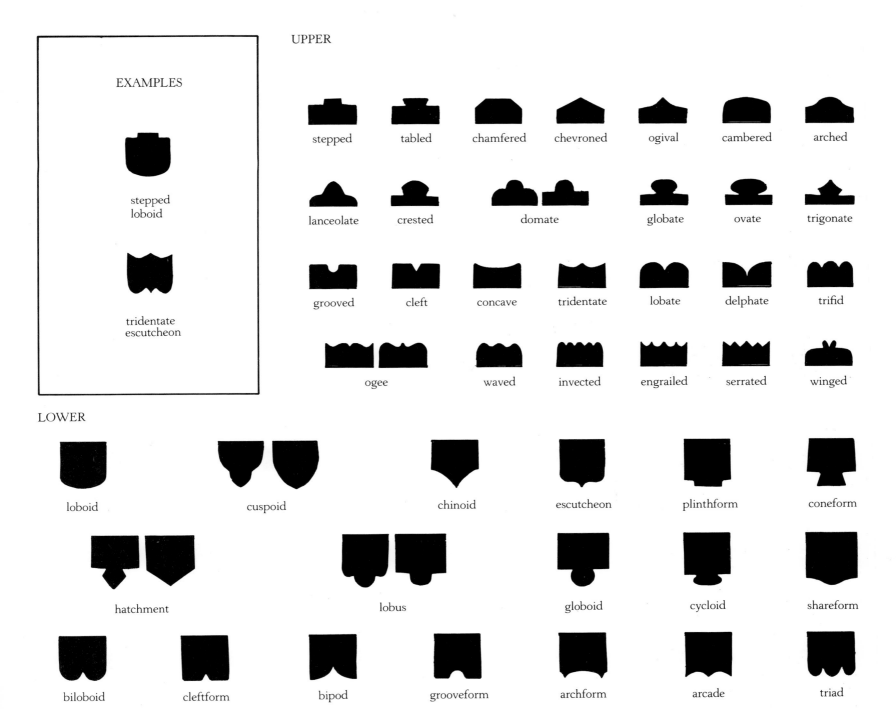

EXAMPLES

stepped
loboid

tridentate
escutcheon

UPPER

stepped · tabled · chamfered · chevroned · ogival · cambered · arched

lanceolate · crested · domate · globate · ovate · trigonate

grooved · cleft · concave · tridentate · lobate · delphate · trifid

ogee · waved · invected · engrailed · serrated · winged

LOWER

loboid · cuspoid · chinoid · escutcheon · plinthform · coneform

hatchment · lobus · globoid · cycloid · shareform

biloboid · cleftform · bipod · grooveform · archform · arcade · triad

APPROXIMATE DATING

It is often useful to be able to obtain a quick approximation of the date of a piece of silver without having to refer to the date-letter chart. This can be accomplished by using the following guide, which is applicable to all British silver made since 1697. If the hallmarks include any of the following, irrespective of any other marks, the item will have been made *before* the date indicated below.

		made before
queen's head (Victoria)		1891
king's head	or	1841
leopard's head crowned		1823 (Newcastle and York 1850)
leopard's head erased		1721

The marks vary in punch shape and detail.

EXAMPLES

queen's head –
before 1891 (Birmingham 1860)

king's head –
before 1841 (Edinburgh 1833)

leopard's head crowned –
before 1823 (London 1812)

leopard's head erased –
before 1721 (Exeter 1714)

London		Earliest date used
		1697
		1720
		1784
		1821
		1838
		1891

Birmingham		Earliest date used
		1773
		1784
		1838
		1891

APPROXIMATE DATING CHART

Chester

		Earliest date used
		1701
		1719
		1779
		1784
		1839
		1890 closed 1962

Dublin

		Earliest date used
		1638
		1731
		1807
		1838
		1891

Edinburgh

		Earliest date used
		1681
		1759
		1784
		1841
		1891

Glasgow

		Earliest date used
		1681
		1811
		1819
		1841
		1891
		1914 closed 1963

Sheffield

		Earliest date used
		1773
		1784
		1840
		1891
		1780
		1829

Exeter

		Earliest date used
		1701
		1721
		1778
		1784
		1837 closed 1882

Newcastle

		Earliest date used
		1702
		1721
		1784
		1841 closed 1884

York

		Earliest date used
		1700
		1778
		1784
		1840 closed 1856
no assays		1714–77

1784–85 George III faces left. Slight variations in proportions and shapes.

DATE LETTERS

Once you have identified the town where a piece of silver was assayed, you can ascertain the date of assay by looking up the date letter in the following charts. For example, London uses a 20-year cycle of letters (omitting J, W, X, Y and Z), and this provides a simple way of identifying dates. The letter E always denotes a century year or a 20-year increment (1800, 1820, 1840, 1860 etc.), while P denotes 1710, 1730, 1750, 1770 etc., and it is necessary only to recognize the alphabet design and punch shape, and then to count forwards or backwards. (The two similar cycles beginning in 1776 and 1816 are distinguished by the latter's having the mark of the leopard's head uncrowned after the date letter.)

LONDON Approximate dating

Earliest date used

1697 — 1784 — 1838
1720 — 1821 — 1891

Alternative punch shape sometimes found 1716–28 and 1776–1875.

Since 1 January 1975 all four British Assay Offices have used the same date letters.

1700, 1800, 1720, 1820, 1740, 1840, 1760, 1860, 1780, 1880

Example [F] = 1800 + 1 = 1801

	A 1716	a 1736	A 1756	a 1776	A 1796
1697	B 1717	b 1737	B 1757	b 1777	B 1797
1698	C 1718	c 1738	C 1758	c 1778	C 1798
1699	D 1719	dd 1739	D 1759	d 1779	D 1799
1700	E 1720	e 1740	E 1760	e 1780	E 1800
1701	F 1721	f 1741	F 1761	f 1781	F 1801
1702	G 1722	g 1742	G 1762	g 1782	G 1802
1703	H 1723	h 1743	H 1763	h 1783	H 1803
1704	I 1724	i 1744	I 1764	i 1784	I 1804
1705	K 1725	k 1745	K 1765	k 1785	K 1805
1706	L 1726	l 1746	L 1766	l 1786	L 1806
1707	M 1727	m 1747	M 1767	m 1787	M 1807
1708	N 1728	n 1748	N 1768	n 1788	N 1808
1709	O 1729	o 1749	O 1769	o 1789	O 1809
1710	P 1730	p 1750	P 1770	p 1790	P 1810
1711	Q 1731	q 1751	Q 1771	q 1791	Q 1811
1712	R 1732	r 1752	R 1772	r 1792	R 1812
1713	S 1733	r 1753	S 1773	s 1793	S 1813
1714	T 1734	t 1754	T 1774	t 1794	T 1814
1715		U 1755	U 1775	u 1795	U 1815
	V 1735				

Letter	Year	Letter	Year	Letter	Year	Letter	Year	Letter	Year	Letter	Year	Letter	Year	Letter	Year
a	1816	A	1836	a	1856	A	1876	a	1896	a	1916	A	1936	a	1956
b	1817	B	1837	b	1857	B	1877	b	1897	b	1917	B	1937	b	1957
c	1818	C	1838	c	1858	C	1878	c	1898	c	1918	C	1938	c	1958
d	1819	D	1839	d	1859	D	1879	d	1899	d	1919	D	1939	d	1959
e	1820	E	1840	e	1860	E	1880	e	1900	e	1920	E	1940	e	1960
f	1821	F	1841	f	1861	F	1881	f	1901	f	1921	F	1941	f	1961
g	1822	G	1842	g	1862	G	1882	g	1902	g	1922	G	1942	g	1962
h	1823	H	1843	h	1863	H	1883	h	1903	h	1923	H	1943	h	1963
i	1824	J	1844	i	1864	I	1884	i	1904	i	1924	I	1944	l	1964
k	1825	K	1845	k	1865	K	1885	k	1905	k	1925	K	1945	k	1965
l	1826	L	1846	l	1866	L	1886	l	1906	L	1926	L	1946	l	1966
m	1827	M	1847	m	1867	M	1887	m	1907	m	1927	M	1947	m	1967
n	1828	N	1848	n	1868	N	1888	n	1908	n	1928	N	1948	n	1968
o	1829	O	1849	o	1869	O	1889	o	1909	o	1929	O	1949	o	1969
p	1830	P	1850	p	1870	P	1890	p	1910	p	1930	P	1950	p	1970
q	1831	Q	1851	q	1871	Q	1891	q	1911	q	1931	Q	1951	q	1971
r	1832	R	1852	r	1872	R	1892	r	1912	r	1932	R	1952	r	1972
s	1833	S	1853	s	1873	S	1893	s	1913	s	1933	S	1953	s	1973
t	1834	T	1854	t	1874	T	1894	t	1914	t	1934	T	1954	t	1974
u	1835	U	1855	u	1875	U	1895	u	1915	u	1935	U	1955		

20

BIRMINGHAM

Approximate dating

Earliest date used

1773

1784

1838

1891

Since 1 January 1975 all four British Assay Offices have used the same date letters.

Letter	Year	Letter	Year	Letter	Year	Letter	Year	Letter	Year	Letter	Year
A	1975	A	1773	a	1798	A	1824	A	1849	a	1875
B	1976	B	1774	b	1799	B	1825	B	1850	b	1876
C	1977	C	1775	c	1800	C	1826	C	1851	c	1877
D	1978	D	1776	d	1801	D	1827	D	1852	d	1878
E	1979	E	1777	e	1802	E	1828	E	1853	e	1879
F	1980	F	1778	f	1803	F	1829	F	1854	f	1880
G	1981	G	1779	g	1804	G	1830	G	1855	g	1881
H	1982	H	1780	h	1805	H	1831	H	1856	h	1882
I	1983	I	1781	i	1806	J	1832	I	1857	i	1883
				j	1807			J	1858		
K	1984	K	1782	k	1808	K	1833	K	1859	k	1884
L	1985	L	1783	l	1809	L	1834	L	1860	l	1885
		M	1784	m	1810	M	1835	M	1861	m	1886
		N	1785	n	1811	N	1836	N	1862	n	1887
		O	1786	o	1812	O	1837	O	1863	o	1888
		P	1787	p	1813	P	1838	P	1864	p	1889
		Q	1788	q	1814	Q	1839	Q	1865	q	1890
		R	1789	r	1815	R	1840	R	1866	r	1891
		S	1790	s	1816	S	1841	S	1867	s	1892
		T	1791	t	1817	T	1842	T	1868	t	1893
		U	1792	u	1818	U	1843	U	1869	u	1894
		V	1793	v	1819	V	1844	V	1870	v	1895
		W	1794	w	1820	W	1845	W	1871	w	1896
		X	1795	x	1821	X	1846	X	1872	x	1897
		Y	1796	y	1822	Y	1847	Y	1873	y	1898
		Z	1797	z	1823	Z	1848	Z	1874	z	1899

a	1900	**A**	1925	**A**	1950	**A**	1975	**A**	1701	**A**	1726

a 1900	**A** 1925	**A** 1950	**A** 1975
b 1901	**B** 1926	**B** 1951	**B** 1976
c 1902	**C** 1927	**C** 1952	**C** 1977
d 1903	**D** 1928	**D** 1953	**D** 1978
e 1904	**E** 1929	**E** 1954	**E** 1979
f 1905	**F** 1930	**F** 1955	**F** 1980
g 1906	**G** 1931	**G** 1956	**G** 1981
h 1907	**H** 1932	**H** 1957	**H** 1982
i 1908			**I** 1983
	J 1933	**J** 1958	
k 1909	**K** 1934	**K** 1959	**K** 1984
l 1910	**L** 1935	**L** 1960	**L** 1985
m 1911	**M** 1936	**M** 1961	
n 1912	**N** 1937	**N** 1962	
o 1913	**O** 1938	**O** 1963	
p 1914	**P** 1939	**P** 1964	
q 1915	**Q** 1940	**2** 1965	
r 1916	**R** 1941	**R** 1966	
s 1917	**S** 1942	**S** 1967	
t 1918	**T** 1943	**T** 1968	
u 1919	**U** 1944	**U** 1969	
v 1920	**V** 1945	**V** 1970	
w 1921	**W** 1946	**W** 1971	
x 1922	**X** 1947	**X** 1972	
y 1923	**Y** 1948	**Y** 1973	
z 1924	**Z** 1949	**Z** 1974	

CHESTER

Approximate dating

Earliest date used

1701

1719

1779

1784

1839

1890

Alternative punch shape used since 1900

Alternative sterling shield used since 1839.

A 1701	**A** 1726
B 1702	**B** 1727
C 1703	**C** 1728
D 1704	**D** 1729
E 1705	**E** 1730
F 1706	**F** 1731
G 1707	**G** 1732
H 1708	**H** 1733
I 1709	**J** 1734
K 1710	**K** 1735
L 1711	**L** 1736
M 1712	**M** 1737
N 1713	**N** 1738
O 1714	**O** 1739
P 1715	**P** 1740
Q 1716	**Q** 1741
R 1717	**R** 1742
S 1718	**S** 1743
T 1719	**T** 1744
U 1720	**U** 1745
V 1721	**V** 1746
W 1722	**W** 1747
X 1723	**X** 1748
Y 1724	**Y** **y** 1749
Z 1725	**Z** 1750

a 1751	a 1776	A 1797	A 1818	A 1839	a 1864	A 1884	A 1901
b 1752	b 1777	B 1798	B 1819	B 1840	b 1865	B 1885	B 1902
c 1753	c 1778	C 1799	C 1820	C 1841	c 1866	C 1886	C 1903
d 1754	d 1779	D 1800	D 1821 1822	D 1842	d 1867	D 1887	D 1904
e 1755	e 1780	E 1801	E 1823	C 1843	e 1868	E 1888	E 1905
f 1756	f 1781	F 1802	F 1824	F 1844	f 1869	F 1889	F 1906
G 1757	g 1782	G 1803	G 1825	G 1845	g 1870	G 1890	G 1907
h 1758	h 1783	H 1804	H 1826	H 1846	h 1871	H 1891	H 1908
i 1759	i 1784	I 1805	I 1827	J 1847	i 1872	I 1892	J 1909
k 1760	k 1785	K 1806	K 1828	K 1848	k 1873	K 1893	K 1910
l 1761	l 1786	L 1807	L 1829	L 1849	l 1874	L 1894	L 1911
m 1762	m 1787	M 1808	M 1830	M 1850	m 1875	M 1895	M 1912
n 1763	n 1788	N 1809	N 1831	N 1851	n 1876	N 1896	N 1913
o 1764	o 1789	O 1810	O 1832	O 1852	o 1877	O 1897	O 1914
P 1765	p 1790	P 1811	P 1833	P 1853	p 1878	P 1898	P 1915
Q 1766	q 1791	Q 1812	Q 1834	Q 1854	q 1879	Q 1899	Q 1916
R 1767	r 1792	R 1813	R 1835	R 1855	r 1880	R 1900	R 1917
S 1768	s 1793	S 1814	S 1836	S 1856	s 1881		S 1918
T 1769 1770	t 1794	T 1815	T 1837	T 1857	t 1882		T 1919
U 1771	u 1795	U 1816	U 1838	U 1858	u 1883		U 1920
V 1772	v 1796	V 1817		V 1859			V 1921
W 1773				W 1860			W 1922
X 1774				X 1861			X 1923
Y 1775				Y 1862			Y 1924
				Z 1863			Z 1925

1926	1951		1717	1720	1747
1927	1952		1718	1721	1748
1928	1953		1719	1722	1749
1929	1954			1723	1750
1930	1955			1724	1751
1931	1956			1725	1752
1932	1957			1726	1753
1933	1958			1727	1754
1934				1728	1757

DUBLIN

Approximate dating

Earliest date used

1638

1731

1807

1838

1891

The Crowned Harp may vary in detail.

Alternative Hibernia 1752–4.

1935	1959	1729	1758
1936	1960	1730–1	1759
1937	1961	1732	1760
1938	1962	1733	1761
1939	closed	1734	1762
1940		1735	1763
1941		1736	1764
1942		1737	1765
1943		1738	1766
1944		1739	1767
1945		1740	1768
1946			
1947	1712–3	1741–2	1769
1948	1714	1733–4	1770
1949	1715	1735	1771
1950	1716	1736	1772

1699
1700
1701
1702
1703
1704–5
1706–7
1708–9
1710–1

Letter	Year	Letter	Year	Letter	Year	Letter	Year	Letter	Year	Letter	Year	Letter	Year	Letter	Year	Letter	Year
A	1773	A	1797	A	1821	a	1846	A	1871	A	1896	A	1916	A	1942	a	1968
B	1774	B	1798	B	1822	b	1847	B	1872	B	1897	b	1917	B	1943	b	1969
C	1775	C	1799	C	1823	c	1848	C	1873	C	1898	c	1918	C	1944	c	1970
D	1776	D	1800	D	1824	d	1849	D	1874	D	1899	D	1919	D	1945	d	1971
E	1777	E	1801	E e	1825	e	1850	E	1875	E	1900	e	1920	E	1946	e	1972
F	1778	F	1802	F	1826	f f	1851	F	1876	F	1901	f	1921	F	1947	F	1973
G	1779	G	1803	G	1827	g g	1852	G	1877	G	1902	g	1922	G	1948	g	1974
H	1780	H	1804	H	1828	h h	1853	H	1878	H	1903	h	1923	H	1949	h	1975
I	1781	I	1805	I	1829			I	1879	H	1904	I	1924	I	1950		
						j	1854							J	1951		
K	1782	K	1806	K	1830	k	1855	K	1880	K	1905	K	1925	K	1952		
L	1783	L	1807	L	1831	l	1856	L	1881	L	1906	L	1926	L	1953		
M	1784	M	1808	M	1832	m	1857	M	1882	M	1907	m	1927	M	1954		
N	1785	N	1809	N	1833	n	1858	N	1883	N	1908	n	1928	N	1955		
O	1786	O	1810	O	1834	o	1859	O	1884	O	1909	O	1929	O	1956		
P	1787	P	1811	P	1835	p	1860	P	1885	P	1910	P	1930–1	P	1957		
Q	1788	Q	1812	Q	1836	q	1861	Q	1886	Q	1911	Q	1932	Q	1958		
R	1789	R	1813	R	1837	r	1862	R	1887	R	1912	R	1933	R	1959		
S	1790	S	1814	S	1838	s	1863	S	1888	S	1913	S	1934	S	1960		
T	1791	T	1815	T	1839	t	1864	T	1889	T	1914	T	1935	T	1961		
U	1792	U	1816	U	1840	u	1865	U	1890	U	1915	U	1936	U	1962		
				V	1841	v	1866	V	1891			V	1937	V	1963		
W	1793	W	1817	W	1842	w	1867	W	1892			W	1938	W	1964		
X	1794	X	1818	X	1843	x	1868	X	1893			X	1939	X	1965		
Y	1795	Y	1819	Y	1844	y	1869	Y	1894			Y	1940	Y	1966		
Z	1796	Z	1820	Z	1845	z	1870	Z	1895			Z	1941	Z	1967		

EDINBURGH

Approximate dating

Earliest date used

 1681

 1759

 1784

 1841

 1981

Since 1 January 1975 all four British Assay Offices have used the same date letters.

1681	1705	1730	1755	1780	1806
1682	1706	1731	1756	1781	1807
1683	1707	1732	1757	1782	1808
1684	1708	1733	1758	1783	1809
1685	1709	1734	1759	1784	1810
1686	1710	1735	1760	1785	1811
1687	1711	1736	1761	1786–7	1812
1688	1712	1737	1762	1788	1813
1689	1713	1738	1763	1789	1814
				1789	1815
1690	1714	1739	1764	1790	1816
1691	1715	1740	1765	1791	1817
1692	1716	1741	1766	1792	1818
1693	1717	1742	1767	1793	1819
1694	1718	1743	1768	1794	1820
1695	1719	1744	1769	1795	1821
1696	1720	1745	1770	1796	1822
1697	1721	1746	1771	1797	1823
1698	1722	1747	1772	1798	1824
1699	1723	1748	1773	1799	1825
	1724	1749	1774	1800	1826
		1750	1755		
1700	1725		1779	1801	1827
1701	1726	1751		1802	1828
1702	1727	1752	1776	1803	1829
1703	1728	1753	1777	1804	1830
1704	1729	1754	1778	1805	1831

A 1832	A 1857	a 1882	A 1906	A 1931	A 1956	A 1975
B 1833	B 1858	b 1883	B 1907	B 1932	B 1957	B 1976
C 1834	C 1859	c 1884	C 1908	C 1933	C 1958	C 1977
D 1835	D 1860	d 1885	D 1909	D 1934	D 1959	D 1978
E 1836	E 1861	e 1886	E 1910	E 1935	E 1960	E 1979
F 1837	F 1862	f 1887	F 1911	F 1936	F 1961	F 1980
G 1838	G 1863	g 1888	G 1912	G 1937	G 1962	G 1981
H 1839	H 1864	h 1889	H 1913	H 1938	H 1963	H 1982
J 1840	I 1865	i 1890	I 1914	J 1939	J 1964	J 1983
K 1841	K 1866	k 1891	K 1915	K 1940	K 1965	K 1984
L 1842	L 1867	l 1892	L 1916	L 1941	L 1966	L 1985
M 1843	M 1868	m 1893	M 1917	M 1942	M 1967	
N 1844	N 1869	n 1894	N 1918	N 1943	N 1968	
O 1845	O 1870	o 1895	O 1919	O 1944	O 1969	
P 1846	P 1871	p 1896	P 1920	P 1945	P 1970	
Q 1847	Q 1872	q 1897	Q 1921	Q 1946	Q 1971	
R 1848	R 1873	r 1898	R 1922	R 1947	R 1972	
S 1849	S 1874	s 1899	S 1923	S 1948	S 1973–4	
T 1850	T 1875	t 1900	T 1924	T 1949		
U 1851	U 1876		U 1925	U 1950		
V 1852	V 1877	v 1901	V 1926	V 1951		
W 1853	W 1878	w 1902	W 1927	W 1952		
X 1854	X 1879	x 1903	X 1928	X 1953		
Y 1855	Y 1880	y 1904	Y 1929	Y 1954		
Z 1856	Z 1881	z 1905	Z 1930	Z 1955		

EXETER
Approximate dating

Earliest
date used

1701

1721

1778

1784

1837

A	1701	a	1725	A	1749	A	1773	A	1797	a	1817	A	1837
B	1702	b	1726	B	1750	B	1774	B	1798	b	1818	B	1838
C	1703	c	1727	C	1751	C	1775	C	1799	c	1819	C	1839
D	1704	d	1728	D	1752	D	1776	D	1800	d	1820	D	1840
E	1705	e	1729	E	1753	E	1777	E	1801	e	1821	E	1841
F	1706	f	1730	F	1754	F	1778	F	1802	f	1822	F	1842
G	1707	g	1731	G	1755	G	1779	G	1803	g	1823	G	1843
H	1708	h	1732	H	1756	H	1780	H	1804	h	1824	H	1844
I	1709	i	1733	I	1757	I	1781–2	I	1805	i	1825	J	1845
K	1710	k	1734	K	1758	K	1783	K	1806	k	1826	K	1846
L	1711	l	1735	L	1759	L	1784	L	1807	l	1827	L	1847
M	1712	m	1736	M	1760	M	1785	M	1808	m	1828	M	1848
N	1713	n	1737	N	1761	N	1786	N	1809	n	1829	N	1849
O	1714	o	1738	O	1762	O	1787	O	1810	o	1830	O	1850
P	1715	p	1739	P	1763	P	1788	P	1811	p	1831	P	1851
Q	1716	q	1740	Q	1764	q	1789	Q	1812	q	1832	Q	1852
R	1717	r	1741	R	1765	r	1790	R	1813	r	1833	R	1853
S	1718	s	1742	S	1766	f	1791	S	1814	s	1834	S	1854
T	1719	t	1743	T	1767	t	1792	T	1815	t	1835	T	1855
		u	1744	U	1768	u	1793	U	1816	u	1836	U	1856
V	1720												
W	1721	w	1745	W	1769	w	1794						
X	1722	x	1746	X	1770	X	1795						
Y	1723	y	1747	Y	1771	y	1796						
Z	1724	z	1748	Z	1772								

Letter	Year		Letter	Year
A	1857		A	1877
B	1858		B	1878
C	1859		C	1879
D	1860		D	1880
E	1861		E	1881
F	1862		F	1882 closed
G	1863			
H	1864			
I	1865			
K	1866			
L	1867			
M	1868			
N	1869			
O	1870			
P	1871			
Q	1872			
R	1873			
S	1874			
T	1875			
U	1876			

GLASGOW
Approximate dating

Earliest date used

Mark	Year
	1681
	1811
	1819
	1841
	1891
	1914

Before 1806 the maker's mark was stamped in duplicate on either side of the date letter.

Letter	Year		Letter	Year
a	1681			
			B	1707
C	1683			
			D	1709
e	1685		E	1763
i	1689			
k	1690			
o	1694		O	1776
q	1696			
s	1698		S	1783
t	1699			
u	1700			
v	1701			
y	1704			
z	1705			

Letter	Year		Letter	Year
A	1819		A	1845
B	1820		B	1846
C	1821		C	1847
D	1822		D	1848
E	1823		E	1849
F	1824		F	1850
G	1825		G	1851
H	1826		H	1852
I	1827		I	1853
J	1828		J	1854
K	1829		K	1855
L	1830		L	1856
M	1831		M	1857
N	1832		N	1858
O	1833		O	1859
P	1834		P	1860
Q	1835		Q	1861
R	1836		R	1862
S	1837		S	1863
T	1838		T	1864
U	1839		U	1865
V	1840		V	1866
W	1841		W	1867
X	1842		X	1868
Y	1843		Y	1869
Z	1844		Z	1870

A 1871	**A** 1897	**a** 1923	**A** 1949		**A** 1702
B 1872	**B** 1898	**b** 1924	**B** 1950		**B** 1703
C 1873	**C** 1899	**c** 1925	**C** 1951		**C** 1704
D 1874	**D** 1900	**d** 1926	**D** 1952		**D** 1705
E 1875	**E** 1901	**e** 1927	**E** 1953		**E** 1706
F 1876	**F** 1902	**f** 1928	**F** 1954		**F** 1707
G 1877	**G** 1903	**g** 1929	**G** 1955		**B** 1708
H 1878	**H** 1904	**h** 1930	**H** 1956		
I 1879	**J** 1905	**i** 1931			
J 1880	**J** 1906	**j** 1932	**J** 1957		
K 1881	**K** 1907	**k** 1933			
L 1882	**L** 1908	**l** 1934	**l** 1958		
M 1883	**M** 1909	**m** 1935	**M** 1959		**M** 1712
N 1884	**N** 1910	**n** 1936	**N** 1960		
O 1885	**O** 1911	**o** 1937	**O** 1961		**O** 1714
P 1886	**P** 1912	**p** 1938	**p** 1962		**P** 1717
Q 1887	**Q** 1913	**q** 1939			**Q** 1718
R 1888	**R** 1914	**r** 1940	**R** 1963		
S 1889	**S** 1915	**s** 1941	1964 closed		
T 1890	**T** 1916	**t** 1942			
U 1891	**U** 1917	**u** 1943			
V 1892	**V** 1918	**v** 1944			
W 1893	**W** 1919	**w** 1945			
X 1894	**X** 1920	**x** 1946			
Y 1895	**Y** 1921	**y** 1947			
Z 1896	**Z** 1922	**Z** 1948			

D 1719
C 1720

NEWCASTLE
Approximate dating
Earliest date used

1702

1721

1784

1841

The date letter and lion passant shapes vary between 1721–8. The lion sometimes faces right.

29

1721	1740	1759	1791	1815	1839	1864
1722	1741	1760–8	1792	1816	1840	1865
1723	1742	1769	1793	1817	1841	1866
1724	1743	1770	1794	1818	1842	1867
1725	1744	1771	1795	1819	1843	1868
1726	1745	1772	1796	1820	1844	1869
1727	1746	1773	1797	1821	1845	1870
1728	1747	1774	1798	1822	1846	1871
1729	1748	1775	1799	1823	1847	1872
					1848	
1730	1749	1776	1800	1824	1849	1873
1731	1750	1777	1801	1825	1850	1874
1732	1751	1778	1802	1826	1851	1875
1733	1752	1779	1803	1827	1852	1876
1734	1753	1780	1804	1828	1853	1877
1735	1754	1781	1805	1829	1854	1878
1736	1755	1782	1806	1830	1855	1879
1737	1756	1783	1807	1831	1856	1880
1738	1757	1784	1808	1832	1857	1881
1739		1785	1809	1833	1858	1882
		1786	1810	1834	1859	1883 closed
		1787	1811	1835	1860	
		1788	1812	1836	1861	
		1789	1813	1837	1862	
		1790	1814	1838	1863	

SHEFFIELD

Approximate dating

Earliest date used

Mark	Earliest date used
(crown)	1773
(crown variant)	1780
(crown & head)	1784
(crown & f)	1829
(crown & head)	1840
(crown)	1891

Assay Office opened in 1773. First two cycles not in sequence.

The crown and date letter are in one punch shape on small objects 1780–1855.

Since 1 January 1975 all four British Assay Offices have used the same date letters.

Letter	Year	Letter	Year	Letter	Year	Letter	Year	Letter	Year	Letter	Year
R	1779	A	1806	a	1824	A	1844	A	1868	a	1893
B	1783	B	1805	b	1825	B	1845	B	1869	b	1894
C	1780	C	1811	c	1826	C	1846	C	1870	c	1895
D	1781	D	1812	d	1827	D	1847	D	1871	d	1896
E	1773	E	1799	e	1828	E	1848	E	1872	e	1897
F	1774	F	1803	f	1829	F	1849	F	1873	f	1898
G	1782	G	1804	g	1830	G	1850	G	1874	g	1899
H	1777	H	1801	h	1831	H	1851	H	1875	h	1900
I	1784	I	1818			I	1852			i	1901
								J	1876		
k	1786	K	1809	k	1832	K	1853	K	1877	k	1902
L	1790	L	1810	l	1833	L	1854	L	1878	l	1903
m	1794										
M	1789	M	1802	m	1834	M	1855	M	1879	m	1904
N	1775	N	1800			N	1856	N	1880	n	1905
O	1793	O	1815			O	1857	O	1881	o	1906
P	1791	P	1808	p	1835	P	1858	P	1882	p	1907
q	1795	Q	1820	q	1836			Q	1883	q	1908
R	1776	R	1813	r	1837	R	1859	R	1884	r	1909
S	1778	S	1807	s	1838	S	1860	S	1885	s	1910
T	1787	T	1816	t	1839	T	1861	T	1886	t	1911
U	1792	U	1823	u	1840	U	1862	U	1887	u	1912
V	1798	V	1819	v	1841	V	1863	V	1888	v	1913
W	1788	W	1814			W	1864	W	1889	w	1914
X	1797	X	1817	x	1842	X	1865	X	1890	x	1915
Y	1785	Y	1821			Y	1866	Y	1891	y	1916
Z	1796	Z	1822	z	1843	Z	1867	Z	1892	z	1917

a 1918	A 1943	A 1968	A 1975		Ꭱ 1700	
b 1919	B 1944	B 1969	B 1976		B 1701	
c 1920	C 1945	C 1970	C 1977		C 1702	C 1778
d 1921	D 1946	D 1971	D 1978		D 1703	D 1779
e 1922	E 1947	E 1972	E 1979			E 1780
f 1923	F 1948	Œ 1973	F 1980		F 1705	F 1781
g 1924	G 1949	G 1974	G 1981		G 1706	G 1782
h 1925	H 1950		H 1982			H 1783
i 1926	I 1951		J 1983		Ꝺ 1708	
k 1927	K 1952		K 1984			J 1784
l 1928	L 1953		L 1985			K 1785
m 1929	M 1954					L 1786
n 1930	N 1955				ꭒ 1711	
o 1931	O 1956					
p 1932	P 1957					
q 1933	Q 1958					
r 1934	R 1959					
s 1935	S 1960				Ꝺ 1713	
t 1936	T 1961					
u 1937	U 1962					
v 1938	V 1963					
w 1939	W 1964					
x 1940	X 1965					
y 1941	Y 1966					
z 1942	Z 1967					

YORK

Approximate dating

Earliest date used

1700

1778

1784

1840

1713–78 no date letters recorded.
1803 and 1806 the lion may face right.

A	1787	**a**	1812	**A**	1837
B	1788	**b**	1813	**B**	1838
C C	1789	**c**	1814	**C**	1839
d	1790	**d**	1815	**D**	1840
e	1791	**e**	1816	**E**	1841
f	1792	**f**	1817	**F**	1842
g	1793	**g**	1818	**G**	1843
h	1794	**h**	1819	**H**	1844
i	1795	**i**	1820	**I**	1845
K	1796	**k**	1821	**K**	1846
L	1797	**l**	1822	**L**	1847
M	1798	**m**	1823	**M**	1848
N	1799	**n**	1824	**N**	1849
O	1800	**o**	1825	**O**	1850
P	1801	**p**	1826	**P**	1851
Q	1802	**q**	1827	**Q**	1852
R	1803	**r**	1828	**R**	1853
S	1804	**s**	1829	**S**	1854
T	1805	**t**	1830	**T**	1855
U	1806	**u**	1831	**V**	1856 closed
V	1807	**v**	1832		
W	1808	**w**	1833		
X	1809	**x**	1834		
Y	1810	**y**	1835		
Z	1811	**z**	1836		

R. Parr
Jeweller & Goldsmith,
at the Diamond Cross,
near Salisbury Court, Fleet-Street,
London
Makes & Sells all Sorts of Jewellers Work,
Plate, Seals, Mourning Rings, Watches &c.
Also English & Dutch Toys,
at Reasonable Rates.

CHRONOLOGY

Queen Anne 1695–1727

1697 Britannia standard introduced. Lion's head erased and Britannia replaces leopard's head and lion passant. Makers to stamp first two letters of surname

1701 Exeter mark of origin changes from Roman X to three-towered castle

1702 Queen Anne crowned

1711 London Goldsmiths' petition to Goldsmiths Company against influx of Huguenot silversmiths

1712 Earliest silver by Paul de Lamerie

1713 York Assay Office closes (until 1778)

1714 George I crowned

1715 Louis XIV of France dies

1720 Britannia standard made optional. Maker's initials again allowed as alternative to first two letters of surname

1725 London Goldsmiths' remonstrance against assay for unregistered Huguenots

1725 Rococo style originated by Juste-Aurèle Meissonnier, French goldsmith, sculptor and architect

Mid-Georgian 1727–1770

1727 George I crowned

1731 Figure of Hibernia added to Dublin mark of origin

1738 Herculaneum excavations begin fashion for ancient Rome

1739 Makers required to register new marks. Initials only allowed

1740 Rococo becoming popular

1742 Thomas Boulsover invents Old Sheffield plate

1755 Pompeii excavated

1758 Robert Adam returns from Italy after classical studies

1759 Matthew Boulton inherits father's business

1759 Thistle replaces Deacon's initials in Edinburgh sterling marks

1760 George III crowned

1761 Hester Bateman registers her first mark

1762 Matthew Boulton meets John Fothergill

1763 Hester Bateman's earliest silver

Adam 1770–1800

1773 Birmingham and Sheffield Assay Offices open

1775 Etruscan styles become popular

1775 Tassie medallions applied to silver

c.1775 Decline of French Rococo style

1778 York Assay Office reopens

1779 Robert and James Adam publish *Works in Architecture*

1780 Hester Bateman silver before this very rare

1780 Sheffield introduces additional mark of origin: date letter and crown in one punch

1784 Duty on silver imposed and mark of sovereign's head introduced

c.1785 Paul Storr apprenticed to Andrew Fogelberg

1788 John Bridge joined by Philip Rundell to found Rundell & Bridge

1790 Peter and Jonathan Bateman's only date

1792 Paul Storr's earliest silver

Regency 1800–1830

1801 Napoleon's art treasures from Egypt fall to British at Alexandria

1805 Rundell, Bridge & Rundell founded

1806 Tatham published *Designs of Ornamental Plate*

1807 Paul Storr made partner in Rundell, Bridge and Rundell

1807 Storr & Co founded

1811 George III pronounced insane. Prince becomes Regent (until 1820)

1819 Scottish lion rampant and sovereign's head added to Glasgow marks

1820 Leopard's head loses crown

1820 George IV crowned. Regency ends

1822 Storr & Mortimer established

c.1826 Rococo revival starts

1830 William IV crowned

Early Victorian 1830–1860

1833 Adam drawings acquired by Sir John Soane

1834 Knight publishes *Encyclopaedia of Ornament*

1837 Victoria crowned

1839 Makers required to use only initials

1839 Mortimer & Hunt established

1840 Dr Smee demonstrates electroplating

1841 Pugin publishes *True Principles of Christian Architecture*

1846 Flaxman's designs for Achilles shield

1849 Birmingham Exhibition of Naturalism

c.1850 Electroplate supersedes Sheffield plate

c.1850 Naturalistic styles popular

1851 Great Exhibition of London features electroplate

1852 Matthew Digby Wyatt publishes *Metalwork and its artistic Design*

1856 York Assay Office closes

1856 Owen Jones publishes *Grammar of Ornament*

Mid-Victorian 1860–1880

1860 Long necks become a popular design feature

1860s Classic styles supersede Rococo. Angular sloping sides popular

1862 International Paris Exhibition features Sheffield plate

1867 Owen Jones writes *Examples of Chinese Ornament*

1871 Christopher Dresser publishes *Principles of Design*

1872 Japanese style becomes popular

1873 Elkingtons now foremost firm

1874 Adam style revived

Late Victorian 1880–1901

1880 W.A.S Benson in business

1887 William Morris designs silver

1887 Guild and School of Handicrafts founded by C.R. Ashbee

1888 George Frampton begins designing metalwork

1889 Arts and Crafts Society exhibits work of Guild of Handicrafts

1889 Hunt & Roskell bought by J.W. Benson

1889 Gilbert Marks starts own workshop

1895 Guild of Handicrafts founded in Birmingham by Arthur Dixon

1895 Art Nouveau becomes popular

1900 Liberty & Co produce catalogue of Cymric Silver

Styles Of Silver 1700–1900

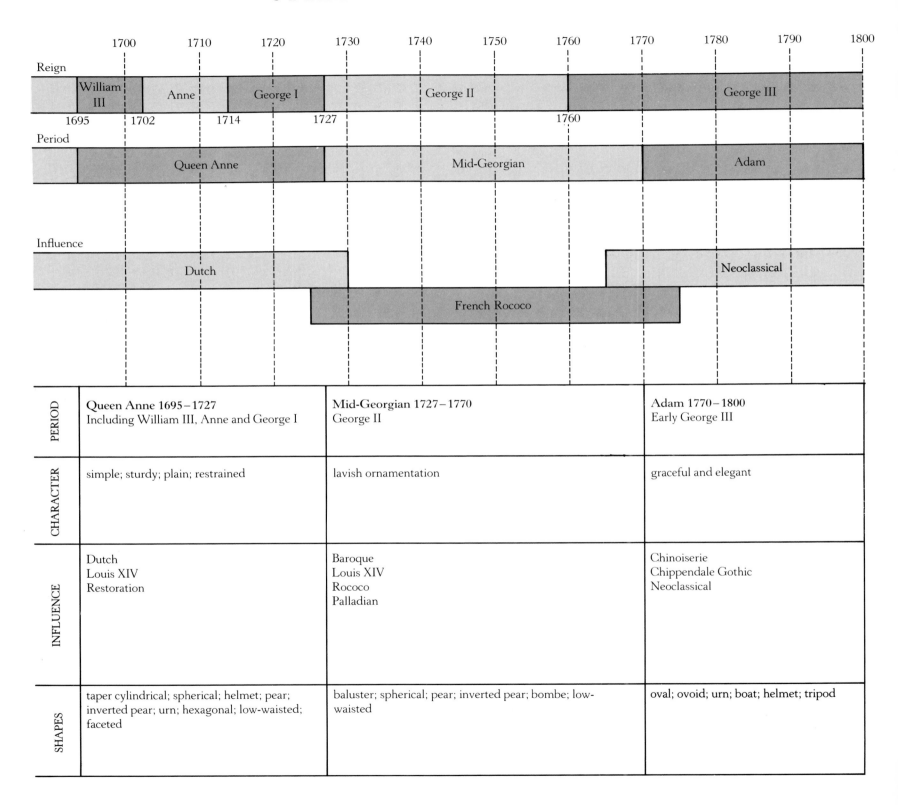

	1700	1710	1720	1730	1740	1750	1760	1770	1780	1790	1800
Reign	William III	Anne	George I		George II				George III		
	1695	1702	1714	1727			1760				
Period		Queen Anne			Mid-Georgian				Adam		
Influence		Dutch			French Rococo			Neoclassical			

PERIOD	**Queen Anne 1695–1727** Including William III, Anne and George I	**Mid-Georgian 1727–1770** George II	**Adam 1770–1800** Early George III
CHARACTER	simple; sturdy; plain; restrained	lavish ornamentation	graceful and elegant
INFLUENCE	Dutch Louis XIV Restoration	Baroque Louis XIV Rococo Palladian	Chinoiserie Chippendale Gothic Neoclassical
SHAPES	taper cylindrical; spherical; helmet; pear; inverted pear; urn; hexagonal; low-waisted; faceted	baluster; spherical; pear; inverted pear; bombe; low-waisted	oval; ovoid; urn; boat; helmet; tripod

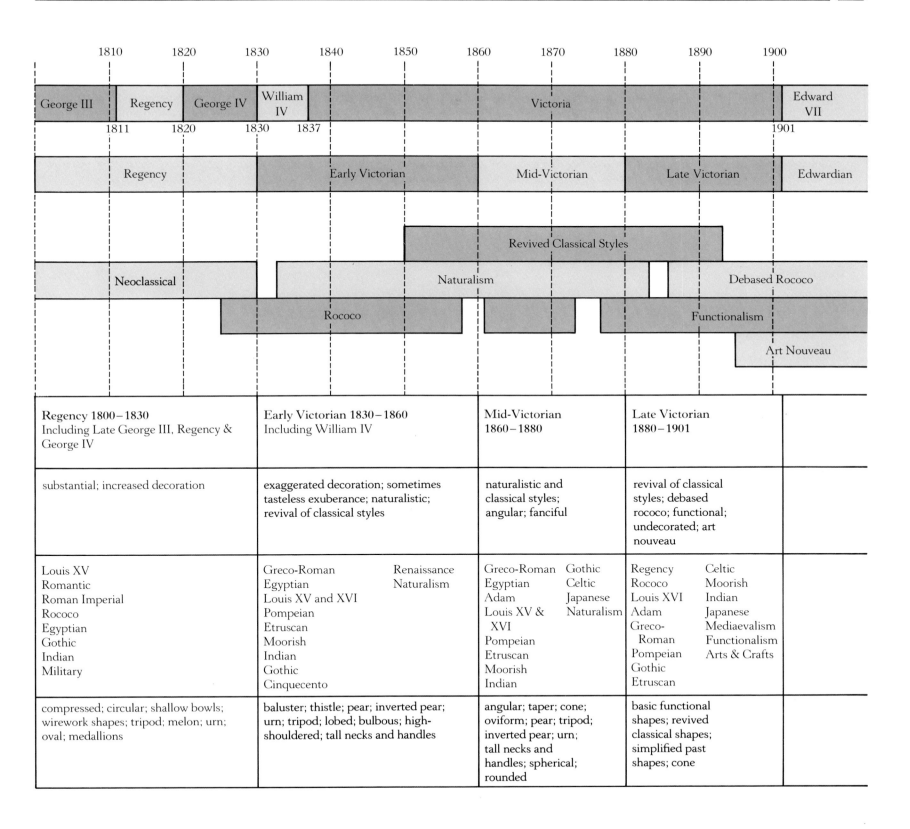

Timeline				
1810	1820	1830	1840	1850 1860 1870 1880 1890 1900

Monarchs: George III | Regency | George IV | William IV | Victoria | Edward VII

1811 · 1820 · 1830 · 1837 · 1901

Periods: Regency | Early Victorian | Mid-Victorian | Late Victorian | Edwardian

Styles: Revived Classical Styles · Neoclassical · Naturalism · Debased Rococo · Rococo · Functionalism · Art Nouveau

Regency 1800–1830 Including Late George III, Regency & George IV	Early Victorian 1830–1860 Including William IV	Mid-Victorian 1860–1880	Late Victorian 1880–1901	
substantial; increased decoration	exaggerated decoration; sometimes tasteless exuberance; naturalistic; revival of classical styles	naturalistic and classical styles; angular; fanciful	revival of classical styles; debased rococo; functional; undecorated; art nouveau	

Louis XV
Romantic
Roman Imperial
Rococo
Egyptian
Gothic
Indian
Military
	Greco-Roman Renaissance
	Egyptian Naturalism
	Louis XV and XVI
	Pompeian
	Etruscan
	Moorish
	Indian
	Gothic
	Cinquecento
		Greco-Roman Gothic
		Egyptian Celtic
		Adam Japanese
		Louis XV & Naturalism
		  XVI
		Pompeian
		Etruscan
		Moorish
		Indian
			Regency Celtic
			Rococo Moorish
			Louis XVI Indian
			Adam Japanese
			Greco- Mediaevalism
			  Roman Functionalism
			Pompeian Arts & Crafts
			Gothic
			Etruscan	

compressed; circular; shallow bowls; wirework shapes; tripod; melon; urn; oval; medallions	baluster; thistle; pear; inverted pear; urn; tripod; lobed; bulbous; high-shouldered; tall necks and handles	angular; taper; cone; oviform; pear; tripod; inverted pear; urn; tall necks and handles; spherical; rounded	basic functional shapes; revived classical shapes; simplified past shapes; cone	

Alms dish A dish or plate for collecting alms. Examples exist dating from the 1600s, but they are rare before this. They are usually plain, with a broad, flat, plain rim, and are often without moulding or edging of any kind. Later ones are decorated and could be parishioners' plates pressed into service. They are quite frequently scratched with cut marks which may have resulted from the cutting of the bread or Host.

ALMS DISH

1717

Argyll A gravy container, usually in the shape of a small coffee pot, cylindrical, vase-shaped or in the form of a baluster. Believed to have been invented by the Duke of Argyll, they kept gravy hot by means of hot water or a hot iron within an inner container. The hot-water jacket usually has a small outlet with a flap for filling on the upper handle ferrule. Because of the inner water jacket, any damage to the outer casing is practically impossible to repair. There are very few before 1760 and they seem to have lost favour in the 1820s.

ARGYLL

1769

1771

1775

1771

1777

1777

1785

1787

1788

1790

1793

1819

Asparagus tongs Resembling outsize sugar tongs, these are believed to be a development of the fish slice, with an additional spring jaw. They are extremely rare before 1790. The handle patterns usually match other items of a table service. The retaining cross-piece should also be partly marked. Cracks across the bend and piercing are imperfections to look out for.

ASPARAGUS TONGS

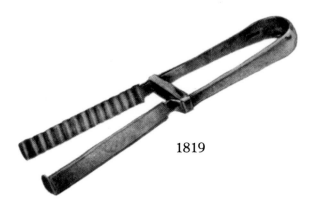

1819

1856

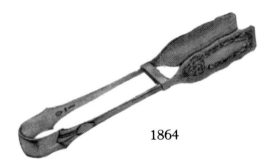

1864

Basin/Bowl Possibly the oldest type of utensil, with an infinite number of purposes. Silver items include bleeding bowls, punch bowls, monteiths, finger bowls, mazers, quaiches, caudle cups, porringers, posset pots, sugar bowls, shaving bowls, sweetmeat dishes, strawberry dishes and wine tasters. (See separate headings.)

BASIN/BOWL

Basting Spoon Usually a long-handled spoon of 15 inches or more in length, often of a tubular tapering form with a spherical end-cap (and sometimes a baluster finial and moulded band about half-way along its length) and an almost oval, rat-tailed bowl. The bowl should be fully hallmarked with a lion's or leopard's head erased on the handle. This type is usually dated between 1695 and 1715. The tubular handles are easily dented or fractured and are very difficult to repair.

BASTING SPOON

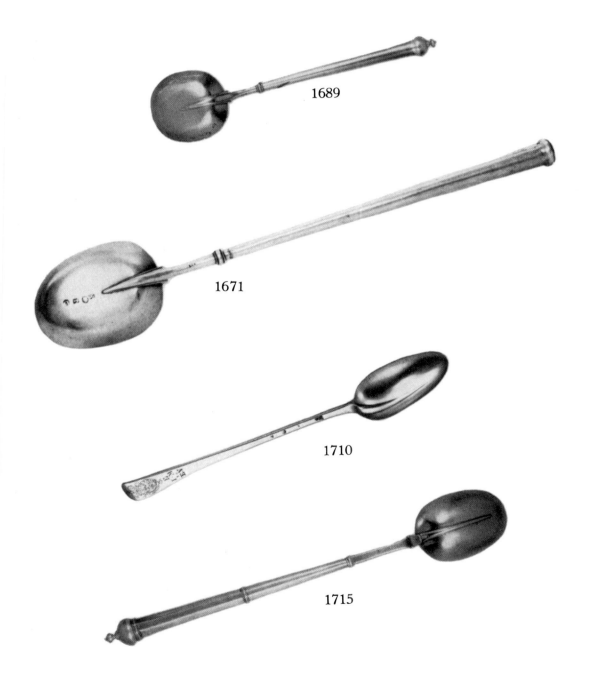

1689

1671

1710

1715

BEAKER

Beaker Elizabethan examples are not uncommon; these are of tapering cylindrical shape or very slightly curved, with simple moulded foot and typical line engraving. Later examples are mostly plain with engraved armorials, crest or monogram. Pairs of beakers decorated with bands and staves like barrels and joined at the lips appeared during the late eighteenth century. These should be hallmarked on both halves.

1576
1610
1618
1637
1645
1641
1674
1677
1682
1653
1685
1691
1743
1702
1776
1775
1795
1801
1804
1811
1825
1871

Bell Bells were often originally part of an inkstand, used to summon a servant to deliver a letter. They show great conformity of design and are usually quite plain and devoid of decoration, apart from late Victorian examples. Early examples date from about 1740, and sometimes have reeded bands. Handles are plain baluster until Victorian times. They should be fully hallmarked, with the clapper also marked. Victorian bells show some variety of shape and decoration.

BELL

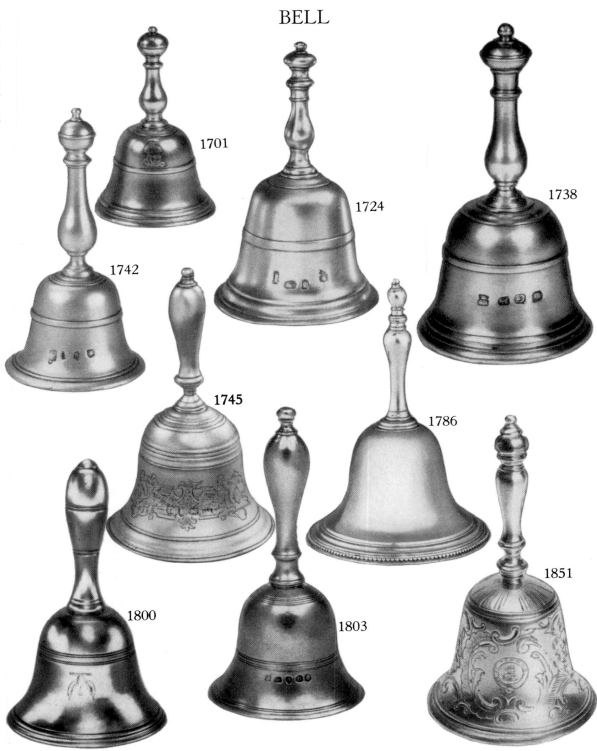

1701

1742

1724

1738

1745

1786

1800

1803

1851

BIGGIN

Biggin Invented by George Biggin, this is a later form of coffee pot, made after about 1800, but remained in favour for only about 30 years. Biggins are cylindrical, with an in-curved top and a loose domed lid with a ball or similar finial, a lip for pouring and a hardwood or ivory C-shaped handle. They sometimes had a stand with a spirit lamp. They are often completely undecorated apart from edge moulding or gadrooning.

1805

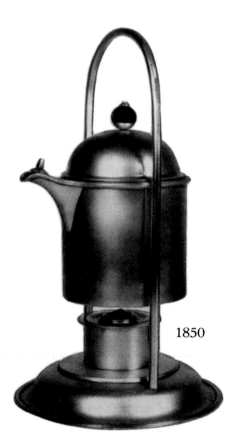

1850

1878

Bleeding bowl Also called a cupping bowl or porringer, this is a shallow cup with a flat, pierced handle and without base or feet. These bowls are not seriously thought to have been for bleeding, but perhaps for wine tasting or as individual porringers or caudle cups. Examples exist from about 1675 to 1725, with conformity of shape throughout. They are usually hallmarked on the rim, and the pierced handle should also bear a mark. The bowl is usually between 4" and 5" in diameter. The bottom of the bowl is particularly subject to wear, dents and fractures.

BLEEDING BOWL

Breakfast dish This was used for keeping the breakfast food hot on the table or buffet. Those made before 1790 often have a loose lid and a spirit lamp. A later type, made after about 1810, has no legs, and has a hinged, rather than loose, lid, a screw-on baluster handle and a hot-water compartment to retain the heat.

BREAKFAST DISH

1772

1757

1789

1820

1873

1825

1885

1900

1903

Butter dish These first appeared in about 1760, and are very varied in design. Early examples have pierced sides and a low, domed cover with a spherical, loop or recumbent cow handle, and contain a glass liner. Later popular designs are milk pails, butter tubs and milk churns with glass liners. Mostly circular and slightly tapering, in shape, they are often decorated with reeded bands or hoops and staves and often have a crest.

BUTTER DISH

1755

1807

1808

1828

1860

1860

Caddy spoon This is a short-handled spoon used for measuring tea from the caddy. Very few are found before about 1770. The shape of the bowl ranges from the plain circular to the extremely imaginative: leaves, feathers, shells, shovels, scoops, jockey caps, hands etc. Some examples have turned hardwood or ivory handles.

CADDY SPOON

Cake basket These were probably also used for bread and fruit. Oval-shaped examples are found from about 1730, although there are rare circular ones dating from before this. Early designs have heavily cast applied edges and scrolling swing handles. The bodies are pierced in geometric and scrolling shapes and have a similar rim foot. The bottoms are not pierced but usually engraved with armorials. Hallmarks are usually on the bottom in a line, but after the 1760s they are sometimes found in the piercing on the foot. Points to look out for are the bottoms, which may be thin or springy or may even have been replaced, and the piercing, which may have missing points or curves and is very difficult to repair. Many of the earlier swing handles are not marked, but on baskets made after the 1760s there should be one or two marks on the handle, although these may be quite difficult to find.

CAKE BASKET

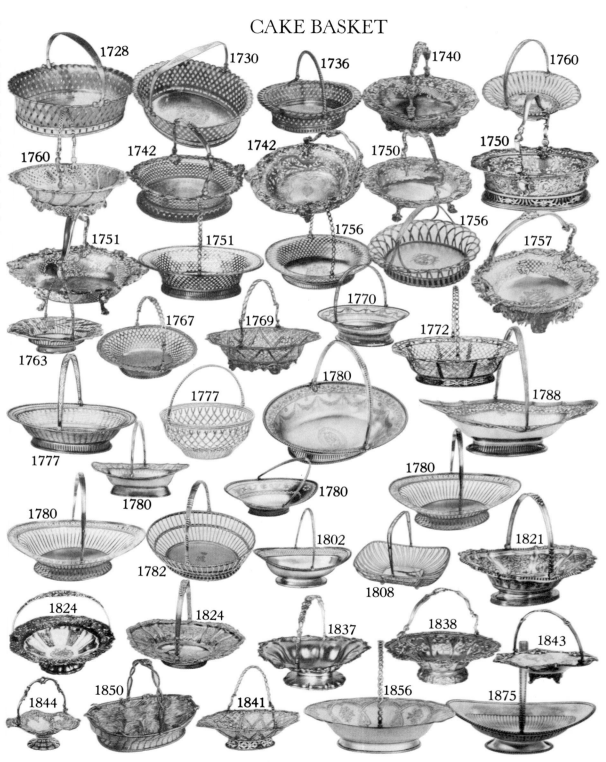

1728 1730 1736 1740 1760
1760 1742 1742 1750 1750
1751 1751 1756 1756 1757
1763 1767 1769 1770 1772
1777 1777 1780 1788
1780 1780 1780 1780 1780
1782 1802 1808 1821
1824 1824 1837 1838 1843
1844 1850 1841 1856 1875

Candelabrum These usually have two, three or more branches in addition to the central socket, which was sometimes replaced by a flame-shaped finial or flambeau. Matching branches were sometimes added later by a different maker. Complete, single-maker candelabra made before 1750 are very rare.

CANDELABRUM

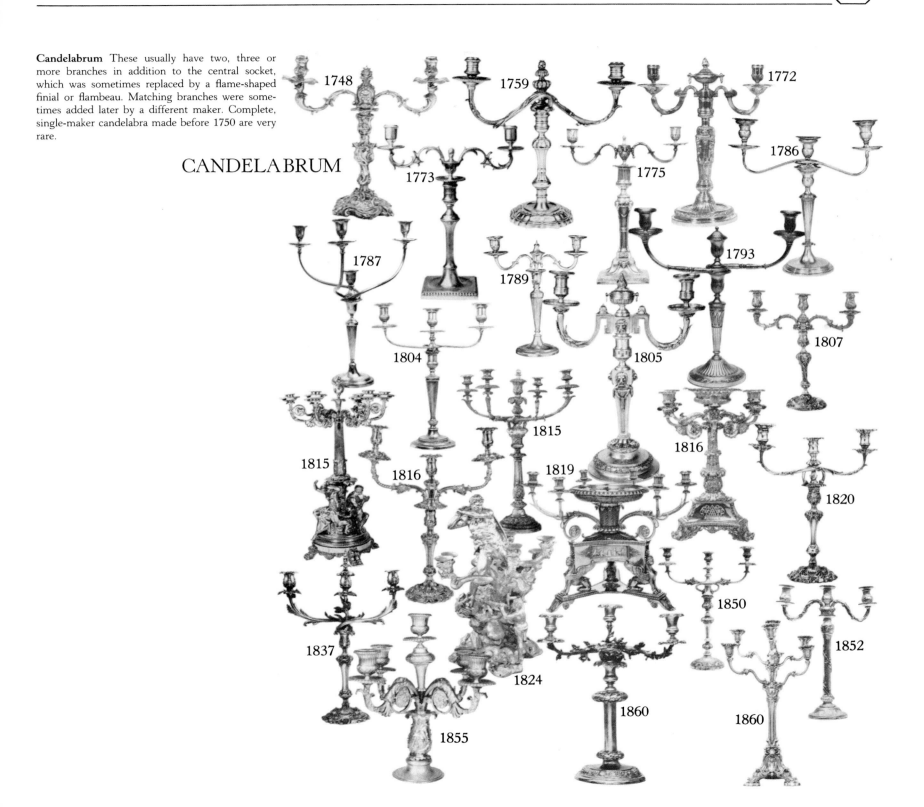

CANDLESTICK

Candlestick Table candlesticks for holding a single candle made before 1660 are rare. Early candlesticks of this type were made in wrought plate and hand-chased, and are susceptible to wear, especially at the corners. After about 1705 they were replaced by the heavier, cast type, which the Huguenot silversmiths had been making since about 1690. Thereafter all candlesticks were cast until about 1760, when wrought plate and die-stamped candlesticks again became popular, following the developments of the Birmingham and Sheffield industries. Cast candlesticks are usually in better condition because they are more durable, although there may be fine cracks in the metal. Hallmarks are usually on the underside. Plate candlesticks may show wear on corners and high spots, and hallmarks suffer wear through cleaning. Rough handling can damage narrow stems. Shapes have generally followed prevailing fashions. Perhaps the most notable names in the manufacture of candlesticks are that of John and William Cafe in the 1750s to 1770s, who were famous particularly for their caryatid style.

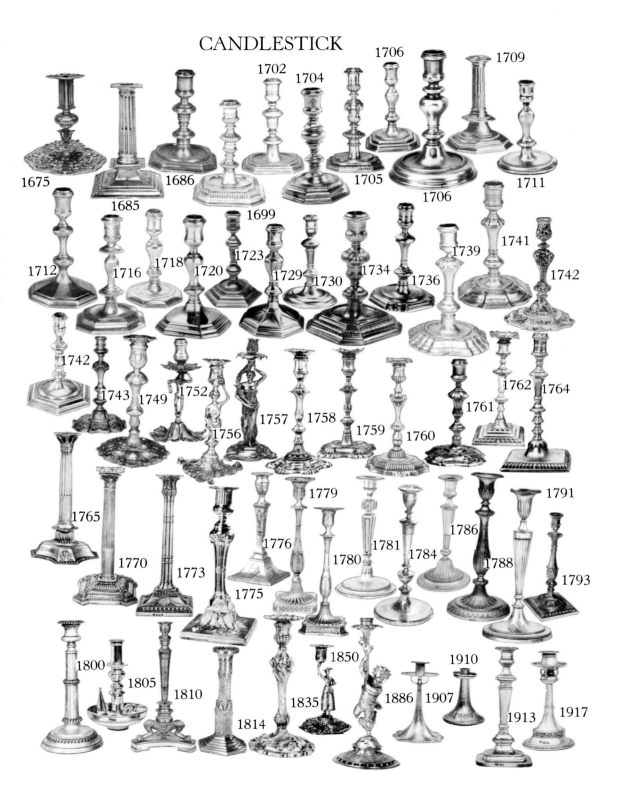

Card case Card cases date from the Victorian era and the custom of the polite social visit. They were designed to protect and present a pristine visiting card, and are usually decoratively embossed, engraved or chased, and fitted with a matching, end-opening hinged lid. Other designs were made without lids or with a spring-closing lid or a hand chain. The most highly prized examples are rectangular, with embossed scroll and leaf decoration, and may include representations of famous buildings such as Windsor Castle or the Scott Memorial.

CARD CASE

1838 1839 1839 1841 1843 1843 1843 1844 1845 1845 1845 1845 1846 1847 1850 1854 1856 1859

Caster These containers for dispensing sugar or pepper through a pierced cover are often found in sets of three in a Warwick cruet stand, with one unpierced caster for powdered mustard. First appearing in about 1660, they were originally of quite plain cylindrical shape. Later shapes changed with the prevailing fashion. Early covers are simply pierced and were kept in place by a slip-over clip or a sleeve fitting outside the lower body. Casters of this type are called lighthouse casters. Later covers are a simple press fit inside the body. The body should be fully hallmarked and the lid should also bear one or two marks, usually on the sleeve. Pepper casters usually have low-domed, simply pierced covers. Casters were very rare before 1660, and after 1775 were largely replaced by sugar baskets and bowls. They are alternatively known as dredgers or muffineers, although the latter were presumably for sprinkling salt on muffins. Points to look out for are odd covers, replacement bases and thin areas on the bulges. Unpierced casters for serving powdered mustard to be mixed on the plate have sometimes been pierced at a later date. Samuel Wood is well-known for making casters from 1730 to 1770.

CASTER

1672 1685 1689 1692 1697 1701 1702 1703 1704 1707 1708 1713 1714 1715 1716 1717 1719 1720 1721 1722 1723 1725 1731 1732 1732 1737 1742 1743 1750 1752 1757 1758 1760 1761 1762 1769 1779 1784 1786 1806 1901 1903 1910

Chamberstick These were intended for use in rooms not often visited, and are usually robust and utilitarian. Early examples date from about 1690, and had a slot in the socket for ejecting candle ends, and a bracket or slot for holding a conical extinguisher. After about 1730 they were made with an opening in the base of the socket for a scissor-type snuffer. Examples with the original extinguisher and snuffer in place are much more valuable. The pan should bear full hallmarks, and all loose pieces should be partly marked.

CHAMBERSTICK

1686
1690
1708
1717
1717
1724
1726
1734
1748
1752
1758
1768
1786
1790
1805
1805
1805
1805
1810
1810
1814
1815
1818
1818
1823
1829
1829
1835
1840
1876
1885
1887

Chocolate pot There are records of chocolate-drinking dating from the 1650s, but chocolate pots made before 1700 are very rare indeed, and their manufacture continued for less than a century. They take the traditional form of the coffee pot, the essential difference being the small additional secondary lid with a finial, which hinges or slides at the top of the conventional lid. This is so a rod could be inserted to stir the thick chocolate. There may also be a detachable hinge-pin on a chain for removing both lids, or a small hinged flap on the spout. The handle is often set at right angles to the spout and may be insulated and bound by a scalloped silver mount.

CHOCOLATE POT

CLARET JUG

Claret jug This is a table jug, usually of glass with silver mounts. Earliest examples date from around the 1830s. The glass bodies are found in many different shapes and are either clear cut or frosted with a great variety of silver mounts. The silver mounts should bear the hallmarks, with separate marks on the lid.

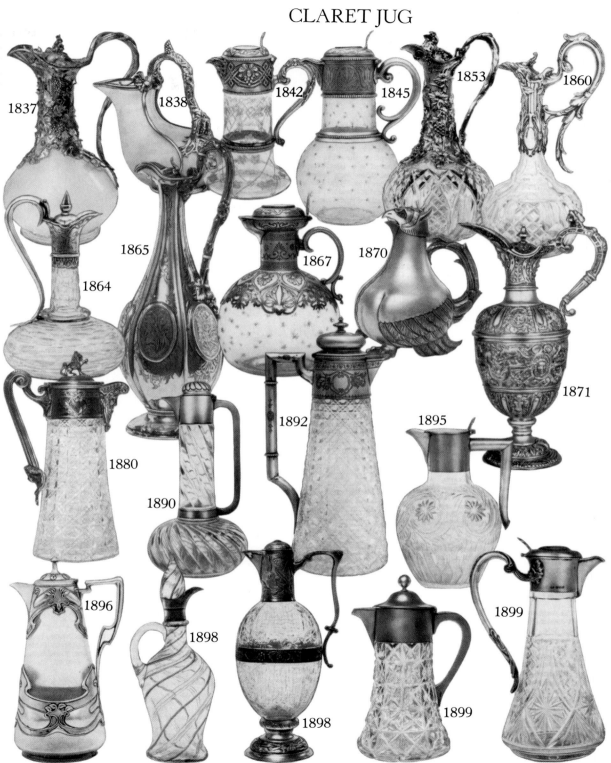

1837 1838 1842 1845 1853 1860 1864 1865 1867 1870 1871 1880 1890 1892 1895 1896 1898 1898 1899 1899

COASTER

Coaster These are also called wine coasters, bottle stands, decanter stands and wine sliders. They were intended for passing the wine (in decanters, rather than bottles) between diners and usually have a turned hardwood base covered with green baize. The base sometimes has a central boss on the inner side in silver for a crest or monogram, and the inside base is sometimes entirely silver and may have full armorials. A heavier type has cast sides with modelled vine leaves and tendrils with hanging grapes. There are also double coasters in a boat or wheeled trolley formation. Early examples dating from the 1750s are usually small and pierced. Points to look out for are split or replacement wooden bases and damage to the lower retaining ring, which may have been caused by the base having been replaced. Hallmarks are particularly vulnerable to the effects of wear and cleaning. Originally often made in pairs or sets of four and made extensively in Old Sheffield plate in the same designs, they seem to have lost favour by the 1840s.

1780

1771

1765

1787

1795

1791

1804

1803

1790

1800

1807

1813

1817

1815

1816

1821

1828

1828

1831

1835

1836

1848

Coffee pot Coffee pots made before 1700 are extremely rare and shapes follow the prevailing fashion. No coffee pot made before 1730 should be embossed or engraved (apart from armorials). The hallmarks on early coffee pots are usually in a group under the base; marks in straight lines should be regarded with suspicion. The early taper cylindrical pots often have marks to the right of the handle, unevenly spaced in a line. Octagonal pots sometimes have one mark on each face. All genuine coffee pots have partly hallmarked lids. Points to look out for are thin patches on the bulges or decoration high spots, fractures near the handles or spout, unmarked or replacement lids, dented bases and later chasing.

COFFEE POT

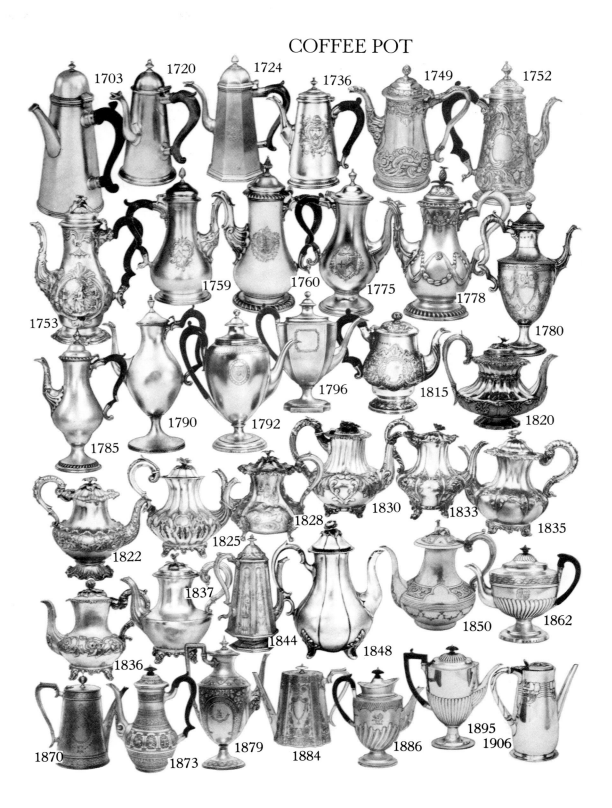

Cow creamer This is a Dutch-influenced type of cream jug made almost exclusively by John Schuppe. Nearly all examples date from the 1760s, although Schuppe registered his mark in 1753. Variations in detail include the addition of a hinged lid on the back, which may be plain or with floral decoration or a large-scale modelled fly. Later reproductions have been made, but these invariably lack the charm of the original.

COW CREAMER

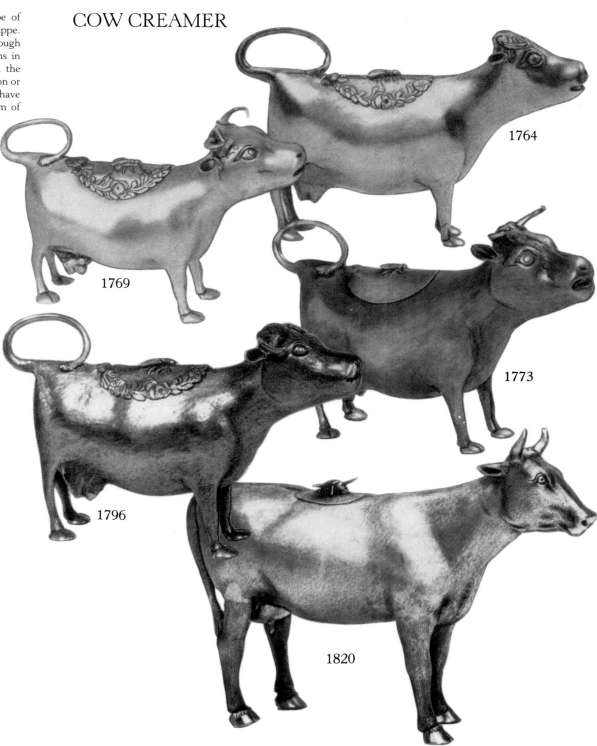

1764

1769

1773

1796

1820

Cream boat and pail The cream jug was used to serve cream until about 1760 when the cream pail appeared as a small pail-shaped container with a swing handle. Tapering and cylindrical in shape, they were sometimes in the form of a pail with hooped bands, sometimes pierced with floral patterns, agricultural and pastoral scenes or with scroll and geometric designs or wirework with applied floral shapes. Mostly up to 3″ high, the pierced type were fitted with a blue glass liner and had handles with pierced or bead decoration. Examples need very close examination for damage to piercing. Cream containers dating from the 1730s were shaped like small sauce boats. Many of this type – heavily cast with Rococo scroll feet and handles – were made by Paul de Lamerie. Old Sheffield plate manufacturers catalogued cream 'basons' in the 1790s. These were oval-shaped on pedestal feet with swing handles.

CREAM BOAT

1740

1753

CREAM PAIL

1754

1776

1800

1845

Cream jug Alternatively known as a creamer or milk jug, this was usually part of a tea set. Cream jugs first appeared in about 1700 as the popularity of tea increased, following its introduction to Europe by the Dutch East India Company. The earliest definite style, now highly prized, was plain baluster with a low collet foot. Called 'pitcher' cream jugs, this type persisted for 30 years or more, finally being replaced by three-legged models, pear-shaped and helmet-shaped jugs etc., according to the fashion. Legs, handles and bases are vulnerable points, as are the bulging sides. Replacement parts should be regarded with suspicion.

CREAM JUG

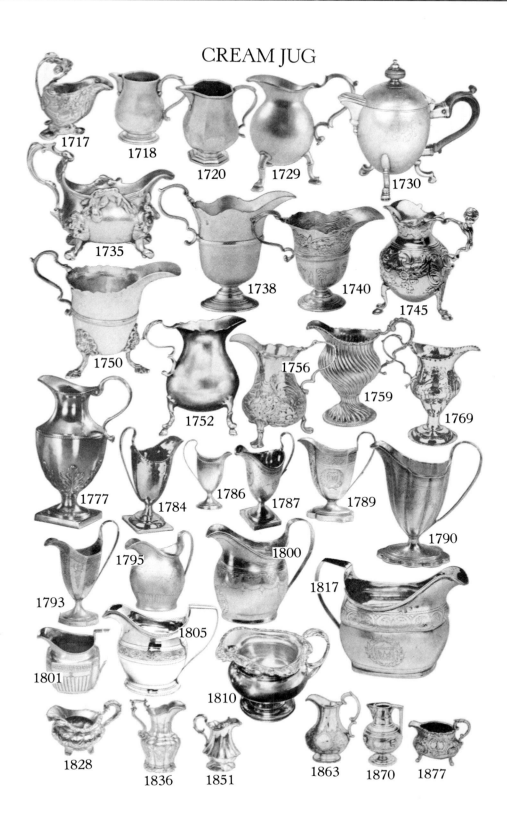

1717 1718 1720 1729 1730 1735 1738 1740 1745 1750 1752 1756 1759 1769 1777 1784 1786 1787 1789 1790 1793 1795 1800 1801 1805 1810 1817 1828 1836 1851 1863 1870 1877

CRUET

Cruet Originally the name given to the vessel containing the wine or the water at the Eucharist, the word 'cruet' is now applied to the frame and containers for table condiments. Earliest examples date from the early eighteenth century or Queen Anne period. These were called Warwick cruets and included three matching silver casters, one unpierced, and two silver mounted bottles for oil and vinegar, in a fitted frame with or without a handle. Some included a cartouche for armorials. There are also two-bottle frames and many other variants. Frame shapes varied according to fashion, and cut-glass silver mounted bottles later replaced the silver casters. Also called soy frames or oil and vinegar frames, the larger ones held up to nine bottles. The vacant rings often found in these frames were for holding the loose covers to prevent soiling of the table. Full hallmarks should be stamped on the underside, and all loose parts should bear some hallmarks. Replacement casters or bottles are often found; these reduce the value of the set.

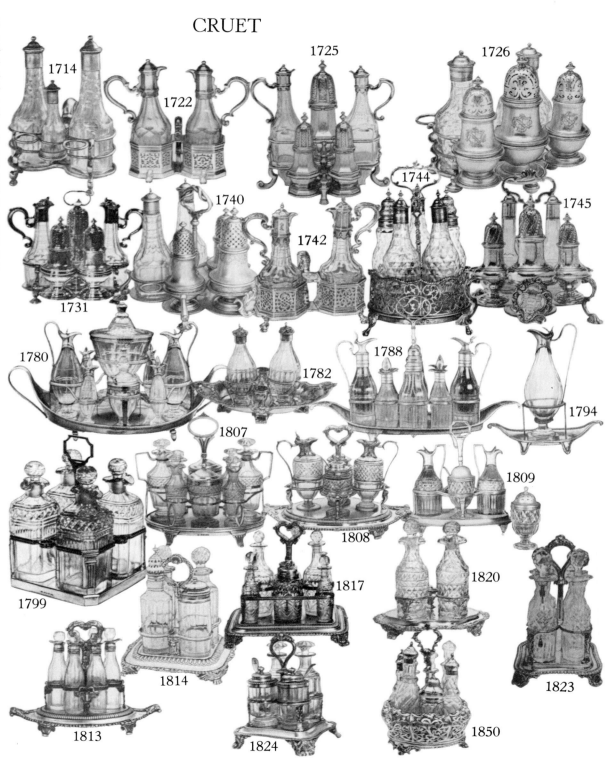

CUP

Cup Silver cups as implements for drinking tea or other hot liquids have fallen from favour owing to their inability to protect the hand and lips from heat, but a number of examples do exist, some with saucers. Two-handled cups, sometimes called loving cups, may have had a ceremonial or commemorative purpose, and follow prevailing styles. A cup raised on a stem, without handles, may be a wine cup or goblet, while a cup used as a chalice at the Eucharist may have a loose cover or paten.

1670   1696   1706   1707   1709

1713   1714   1718   1725   1727

1732   1739   1740   1743   1750

1765   1770   1773   1784   1788   1789

1790   1800   1802   1811   1823   1825

DISH

Dish Distinct from plates by virtue of their larger size (anything over 12″ in diameter, when circular, or wide, when oval), dishes are usually plain apart from edge decoration and a raised rim, often bearing a coat of arms or a crest. They are often found in matching or graduated sets or with matching plates, and occasionally have an enlarged shell at each end, or short feet. There are also examples with a fitted or hinged mazarine or a hot-water container. Few remain without signs of cuts or scratches. A thin or springy base or a particularly highly polished surface may be evidence of attempts to remove defects. Hallmarks are usually found in a line on the underside near the rim. Early examples date from about 1740.

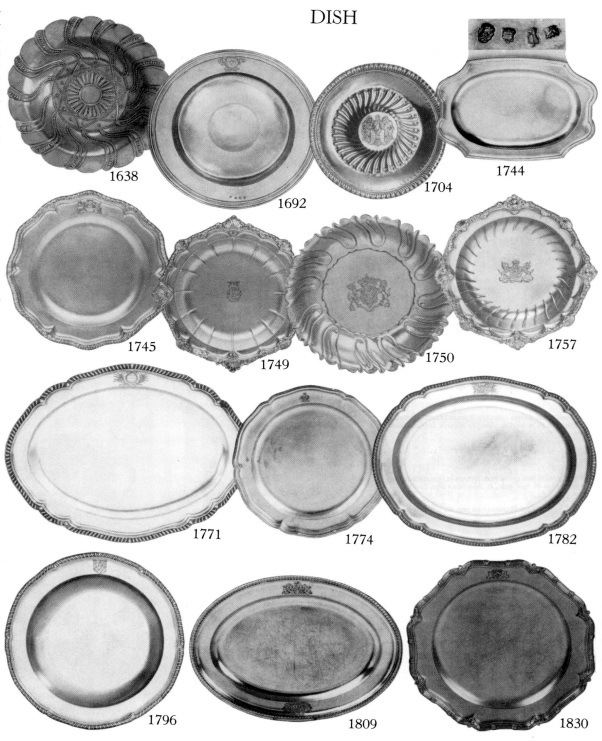

1638

1692

1704

1744

1745

1749

1750

1757

1771

1774

1782

1796

1809

1830

Dish cover Designed for covering dishes in order to protect food and retain heat, these are usually oval and dome-shaped, varying in length from 10" to 24", with detachable reeded or foliate handles secured by a screw and wing nut. They may possibly have originated as part of a meat dish or heated meat stand. Few examples date from before about 1760. Silver covers seem to have remained quite plain, the only decoration being engraved armorials or a crest, but the Old Sheffield plate examples made after about 1800 are more decorated and more varied, with flared bases, double curved domes, large gadrooning, fluting and modelled fruit-shaped handles.

DISH COVER

1794

Dish cross This was designed to retain the heat of food before it was served, and was an improvement on the earlier chafing-dish. It consists of two crossed, square-section arms, centrally pivoted, with adjustable legs and dish supports, and a central spirit lamp, the whole being flat-folding for economy of space. Some examples have a central pierced disc for a separate lamp. The earliest ones appeared in about 1735 but most seem to date from between 1755 and 1780. There should be hallmarks on all the separate parts. The majority of Old Sheffield plate examples date from the 1770 and 1780s.

DISH CROSS

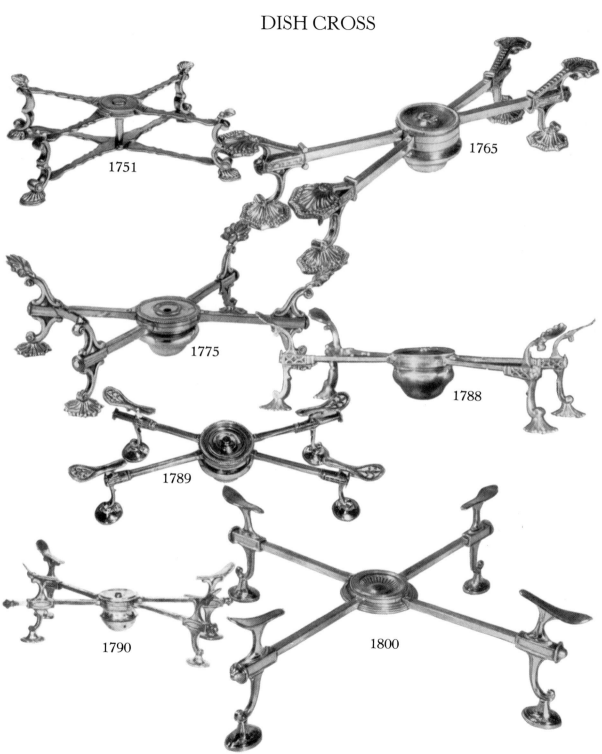

Dish ring Often called potato rings, these were used to protect the table from the heat of dishes. Originating in Ireland, where they were normally made, they first appeared in about 1750. Most examples appear to date from the 1770s and 1780s, but a few have been noted after 1800. There are some rare examples in Old Sheffield plate, possibly made for export to Ireland.

DISH RING

1763

1770

1773

1776

1795

1899

Egg frame Also called egg cruets, these accommodated from two to eight egg cups. Some also include egg spoons hanging in slots, and a salt cellar or a toast rack. The egg cups and spoon bowls usually have gilded interiors, to protect against corrosion. The cups may fit in rings or over a stud in the base of the cruet, which may be either solid or in the form of a frame with a central handle. Early examples date from the 1740s, and they persisted into the reign of Victoria. The base or frame should be fully hallmarked, with additional marks on each separate piece. The frames are easily damaged. Replacement parts reduce the value of the set.

EGG FRAME

1805

1810

1807

1815

1813

1829

1855

1875

Entrée dish Originally known as double dishes, hash dishes or steak dishes, these were intended for the serving of a preliminary course. Very few were made before 1775. The earliest examples are oval, while later examples are octagonal or cushion-shaped, with an increasing incidence of gadrooning, fluting and applied cast borders. The handles are detachable, the earliest ones screwing in, the later ones fitting into a slot. The fitted lids are also detachable, and would have been used as separate dishes. In sets of two or four, the separate pieces are numbered, since they are not always interchangeable. Influential customers sometimes ordered the handles to be made in the shape of their crest. Interior scratches and cuts are common and a highly polished inside surface should be regarded with suspicion. The base should bear full hallmarks, and there should be some marks on the cover and handle. They were made in great variety in Old Sheffield plate.

ENTREE DISH

Epergne The earliest examples appeared in the 1750s, taking the form of several flat dishes supported on scrolling branches from a central stand holding a similar but larger dish. The whole stands on four scrolling and voluted legs, usually with shell feet. In the 1760s and 1770s, still supported on elaborate legs, epergnes reached extremes of imaginative Rococo design, with individual baskets hung from scrolling branches. Many of the original dishes and baskets remain and are delightful pieces in their own right. The central stand should be fully hallmarked and all separate pieces partly marked. In the Adam period (1770–1800) the legs were fluted with claw and ball feet, and the bowls and baskets boat-shaped. After about 1800 they seemed to take the form of a centre-piece, often with cut glass baskets. Examples with all the original parts are now very rare.

EPERGNE

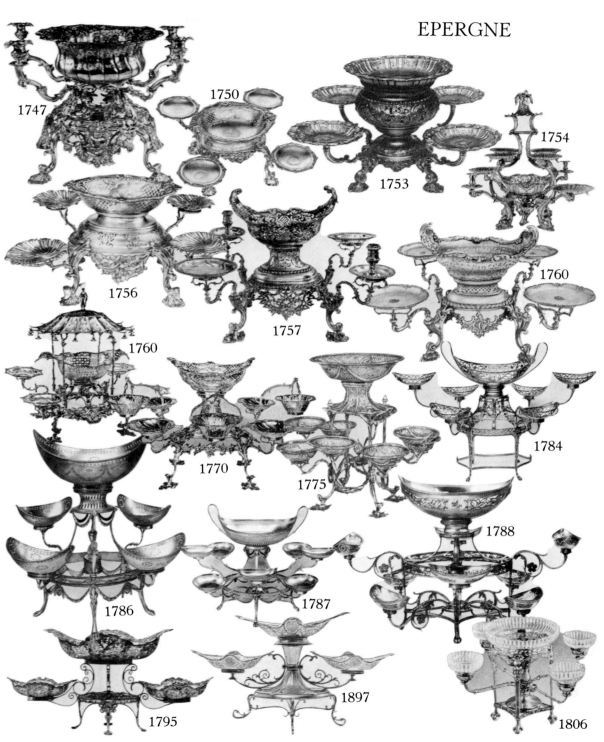

1747

1750

1753

1754

1756

1757

1760

1760

1770

1775

1784

1786

1787

1788

1795

1897

1806

Ewer Intended for finger-washing before a meal, these were sometimes called rosewater ewers and sometimes had a matching basin. Few were made before 1700. Shapes follow the prevailing fashion, and there are examples both with and without hinged lids. Without a matching basin they are sometimes called beer jugs or water pitchers. The bulges and handle joints are subject to dents and fractures, and there may be thin patches where armorials have been removed. The body should bear full hallmarks and the lid should also have some marks, preferably the maker's mark.

EWER

Fish slice There are examples dating from the 1750s with pierced, fan-shaped blades, but oval, spade-shaped and trowel-shaped blades subsequently became more usual. Some of the early models have piercing representing fish, eels, shrimps and other sea creatures swimming amongst seaweed. Fish, lattice, scroll and geometric piercing are regularly found in later examples. Some of the silver handles may be embossed with similar patterns, but these may be the work of a different maker. Ivory or bone handles are also found, sometimes with a trowel-shape attached to the blade. After about 1800, a matching fork was added; the pair were then known as fish servers and sometimes sold in a fitted case.

FISH SLICE

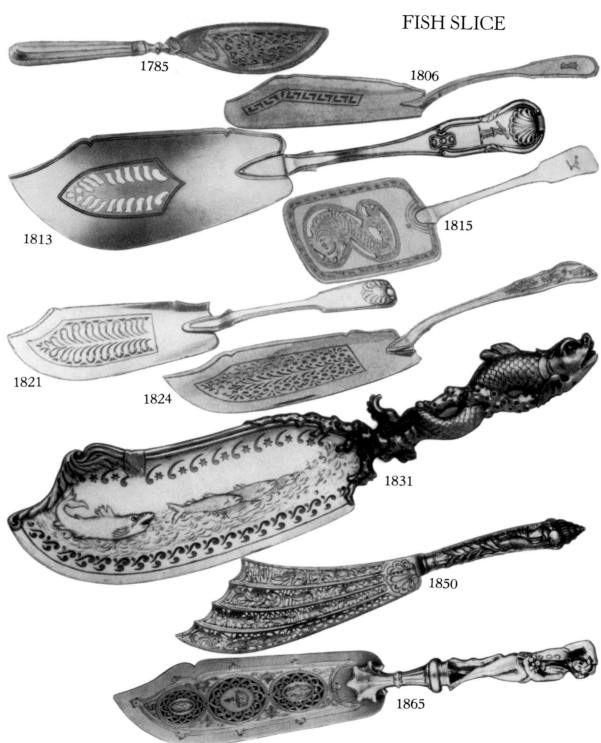

1785

1806

1813

1815

1821

1824

1831

1850

1865

Flagon Also known as livery pots, the earliest examples date from Elizabethan times. Shaped like a large tankard, a flagon has a low-domed, hinged lid, occasionally with a finial, and with a thumb piece. They are usually of plain, tapering cylindrical shape, conforming closely to early tankard plain shapes but with a wide spreading foot. Intended to contain wine, their continuing use is for replenishing the chalice at communion. They rarely have any decoration, although there are examples with armorials or a parish name or inscription. The hallmarks are generally to the right of the handle. The lid should also be marked.

FLAGON

1660

1665

1667

1688

1730

1777

1830

Fruit basket This is a basket either without a handle or with one fixed top handle or two side handles. Examples in contemporary styles exist from about 1730 in delicate pierced, fluted, and wirework patterns. Many were made in Old Sheffield plate. Finely pierced examples often have pieces missing and rim feet may suffer from denting. Hallmarks may be difficult to find and may have been pierced out.

FRUIT BASKET

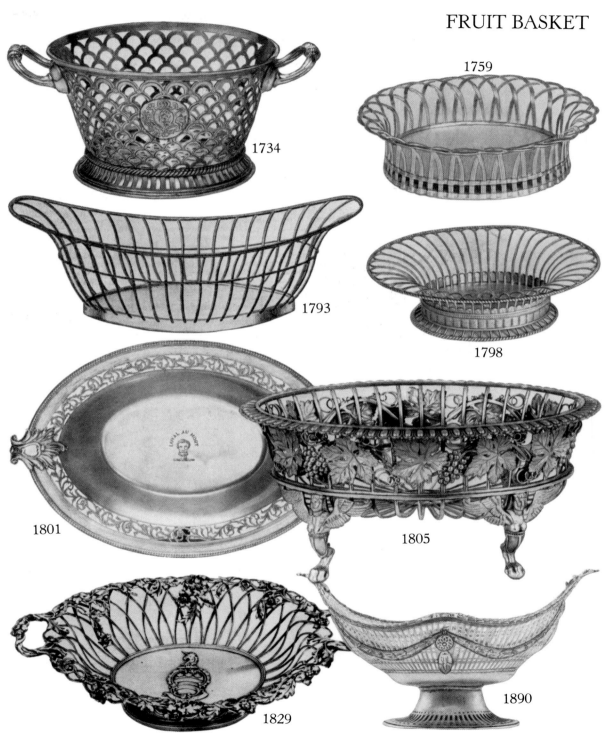

1734

1759

1793

1798

1801

1805

1829

1890

Honey pot Realistically fashioned in the form of a straw honey skep, most examples date from between 1795 and 1805. Paul Storr began making these honey pots, some in silver gilt, at the beginning of his working life, and in Christie's records these are dated from 1793 to 1803. The Victoria and Albert Museum has one of his, dated 1799, which has a looped handle representing plaited straw. The edge of the dish is usually moulded in the same way. The handle is usually modelled as a rather outsize bee, but there are also handles in the form of berries and bees crawling on berries. The honey was usually contained in a separate glass dish within. An Old Sheffield plate honey pot made by Watson and Bradbury in Sheffield in 1800 had a base plate with three legs.

HONEY POT

1797

1799

1802

1830

1850

1858

Inkstand Alternatively called a standish. A few examples exist dating from before 1660, but they are quite rare before 1700. The containers were for ink, wafers (for sealing letters), pounce (for drying the ink) and tapers. There was also a bell for summoning a servant for posting. After the comparatively plain early examples they showed much variety. The type in the form of a plain casket with hinged lids for the containers is called a treasury inkstand. The gallery inkstand is divided into pierced compartments and was popular in the 1760s. The globe inkstand is a most delightful modelled globe standing on a pedestal foot, the upper half of the globe sliding away to reveal the containers within. Most date from around 1790, some standing on a square plinth with a drawer. All the separate parts should be hallmarked. Points to look out for include replacement parts, including legs. Attempts have been made to make the early type from snuffer trays.

INKSTAND

1690
1718
1726
1726
1739
1746
1748
1751
1766
1775
1772
1785
1786
1788
1790
1803
1804
1813
1826
1814
1816
1820
1830
1838
1843
1847
1848
1849
1860
1863
1872
1880
1894
1897

JUG

Jug Jugs were probably originally intended principally for wine, although they can be used to contain almost any kind of liquid. Examples made before 1700 are rare, but there are some Elizabethan Tigerware jugs with silver mounts and hinged lids. After about 1700, they were made in the shape in fashion at the time. Special attention should be given to protruding surfaces, where there may be thin areas, and to deformed handle attachments. Pouring lips have sometimes been removed or added. The body should bear full hallmarks, with some marks also on the lid.

KETTLE

Kettle These were originally used for replenishing the tea pot at the table, and were sometimes made as part of a matching tea set. A few rare examples date from before 1700, those made around this time displaying a Dutch influence. At first they were made with a separate stand and lamp, but later were hinged to stand and secured by a locking pin on a chain. In some early examples the covers are loose, but later hinge sideways. The lamps should be separate from the stand. The body should be fully hallmarked, usually in the centre of the base, but the marks may have been damaged by heat. All hinged or loose parts should also bear some marks. The wide parts of the body are especially vulnerable to wear, dents and fractures. Points to look out for are replacement lids, lamps and handles, although replaced cane or raffia handle covering should not significantly reduce the value.

Marrow scoop This piece of cutlery was specifically designed for the purpose of extracting the marrow from bone cavities after boiling and serving. The most common is the double-ended type, with scoops of varying width, but there are also spoons with scoop handles, and a single reported example of a fork with a scoop handle, made in about 1670. Another rarity is a marrow scoop forming part of the tubular handle of a basting spoon dated 1751. They are rare before 1700 but persist until the reign of Victoria. They are often crested or initialled on the wide bowl and the hallmarks are usually on the stem.

MARROW SCOOP

1714

1741

1758

1788

1754

MAZARINE

Mazarine A flat, usually oval, dish, pierced with geometric and scrolling shapes, this was used for straining the fish on the fish server. It was usually a part of a serving dish, and was sometimes hinged as part of a heated serving stand. Coats of arms or crests often form part of a central oval cartouche. A report of 1673 suggests that mazarines were then used for straining ragout; they were in more widespread use in the early 1700s.

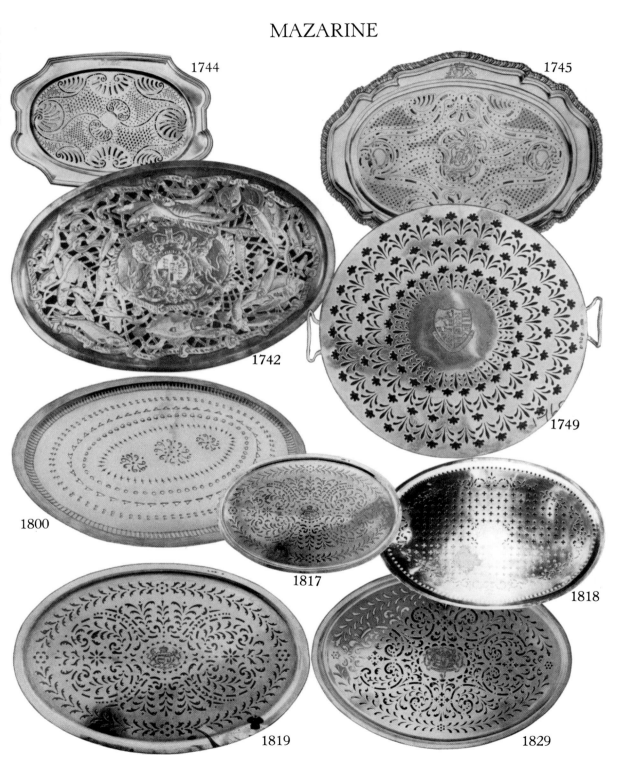

1744

1745

1742

1749

1800

1817

1818

1819

1829

Monteith Punch bowls with a detachable notched rim are known as monteiths, reportedly after a Scotsman of that name who wore a cloak with a similarly notched hem. The notches served to hold wine glasses, bowl downwards in the liquid, for cooling. There should also be hallmarks on detachable rims and loose handles.

MONTEITH

Mug A mug is usually of half-pint size or a little larger. Almost every vessel of this type with more than a pint capacity generally had a cover, so any rather large pieces may be tankards with the lids removed owing to damage. The earliest silver mugs, which appeared in the 1680s, are spherical or globular, with a rather smaller wide and straight reeded neck and a simple loop handle. Some have chinoiserie decoration but they are often quite plain. Until about 1800, all mugs were raised in one piece and should therefore have no side seams. They were usually styled in accordance with the tankard shapes and decoration of the time. Points to look out for are thin areas where crests or initials may have been removed.

MUG

Mustard pot Mustard was used as a condiment by the Anglo Saxons, and in Norman times was used mixed with honey, wine and vinegar. In the early eighteenth century it was served in its powdered form and mixed before use. It usually arrived at the dining table in the unpierced caster of the three forming the Warwick cruet. It was not served in its ready-mixed form until about 1760, when a specially made container became necessary. No mustard pots are found dating from before this time. The early models were cylindrical or drum-shaped. Novelty shapes appeared in Victorian times, and there are also art nouveau examples. The unpierced ones had gilded interiors, while blue glass liners are found in the pierced ones. The pierced type are sometimes rather weak near the lid hinge and handle top, and require close inspection for fractures or replacement parts. The body should be fully hallmarked and the lid partly marked.

MUSTARD POT

Nutmeg grater Nutmeg was introduced sometime before 1600 and was a convenient means of flavouring food and drink, its only disadvantage being that, while it was desirable to carry a personal supply, it had to be freshly ground. Silversmiths solved this problem by making a pocket container which included a grater. Silver graters soon wore out and had to be replaced by steel ones, but they had to be made separately in order to satisfy the Assay Office rule against uniting base metal with silver. Earliest examples date from about 1760 and are of simple cylindrical shape with cap ends, but examples made before the 1770s are rare. In the late eighteenth century Samuel Massay made many graters in many different shapes, and the Birmingham silversmiths, prolific in small items such as these, also produced them in enormous variety. They were also incorporated into corkscrews. The hallmarking is disappointing, very few pieces having more than the maker's mark, and many of these being unidentifiable.

NUTMEG GRATER

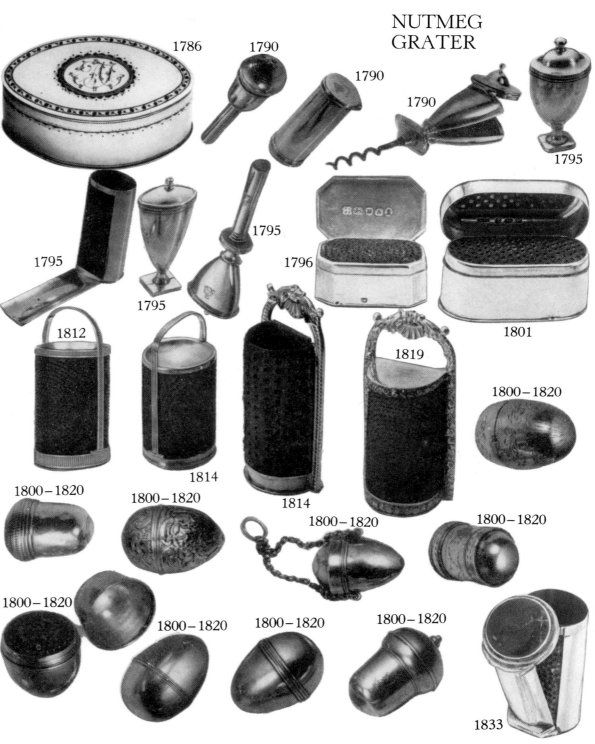

Pap boat This was a small, shallow, sauce-boat shaped vessel with a taper spout and without a handle or foot. Examples made before 1715 are rare. Early pap boats are quite plain, without edge moulding, but later ones are sometimes gadrooned. They are usually hallmarked at the wide end near the rim. None originally had base or feet, but these have sometimes been added, in which case the vessel may be called a cream boat. If a handle has been added it is discernible by its proximity to the marks. Sauce boats are rarely found dated later than 1820.

PAP BOAT

1733

1788

1833

Pepper pot The kitchen pepper pot, which appeared shortly after 1700, is highly valued. In accordance with its humble kitchen use it is of simple design, usually plain cylindrical with a low-domed, simply pierced, slip-on cover and a loop handle. Later, shapes became more varied. The hallmarks should be stamped in a group on the underside of the base and there should also be a mark on the cover, usually inside. Those intended for table use usually have a bun-shaped cover and are known as bun peppers for this reason. They are usually simply pierced. With pear-shaped bodies they are found from the 1720s, later appearing in many other forms, such as egg-shaped, cylindrical, conical etc., through the fanciful Victorian styles and art nouveau patterns.

PEPPER POT

PLATE

Plate Plates have been in use since the communal bowl fell from favour. There are some ornate circular examples dating from the 1600s, with wide, deeply embossed, raised rims, depicting birds, fish, animals and fruit, often with a coat of arms in the centre. In spite of being so ornate, these were for everyday family use. In about 1730, simple, practical, plain circular ones appeared, but shortly after this they were superseded by the familiar circular gadrooned type. Armorials and crests were often engraved on the rims, and edge moulding often included shell and acanthus leaf motifs, but it is much easier to find matching sets with simple gadrooned edges. The centres quite often bear scratches or cuts but, unless very unsightly, these do not unduly reduce the value. Attempts to remove them may reduce the value more, but there is sometimes evidence of such attempts and thin, shiny or springy centres should be examined carefully. Plates bearing the Royal Arms may have been part of an ambassadorial issue that were not returned. Dinner plates are about 9½″ in diameter; larger pieces are second course dishes. Hallmarks are usually on the underside, in a line near the rim or, very occasionally, in a group in the centre.

1663

1690

1721

1732

1745

1790

1806

1804

1807

1814

1816

Pomander The pomander, whose name is derived from the French *pomme d'ambre*, meaning amber apple, is a container for sweet-smelling spices, designed to counteract any unpleasant odours. They are found in many forms: segmented spheres, fruit shapes, skulls, boxes and many others. The forerunner of the vinaigrette, the pomander was originally simply the compartment for aromatic vinegar in the spice box, other compartments containing an assortment of solid spices. It was also associated with the vinegar stick, a walking-stick in the head of which was a compartment, with a pierced cover, for aromatic vinegar. Vinegar sticks were probably carried principally by clergymen and physicians. Although no very early examples are known, there are references in the Privy Purse expense accounts to pomanders in the possession of Catherine Howard, Mary Tudor and Henry VII. There are many reliable references to vinaigrettes from as early as 1722, but these did not come into general use until about 1790, and pomanders were probably in use both then and afterwards.

POMANDER

1620

Porringer Also known as caudle cups or posset pots, these were used for holding porridge, caudle (a mixture of broth, milk, eggs and wine, given to convalescents) or posset (a dietetic drink of hot milk curdled in white wine, sherry and old ale, then sweetened, spiced and thickened). Defects to look for are thin areas on the bulges or decoration high spots, fractures or repairs near the handle joints, replacement handles and any displacement of the base rim. Crudely cast, beaded caryatid handles are typical of porringers of the 1660s to 1680s, but may be replacements. Hallmarks are usually in a line, sometimes uneven, near the upper rim. Marks on the base should be regarded with suspicion. Covers should also be fully hallmarked.

PORRINGER

PUNCH BOWL

Punch bowl These came into general use around the 1680s and were intended to hold sufficient punch for a gathering or party. The word 'punch' is derived from the Hindi *panch*, meaning five, as there were five traditional ingredients: spirit, lemon juice, spice, sugar and water. Punch bowls are usually of good gauge, but there may be areas of thinness, for example where armorials have been removed. Hallmarks on the body are usually in a group under the base, or, in later examples on the foot rim.

1696

1698

1699

1700

1701

1702

1703

1723

1729

1776

1779

1804

1886

1899

Quaich These early drinking vessels, Scottish in origin, are found from the early 1600s, taking the form of shallow circular bowls, between 2″ and 6″ in diameter, made from wooden staves bound with silver mounts. Nearly all are dated before 1700, although there are some from as late as the 1750s, the later ones sometimes entirely silver, either engraved to represent wooden staves or quite plain. Most have two flat curving handles at the level of the rim. Examples with Scottish provincial hallmarks are particularly sought after. It has been suggested that the quaich may be the Scottish equivalent of the English mazer.

QUAICH

1700

1704

1709

1710

1826

Rattle Early rattles consist of a piece of coral for sucking, a whistle for blowing and bells for shaking. (Coral has been attributed with medicinal properties since Roman times.) A rattle of this type is illustrated in a Royal portrait of the early 1500s. The same general design persisted into Victorian times, but the construction of rattles out of thin-gauge metal and the flimsiness of the bell attachments, together with rough treatment in the hands of infants, gave them a short life expectation. Those remaining have often lost their coral, which is most difficult to replace; ivory has sometimes been substituted. Bells may be missing or may have been replaced, and the metal is subject to buckling and tearing. Hallmarks are sometimes extremely difficult to find. Occasionally there is only the maker's mark, which is most likely to be on the whistle lip.

RATTLE

1700

1745

1765

1785

1810

Salt cellar These date from medieval times although many early ornamental examples now only exist in museums and collections. The collectors' interest starts with the trencher salts in use after about 1690. These are usually one piece items with a circular or oval bowl. They are generally marked under the bowl which may be quite thin from wear and cleaning and may possibly be worn through on the marks. This pattern is found until about 1735 when the three or four legged type became fashionable. The 1760s introduced four legged oval pierced salt cellars with blue glass liners and the late eighteenth-century Adam style brought the oval boat shape on pedestal feet, decorated with flutes, embossed or with bright cut floral swags. After 1800 styles became more elaborate and substantial and earlier shapes were also revived. Salt cellars were also fully catalogued in old Sheffield plate and are found with a variety of interiors which may be tin, silver plate, gilding or a blue glass liner. Gilded interiors, found after about 1740, are often worn away by cleaning. Salt cellars were made by Hester Bateman in fashionable styles of the time and Paul Storr made many notable sets with highly Rococo and realistic shell patterns.

SALT CELLAR

SALVER

Salver This is a flat tray, with or without short feet, sometimes with a central pedestal foot, when it is called a tazza, or with handles, when it is called a tray. Small salvers are sometimes known as waiters, presumably because they were used by servants in waiting. Salvers made before 1700 are rare and varied in style; later ones were made in simple geometric shapes, becoming more complex according to fashion, and from time to time reverting to previous tastes. Points to look out for include thin or springy areas where armorials have been erased, re-engraved monograms, split or repaired applied moulding and worn-through corners or angles. Originally plain salvers may have been chased or engraved at a later date, and legs may have been repaired or replaced. Hallmarks are usually, but not always, on the underside.

Sauce boat Sauce boats made in the 1720s are double-lipped, with a moulded serpentine upper edge, a scroll handle at each side and a low rim or pedestal foot. This type persisted into the 1750s, but oval, single-lipped designs appeared in the 1730s. Sauce boats made before 1720 are rare. Around the 1740s they appeared with four feet and flying scroll handles. Likely trouble spots are the points where the feet and handle join the body, where there might be dents or fractures. Feet and handles may have broken off or may have been repaired or replaced, replacements sometimes discernible only by a narrow ring of solder. Shaped edges may have split and show evidence of repairs, and bodies may be thin where crests have been erased. Hallmarks are usually in a line on the underside or, in later examples, beneath the lip.

SAUCE BOAT

1720

1727

1729

1731

1735

1738

1739

1740

1742

1745

1749

1750

1752

1754

1766

1769

1770

1771

1775

1784

1786

1793

1795

1813

1829

1835

1854

SAUCEPAN

Saucepan Also called a brandy warmer, the saucepan was reputedly originally used for warming brandy. Few examples exist dating from before 1700, but there is very little variation in style from the time they first appear until they fade out around the 1820s. Most have a bulbous body, but some are cylindrical or have an everted rim. The handle is at right angles to the spout and is usually made of turned hardwood with a silver ferrule joining it to the body. The body was raised from the sheet and has a pressed or cast lip. Some examples have a loose cover with a silver, ivory or hardwood knob and some have a stand. Smaller saucepans are called pipkins. Handle joints may be pushed in or fractured, and body high spots may be thin through wear or cleaning. A wooden handle is very likely to be a replacement, and hallmarks are often burnt or rubbed.

1717

1728

1737

1743

1769

1775

1815

1824

SHELL

Shell Realistically cast or modelled – roughly life-size – in silver plate, these scallop shells were used to hold butter. An example by David Willaume I, recorded in 1718, was cast with feet in the form of whelks in a marine encrustation. Paul de Lamerie made many similar ones, some in sets of four, in the 1730s. This design was continued by other makers, but later shells were modelled, rather than cast, and had spherical or cockle feet. The semicircular edge is usually scallop cut and without moulding, while the opposite edge varies greatly in shape and has a wide variety of floral, shell or gadroon decoration, often with a crest or monogram.

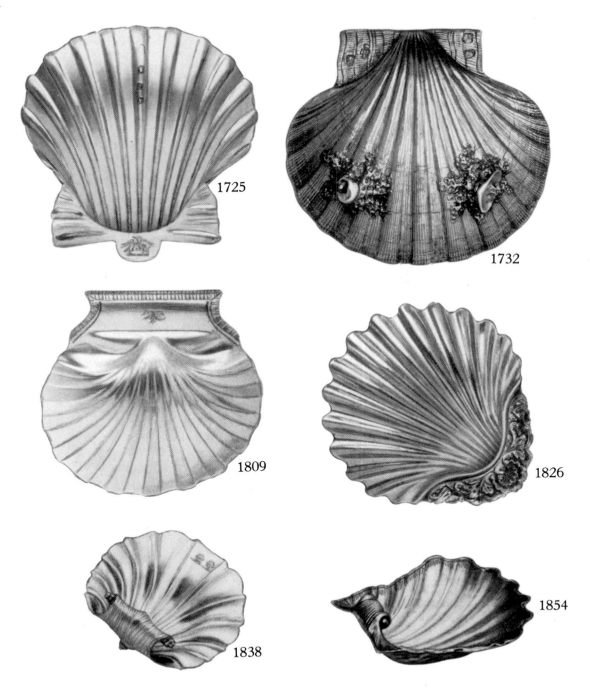

1725

1732

1809

1826

1838

1854

SNUFF BOX

Snuff box Although there is evidence that snuff was taken from as early as the 1560s, there are very few examples of silver snuff boxes made before the 1720s. Some of the London silversmiths, such as Edward Edwards and William Eley, made them in large numbers, as did the Birmingham silversmiths, notably Nathaniel Mills, whose high-quality work lasted well into Victorian times. The level of technical craftsmanship and the boxes' aesthetic qualities determine their value, and undamaged examples with well-fitting lids are the most sought after. The larger boxes, into which cigarettes will fit, the table models and those in fox-head shapes are very popular. Badly-fitting lids and badly worn decoration are points to look out for.

Snuffer Snuffers were used for trimming the wicks of candles to prevent guttering (caused by the curling of the wick which resulted in smoking and loss of wax). The snuffers were required to cut the hot wick and retain it. The point was used for pricking out the burnt-out candle end. In 1749 Benjamin Cartwright invented a 'mechanical' snuffer, which had an additional plate to extinguish the burning wick. Apart from the examples in the museums made in the 1500s, there are very few silver snuffers dating from before 1680. They are of sturdy construction and often have armorials engraved on the box. Some were furnished with a stand, into which the snuffer fitted vertically, but these stands were later replaced by snuffer trays, which appeared in about 1700. Snuffers should bear full hallmarks on one half and be partly marked on the other. The introduction of the non-guttering wick in the 1830s made snuffers with stand and tray redundant.

SNUFFER

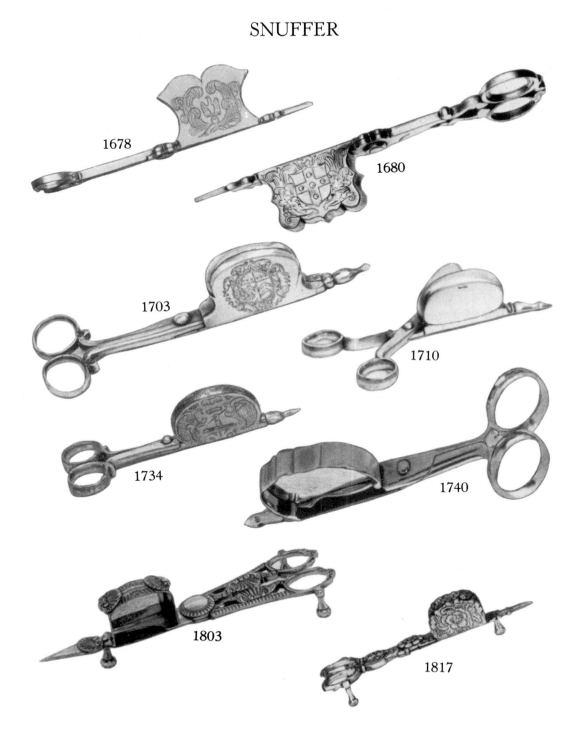

1678

1680

1703

1710

1734

1740

1803

1817

Snuffer stand This was a stand for holding the candle snuffer, retaining it in a vertical position. Variations in detail include the addition of a candle socket and drip pan or of a conical extinguisher on a chain, but refinements such as these disappeared soon after 1700. Examples made before 1680 are rare; they persisted until about 1730 although snuffer trays appeared as an alternative in about 1700. The stand should be fully hallmarked on the underside of the base.

SNUFFER STAND

1674

1686

1697

1690

1700

1703

1715

1724

Snuffer tray A few snuffer trays are known to have been made around the 1680s, but most are dated after 1700. They served the same purpose as snuffer stands, but survived much longer, into Victorian times, a large number and variety being made in Old Sheffield plate. After falling into disuse around the 1830s, they may have been kept for use as pen or spoon trays.

SNUFFER TRAY

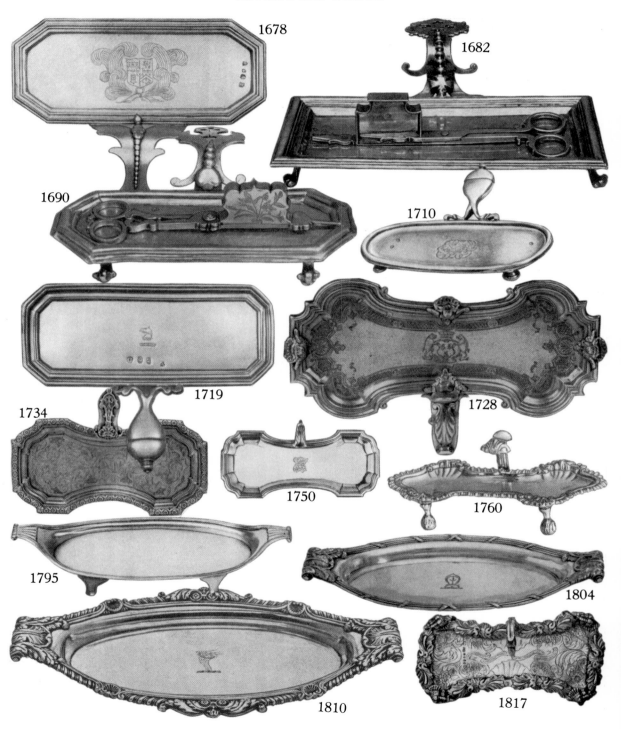

1678

1682

1690

1710

1719

1728

1734

1750

1760

1795

1804

1810

1817

STIRRUP CUP

Stirrup cup These are used for a pre-hunt drink while in the saddle. Most commonly in the shape of a fox's head, stag's head and hooves are also found. The earliest fox head cup noted is dated 1760. Early examples tend to be narrower with a smaller opening. They later become wider and less stylised. Usually wrought in silver plate, there are also cast examples with very detailed features. Pairs are extremely rare. The hallmarks are usually stamped round the plain drinking band at the fox's neck. Points to look out for are thin or worn through nose and ear tips.

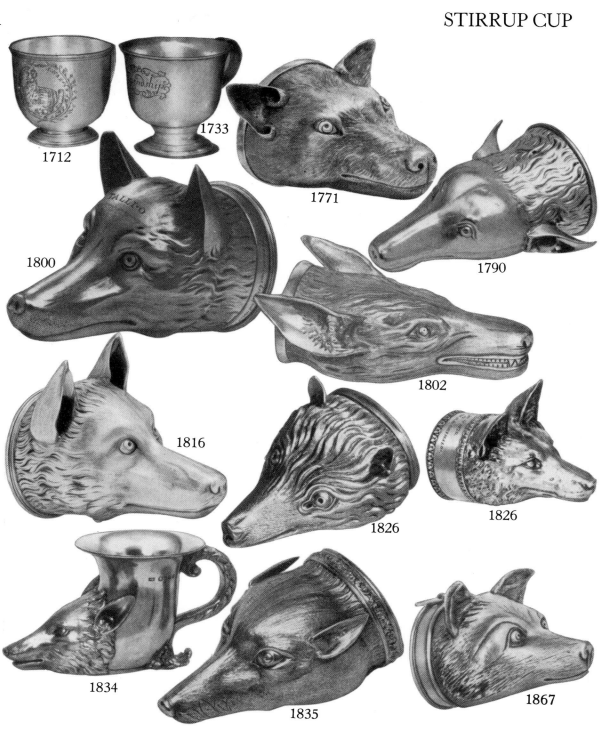

1712

1733

1771

1790

1800

1802

1816

1826

1826

1834

1835

1867

STRAINER

Strainers Usually called lemon or orange strainers, the few known examples of these made before 1700 are plain circular, with simple geometric piercing in the shallow bowl and two unpierced, shaped handles, level with the rim. Later examples have larger, shallower bowls with more decorative piercing and single or double cast scroll handles. They are sometimes pierced out and sometimes hallmarked inside the bowl. The handles should be hallmarked. A gravy strainer is a serving spoon with a gallery-pierced straining plate fixed longitudinally across the bowl. The mote spoon or mote skimmer is of teaspoon size and has a scroll-pierced bowl for removing a mote from a cup of tea or Communion wine. The pointed handle was for removing a blockage in the teapot spout. Most are dated between about 1690 and 1770 and are usually disappointingly hallmarked on the stem, which often makes them very hard to identify. There is also a mote spoon with a marrow-scoop handle, made in 1740.

1714

1718

1721

1732

1748

1760

1770

1789

1790

1819

Strawberry dish These are distinctive and often puzzling dishes, displaying a close conformity of pattern, and which could be used to contain many other eatables apart from strawberries. Their construction is notable for its simplicity. They are usually found without either edge mouldings or raised bases. The curving sides have distinctive, widely-spaced flutes, and the flat centres are usually plain apart from engraved or flat chased armorials. Few examples are found before 1700; most seem to be dated between 1720 and 1740. Earlier examples have punched decoration. Later examples have scalloped, serpentine and sometimes everted edges, and may have elaborate, flat chased spiral fluting. They usually measure between 6″ and 10″ in diameter. Troubles that may be encountered include splits in the flutes and thin or springy areas where armorials have been ground out. Robert Garrard made many high-quality copies of George II patterns.

STRAWBERRY DISH

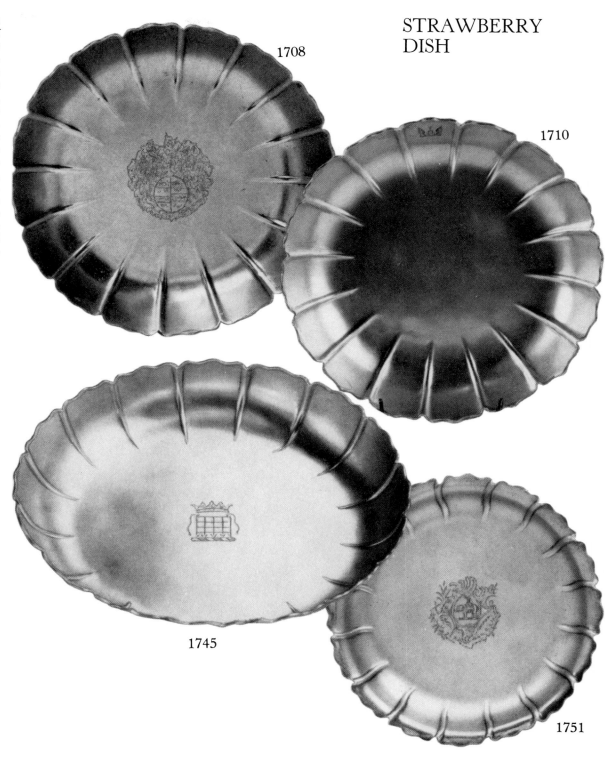

1708

1710

1745

1751

Sugar bowl In the wake of a variety of ornate patterns, the design of sugar containers settled down just after 1700 to a simple plain, undecorated circular or octagonal bowl with a low moulded foot. Most have a matching loose cover, also with a rim foot, although some covers have baluster finials. Many are without covers and have wide flat rims with serpentine edges. Examples with widely-spaced flutes have been noted dating from the 1730s. After the 1750s, embossed baluster lidded shapes are found; these were probably the central containers in boxed tea caddy sets. 'Irish' bowls appeared at about this time in the form of plain bowls or bowls with wide spiral flutes, with an everted serpentine edge and three shell-headed hoof feet, and without a cover. Their purpose was probably to hold the pieces of sugar broken from the sugar loaf, and they seem to precede the two-handled sugar basins that form part of tea-sets. They are usually hallmarked under the foot, and the covers should also be fully or partly marked.

Sugar nips Pieces of sugar broken from the sugar loaf were picked up with sugar tongs, the design of which seems to have been inspired by the andiron or coal tongs. The earliest examples, dating from the 1720s, are of this type, having a spring action, and there is an example with a central pin for clearing teapot spouts. Those of pivoted scissor type known as sugar nips, which appeared in about the 1750s, have charming scrolling legs and shell grips. They are sometimes crested on the circular pivot plate. The type with pierced cast legs, shell grips and a spring-bow handle appeared in about 1775, together with the early spring-bow type with taper or shaped legs and plain or bright cut engraved oval grips. An examination of those of the cast and scissor type frequently reveals evidence of repair, and there is often a crack on the bend of the spring-bow type. Sugar nips are usually hallmarked on the ring handles or shell grips, often with the maker's mark or lion only.

SUGAR NIPS

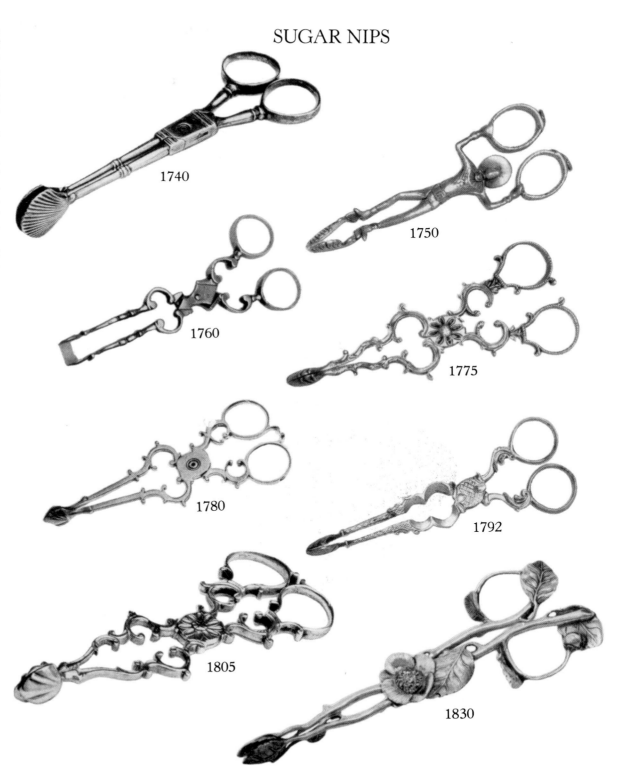

1740

1750

1760

1775

1780

1792

1805

1830

Sugar vase This sugar container is sometimes found as part of a matching set along with two tea caddies, and sometimes in a fitted case. They appeared in about the 1750s and are often found without the caddies. The shape of those made in the 1750s is compressed baluster and rather wider than that of the caddies, with floral embossing and a matching cover and finial. The 1760s brought the delightful Adam urn-shaped vase with embossed drapes and anthemions and two short scroll handles at the shoulders, and high-domed drape-embossed covers with baluster finials. Around the 1770s another Adam urn-shape appears, with loop handles or short volute handles on the shoulders of a plain or half-fluted body. Perhaps the best-known sugar vases are the set of eight mady by Benjamin and James Smith in 1809–10, which are now in the Royal Collection, and a similar pair made by Paul Storr in 1814. These are almost thistle-shaped and are richly chased with acanthus scrolls above fluting. They have a wide integral stand with shell-embossed acanthus feet.

SUGAR VASE

1757

1758

1761

1766

1772

1772

1779

1785

1806

1872

1788

Sweetmeat basket The pattern with a swing handle, which dates from the 1770s, is usually vase-shaped with a pedestal foot or tripod feet. The body may be pierced, in which case a blue glass liner is fitted. Examples dating from the Adam period (1770–1800) have drapes, swags and medallions and are generally boat-shaped, multifoil or octagonal. The handles are quite often unmarked. Handles and legs or pedestal feet may possibly be replacements.

SWEETMEAT BASKET

1741 · 1771 · 1750 · 1736 · 1764 · 1773 · 1777 · 1781 · 1783 · 1784 · 1785 · 1785 · 1788 · 1790 · 1790 · 1791 · 1796 · 1798 · 1800 · 1806 · 1817

Sweetmeat dish These are generally dated between 1630 and 1700. Mostly smaller than 8″ in diameter, they are usually circular and shallow without a base or feet and are often rather crudely embossed with straight fluting, scrolling or punch beading. Simple cut-out shell-shaped or pointed handles are soldered on at opposite sides. Sweetmeat dishes appear in the sales rooms from time to time although their exact use is often uncertain. Their nearest relative in shape and construction is the wine taster which they mostly pre date.

SWEETMEAT DISH

1629

1632

1632

1638

1652

1678

Tankard All tankards have hinged covers, most with a thumb-piece for opening before drinking. A few have domed covers with a finial. Shapes have remained remarkably constant since Elizabethan times, the body being tapering cylindrical with a scroll handle. Examples dating from the 1580s are usually silver gilt with chased strapwork and cover finials. After 1700, baluster and barrel shapes appear. Thin areas may be found in places where armorials have been removed, and lids may have been damaged, repaired or completely replaced. A lid may have been removed and a lip added to make a jug. There may be body fractures near the handle joints. The hallmarks should be in a straight line to the right of the handle. Tankards made before 1730 with hallmarks on the underside should be regarded with suspicion. Lids should bear full hallmarks on the outside. Hallmarks are rarely on the inside except when the cover is domed, in which case the marks are found inside in a group. Most tankards made before 1730 have the maker's mark struck on the handle. The bodies of mugs and tankards made before about 1800, when reeded models appeared, were raised in one piece and should therefore have no side-seams or let-in bottoms.

TANKARD

Taper stick These were used to hold a taper or small candle for melting sealing wax. They were made in the same patterns and proportions as candlesticks, but were little more than half their height. They are quite often found in pairs. Alternative designs take the shape of a chamber candlestick or are part of an inkstand, in which case they may have an attached conical extinguisher on a chain. Examples made before 1700 are not numerous, but subsequently they occur frequently until the 1770s, when coiled tapers appeared and were held in stands called wax jacks. The earlier cast type of taper sticks are hallmarked under the base, and the loaded type on the base edge or rim.

TAPERSTICK

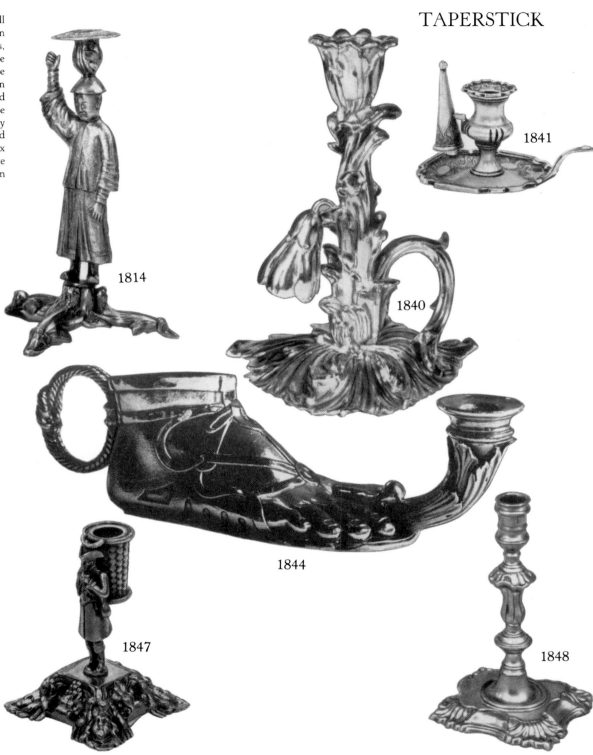

1814

1841

1840

1844

1847

1848

Tazza A tazza is a shallow drinking vessel on a pedestal foot. Examples of these are found dating from the 1560s onwards. The name 'tazza' is now also given to the footed salver, and examples of these exist from the 1650s onwards; these are plain circular with a plain moulded or gadrooned rim. The matching spreading pedestal foot has a screw attachment. There are octagonal and other, variously shaped plates and even pierced ones. Hallmarks should be on the upper or lower surface near the rim. The foot should be marked with a lion or leopard's head erased. The screw-in socket may have cut-card strengthening pieces to prevent buckling of the plate centre. Tazze were made just after 1700 by Philip Rollos, David Willaume and Nicholas Clausen. The later, vine-decorated, pierced type were made just after 1800 by Digby Scott and Benjamin Smith.

TAZZA

1661

1697

1703

1712

1720

1724

1784

1805

TEA CADDY

Tea caddy When tea first arrived in Europe from the East it was very expensive and required a compact and secure container with a lock. A caddy is a case named after the Malay word *Kati*, a weight by which tea was sold. The tea was kept in a glass or metal container called a canister, inside the caddy. There was one canister for each type of tea, and possibly also one for sugar. Tea canisters made before 1700 are rare. They seem to have been kept singly until the 1730s, when pairs, threes and cases are found. The early undecorated rectangular or octagonal examples have a circular, domed slip-on cover, which could be used as a measure. This cover fitted onto a sliding flat top to facilitate filling, although some canisters had sliding bases for this purpose. Shapes later varied with current tastes. Perhaps the most notable example is the set by Paul de Lamerie, which comprises three delicately chased canisters with armorials, a cream jug, twelve teaspoons, two knives, a pair of sugar nips and a mote spoon, all contained within a mahogany fitted case with silver scroll feet and a silver lock plate and key. As caddies became larger, in the 1760s, they began to include individual locks. The most fashionable design at this time was a representation of a cube-like tea chest with a chinoiserie pattern and a tea-leaf handle. Notable oval models were made by Andrew Fogelberg, Paul Storr's master, in 1781; these have a domed, hinged lid, an acorn finial, guilloche decoration, a Tassie medallion and a lock. The Bateman family also made oval designs, with domed, hinged lids with locks and a pineapple finial. The bodies should be fully hallmarked, with lids and slides also partly marked. Embossed decoration may possibly be worn through on the high spots. Worn bright cut or engraved decoration reduces the value of the piece. Badly-fitted hinged lids are almost impossible to repair.

1698 1699 1700 1710 1715 1720 1722 1724
1726 1728 1729 1735 1738 1739 1741
1742 1743 1744 1746 1755 1756 1757 1763
1765 1766 1769 1771 1771 1771 1774
1775 1776 1782 1783 1785 1786 1787
1788 1789 1790 1791 1792 1793 1794
1795 1800 1809 1803 1835 1850 1865 1865 1899

Teapot The father of all teapots must be the example in the Victoria and Albert Museum, maker TL, dated 1670, inscribed as having been presented to the Committee of the East India Company. Silver gilt, it is very simply wrought, with straight tapering sides, a straight spout and a cone-shaped lid, which is hinged to the top handle ferrule. The handle is set at right angles to the spout. It is known to be a teapot only because of the inscription. After 1700 some pear-shaped and octagonal pear-shaped teapots appeared, made by Jacob and Samuel Margas, James Seabrook and David Willaume. Spherical or bullet-shaped teapots also appeared at about this time. Later Paul Storr made a compressed circular lobed one, dated 1837, as a wedding present for his son. Hester Bateman and the Bateman family made some lovely oval teapots with bright cut engraved decoration. Problems associated with teapots are the result of wear on the hinges, lids and knobs or finials, as well as on the handle ferrules and rivets. Sides may be thin or patched, especially on the angles or corners; this may be more visible on the inside. The bodies should be fully hallmarked, and there should also be marks on the inside of the lid.

TEAPOT

Toast rack Very few toast racks are known before 1770. They are one of the more humble items of silverware, and do not appear in Matthew Boulton's Soho pattern books. Those that have survived have nearly always been damaged and repaired. There is, however, a notable pair made by Paul Storr in 1810, which have solid oval gadrooned and reeded bases with raised acanthus ends and lion's paw feet. The seven-bar wirework racks have a central handle composed of long water leaves. Toast racks without solid bases have a flat strip frame resting upon spherical, claw and ball or lion's paw feet. The racks are wirework in various shapes and have loop handles. After the 1780s a large variety appeared made in old Sheffield plate. Ingenious patterns, some with folding frames, following the invention of plated wire, and were patented by Samuel Roberts in 1807. Some of them were also combined with egg frames.

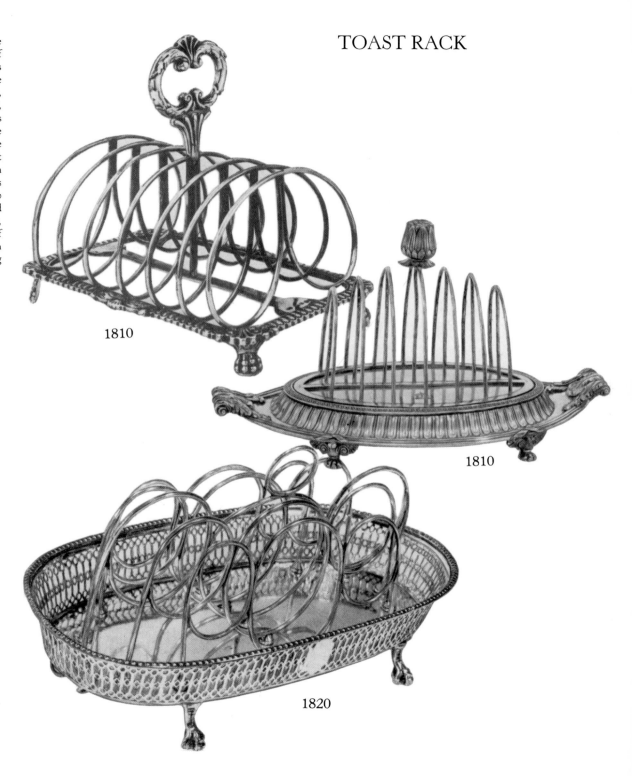

1810

1810

1820

TOBACCO BOX

Tobacco box Tobacco was brought to England by Sir Walter Raleigh and popularised by Sir Francis Drake. It was in general use until James I increased the tax on it from twopence to six shillings and tenpence per pound. It then receded to the back rooms and parlours, and this may have had some influence on the appearance of the personal tobacco box. Most examples seem to be dated between 1650 and 1730. Although they serve a similar purpose, they are usually a little larger than snuff boxes. Tobacco boxes are nearly always oval but sometimes circular – and have a loose cover. A box with a hinged cover is usually a snuff box. Edge decoration is usually not very prominent, taking the form of fine beading or cable moulding, but the covers are often quite elaborately engraved with a monogram or crest or full coat of arms in a decorative cartouche or with full mantling. A few boxes were made with silver mounted tortoiseshell covers. They were also made in the same designs in old Sheffield plate from about 1780.

1675

1696

1706

1709

1828

Tray There are some examples of very finely fashioned dishes with handles dating back to the 1600s, but the trays that we associate with the service of tea did not come into use much before the 1780s. They may be quite large, since they may have had to accommodate a kettle on a stand and a four-piece tea-set. Large examples measure about 22″ across the handles, and small ones about 16″. They were made with and without short feet. Paul Storr made some notable trays, such as the oval 20″ example, made in 1818, with a heavily cast border of grapes, vine leaves and tendrils and handles of entwined snakes. It has short volute feet and the plain centre is engraved with a large coat of arms of the 1st Marquis of Ailesbury KT. Other notable examples of heavy-gauge trays with cast borders were made by Robert Garrard in the 1840s. In the 1780s Matthew Boulton perfected a method of fitting silver edges to old Sheffield plate trays, which then became known as 'silver borders', and a method of doing this was patented by Samuel Roberts in 1824.

TRAY

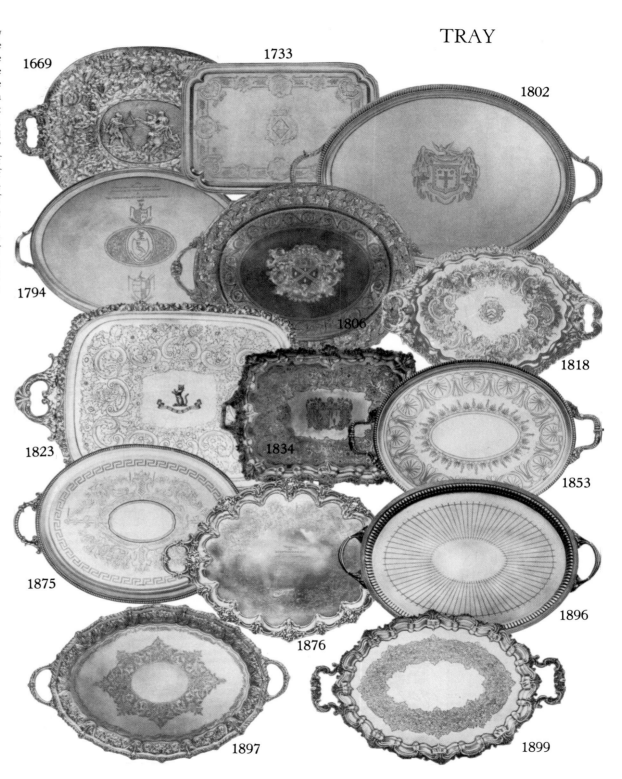

1669

1733

1802

1794

1806

1818

1823

1834

1853

1875

1876

1896

1897

1899

Tumbler These are cups without handles, of uniform character. Raised from a flat heavy-gauge sheet, the sides were thinned and graduated towards the outer edge, and the bottom rounded, to ensure a very low concentration of weight and centre of gravity. They are usually quite plain, without edge decoration or moulding; the surface is matted and engraved with crest or coat of arms. Examples made before 1670 are uncommon, but after that they are found up to the 1760s or 1770s. The hallmarks are usually under the rounded bottom in a group. There is a notable pair, dated 1766, joined at the rims by a band, which bears the hallmarks. One of the best-known examples, now in the Victoria and Albert Museum, London, is a tumbler dating from around 1790, which has the maker's mark only (TT), beneath a coronet. This piece is finely engraved with formal scrolling foliage surrounding a draped cherub. There is also a notable plain example by Peter and Jonathan Bateman, dated 1790, their only date. The two brothers worked together for only three months, so their silver is particularly rare.

TUMBLER

Tureen Any doubt about what these versatile items were intended to contain is easily dispelled by the realistic modelling on the body and cover. Examples made in the 1740s include representations of every kind of animal, vegetable and fruit served at the table. One of the earliest known soup tureens was made by Anthony Nelme in 1703. Examples have been noted throughout the 1720s, and Paul de Lamerie made some with Rococo patterns including vegetables and ram's heads. Perhaps the most notable is the soup tureen made by Paul Crespin in 1740, depicting two oxen supporting all kinds of vegetable and fruit, which is now in the Toledo Museum of Art, Ohio, USA. Sauce tureens are similar in design, but smaller; these are found from the 1760s onwards. Both kinds were made in pairs and in sets. Points to look out for are sides that may have worn thin. Joints where the feet meet the body may be fractured or repaired. The body should be fully hallmarked and the cover fully or partly marked. Matthew Boulton made many fine Adam style tureens and offered a large range in his pattern books. Paul Storr, Thomas Heming, Robert Garrard and Wakelin and Taylor also made many fine examples. All the popular patterns were also obtainable in old Sheffield plate after about 1775.

TUREEN

Urn Urn-shaped vessels with taps have been made since the late 1600s. David Willaume made several from 1701, and Thomas Bolton made one with three taps in 1702; these were probably used for serving wine. Tea urns did not become established until about the 1760s, although there is a very unusual egg-shaped example from Edinburgh with a curly frame, dated 1732. They seem to have taken the place of tea kettles, and there is one example of the intermediate stage consisting of a kettle on a lampstand with a tap to the spout. Not many tea urns dating from the 1770s and 1780s have any means of heating, but the old Sheffield plate makers appear to have taken the idea of heating very seriously and produced tea urns with compartments for heated iron bars and even charcoal. They followed the shapes and patterns of the times, and a further development was the tea machine which appeared in 1798 and comprised three separate spherical containers, each supported on four Adam period legs on a single base, and a central bowl. The central container had a capacity of six pints, and each of the others of three pints, and all had separate taps and lamp heaters. Matthew Boulton had a large variety of tea urns in his standard pattern book. Hester Bateman made some elegant examples in the 1780s and 1790s, while perhaps the most notable are those made by Paul Storr in his Regency and Egyptian styles, which have rather shallow containers, heavy gadrooning and fluting, dolphin spouts, ivory palmette tap-handles and palm-leaf volute lion's paw feet, and are known as the Paul Storr type. Tea urns were made throughout the Victorian period in shapes reproducing earlier styles and some were included in tea-sets. Plated examples in Etruscan styles continued to be produced into the 1920s.

URN

Vesta case Named after the match, which in turn was named after Vesta, the Roman goddess of the hearth and home, this was a convenient container for a small supply of matches, which could be ignited by being scraped against the rasp-like surface provided at the end of the box. Usually rounded rectangular, measuring about 2″ × 1½″, they have an end-opening spring-loaded lid. They may be quite plain or decorated in one of a large variety of patterns. They all seem to date from the late-Victorian era, from 1880 into the early 1900s.

VESTA CASE

1870

1880

1884

1885

1886

1887

1887

1895

1895

1895

1896

1896

1897

1897

1900

1905

1908

1917

Vinaigrette The precursor of our air-freshener, the vinaigrette was used to counteract unpleasant odours. Most date from between 1800 and 1840, although there are a few made in the 1780s and 1790s and examples have also been noted almost up to 1900. They were a development of the earlier pomanders or spice boxes, being considerably more convenient to carry and use. Ranging in length from about 1″ to 4″, they are usually rectangular with a hinged lid, and contain a hinged grille to retain a sponge which would have been soaked in aromatic vinegar 'agaynst the pestylents ayers'. To prevent corrosion, the inside was usually gilded. The hinged grilles vary between simple piercing and the most delicate filigree work. The aromatic vinegar was known as Dr Henry's vinegar, having been introduced by him in 1785 as a refreshing and pungent perfume for faintness and 'to correct the bad quality of the air'. Vinaigrettes seem to have been too humble to have interested the great silversmiths, but the high quality of work required did attract many of the Birmingham makers, including Nathaniel Mills, Samuel Pemberton, Joseph Willmore, Thomas Willmore and Francis Clark. Vinaigrettes were made in an innumerable variety of shapes and, apart from the rectangular ones, there are examples of fish, bells, helmets, beehives, books, hand bags, walnuts, oranges, hearts, flowers, horns, shells, barrels and acorns, as well as silver mounted bottles and those with semiprecious stones. The rectangular variety remained the most popular, and there are examples with representations of a scene or famous building on the lid, which seem to date from the 1830s and 1840s.

VINAIGRETTE

Wall sconce This was used as an additional light source, supplementing the table candelabrum and the chandelier. Most seem to be dated between the 1690s and 1720s although earlier examples are known. They are listed in large numbers in the Royal inventories, in which it is recorded that in 1721 there were 67 wall sconces of various types at St James's Palace, 24 at Kensington Palace, 18 at Hampton Court and 50 at Windsor Castle. Many Royal wall sconces were disposed of in 1808 to Rundell and Bridge, to raise funds for the separate establishment of the Prince of Wales in Kensington Palace. Four of these, however, were then sold to the Earl of Lonsdale, for whom Paul Storr added the coronets and Garter motto, probably replacing the Royal cipher. These four sconces dated from 1668 and around 1670. Another type included framed mirrors as a better means of reflecting light. Makers of wall sconces include many famous names such as Isaac Liger, John Fawdery and Anthony Nelme. Some were made from light-gauge sheet and had embossed decoration and many may not have survived, but others are of much more substantial construction.

WALL SCONCE

1665

1668

1680

1692

1707

1837

WAX JACK

Wax jack Also known as a wax winder, this is an open-work bougie box, with coiled taper retained by a central bar within an open-work frame, passing through an opening in the top and held in position by a spring clip. The frame is usually supported by a circular or rectangular pan or base, with a handle similar to that of chamber candlestick. The frame may include a slot for the bracket of a conical extinguisher retained by a chain. Wax jacks take many forms, with the coiled taper disposed either horizontally or vertically. Most examples date between the 1770s and 1830s. Exact counterparts of silver wax jacks are found in old Sheffield plate.

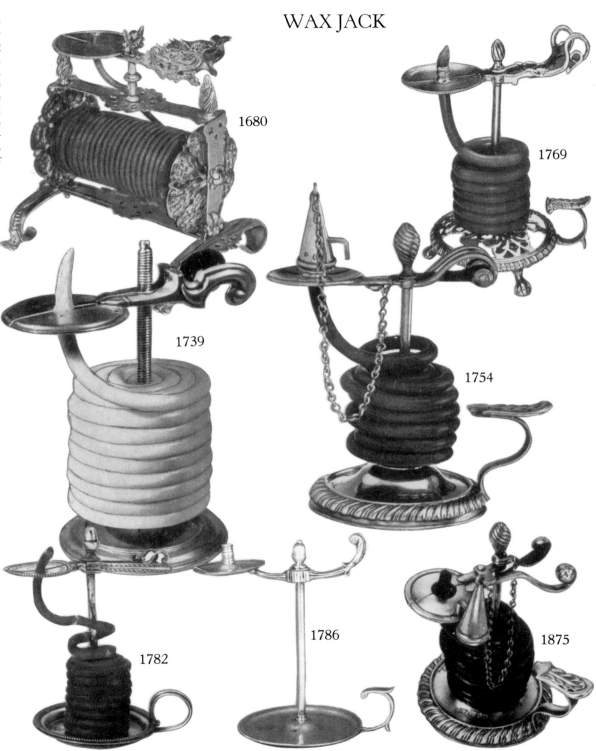

1680

1769

1739

1754

1782

1786

1875

Wine cistern The importance attached to wine in domestic life led to the production of some extraordinary pieces of equipment, the largest and most imposing of which is probably the wine cistern. The process of cooling wine whilst it was still in the bottle required a container of bath-like proportions. Being too large and heavy for the table, they were made to stand on the floor. Very many were made, but their greatest value, their weight of silver, also turned out to be their greatest disadvantage, and many owners decided that they preferred to retain the value in a more convenient form and converted their cisterns into numerous smaller items by way of the melting pot. There is evidence in official lists that because of their great size they were also used for washing plates and dishes. One of the largest and heaviest must be the cistern made by Charles Kandler in 1734, which is 5′ 5″ wide and weighs 8,000 oz. This is a cast oval bowl overhung with vine stems, leaves and grapes, with handles representing female figures holding bunches of grapes. The bowl rests on feline animals chained to the base. It was made to the order of Henry Jerningham and is now in the USSR, but there are copies in the Victoria and Albert Museum and in the Metropolitan Museum, New York. Another example weighing about 8,000 oz. was made by John Bridge to the order of George IV in 1828. It is silver gilt and measures 4′ 6″ in width. Perhaps the best known is the cistern made by Paul de Lamerie in 1719, now in the Minneapolis Museum of Art, which takes the form of a compressed circular bowl with a wide overhanging lobed rim, with flying scroll and volute handles and a moulded pedestal foot. The bowl is decorated with shells, scrolls and human masks. It is 38″ wide and weighs 700 oz. Other notable silversmiths making cisterns around 1700 include Philip Rollos, David Willaume, George Garthorne, Benjamin Pyne and Anthony Nelme.

WINE CISTERN

1697

1715

1715

1794

1719

Wine cooler The wine cooler usually accommodated only one bottle at a time although the Royal collection has a silver gilt oval pair, made by Digby Scott and Benjamin Smith in 1805, which accommodated two bottles each. Alternatively called ice pails, they were sometimes made in pail-shapes. They include an inside liner and a flat cover ring or cape, and are often found in pairs or sets. Among the most notable are the silver gilt Warwick Vase wine coolers mady by Paul Storr in 1812 as part of the banqueting service supplied to the first Earl of Harwood. These were modelled on a 7′-high marble vase found in Hadrian's villa near Rome in 1770, which was brought to Warwick castle by the Earl in 1774 and placed on a specially prepared pedestal. Wine coolers were made in many other classical vase-shapes, and what is thought to be Paul Storr's largest single piece is a wine cooler 3′ 1½″ in diameter, weighing 1,707 oz., which was made in 1815 for the citizens of Denbigh to present to Sir Watkin Williams-Wynn for his patriotism. It is a shallow circular bowl with an overhanging egg-and-tongue border, the lower half with alternate fluting, without handles and with a pedestal foot. Most wine coolers date from the 1770s into the Victorian era, although there is a pair made in 1713 by Lewis Mettayer, bearing the Royal Arms of Queen Anne. Other notable makers include Frederick Kandler, John Bridge, Benjamin Smith and Rundell, Bridge and Rundell. Wine coolers were also made extensively in old Sheffield plate in very similar patterns.

WINE COOLER

Wine cups It is difficult to ascertain when wine cups began to be produced, since further delving always seems to reveal earlier ones. Early examples take the form of Communion cups, chalices, goblets and grace cups. They were the standard drinking vessels used at the more affluent domestic tables and taverns until the invention in 1676 of flint glass, which was much cheaper. Wine cups dating from the early 1600s are regularly to be found in salesrooms. These are of the plain taper bowl type with a baluster stem. Cups of the rather deeper, curved taper bowl type, with narrow bands of formal floral scrolls, dating from the late 1500s, are also occasionally to be found. Some of these have a cover or paten with a collet foot. In the mid-1660s an interesting, rather crudely-made type appeared, with a straight taper bowl and a wide conical base, often with rather unskilled-looking chasing of foliage or punch decoration in panels. Cups made after the mid-1770s lost their ecclesiastical appearance and assumed the shapes in fashion at the time. Reproductions of earlier patterns were, however, regularly produced. Bowls often have thin areas where crests and monograms have been removed. Dents in the foot rim or slightly leaning stems can be rectified, but nothing can be done about a fracture in a hollow stem. Old Sheffield plate goblets were made in various popular styles after about 1775, and examples of these, mostly with Adam-style decoration were included in Matthew Boulton's pattern book.

WINE CUP

WINE FUNNEL

Wine funnel Also called wine strainers, these were used in both the home and the tavern to decant to the bottle and from the bottle to the decanter. Most funnels are circular and are either in one piece, with a removable pierced strainer or gauze, or in two pieces, comprising a pierced bowl and a removable spout. Alternatively the bowl may include a removable inner ring to retain a muslin straining cloth. Examples made in the 1770s and 1780s are usually plain or have a reeded rim, although one early Hester Bateman example made in 1774 has a wavy circular gadrooned rim. Wine funnels usually include a small shaped or egg-pattern hook hanging down from the rim. Later examples are more elaborately decorated and have wider, applied foliate rims. Most examples date from between 1770 and 1820. There is an unsubstantiated report of one dated 1651, and there is a rather large, plain circular one-piece example made in 1739. Boulton and Fothergill made the type with a muslin strainer in the 1770s. Funnels were offered in the old Sheffield plate pattern books in several different patterns up to the 1840s, when they could be ordered with either plated or gilded bowl interiors, the gilded bowls costing four shillings and sixpence extra. Silver wine funnels should be fully hallmarked on the bowl, and others parts should also bear some marks. Care should be taken to check that all the parts match. Wine funnels are sometimes found with a matching stand or tray with a domed centre and/or short legs.

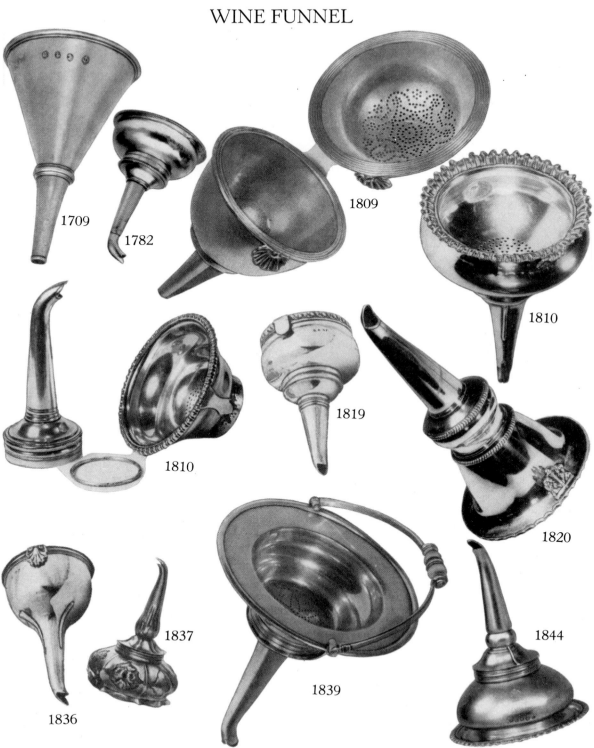

1709

1782

1809

1810

1810

1819

1820

1836

1837

1839

1844

Wine label Different methods of distinguishing the wine decanter from the vinegar decanter ranged from the use of different coloured glass to indicating the contents in gold letters or by engraving. All finally gave way to the wine label, which simply hung on the decanter and was changed as required. Wine labels were first known as bottle tickets. After the simple rectangular shape, designs proliferated and construction methods varied from the use of wrought plate to piercing, embossing and casting. With such a variety, wine labels are difficult to classify, but the most frequently occurring shapes, other than rectangular, are oval, crescent, ring, multifoil, scroll, vase, escutcheon, leaf, shell, festoon, vine, crest, letter profile and word profile. Another similar but rather smaller range was intended for sauce bottles. In addition to all the usual names of wines, some interesting, less common ones have been noted, such as Shrub, Noyeau, Rhenish, Vidonia, Frostiniac, Nig and Calamity Water. Paul Storr made a number of wine labels, including a set of fourteen, made in 1810, which were exceptionally large, each measuring more than 3″ in width and weighing 4½ oz. In the 1780s Hester Bateman made wine labels in conventional wrought and pierced patterns. It is thought that Sandilands Drinkwater may have made wine labels, because of the punch shape of one of his unregistered marks of around 1745, which consists of a script SD beneath a crown within a wine-label shape. Other silversmiths who made wine labels were Richard Binley, who was apprenticed to Sandilands Drinkwater, Margaret Binley, (presumably his widow, since their marks do not appear on any other silver) and Phipps and Robinson. Most wine labels are dated between 1750 and 1850, although a few examples have been noted from 1745, and they are still being made. Each wine label should include ring attachments for the chain. The label eyelets may show some damage, while chains may be replacements. Hallmarks are usually on the back but are occasionally stamped on the front amongst the foliage.

WINE LABEL

Wine taster The evaluation of wine depends primarily on taste, and most wine-growing countries have produced small wine-tasting vessels to facilitate the tasting process. Occasionally oval, but more usually circular, they are shallow vessels, and may have handles. Their shape is designed to emphasise individual characteristics such as flavour, colour bouquet or aroma. The taster known as the Portuguese type although it is thought to have originated in England has a domed centre designed to reflect the colour of the wine. The type without handles, which has spreading sides, may sometimes be mistaken for a trencher salt. Most seem to be dated between 1660 and 1680, but a few have been noted as early as 1642 and as late as 1820. They are sometimes of surprisingly flimsy construction and may have crude chased or punched bead decoration and simple wire scroll handles. The handles and handle joints should be carefully inspected for evidence of repairs or replacements. The hallmarks are often clumsily and unevenly stamped.

WINE TASTER

1639

1643

1652

1662

1659

1664

1672

1828

IMPORTANT MAKERS

Queen Anne 1695–1727

1697 John Fawdery I
William Fawdery
John Sutton
Timothy Ley
John Bodington
David Willaume I
Benjamin Pyne

1698 John Eckfourd

1699 Seth Lofthouse

1700 Lewis Mettayer

1701 Simon Pantin I

1706 Jacob Margas

1707 Thomas Folkingham
Gabriel Sleath

1708 Augustine Courtauld

1713 Paul de Lamerie
William Looker
David Tanqueray

1715 Benjamin Blakely

1716 Paul Hanet

1718 Starling Wilford
John Hugh Le Sage

1719 Thomas Tearle
William Darker

1720 Paul Crespin
Thomas Bamford I
Edward Feline
Edward Vincent (c.)

1721 Peter Archambo I
Abraham Buteux
John Tuite (c.)

1723 Francis Nelme

1724 Gawen Nash
Edward Aldridge

1726 Ayme Videau

1727 Charles Kandler

Mid-Georgian 1727–1770

1731 Robert Abercrombie
George Hindmarsh

1732 William Gould

1733 Samuel Wood

1735 William Garrard

1736 David Hennell I

1737 James Shruder
Thomas Whipham

1738 Phillips Garden
Ebenezer Coker
George Baskerville

1739 John Swift

1740 John Cafe

1743 William Grundy

1745 Thomas Heming

1747 Edward Wakelin
Samuel Herbert

1749 Walter Brind

1751 John Wirgman

1752 Paul Callard

1753 John Schuppe

1754 Pierre Gillois
Simon Le Sage

1755 John Delmester

1757 William Cafe

1760 Parker & Wakelin (c.)

1761 Hester Bateman

1762 Augustin Le Sage (c.)

1763 William Abdy I

1766 Crouch & Hannam (c.)

1768 Burrage Davenport

Adam 1770–1800

1770 Andrew Fogelberg (c.)

1771 Orlando Jackson (c.)

1772 Robert Hennell I

1773 John Arnell
Courtauld & Cowles
Robert Cruickshank (c.)
Thomas Chawner

1774 John Denziloe

1775 Henry Greenway

1776 **John Carter II**
Wakelin & Taylor
Nicholas Dumee
Thomas Northcote

1777 George Cowles
Makepeace & Carter

1778 William Eley I
John Scofield

1782 Richard Crossley

1784 Samuel Godbehere

1786 Samuel Davenport
Henry Chawner

1790 Matthew Boulton (B)

1791 Urquhart & Hart

1792 Wakelin & Garrard
Frisbee & Storr
Crispin Fuller
Smith & Hayter

1793 Paul Storr

1797 Eley & Fearn

1798 John Emes

Dates refer to earliest mark registration.
London makers unless otherwise noted.
(B) Birmingham.
(S) Sheffield.
(c.) = circa.

Regency 1800–1830

1800 Peter, Anne & William Bateman

1802 Robert Garrard I, Digby Scott & Benjamin Smith

1804 Rundell, Bridge & Rundell Charles Fox I

1805 Richard Sibley I Burwash & Sibley

1807 Benjamin Smith II

1808 Eley Fearn & Chawner John Crouch II Emes & Barnard

1809 Benjamin & James Smith

1810 T. & J. Creswick (S)

1811 Samuel Hennell

1813 William Elliott

1815 William Bateman I William Chawner II

1818 John & Henry Lias

1823 John Bridge

1825 Nathaniel Mills (B) W.K. Reid

1826 A.B. Savory

1829 Rawlings & Summers

Early Victorian 1830–1860

1832 Thomas Bradbury (S) George Unite (B)

1836 William Hutton

1840 G.W. Adams E.H. Baily Alfred Brown

1841 W.R. Smiley (c.) George Angel

1842 John S. Hunt Owen Jones

1843 Elkington Mason

1846 Henry Cole

1850 C.F. Hancock

1851 Albert Wilms (B) Smith & Nicholson

1854 H.H. Armstead Martin, Hall & Co (S)

1856 Mappin Bros (S)

1857 W. Hutton & Sons (S)

1858 Raphael Monti W. & G. Sissons (S)

1859 Roberts & Briggs (S)

Mid-Victorian 1860–1880

1860 John Hardman & Co (B) (c.)

1861 George Fox (c.)

1863 Briddon Brothers (S) C.S. Harris

1864 Roberts & Belk (S) E.S. Pegler of Halifax

1865 Hunt & Roskell

1866 Goldsmiths' Alliance

1867 J. Round & Son (S) James Dixon & Sons (S)

1870 Hennell, Frazer & Haws

1879 Christopher Dresser Aldwincle & Slater

1880 W.A.S. Benson

Late-Victorian 1880–1901

1881 E.C. Purdee Hukin & Heath

1882 Carrington & Co

1887 William Comyns & Sons Guild of Handicraft

1890 Fordham & Faulkner (S)

1895 Liberty & Co Arthur Dixon (B)

1896 C.R. Ashbee

1897 Gilbert Marks George Frampton

1898 Omar Ramsden & Alwyn Carr

1900 Henry Lambert (c.) C.F.A. Voysey

1901 Goldsmiths & Silversmiths Co Ltd

THE MASTERS

In England silver makers have had to comply with trade regulations since 1300 when it was found necessary to control the trade and to protect customers. Anyone wishing to enter the trade as a master craftsman was obliged to 'put himself apprentice' to a master, i.e. someone who had already been granted freedom to practise by his trade association or guild, by virtue of having satisfactorily worked through the term of his apprenticeship (which in the early eighteenth century was usually at least seven years). The apprenticeship fee paid to the master at that time was usually about £30, but varied considerably. It was also possible to obtain freedom to practise the trade by service or by patrimony.

On receiving freedom to practise, a metalworker could either continue working for another silversmith, as a master craftsman or a journeyman, or set up in business on his own account, in which case he had to register a maker's mark of his own in the Register of Marks at Goldsmiths' Hall, where he had to sign and give his title and a specimen of his mark, perhaps in several sizes. His title would be given as a plateworker, largeworker, smallworker, spoonmaker or bucklemaker and so on. During his working life, a master may have had to register a number of different marks to take account of changing circumstances. Entering into partnership would also necessitate the registration of new marks. Scottish goldsmiths and silversmiths have always been organized quite independently and were known as Hammermen. The Dublin Goldsmiths' Company also has it's own charter, which is dated 1637, although a much earlier one is known to have existed.

Methods of trading took many forms. At the highest level the Royal Goldsmiths or a company in the Royal patronage would simply be instructed to submit samples or proposals for silver to fulfil requirements. A very important piece may have had to be designed by a sculptor or artist. Lower down the scale, a person of high rank might call for a selection from stock to be sent before making a choice. Important firms in the trade had representatives in the highest circles who would report likely requirements. John Bridge (of Rundell and Bridge in Ludgate Hill) was personally favoured in Royal circles by George III, having been recommended by his cousin who had a farming interest with the King, and was thus able to obtain the trade of the Royal family and many in Court circles. It is said that whenever the King heard of a marriage taking place he would virtually command the couple to go to Ludgate Hill for their plate and jewels.

Individual makers often widened the scope of their trade by offering other services. Examples include Jeweller, Goldsmith and Toyman (Thomas Harrache at the Golden Ball & Pearl in Pall Mall), Pawnbroker and Silversmith (John Flude, 2 Grace Church Street) and Goldsmith and Artificial Teeth Maker (P. Pilleau at the Golden Cup in Shandois Street). The actual places of manufacture of much fine silver in the early eighteenth century and later are uncertain. The business addresses of many influential and well-known makers are given on their trade cards as well-known city taverns. No separate manufacturing premises are mentioned, and it must be presumed that most of the dealing was done at the taverns. The trade card of Phillips Garden shows a very dignified retail shop with customers and a shop assistant behind a counter and well-stocked show cabinets. The address, however, is 'At the Golden Lion in St Paul's Church Yard'! A footnote states: 'N.B. Work performed in my own House'. On John Briscoe's trade card his address is given as 'At his Old Shop The Three Kings & Golden Ball, opposite Forster Lane in Cheapside'. Hester Bateman is known to have both lived and produced silver at 107 Bunhill Row. Other members of her large family also occupied houses in Bunhill Row but it is not clear whether any of their houses were used for manufacturing.

The maker's mark consists of the maker's initials or, between 1697 and 1720, the first two letters of his or her surname, in Roman, Script or Gothic letters, with or without additional decoration, within a punch of varying shape (indicated in the alphabetical list).

EXAMPLES

Roman, bifoil
Paul Storr

Script, quatrefoil, 2 pellets
Rebecca and William Emes

Roman, cuspoid, 2 pellets, bell
Joseph Bell I

When the same initials indicate two or more different silversmiths, the date of the piece (see the section *How to Date Silver*) will help to distinguish one from another. Indistinct or rubbed makers' marks are difficult to identify. When only the first letter is legible, the alphabetical list of makers' marks (see pages 136 to 282) can be used to identify the possible makers, and the letter type, date, punch shape and any additional marks will help to differentiate between them. When only the second letter is legible, the alphabetical list of silversmiths (see pages 283 to 322) can be used to identify the possible surnames, and the letter type, date, punch shape and any additional marks will again indicate which of these is the most likely maker.

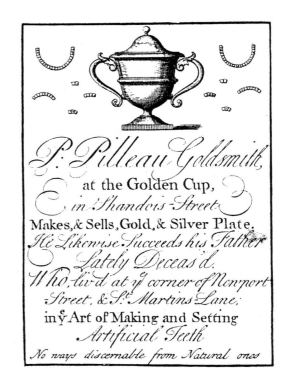

Key to Town of Registration

L London A Aberdeen B Birmingham Ch Chester Co Cork Db Dublin Du Dundee Ed Edinburgh Ex Exeter Gl Glasgow Gr Greenock Gy Galway H Hull M Montrose Nc Newcastle Nw Norwich P Perth S Sheffield Y York

Maker's initial(s) & maker(s)	Town of registration	Date of mark registration	Earliest example	Latest example	Letter style G Gothic R Roman S Script	Punch shape	Additional features/notes
A							
Andrew Archer	L	1720	1703	1719	R	stepped hatchment	crowned circle
	L	1703					AR
Matthew Alanson	Db	1731	1731	1736	R	circle	crown
A A							
Arthur Annesley	L	1758	1758	1760	S	profiloid	pellet
Andrew Allison	Gl	–	1836	–	R	rectangle	–
A B							
Abraham Buteau	L	1721	1722	1731	R	quatrefoil	crown, mullet
	L	1721	–	–	–	–	BV
Alexander Brown	Db	1726	1727	1736	R	trifid rectangle	crown
Abel Brokesby	L	1727	1727	1728	R	globate cleftform	heart
Ambrose Boxwell	Db	1768	1767	1788	R	lobate biloboid	pellet
Ab (conjoined)							
Robert Abercrombie	L	1740	1731	1754	R	oval	
	L	1731	–	–	–	–	RA
A B **A H B** Hunt & Roskell (Alfred Benson & Arthur Henry Benson)	L	1895	–	–	R	–	crown
A B **H H W** Hunt & Roskell (Alfred Benson & H. H. Wintle)	L	1889	–	–	R	–	crown
	L	1842	–	–	–	–	ISH
	L	1865	–	–	–	–	IH RR
	L	1882	–	–	–	–	RR AR IMH
	L	1897	–	–	–	–	H & R Ltd
A B **G B** Alice Burrows & George Burrows II	L	1801	1801	1837	R	square	2 pellets

Maker's initial(s) & maker(s)	Town of registration	Date of mark registration	Earliest example	Latest example	Letter style G Gothic R Roman S Script	Punch shape	Additional features/notes
A B S							
Adey Bellamy Savory	L	1826	1827	1853	R	rectangle	2 pellets
	L	1826	–	–	R	oval	2 pellets
	L	1826	–	–	R	waveform	2 pellets
	L	1836	–	–	R	bevelform	2 pellets
A C							
Augustine Courtauld	L	1729	1710	1743	R	trifid coneform	fleur de lis
	L	1739	–	–	S	cinquefoil	fleur de lis
	L	1708	–	–	–	–	CO
James Arthur Calame	L	1764	1764	1774	R	quatrefoil	incuse
	L	1764	–	–	–	–	IAC
Ann Chesterman	L	1775	–	1776	R	lozenge	mullet, pellet
Alexander Cameron	Du	–	1797	1833	R	rectangle	–
	Du	–	–	–	–	–	CAM DUN ERON DEE
A C E F							
Alexander Coates & Edward French	L	1734	1734	–	R	quatrefoil	–
A C I N							
Ann Craig & John Neville	L	1740	1740	1742	R	square	crown, fleur de lis
	L	1743	–	–	R	square	–
A D							
Charles Adam	L	1703	1698	1719	R	spikeform	–
Archibald Douglas	L	1826	1826	1833	R	rectangle	
	L	1836	–	–	R	oval	–
	L	–	–	–	R	–	cameo
Abraham Dyson	S	1835	–	1836	R	ovoid	–
A E							
Alexander Edmonston	Ed	1779	1795	1805	R	rectangle	–
A E J							
A. Edward Jones Ltd	B	–	1904	1936	–	oval	–
AEP & Co Ltd							
A.E. Poston & Co Ltd	S	–	1954	1960	R	domate loboid	large P
	B	–	1947	1952	R	domate loboid	large P
AE R							
Aeneas Ryan	Db	1792	1787	1807	R	rectangle	pellet, AE (conjoined)

Maker's initial(s) & maker(s)	Town of registration	Date of mark registration	Earliest example	Latest example	Letter style G Gothic R Roman S Script	Punch shape	Additional features/notes
A F							
Alexander Forbes	Ed	1692	1703	1705	R	winged invectoid	pellet
	A	1728	–	–	R	lobate escutcheon	–
Andrew Fogelberg	L	–	1766	1811	R	rectangle	pellet
Alexander Field	L	1780	1790	1808	R	rectangle	–
A F **S G**							
Andrew Fogelberg & Stephen Gilbert	L	1780	1778	1792	R	trifid biloboid	crown, 2 pellets
	L	1780	–	–	R	trifid biloboid	2 pellets
A G							
Alexander Gairdner	Ed	1754	1762	1799	R	rectangle	pellet
Adam Graham	Gl	1763	1784	1789	R	rectangle	–
A G B							
Benney Gerald	L	–	1956	1974	R	trefoil	–
A G & Co							
Alexander Goodman & Co	S	1800	1802	1819	R	rectangle	–
Goodman, Gainsford & Co	S	1797	1800	1834	R	rectangle	–
	S	1797	–	–	–	–	GG & Co
A G E							
Anthony Elson	L	–	1973	–	–	–	–
A H							
Arthur Heaslewood	Nw	1661	1661	1670	R	engrailed escutcheon	–
Alexander Henderson	Ed	1792	1792	1812	R	rectangle	–
Alexander Hewat	L	1810	1810	–	R	rectangle	pellet
Aaron Hatfield	S	1823	1820	1850	R	ovoid	pellet
Ashforth & Harthorn	S	1826	1824	1831	R	rectangle	–
Martin Bros & Co	S	1846	1845	1876	R	ovoid	pellet
A **H N**							
A. Haviland–Nye	L	–	1960	1980	R	lanceolate biloboid	–
A J							
Alexander Johnston	L	1733	1748	1771	S	ovoid	–
	L	1748	–	–	S	trefoil	pellet
A J S							
Alexander J. Strachan	L	1799	1800	1838	R	rectangle	2 pellets

Maker's initial(s) & maker(s)	Town of registration	Date of mark registration	Earliest example	Latest example	Letter style G Gothic R Roman S Script	Punch shape	Additional features/notes
A & J Z							
A. & J. Zimmerman	B	–	1897	1934	R	tridentate escutcheon	–
A K							
Alexander Kincaid	Ed	1692	1700	1734	R	heart	bird in flight
Ann Kersill	L	1747	1747	–	R	lozenge	pellet
Andrew Killik	L	1749	1750	1752	R	rectangle	pellet
Abstainando King	L	1791	1792	1828	R	rectangle	–
	L	–	–	–	R	oval	–
Alexander Kelty	Nc	–	1803	–	R	rectangle	pellet
A L							
Andrew Law	Ed	–	1682	1694	R	trifid escutcheon	crown
Thomas Allen	L	1697	1694	1719	R	waved chinoid	crown, cross
	L	1697	–	–	R	trifid triad	crown, pellet
	L	1697	–	–	R	hatchment	crown, pellet
John Albright	L	1718	1717	1724	R	rectangle	–
	L	1720	–	–	–	–	IA
Aaron Lestourgeon	L	1771	1768	1777	R	globate coneform	mullet
	L	1769	–	–	R	circle	crown
	L	1776	–	–	R	circle	crown
Augustin Le Sage	L	–	1761	1779	R	quatrefoil	goblet, pellet, mullet
	L	–	–	–	R	circle	crown
A & L							
Arnold & Lewis of Manchester	L	–	1911	–	–	–	–
A W L							
William & Aaron Lestourgeon	L	1767	–	1769	R	octagon	–
A M							
Arthur Murphy	Db	–	1805	–	R	oval	–
Alexander Mitchell	Gl	1822	1837	1838	R	rectangle	–
A McD							
Angus McDonald	Gl	1824	1824	1852	R	rectangle	–
A N (N smaller)							
William Andrews	L	1697	1697	1713	R	spiked ovoid	–
AN (monogram)							
Francis Nelme	L	1723	1725	1739	S	waveform	–
	L	1739	–	–	–	–	FN

Maker's initial(s) & maker(s)	Town of registration	Date of mark registration	Earliest example	Latest example	Letter style G Gothic R Roman S Script	Punch shape	Additional features/notes
ANe (monogram)							
Anthony Nelme	L	1697	1683	1738	R	spikeform	–
	L	1697	–	–	R	waveform	–
	L	–	–	–	–	–	Ne or J Newton
A & O							
Atkin & Oxley	S	1824	1828	1839	R	rectangle	–
A P							
Abraham Portal	L	1749	1754	1767	R	rectangle	–
Abraham Peterson	L	1790	1789	1810	R	rectangle	pellet
A P **F P**							
A. & F. Parsons	L	–	1911	1939	R	tridentate cuspoid	–
A P **P P**							
Abraham Peterson & Peter Podio	L	1783	1783	1796	R	square	–
A^R_OP							
Hugh Arnett & Edward Pocock	L	1720	1719	1734	R	quatrefoil	pellet
	L	1720	–	–	–	–	H^A_PE
A R							
Alexander Reid III	Ed	1677	1665	1681	R	chevroned cuspoid	crown, fleur de lis
	Ed	1660	–	–	–	–	AR (conjoined)
Andrew Raven	L	–	1698	1706	R	biloboid	–
	L	1697	–	–	–	–	RA
	L	1697	–	–	–	–	Ra
Andrew Archer	L	1703	1703	1719	R	oval	–
	L	1720	–	–	–	–	A
Peter Archambo I	L	1721	1721	1768	R	crested triad	crown, mitre
	L	1722	–	–	–	–	PA
Alexander Richards	Db	–	1737	1765	R	oval	pellet
	Db	–	–	–	R	kidney	–
Ann Robertson	Nc	–	1786	1815	R	ovoid	pellet
Ar							
Francis Archbold	L	1697	1699	1714	R	spiked circle	fleur de lis
AR (conjoined)							
Alexander Reid III	Ed	1660	1665	1681	R	chevroned cuspoid	crown, fleur de lis
	Ed	1677	–	–	–	–	AR

Maker's initial(s) & maker(s)	Town of registration	Date of mark registration	Earliest example	Latest example	Letter style G Gothic R Roman S Script	Punch shape	Additional features/notes
A S							
Anthony Stanley	Db	–	1696	1715	R	serrated loboid	–
	Db	–	–	–	R	bevelled triad	cross, fleur de lis
Thomas Ash	L	1697	1702	1714	R	ogee triad	2 pellets, fleur de lis
	L	1697	–	–	R	bevelled globoid	triangle
	L	1706	–	–	R	waved triad	mullet
	L	1697	–	–	–	–	Ash
Ambrose Stevenson	L	1720	1708	1720	R	quatrefoil	2 pellets
	L	1707	–	–	–	–	St
Albertus Schurman	L	1756	–	1764	R	oval	pellet
	L	–	–	–	R	bifoil	–
Alexander Saunders	L	1757	1759	1766	S	profiloid	–
	L	1778	–	–	R	rectangle	pellet
Alex Spence	Ed	1783	1790	1809	R	rectangle	–
Alexander Smith	L	–	1873	1891	R	rectangle	–
A & S							
Thomas Aston & Son	B	1858	1858	–	R	rectangle	–
Ash							
Thomas Ash	L	1697	1702	1714	R	oval	–
	L	1697	–	–	–	–	AS
A S **J S** **A S**							
Adey Joseph II & Albert Savory	L	1833	1833	1834	R	quadriform	–
	L	1834	–	–	–	–	–
A^N_AS							
Anne Smith & Nathaniel Appleton	L	1771	1766	1783	R	cruciform	pellet
A T							
William Atkinson	L	1725	1726	1729	R	profiloid	cup
	L	1725	–	–	–	–	WA
Anne Tanqueray	L	–	1726	1732	R	lozenge	mullet, thistle
	L	–	–	–	–	–	TA
Abraham Tuppy	Db	1761	–	1786	R	rectangle	pellet
Abraham Taylor	L	1796	1797	1799	R	rectangle	–
Alexander Ticknell	Db	1784	–	1797	R	oval	–
AT (monogram)							
Anthony Tripe	Ex	1712	1695	1731	S	hatchment	–
	Ex	–	–	–	–	–	Tr

Maker's initial(s) & maker(s)	Town of registration	Date of mark registration	Earliest example	Latest example	Letter style G Gothic R Roman S Script	Punch shape	Additional features/notes
A T & S A. Taylor & Son	Gl	–	–	1900	R	rectangle	–
A U Archibald Ure	Ed	1715	1725	1739	R	rectangle	–
Au John Audrey	Ex	–	1701	1705	G	oval	2 pellets
A V Ayme Videau	L	1726	1733	1759	R	globate rhombus	mullet
	L	1739	–	–	S	trefoil	mullet, pellet
A Z Alex Zeigler	Ed	1782	1768	1827	R	rectangle	–
B John Borthwick	Ed	1681	1681	1696	S	spiked profiloid	–
	Ed	–	–	–	S	multifoil	–
Thomas Bolton (*or* Boulton)	Db	1686	1696	1725	S	invected triad	–
	Db	–	–	–	S	tabled loboid	–
	Db	–	–	–	S	waved triad	–
	Db	–	–	–	–	–	TB monogram
	Db	–	–	–	–	–	TB
B A John Barnard I	L	1720	1699	1713	R	heart	pellet
	L	1697	–	–	–	–	Ba
	L	1720	–	–	–	–	IB
John Bache	L	1700	1701	1725	R	globate globoid	fleur de lis, mullet
	L	1711	–	–	R	ovoid	2 mullets
	L	–	–	–	R	globate globoid	2 mullets
	L	1720	–	–	–	–	IB
Joseph Barbit (*or* Barbut)	L	1703	1706	1720	R	profiloid	crown, floret
	L	–	–	–	R	cinquefoil	mullet
	L	–	–	–	–	–	IB
Richard Bayley	L	1708	1710	1750	R	quatrefoil	–
	L	1720	–	–	–	–	RB
Edward Barnett	L	1715	1711	1717	R	bifoil	–
B A (A smaller) William Bainbridge I	L	1697	1698	1711	R	spiked ovoid	–
Ba Francis Batty I	Nc	1674	–	–	R	loboid	mullet
Francis Batty II	Nc	1708	1712	1736	S	oval	–
	Nc	–	–	–	–	–	FB

Maker's initial(s) & maker(s)	Town of registration	Date of mark registration	Earliest example	Latest example	Letter style G Gothic R Roman S Script	Punch shape	Additional features/notes
John Barnard I	L	1697	1699	1713	G	heart	plant
	L	–	–	–	R	triad	pellet
	L	1720	–	–	–	–	IB
	L	1720	–	–	–	–	BA
Thomas Bamford I	L	1720	1716	1732	R	oval	–
	L	1720	–	–	G	oval	–
	L	1720	–	–	–	–	TB
B B							
Benjamin Blakeley	L	1720	1716	1725	R	rectangle	–
	L	1739	–	–	S	oval	–
	L	1739	–	–	R	ovoid	–
	L	1715	–	–	–	–	BL
Benjamin Bentley	L	1728	1710	1716	R	globate archform	–
	L	1698	–	–	–	–	BE
Benjamin Brewood II	L	1755	1758	1767	R	delphate biloboid	annulet
	L	1755	–	–	R	oval	–
	L	1757	–	–	R	rectangle	2 pellets
Briddon Bros	S	1863	1863	–	R	rectangle	pellet
Baker Bros	Ch	–	1902	1926	R	rectangle	pellet
B$^{T}_{R}$B							
Bennett Bradshaw & Robert Tyrill	L	1739	1736	1740	S	ogival chinoid	–
	L	1737	–	–	–	–	R$^{B}_{B}$T
B C							
Benjamin Cartwright I	L	1739	1740	–	G	rectangle	–
Benjamin Cartwright II	L	1754	–	1766	R	rectangle	2 pellets
	L	1756	–	–	R	delphate cleftform	–
	L	1770	–	–	R	delphate bipod	–
Benjamin Cooper I	L	1724	–	1759	R	rectangle	–
Benjamin Cooper II	L	1764	1767	1785	R	rectangle	–
B C & N							
James Barber, George Cattle & William North	Y	–	1825	1833	R	square	–
	Y	–	–	–	–	–	J B G C W N
	L	–	–	1835	–	–	–
B D							
Burrage Davenport	L	–	1768	1784	R	oval	pellet
Benjamin Davis	L	1823	–	1826	R	rectangle	pellet
Benjamin Reece Dexter	L	1835	1835	1838	R	ovoid	–

Maker's initial(s) & maker(s)	Town of registration	Date of mark registration	Earliest example	Latest example	Letter style G Gothic R Roman S Script	Punch shape	Additional features/notes
B E							
Benjamin Bentley	L	1698	1710	1716	R	ogee triad	mullet
	L	1728	–	–	R	globate rectangle	–
	L	–	–	–	R	circle	pellet, thread circle
	L	1728	–	–	–	–	BB
George Beale	L	1699	1714	1729	R	oval	–
	L	–	–	–	R	lobate triad	3 pellets
	L	1713	–	–	–	–	Be
James Beschefer	L	1704	–	1706	R	trigonate globoid	crown, 2 mullets
Joseph Bell I	L	1716	1716	–	R	cuspoid	2 pellets, bell
William Bellassyse	L	1717	1722	1723	R	profiloid	mitre
	L	1723	–	–	–	–	WB
Be							
Thomas Bevault	L	1712	–	1714	R	waved rectangle	–
George Beale	L	1713	1714	1729	R	lobate triad	2 mullets, fleur de lis
	L	1699	–	–	–	–	BE
B F							
Bernard Fletcher	L	1725	–	1727	R	ovate rectangle	crown
B & F							
Matthew Boulton & John Fothergill	Ch	1769	1769	1781	R	rectangle	3 separate crowns
	B	1773	–	–	–	–	MB IF
B G							
Benjamin Godfrey	L	1732	1730	1768	R	globate rectangle	crown, pellet
	L	1739	–	–	S	quatrefoil	crown, pellet, annulet
	L	1739	–	–	S	rectangle	–
Benjamin Gignac	L	1745	1745	1776	R	domate rectangle	mullet, pellet
	L	–	–	–	R	globate rectangle	floret, pellet
	–	–	–	–	R	stepped rectangle	–
B H & H							
Batty Howard & Hawksworth	S	1815	1811	1829	R	square	–
B I							
Joseph Bird	L	1697	1697	1723	R	waved triad	2 hearts, tree, bird
	L	–	–	–	R	bifoil	–
	L	1697	–	–	–	–	Bi
	L	1724	–	–	–	–	IB

Maker's initial(s) & maker(s)	Town of registration	Date of mark registration	Earliest example	Latest example	Letter style G Gothic R Roman S Script	Punch shape	Additional features/notes
Richard Bigge	L	1700	–	1702	G	oval	thread oval
John Bignell	L	1718	1720	1732	R	bifoil	–
	L	1720	–	–	–	–	IB
Bi							
Eli Bilton	Nc	1683	1686	1711	R	cuspoid	2 mullets
	Nc	1683	–	–	R	hatchment	2 mullets
	Nc	1683	–	–	R	uneven loboid	2 mullets
	Nc	1683	–	–	–	–	EB
Joseph Bird	L	1697	1697	1723	G	globate globoid	fleur de lis, bird
	L	1697	–	–	–	–	BI
	L	1724	–	–	–	–	IB
Francis Billingsley	L	1697	–	1698	G	ogee triad	–
B L							
Anthony Blackford	L	1702	1703	1704	R	heart	pellet, bird
Samuel Blachford of Plymouth	Ex	1706	1720	1730	R	ogee chinoid	mullet
	Ex	–	–	–	–	–	SB
Benjamin Blakely	L	1715	1716	1725	R	oval	–
	L	1720	–	–	–	–	BB
Benjamin Laver	L	1781	1781	1794	R	rectangle	pellet
	L	1789	–	–	R	globate rectangle	fleur de lis, pellet
B M							
Barth Mosse	Db	1734	–	1735	R	rectangle	–
Benjamin Mordecai	L	1770	1779	1782	R	rectangle	–
	L	–	–	–	R	oval	–
Benjamin Montague (*also* Mountigue)	L	1771	1781	1789	R	rectangle	–
	L	1774	–	–	R	bevelform	–
	L	1776	–	–	R	bevelform	pellet
	L	1772	–	–	–	–	MB
	L	1773	–	–	–	–	cameo
Barak Mewburn	L	1826	–	1830	R	ovate rectangle	crown
	L	1830	–	–	R	rectangle	–
B M W							
Army & Navy Co-operative Soc. Ltd	L	–	1892	1928	–	–	–
B N							
Bowles Nash	L	1721	1721	1725	R	heart	fleur de lis
	L	1721	–	–	–	–	NA

Maker's initial(s) & maker(s)	Town of registration	Date of mark registration	Earliest example	Latest example	Letter style G Gothic R Roman S Script	Punch shape	Additional features/notes
B O							
John Bodington	L	1697	1697	1713	R	trifid shareform	mitre, fleur de lis
Michael Boult	L	1713	1714	1718	R	trefoil	anchor
	L	1720	–	–	–	–	MB
George Boothby	L	1720	1722	1752	R	globate rectangle	bird
	L	1720	–	–	–	–	GB
B P							
Benjamin Pemberton	Ch	–	1723	1753	R	rectangle	–
Benjamin Preston	L	1825	1825	1862	R	rectangle	–
B R							
Benjamin Braford	L	1697	1697	1698	R	quatrefoil	crown, crescent
Jonathan Bradley	L	1697	1696	1697	R	tridentate triad	crown
Thomas Brydon	L	–	1696	1697	R	oval	dotted oval
	L	1697	–	–	–	–	Br
B. Rooke & Son	S	1818	1818	1823	R	rectangle	pellet
Br							
Thomas Brydon	L	1697	1696	1697	R	oval	dotted oval
	L	–	–	–	–	–	BR
John Broake	L	1699	1699	1711	G	invected chinoid	shield
Philip Brush	L	1707	–	1710	R	ogee triad	pellet
B S							
Benjamin Sanders	L	1737	1738	1740	R	globate rectangle	star
	L	1739	–	–	G	quatrefoil	–
	L	–	–	–	S	circle	–
Bartholomew Stokes	Db	–	–	1752	R	trifid ovoid	fleur de lis, pellet
Benjamin Stephenson	L	1775	1774	1776	R	rectangle	pellet
Benjamin Simpson	L	1800	–	1803	R	rectangle	–
Benjamin Smith II	L	1807	1806	1840	R	profiloid	pellet
	L	1812	–	–	R	rectangle	–
Benjamin Smith III	L	1818	1821	1846	G	rectangle	–
	L	1837	–	–	R	quatrefoil	–
B & S							
Brook & Son	Ed	–	1888	1937	R	waved rectangle	–
	S	–	1906	1934	–	–	–
I B							
I S							
Benjamin Smith II & James Smith III	L	1809	1794	1835	R	square	2 pellets
B T							
Benjamin Tate (*or* Tait)	Db	1787	1785	1788	R	rectangle	–
	Db	–	–	–	R	waved rectangle	–

Maker's initial(s) & maker(s)	Town of registration	Date of mark registration	Earliest example	Latest example	Letter style G Gothic R Roman S Script	Punch shape	Additional features/notes
Bu							
William Busfield	Y	1679	1677	1705	R	rectangle	fleur de lis, 2 pellets
	Y	1679	–	–	–	–	WB
	Y	1679	–	–	–	–	WB (conjoined)
Thomas Burridge	L	1706	1712	1732	R	ogee triad	mullet, 3 pellets
	L	1717	–	–	R	trefoil	mullet
	L	1720	–	–	–	–	TB
B V							
Abraham Buteux	L	1721	1722	1731	R	globate globoid	crescent, mullet
	L	1721	–	–	–	–	AB
B W							
Benjamin Watts	L	1720	1704	1718	R	quadriform	stag's head
	L	1698	–	–	–	–	Wa
Benjamin West	L	1738	1737	1751	R	oval	–
	L	1739	–	–	S	bifoil	pellet
B Y							
Benjamin Yate	L	–	1624	1634	R	stepped loboid	gate
	L	–	–	–	R	hatchment	gate
C & Co							
Creswick & Co	S	1863	–	1865	R	rectangle	I F P
	S	1858	–	–	–	–	C & Co
Carrington & Co	L	–	1882	1959	R	concave archform	–
	L	–	–	–	–	–	JBC
	L	–	–	–	–	–	JBC &S L
C A							
John Carter I	L	1697	–	1741	R	tridentate hatchment	mullet
John Carman I	L	1716	–	1720	R	ovoid	–
	L	1720	–	–	–	–	IC
Isaac Callard	L	1726	1732	1769	R	waved cuspoid	2 mullets, fleur de lis
	L	1726	–	–	–	–	IC
Charles Alchorne	L	1729	1730	1738	R	globate triad	floret, mullet
Coline Allan	A	1748	1748	1750	R	rectangle	–
	A	–	–	–	R	bifoil	–
Charles Aldridge	L	1786	1787	1809	R	rectangle	–
CA (A within)							
Christopher Canner I	L	1697	–	1698	R	circle	–
Ca (a within)							
Christopher Canner II	L	1716	1718	1723	R	circle	–
	L	1720	–	–	–	–	ƆC (monogram)

Maker's initial(s) & maker(s)	Town of registration	Date of mark registration	Earliest example	Latest example	Letter style G Gothic R Roman S Script	Punch shape	Additional features/notes
John Carnaby	Nc	1717	1719	1724	R	hatchment	–
	Nc	1717	–	–	–	–	JC
C^{HA}_G							
Charles Aldridge & Henry Green	L	1775	1767	1788	R	quatrefoil	pellet
CAM DUN **ERON DEE**							
Alexander Cameron	Du	–	1797	1833	R	2 rectangles	–
	Du	–	–	–	–	–	AC
C B							
Charles Blair	Ed	1707	1709	1724	R	chinoid	–
Cornelius Bland	L	1772	1788	1800	R	ovoid	–
	L	1788	–	–	R	rectangle	–
	L	1788	–	–	R	rectangle	pellet
Charles Boyton	L	1825	1826	1933	R	rectangle	–
C B **E P**							
S. Roberts & C. Belk	S	1879	1865	1975	R	square	2 pellets
	S	1864	1865	1975	R	rectangle	R&B
	S	1864	–	–	R	3 bevelled squares	R&B
	S	1867	–	–	–	–	SR CB
C & B							
Cocks & Bettridge	B	1813	1814	1823	R	rectangle	–
	B	1813	–	–	R	billet	–
C B **T B**							
Christopher & Thomas W. Barker	L	1800	1800	1804	R	square	–
C C							
Colin Campbell	Ed	1711	1711	1722	R	bifoil	–
	Ed	1714	–	–	R	cambered loboid	mullet
Charles Clark	L	1739	–	1768	G	rectangle	–
	L	1758	–	–	R	rectangle	–
	L	1758	–	–	R	rectangle	pellet
	L	1763	–	–	R	ovoid	pellet
Charles Chesterman I	L	1741	1752	1792	R	rectangle	pellet
	L	1752	–	–	S	rectangle	–
Charles Chesterman II	L	1801	1811	1828	R	oval	–
C. Cummins I	Db	–	1836	–	R	bifoil	–
Clement Cheese	L	1823	1826	1828	R	rectangle	–
C. Cummins II	Db	–	1848	1863	G	rectangle	–

Maker's initial(s) & maker(s)	Town of registration	Date of mark registration	Earliest example	Latest example	Letter style G Gothic R Roman S Script	Punch shape	Additional features/notes
⊃C (monogram)							
Christopher Canner II	L	1720	1718	1723	R	octagon	–
	L	1716	–	–	–	–	Ca (a within)
C C P							
C. C. Pilling	L	–	1900	1910	R	domate loboid	–
	S	–	1912	–	–	–	–
C D							
Charles Dickson	Ed	1719	1721	1748	R	heart	pellet
	Ed	1738	–	–	R	ogee escutcheon	–
	Du	1722	–	–	S	rectangle	–
C E							
Charles Eley	L	1825	1824	1828	R	rectangle	–
C F							
C. Fox	Db	–	1747	1774	R	bevelform	–
Charles Freeth	B	–	1775	1798	R	rectangle	–
Crispin Fuller	L	1792	1793	1835	R	rectangle	–
	L	1796	–	–	–	–	–
Charles Fox I	L	1804	–	1808	R	rectangle	–
Charles Fox II	L	1822	1822	1861	R	bifoil	–
	L	1823	–	–	R	oval	pellet
C F H							
Charles Frederick Hancock	L	1850	1854	1912	R	globate rectangle	–
	L	1850	–	–	R	rectangle	–
	L	1870	–	–	R	globate loboid	3 pellets
	L	1870	–	–	R	hexagon	–
C F **I F**							
Charles & John II Fry	L	1822	–	1823	R	square	–
C‡F (T)							
James Turner & Charles Fox I	L	1801	1801	–	R	quatrefoil	pellet
C G							
Charles Gibbons	L	1732	–	1734	R	lobate coneform	cup, pellet, mullet
Charles Goodwin	L	1799	–	1836	R	rectangle	–
	L	1803	–	–	R	bevelform	pellet
Charles Gibson	L	1828	1828	–	R	rectangle	–
Charles Gordon	L	1828	1837	1840	R	rectangle	–

Maker's initial(s) & maker(s)	Town of registration	Date of mark registration	Earliest example	Latest example	Letter style G Gothic R Roman S Script	Punch shape	Additional features/notes
C H							
Christopher Harrington	Y	1595	1597	1663	R	hatchment	billet
	Y	–	–	–	R	biloboid	–
	L	–	–	–	R	hatchment	billet
James Chadwick	L	1697	1697	1702	R	lobate triad	crown
John Chartier	L	–	1699	1714	R	trifid rectangle	fleur de lis
	L	–	–	–	R	ovate ovoid	crown, fleur de lis, 2 pellets
	L	1723	–	–	–	–	IC
William Charnelhouse	L	1703	1706	1711	R	quatrefoil	2 mullets
Charles Hatfield	L	1727	1723	1738	R	globate loboid	2 mullets
	L	1727	–	–	R	globate globoid	2 mullets
	L	1739	–	–	S	cambered biloboid	fleur de lis
Caleb Hill	L	1728	1730	1733	R	globate rectangle	mullet
Christian Hillan	L	1736	1739	1741	R	trifid plinthform	multifoil, pellet
	L	1739	–	–	S	profiloid	bird, pellet
Charles Hougham	L	1769	1776	1813	R	rectangle	–
Christopher Haines	Db	1784	1770	1811	R	rectangle	–
	Db	–	–	–	R	rectangle	pellet
C H **J E**							
Hawkesworth, Eyre & Co Ltd	S	1867	1834	1931	R	quatrefoil	–
	S	1833	–	–	–	–	H E & Co
	S	1869	–	–	–	–	JKB
	S	–	–	–	–	–	J K B T H G W
	L	–	1858	1925	–	–	–
	B	–	1933	1937	–	–	–
cTh **J W**							
C. H. & J. W. Thomas	L	–	1911	1925	R	cuspoid	–
C I							
Charles Jackson	L	1720	1713	1728	R	globate globoid	3 pellets
	L	1739	–	–	S	circle	–
	L	1714	–	–	–	–	IA
C J R							
Christian J. Reid	Nc	–	1869	1870	R	billet	–
	Nc	–	–	–	R	trefoil	crown

Maker's initial(s) & maker(s)	Town of registration	Date of mark registration	Earliest example	Latest example	Letter style G Gothic R Roman S Script	Punch shape	Additional features/notes
C K							
Charles Frederick Kandler I	L	1727	1694	1777	R	winged triad	mullet
	L	1735	–	–	–	–	FK
	L	1751	–	–	–	–	KA
Charles Kandler II	L	1778	–	–	R	ovoid	–
Carl Christof Krall	L	–	1894	1915	R	rectangle	pellet
C L							
Jonah Clifton	L	1703	1703	1725	R	trifid ovoid	crown, floret
	L	1720	–	–	–	–	IC
Nicholaus Clausen	L	1709	1713	1719	R	trifid loboid	crown, shield
	L	1720	–	–	–	–	NC
Henry Clarke I	L	1709	1711	1722	R	ogee chinoid	mullet
	L	1723	–	–	–	–	HC
Joseph Clare I	L	1713	1714	1737	R	heart	pellet
	L	1720	–	–	–	–	†C
	L	1721	–	–	–	–	IC
Charles Lemaitre	Db	1735	1733	1736	R	rectangle	fleur de lis
Christopher Locker	Db	1739	1730	1751	R	crested rectangle	crown
Charles Lias	L	1837	1837	1884	R	rectangle	–
Charles Lamb	Db	1893	1894	1902	R	rectangle	pellet
A^CR^LE							
Joseph Clare II	L	1767	–	1768	R	ovoid	–
	L	1763	–	–	–	–	IC
CLARK							
John Clark	Ed	1751	1755	1765	R	rectangle	–
C L C							
C. L. Connel	L	–	1902	–	–	trefoil	–
	B	–	1913	1936	–	–	–
C M							
Charles Mackenzie	L	1736	–	1773	R	ovoid	–
Charles Martin	L	–	1727	1738	R	trifid rectangle	crown, pellet
	L	1741	–	–	S	ovoid	pellet
Christopher Makemeid	L	1758	–	1772	R	rectangle	pellet
	L	1771	–	–	R	oval	pellet
Charles Mullin	Db	–	1772	1805	R	rectangle	–
Charles Marsh	Db	1816	1817	1833	R	rectangle	–
	Db	–	–	–	R	rectangle	pellet
Mappin Bros	S	1883	1889	1954	R	bevelform	–
	S	1856	–	–	–	–	MB M&B EM JM FC CH WG JLL EM WG FC M Mn JM JLL HC Bros Bros

Maker's initial(s) & maker(s)	Town of registration	Date of mark registration	Earliest example	Latest example	Letter style G Gothic R Roman S Script	Punch shape	Additional features/notes
C N							
Charles Needham	S	1810	–	–	R	rectangle	pellet
C O							
John Cole	L	1697	1697	1706	R	heart	mullet
John Cory	L	1697	1698	1704	R	circle	crown
Lawrence Coles	L	1697	1674	1709	R	delphate biloboid	–
Stephen Coleman	L	1697	1681	1701	R	ogee chinoid	spoon
Edward Courthorpe	L	1697	–	1701	R	rectangle	–
Robert Cooper	L	1697	1682	1716	R	lobate shareform	chain, mullet, 5 pellets, 2 annulets
George Cox	L	1698	1698	1715	R	ogee triad	2 pellets
Thomas Corbett	L	1699	–	1703	R	hatchment	bird, 3 pellets
	L	1699	–	–	–	–	similar, incuse
Matthew Cooper I	L	1702	–	1703	G	ovate shareform	crown
	L	1720	–	–	–	–	MC
Edward Cornock	L	1707	1707	1733	R	circle	thread circle
	L	1723	–	–	–	–	EC
Augustine Courtauld	L	1708	1710	1743	R	globate ovoid	fleur de lis
	L	1729	–	–	–	–	AC
Thomas Cooke I	L	1713	–	–	R	heart	pellet
	L	1727	–	–	–	–	TC
John Corporon	L	1717	1717	–	R	crested triad	crown, mullet, fleur de lis
Isaac Cornafleau	L	–	1719	1723	R	profiloid	crown, mullet
	L	–	–	–	–	–	IC
Matthew Cooper II	L	1725	–	1731	R	rectangle	–
	L	1725	–	–	–	–	MC
C P							
Charles Plimpton	L	1805	1805	–	R	rectangle	–
Charles Price	L	1812	1812	1828	R	rectangle	pellet
	L	1823	–	–	R	bifoil	pellet
C R							
Charles Rhoades	Y	1677	1678	1707	R	heart	–
	Y	1677	–	–	–	–	RH
Clement Reed	Y	1698	1695	1698	R	cambered loboid	mullet, 2 pellets
Paul Crespin	L	1720	1721	1766	R	globate globoid	2 mullets
	L	1740	–	–	S	kidney	–
	L	–	–	–	–	–	PC
Christian Reid	Nc	–	1799	1818	R	oval	–
	Nc	–	–	–	R	rectangle	pellet

Maker's initial(s) & maker(s)	Town of registration	Date of mark registration	Earliest example	Latest example	Letter style G Gothic R Roman S Script	Punch shape	Additional features/notes
Charles Rawlings	L	1817	1817	1828	R	oval	–
	L	1819	–	–	R	rectangle	–
C R (R smaller) Jonathan Crutchfield	L	1697	–	1704	R	spiked oval	–
C R A C.R. Ashbee	L	–	1863	1942	–	–	–
C & R / C Charles & Richard Comyns	L	–	1918	1926	R	trefoil	–
C R / D R Christian Ker Reid & David Reid	L	1815	1799	1829	R	square	–
	Nc	1828	–	–	R	square	–
	Nc	–	–	–	R	quatrefoil	–
	L	1828	–	–	R	quatrefoil	–
C R / D R / C R Christian Ker Reid, David Reid, Christian Bruce Reid	Nc	–	1809	1834	R	sexfoil	–
C R / G S Charles Reily & George Storer	L	1829	1824	1862	R	quatrefoil	–
CR / WS Charles Rawlings & William Summers	L	1829	1829	1863	R	square	–
C S Clement Stonor	L	–	1683	1689	R	oval	dotted oval, arrow
Charles Sprage	L	1734	–	1736	R	arched shareform	mullet
Christopher Skinner	Db	1736	1737	1768	R	lozenge	2 mullets
	Db	–	–	–	S	quatrefoil	2 mullets, roman S
Charles Shipway	L	1826	1835	1839	R	rectangle	pellet
	L	1836	–	–	R	rectangle	–

Maker's initial(s) & maker(s)	Town of registration	Date of mark registration	Earliest example	Latest example	Letter style G Gothic R Roman S Script	Punch shape	Additional features/notes
C_HS $_SC_H$ Charles Stuart Harris	L	–	1863	1936	R	trefoil	–
C T Charles Townsend	Db	1770	1770	1776	R	rectangle	–
C T **I W** Carden Terry & John Williams	Db	–	1795	1819	R	square	–
	Co	–	–	–	–	–	T & W
	Co	–	–	–	–	–	C$_&$T I$_&$W
C_GT_FF Charles T. Fox & George Fox	L	–	1841	1906	R	ogee loboid	–
	L	–	–	–	R	ogee escutcheon	pellet
$C_&T$ $I_&W$ Carden Terry & John Williams	Co	–	1795	1819	R	rectangle	–
	Co	–	–	–	–	–	C T I W
	Db	–	–	–	–	–	C T I W
	Co	–	–	–	–	–	T & W
T^CW Thomas & William I Chawner	L	1764	1760	1771	R	square	–
	L	1763	–	–	–	–	W^{T}C$_C$
	L	1765	–	–	–	–	CT WC
	L	1768	–	–	–	–	T^W_CC
C V Louis Cuny	L	1703	1697	1729	R	profiloid	crown, pellet, fleur de lis
	L	1703	–	–	R	tridentate ovoid	crown
	L	1732	–	–	–	–	LC
Daniel (Peter) Cunningham	L	1717	–	1720	R	profiloid	dog
	L	1720	–	–	–	–	DC
C W Christopher Whitehill	Y	1676	1684	1693	R	tridentate triad	pellet
Charles Woodward	L	1741	1742	1776	R	rectangle	–

Maker's initial(s) & maker(s)	Town of registration	Date of mark registration	Earliest example	Latest example	Letter style G Gothic R Roman S Script	Punch shape	Additional features/notes
Charles Wright	L	1775	1768	1782	R	rectangle	–
	L	1780	–	–	R	rectangle	pellet
Charles Watts	L	1788	–	1803	R	rectangle	–
	L	1783	–	–	–	–	incuse, pellet
D A							
Isaac Davenport	L	1697	1697	1720	R	ogee triad	2 pellets, mullet
	L	1697	–	–	R	trifid triad	–
	L	1705	–	–	R	ogee triad	–
Isaac Dalton	L	1711	1706	1719	R	delphate chinoid	–
	L	1711	–	–	R	domate triad	fleur de lis, pellet
	L	–	–	–	R	ogee loboid	pellet
Josiah Daniel	L	1715	1715	1719	R	domate invectoid	mullet
	L	1724	–	–	–	–	ID
William Darker	L	1719	1719	1733	R	profiloid	acorn
	L	1720	–	–	–	–	WD
Fleurant David	L	–	1724	1725	R	profiloid	crown, pellet
	L	–	–	–	–	–	FD
D & A							
Daniel & Arter	B	–	1912	1934	R	3 bevelled squares	–
	S	–	1892	1900	–	–	–
D B							
David Bell	L	1756	1756	1778	R	rectangle	–
Daniel Bates	L	1778	1777	–	R	rectangle	–
D E B / A							
William Denny & John Bache	L	1697	1698	1699	R	quatrefoil	–
D C							
Daniel (Peter) Cunningham	L	1720	1720	–	R	profiloid	dog, floret
	L	1717	–	–	–	–	CV
Daniel Chartier	L	1740	1739	–	S	trifid rectangle	fleur de lis
David Crawford	Nc	–	1763	1784	R	rectangle	–
	Nc	–	–	–	R	trifid rectangle	crown
D C R							
D. Crighton Rait	Gl	1832	1830	1897	R	rectangle	–
	GL	–	–	–	–	–	D C R & S
D C R & S							
D. C. Rait & Son	Gl	–	1830	–	R	rectangle	–
	Gl	–	–	–	–	–	D C R

Maker's initial(s) & maker(s)	Town of registration	Date of mark registration	Earliest example	Latest example	Letter style G Gothic R Roman S Script	Punch shape	Additional features/notes
D D							
Dru Drury II	L	1767	–	–	S	bifoil	–
Daniel Denney	L	1786	1786	–	R	ovoid	–
	L	–	–	–	R	rectangle	–
David Darling	Nc	–	1802	1804	R	oval	pellet
D E							
William Denny	L	1697	1700	1705	R	quatrefoil	2 mullets
Samuel Dell	L	1697	1698	1703	R	delphate triad	pellet
Daniel Egan	Db	1800	1789	1816	R	oval	–
	Db	–	–	–	R	cleft rectangle	pellet
D G							
David Green	L	1720	1718	1728	R	rectangle	–
	L	1701	–	–	–	–	Gr
Dinah Gamon	L	1740	1740	1742	R	lozenge	2 mullets
D H							
David Hennell I	L	1736	1736	1762	R	rectangle	–
	L	1739	–	–	G	domate triad	fleur de lis
	L	1756	–	–	R	rectangle	pellet
Daniel Holy & Co	S	1776	1776	1825	R	rectangle	–
	S	1778	–	–	–	–	DH & Co
Daniel Hockly	L	1810	1810	1818	R	rectangle	pellet
D H & Co							
Daniel Holy & Co	S	1778	1776	1825	R	rectangle	–
	S	1776	–	–	–	–	DH
D H / **C H**							
Hands & Son	L	–	1825	1881	R	quatrefoil	2 pellets
D R H							
David II & Robert I Hennell	L	1763	1763	1810	R	cruciform	pellet
	L	1795	–	–	–	–	R H D H
H H / **T B**							
Daniel Hockly & Thomas Bosworth	L	1815	1815	–	R	square	–
D I							
Isaac Dighton	L	1697	1697	1705	R	ogee biloboid	winged mask, leaf spray
	L	1697	–	–	R	domate triad	winged mask, 3 pellets, arrow

Maker's initial(s) & maker(s)	Town of registration	Date of mark registration	Earliest example	Latest example	Letter style G Gothic R Roman S Script	Punch shape	Additional features/notes
John Diggle	L	1697	–	1702	R	delphate hatchment	fleur de lis, 3 pellets
Di							
Arte (Arthur) Dicken	L	1720	–	1723	S	globate rectangle	fleur de lis
D & W J							
Daniel & John Wellby	L	–	1878	1950	R	bevelled escutcheon	–
D K							
David King	Db	1690	1693	1739	R	oval	–
	Db	–	–	–	R	ovoid	crown
Daniel Ker	Ed	1764	1767	1773	R	rectangle	–
D L							
Dennis Langton	L	1729	–	1734	G	rectangle	–
	L	1732	–	–	R	rectangle	pellet
	L	1716	–	–	–	–	La
Dorothy Langlands	Nc	–	1804	1811	R	oval	pellet
D M							
Dorothy Monjoy	Db	–	1725	1730	R	domate oval	crown, pellet
David Mowden	L	1739	1751	1773	R	rectangle	pellet
	L	1774	–	–	R	profiloid	pellet
Dorothy Mills	L	1752	1751	1775	S	bifoil	–
David Marshall	Ed	1782	1785	1786	S	rectangle	–
DM monogram							
David Mitchell	Ed	1700	1720	1739	R	heart	–
DMcD							
D. McDonald	Gl	1828	1819	1841	R	rectangle	pellet
D M **T S**							
Dorothy Mills & Thomas Sarbitt	L	–	1745	1750	R	quatrefoil	quatrefoil
Do							
John Downes	L	1697	1697	1707	R	oval	2 fleurs de lis
D P							
Daniel Piers	L	1746	1749	1799	R	trifid archform	pellet
	L	–	–	–	R	bevelform	–
Daniel Popkins	Db	1759	1758	1775	R	rectangle	pellet
David Peter	Db	1767	1761	1806	S	rectangle	–
Daniel Pontifex	L	1794	1794	1811	R	rectangle	–

Maker's initial(s) & maker(s)	Town of registration	Date of mark registration	Earliest example	Latest example	Letter style G Gothic R Roman S Script	Punch shape	Additional features/notes
D P W Edward Dobson, William Pryor & James Williams	L	1755	1754	1755	R	rectangle	–
D R David Reid	Nc	–	1846	1867	R	ovoid	–
D S Dorothy Sarbitt	L	1753	1753	1754	R	oval	–
D S **B S** Digby Scott & Benjamin Smith II	L	1802	1802	1808	R	square	&
	L	1803	–	–	R	square	pellet
D S C G Millicent Sutherland	B	–	1914	1915	–	–	coronet, incuse
D S R S **D$_S$R S** Daniel Smith & Robert Sharp	L	1768	1757	1789	R	rectangle	RC
	L	1780	–	–	R	quatrefoil	pellet
	L	1780	–	–	S	quatrefoil	2 pellets
D T David Tanqueray	L	1720	1715	1724	R	globate globoid	floret, thistle
	L	1713	–	–	–	–	TA
D U **N H** Duncan Urquhart & Naphtali Hart	L	1791	1789	1812	R	square	pellet
	L	–	–	–	–	–	U & H
	L	–	–	–	–	–	others similar
D V Matthieu Durousseau	L	1705	–	–	R	lobate oval	double thread oval
D W David Willaume I	L	1720	1698	1744	R	profiloid	2 mullets, fleur de lis
	L	1697	–	–	–	–	WI
David Willaume II	L	1728	1725	1743	R	rectangle	–
	L	1739	–	–	S	quatrefoil	2 mullets
	L	1728	–	–	–	–	WI
Dennis Wilks	L	1737	1737	1741	R	waved triad	4 pellets
	L	1739	–	–	G	ogee triad	pellet

Maker's initial(s) & maker(s)	Town of registration	Date of mark registration	Earliest example	Latest example	Letter style G Gothic R Roman S Script	Punch shape	Additional features/notes
David Whyte	L	–	1762	1768	S	rectangle	–
D & W							
Thomas Devonshire & William Watkins	L	1756	1757	1760	S	ovoid	–
	L	1756	–	–	–	–	TD WW
W^D_I							
William & John Deane	L	1762	1762	1764	R	globate rectangle	pellet
	L	1759	–	–	–	–	W^D_JD
D^W_HW							
David Whyte & William Holmes	L	–	1763	1767	R	cruciform	pellet
E & Co							
Elder & Co	Ed	–	1831	1865	R	waved rectangle	–
Elkington & Co	B	–	1844	1970	R	rectangle	crown
	B	–	–	–	–	–	E & Co Ltd
	L	–	1864	1910	–	–	–
	S	–	1892	1921	–	–	E$^&$Co
	Db	–	–	1908	–	–	E$^&$Co
E & Co Ltd							
Elkington & Co Ltd	–	as above					
E A							
John East	L	1697	1697	1725	R	ogee shareform	pellet, fleur de lis
	L	1721	–	–	–	–	IE
Edward Aldridge I	L	1724	1734	1772	R	rectangle	–
	L	1739	–	–	S	bevelform	pellet
	L	–	–	–	R	rectangle	pellet
	L	–	–	–	R	lozenge	pellet
	L	–	–	–	S	rectangle	–
	L	–	–	–	G	tridentate biloboid	–
E / **A**							
Edward Anthony	Ex	1612	1610	1667	R	circle	dotted circle
	Ex	–	–	–	R	bevelled chinoid	–
	Ex	–	–	–	R	bevelled loboid	–
E^I_SA							
Edward Aldridge I & John Stamper	L	1753	1753	1759	R	cambered loboid	–

Maker's initial(s) & maker(s)	Town of registration	Date of mark registration	Earliest example	Latest example	Letter style G Gothic R Roman S Script	Punch shape	Additional features/notes
E B							
Eli Bilton	Nc	1683	1686	1711	R	rectangle	–
	Nc	–	–	–	R	loboid	mullet
	Nc	–	–	–	R	loboid	bat
	Nc	–	–	–	R	cleft triad	mullet
	Nc	–	–	–	R	lanceolate cuspoid	2 mullets, 2 pellets
	Nc	–	–	–	R	lanceolate triad	2 mullets
	Nc	1683	–	–	–	–	Bi
Edward Barrett	Db	1702	1700	1738	S	oval	–
	Db	–	–	–	R	rectangle	–
Edward Bennett I	L	1727	1731	1750	R	domate loboid	2 annulets
	L	1731	–	–	R	domate loboid	crown
	L	1747	–	–	S	ovoid	pellet
	L	1739	–	–	G	ovoid	–
Elizabeth Buteux (*later* Godfrey)	L	1731	1731	1732	R	quatrefoil	lancet, pellet, mullet
Edward Barton	L	1822	1821	1832	R	rectangle	–
	L	1834	–	–	R	rectangle	pellet
E B **J B**							
Edward & John Barnard	L	–	1851	1869	R	quatrefoil	–
	L	–	–	–	–	–	E & B J & B
E & B **J & B**							
Edward & John Barnard	L	–	1851	1869	R	quatrefoil	–
	L	–	–	–	–	–	E B J B
J **EBW** **J**							
John I, Edward III, Walter & John II Barnard	L	–	1862	1875	R	quatrefoil	2 pellets
E C							
John Eckfourd I	L	1698	1703	1719	R	quatrefoil	–
	L	–	–	–	–	–	IE
Erasmus Cope	Db	1707	1717	1736	R	cambered quadriform	crown
	Db	–	–	–	R	bifoil	pellet
	Db	–	–	–	R	heart	pellet
Edward Cornock	L	1723	1707	1733	R	oval	thread oval
	L	1707	–	–	–	–	CO
Edward Conen	L	1724	1724	–	R	globate square	fleur de lis, 2 pellets

Maker's initial(s) & maker(s)	Town of registration	Date of mark registration	Earliest example	Latest example	Letter style G Gothic R Roman S Script	Punch shape	Additional features/notes
John Eckfourd II	L	1725	1724	1747	R	kidney	mullet
	L	1725	–	–	–	–	IE
Ebenezer Coker	L	1738	1748	1775	R	oval	–
	L	1738	–	–	R	rectangle	–
	L	1739	–	–	S	ovoid	–
	L	1745	–	–	S	[lobed punch]	–
	L	–	–	–	R	invected rectangle	–
Elias Cachart	L	1742	1740	1765	S	quatrefoil	2 pellets
Elizabeth Cooke	L	1764	1763	1772	R	rectangle	–
	L	1764	–	–	R	rectangle	pellet
	L	–	–	–	R	invected rectangle	pellet
Edward Cooper	L	1775	–	1776	R	globate coneform	mullet
Edward Capper	L	1792	–	1820	R	rectangle	–
Edward Crofton	Db	1827	1815	1831	R	rectangle	–
E_BC Edward Charles Brown	L	–	1867	1882	R	trefoil	–
e_pc E. C. Purdee	L	–	1881	1900	G	trefoil	–
E C / T H Ebenezer Coker & Thomas Hannam	L	1759	1759	–	R	square	2 pellets
E D John Edwards I	L	1697	1701	1744	G	ogee chinoid	–
Edward Dowdall	Db	–	1715	–	R	circle	cross
John Edwards II	L	1724	*	*	R	globate rectangle	floret
	L	1724	–	–	–	–	IE
Edward Darvill	L	1757	–	1773	R	ovoid	–
Ed Richard Edwards	L	1716	1716	1717	R	globate globoid	2 pellets
	L	1723	–	–	–	–	RE
E E Edward Edwards	L	1697	–	–	G	ogee shareform	–
Edward Edwards I	L	1816	1816	*	R	rectangle	–
Edward Edwards II	L	1828	1828	1857	R	rectangle	–
Elizabeth Eaton	L	–	1829	1857	R	bifoil	–
E_JB_WE Edward I, Edward II, John & William Barnard	L	1829	1828	1895	R	quatrefoil	–

Maker's initial(s) & maker(s)	Town of registration	Date of mark registration	Earliest example	Latest example	Letter style G Gothic R Roman S Script	Punch shape	Additional features/notes
E E							
J E							
Messrs Eady	L	–	1858	1862	R	square	–
E F							
Edward Feline	L	1720	1721	1750	R	ovate triad	phoenix, mullet
	L	1739	–	–	S	profiloid	mullet
	L	–	–	–	–	–	Fe
Edith Fletcher	L	–	1729	1730	R	lozenge	fleur de lis, pellet
Edward Fernell	L	1780	1779	1802	R	rectangle	pellet
	L	1780	–	–	R	bifoil	pellet
	L	1781	–	–	R	rectangle	pellet
	L	1787	–	–	R	rectangle	–
Edward Farrell	L	1813	1814	1845	R	rectangle	pellet
	L	1819	–	–	R	quatrefoil	pellet
E G							
Edward Gibbon	L	1723	1723	1730	R	globate rectangle	mullet, pellet
	L	1719	–	–	–	–	Gi
Elizabeth Goodwin	L	1729	1729	1730	R	lozenge	2 mullets
Elizabeth Godfrey (*formerly* Buteux)	L	1741	1741	1765	R	lozenge	baluster, mullet
E H							
Edward Hall	L	1721	–	1722	R	rectangle	–
	L	1721	–	–	–	–	HA
Elizabeth Hartley	L	1748	1748	1751	R	lozenge	–
Edward Hutton	L	–	1855	1896	R	hexagon	–
	L	–	–	–	R	tridentate escutcheon	pellet
E I							
Edward Jennings	L	1720	1723	1730	R	ovate ovoid	crown, pellet
	L	1710	–	–	–	–	Ie
	L	1720	–	–	–	–	IE
Edward Jay	L	–	1775	1795	R	rectangle	–
	L	1757	–	–	–	–	EJ
Elizabeth Jones	L	1783	1784	1795	R	rectangle	–
E J							
Elizabeth Jackson	L	1748	1748	1750	R	lozenge	pellet
Edward Jay	L	1757	1775	1795	R	lobate ovoid	pellet
	L	–	–	–	–	–	EI
Edmond Johnson I	Db	1825	1833	1853	R	rectangle	pellet

Maker's initial(s) & maker(s)	Town of registration	Date of mark registration	Earliest example	Latest example	Letter style G Gothic R Roman S Script	Punch shape	Additional features/notes
Edmond Johnson II	Db	1882	–	1906	R	rectangle	pellet
	Db	1881	–	–	–	–	E Johnson
	Db	1893	–	–	–	–	EJ (monogram)
	L	–	1896	–	–	–	–
	S	–	1925	1927	–	–	–
EJ (monogram)							
Edmond Johnson II	Db	1893	–	1906	R	square	–
	Db	1882	–	–	–	–	EJ
	Db	1881	–	–	–	–	E Johnson
	L	–	1896	–	–	–	–
	S	–	1925	1927	–	–	–
E Johnson							
Edmond Johnson II	Db	1881	–	1906	R	[no shape]	–
	Db	1882	–	–	–	–	EJ
	Db	1893	–	–	–	–	EJ (monogram)
	L	–	1896	–	–	–	–
	S	–	1925	1927	–	–	–
E B J & W							
E. J. & W. Barnard	L	–	1835	1871	R	quatrefoil	–
E K R							
E. K. Reid	L	–	1855	1873	R	bifoil	–
E L							
Edward Lothian	Ed	1731	1735	1749	R	trifid ovoid	crown, pellet
Edward Lambe I	L	1740	–	1741	S	oval	pellet
	L	1742	–	–	S	[inverted pear]	floret
	L	–	–	–	S	concave archform	–
Edward Lowe	L	1760	1770	1783	R	rectangle	pellet
Edward Leapidge	L	1767	1769	1776	R	rectangle	–
Edward Lees	L	1803	1803	1807	R	ovoid	pellet
	L	1806	–	–	–	–	others similar
Edward Livingstone	Du	–	1809	1840	R	rectangle	–
El							
John Elston I	Ex	–	1702	1728	G	circle	crown
	Ex	–	–	–	–	–	IE IE
	Ex	–	–	–	–	–	JE
E M							
Edmund Medlycot	L	1748	1750	1752	R	domate rectangle	mullet, pellet
Elizabeth Morley	L	1794	1796	1817	R	rectangle	pellet
Edward Mayfield	L	1796	1795	1808	R	rectangle	–
Edward Murray	Db	1812	1816	1822	R	rectangle	–

Maker's initial(s) & maker(s)	Town of registration	Date of mark registration	Earliest example	Latest example	Letter style G Gothic R Roman S Script	Punch shape	Additional features/notes
E M & Co							
Elkington Mason & Co	B	1843	1844	1862	R	billet	–
	B	–	–	–	G	3 rectangles	–
	S	1859	–	–	R	billet	–
EM JM (EM / JM)							
Mappin Bros	S	1867	1889	1954	R	2 rectangles	–
	S	–	–	–	R	square	–
	S	1859	–	–	–	–	MB M&B CM FC CH WG JLL / FC WG M MN / HC JLL Bros Bros
En							
Thomas England	L	1725	1727	1746	R	trigonate rectangle	crown
	L	1725	–	–	–	–	TE
E N / V A							
William England & John Vaen	L	1714	1714	–	R	square	–
E O							
Ebenezer Olivant	Ed	1737	–	1749	R	rectangle	–
Elizabeth Oldfield	L	1750	1750	1754	R	rectangle	–
E P							
Edward Penman	Ed	1707	1707	1729	R	bifoil	–
Edmund Pearce	L	1720	1705	1722	R	cambered square	–
	L	1720	–	–	R	chevroned rectangle	pellet
	L	1705	–	–	–	–	PE
Edward Peacock	L	1724	1724	–	R	oval	pellet
	L	1710	–	–	–	–	Pe
Edward Pocock	L	1728	1714	1738	R	globate rectangle	lion rampant
Edward Power	Db	1816	1817	1835	R	rectangle	–
E R							
Emick Romer	L	–	1759	1776	R	profiloid	–
E S							
Edward Stammers	L	1816	1819	1850	R	rectangle	pellet
Edward Smith	B	1826	1826	1865	R	rectangle	–
E T							
Elizabeth Tuite	L	1741	–	–	R	square	pitcher
Elizabeth Tookey	L	–	1770	–	R	lozenge	–
	L	–	–	–	R	rectangle	pellet
Edward Thomason	B	1821	1813	1848	R	rectangle	pellet
	B	–	–	–	R	rectangle	–

Maker's initial(s) & maker(s)	Town of registration	Date of mark registration	Earliest example	Latest example	Letter style G Gothic R Roman S Script	Punch shape	Additional features/notes
E V							
Edward Vincent	L	–	1713	1740	R	oval	crescent, annulet, pellet, thread oval
	L	1739	–	–	S	oval	2 pellets
	L	–	–	–	R	oval	crescent, pellet
	L	–	–	–	–	–	VI
E W							
Edward Workman	Db	1702	1708	1719	S	globate globoid	2 mullets
Thomas Ewesdin	L	1713	1717	1725	R	trefoil	floret
Edward Wood	L	1722	1723	1759	R	circle	mullet, pellet, arrow, thread circle
	L	1735	–	–	R	circle	mullet, pellet, fleur de lis
	L	1740	–	–	G	circle	crown, crescent
	L	1722	–	–	–	–	WO
Edward Wakelin	L	1747	1741	1762	G	trifid rectangle	crown
E Y							
Edward Yorke	L	1730	1709	1731	R	hatchment	mullet
	L	1705	–	–	–	–	YO
F							
William Fawdery	L	1720	1700	1726	R	[waved spurform]	–
	L	1697	–	–	–	–	FA
	L	–	–	–	–	–	WF
Hester Fawdery	L	1727	1727	–	R	lozenge	–
F A							
William Fawdery	L	1697	1700	1726	R	circle	crown, thread circ
	L	1720	–	–	R	circle	–
	L	–	–	–	R	circle	pellet, thread circle
	L	1720	–	–	–	–	F
	L	–	–	–	–	–	WF
John Fawdery I	L	1697	1698	1734	R	bevelled square	smaller A
John Farnell	L	1719	1715	1727	R	trefoil	pellet
	L	1714	–	–	–	–	Fa
	L	1720	–	–	–	–	IF
Thomas Farren	L	1707	1710	1742	R	domate lobus	fleur de lis, mullet
	L	–	–	–	R	domate lobus	clover, floret
	L	1720	–	–	–	–	TF

Maker's initial(s) & maker(s)	Town of registration	Date of mark registration	Earliest example	Latest example	Letter style G Gothic R Roman S Script	Punch shape	Additional features/notes
Fa							
Thomas Fawler	L	1707	1707	1709	R	concave loboid	–
John Farnell	L	1714	1715	1727	R	heart	thread heart
	L	1719	–	–	–	–	FA
	L	1720	–	–	–	–	IF
FB							
Francis Batty II	Nc	1708	1712	1736	G	rectangle	–
	Nc	1708	–	–	–	–	Ba
Francis Blackbeard	L	1824	1824	–	R	cleft cleftform	–
F B **N D**							
Francis Butty & Nicholas Dumee	L	1761	1765	1772	R	square	pellet
F C							
Francis Crump	L	1741	1742	1790	S	profiloid	pellet, annulet
	L	1745	–	–	R	oval	thread oval, pellet
	L	1751	–	–	R	bifoil	–
	L	1756	–	–	R	rectangle	pellet
Francis Clark	B	1826	1830	1848	R	rectangle	–
	B	1840	–	–	R	rectangle	–
F C **C H**							
Mappin Bros	S	1885	1889	1954	R	bevelled quadriform	MB M&B WG JLL WG M Mn JLL Bros Bros EM JM EM CM JM
FC CH							
Mappin Bros	S	1889	1889	1954	R	2 rectangles	as above
F D							
Fleurant David	L	–	1724	1725	R	rectangle	pellet
	L	–	–	–	–	–	DA
Francis Douglas	L	1837	1837	1861	R	rectangle	pellet
F E							
Frederick Elkington	L	–	1872	1882	R	bifoil	–
	B	–	1869	1888	–	–	–
Fe							
Edward Feline	L	1720	1721	1750	R	ovate globoid	phoenix, mullet
	L	–	–	–	R	trefoil	fleur de lis
	L	1720	–	–	–	–	EF

Maker's initial(s) & maker(s)	Town of registration	Date of mark registration	Earliest example	Latest example	Letter style G Gothic R Roman S Script	Punch shape	Additional features/notes
F E T & Co F. E. Timm	S	1857	1894	1929	R	woolsack	–
F & F Findlay & Field	Gl	–	1848	–	R	rectangle	–
F G Francis Garthorne	L	–	1677	1723	R	ogee triad	mullet
	L	1697	–	–	–	–	GA (A within)
Francis Gerard	Db	1704	1712	1715	R	ogee escutcheon	M & 2 dogs
F H Francis Howden	Ed	1781	1785	1820	R	rectangle	–
Francis Higgins	L	1817	1818	1940	R	rectangle	–
	L	1835	–	–	R	rectangle	pellet
F I Joshua Field	L	1701	–	1716	R	trifid globoid	fleur de lis, mullet
F K Charles (Frederick) Kandler	L	1735	1694	1777	R	domate hatchment	crown, mullet
	L	1739	–	–	S	globate triad	fleur de lis
	L	1758	–	–	S	domate rectangle	trefoil
	L	1727	–	–	–	–	CK
	L	1751	–	–	–	–	KA
Frederick Knopfell	L	1752	1765	1768	R	domate rectangle	fleur de lis
F L Francis Leake	L	–	1658	–	R	concave shareform	3 pellets, bird
William Fleming	L	1697	1701	1728	R	trifid loboid	crown, pellet
John Flight	L	1710	1702	–	R	trefoil	mullet
F & M Fergusson & MacBean of Inverness	Ed	–	1891	–	R	rectangle	–
F N Francis Nelme	L	1739	1725	1739	R	tridentate arcade	–
	L	1723	–	–	–	–	AN (monogram)
F O Thomas Foote	Ex	–	1701	1703	R	bevelform	–
Thomas Folkingham	L	1707	1707	1734	R	domate loboid	mitre, 2 mullets, 2 pellets
	L	1721	–	–	–	–	TF
William Fordham	L	1707	1726	1731	G	circle	–
	L	–	–	–	–	–	WF

Maker's initial(s) & maker(s)	Town of registration	Date of mark registration	Earliest example	Latest example	Letter style G Gothic R Roman S Script	Punch shape	Additional features/notes
F P							
Francis Pages	L	1729	1730	1754	R	rectangle	pellet
	L	1739	–	–	S	oval	pellet
Frances Purton	L	1783	1788	1809	R	oval	–
Francis Powell	L	1818	1817	1823	R	rectangle	–
F P **T J**							
Frances Purton & Thomas Johnson	L	1793	1793	1794	R	square	–
F R							
William Francis	L	1697	–	1709	R	lobate triad	heart
Ralph Frith	L	1728	1728	–	R	rectangle	pellet
	L	1728	–	–	–	–	RF
Fr							
James Fraillon	L	1711	1702	1727	G	hatchment	mullet
	L	1723	–	–	–	–	IF
F S							
Francis Spilsbury I	L	1729	1729	*	R	heart	pellet, ovoid
	L	1739	–	–	R	trifid waveform	crown, pellet
	L	1739	–	–	–	–	SP
Francis Spilsbury II	L	1767	1768	1776	R	quatrefoil	pellet
Francis Stamp	L	1780	1779	1780	R	cleft rectangle	pellet
	L	1780	–	–	R	rectangle	pellet
F & S							
Fattorini & Sons	Ch	–	1909	1911	–	–	–
	B	–	1911	1916	–	–	–
F T							
Francis Turner	L	1720	1718	1734	R	bevelled hatchment	2 mullets, pellet
	L	–	–	–	R	bevelform	2 pellets
	L	1709	–	–	–	–	Tu
Francis Thurkle	L	1783	–	1793	R	bevelform	cameo
F W							
Fuller White	L	1744	1743	1773	R	waved rectangle	–
	L	1751	–	–	R	waved rectangle	pellet
	L	1758	–	–	S	rectangle	–
	L	–	–	–	S	oval	–
F W **& D**							
Fenton, Danby & Webster	S	1823	–	1825	R	square	pellet

Maker's initial(s) & maker(s)	Town of registration	Date of mark registration	Earliest example	Latest example	Letter style G Gothic R Roman S Script	Punch shape	Additional features/notes
G A							
William Gamble	L	1697	1698	1721	R	oval	crown, 2 pellets, thread oval
Daniel Garnier	L	1697	1697	1698	R	trifid ovoid	crown, fleur de lis, 2 pellets
George Garthorne	L	1697	1681	1709	R	ovate triad	crown, crescent
George Angel	L	–	1841	1892	R	bifoil	–
	L	–	–	–	R	quatrefoil	quatrefoil, thread, 2 mullets
George W. Adams	L	1840	1840	1892	R	bifoil	–
G. Alcock	Db	–	1841	1842	R	rectangle	–
G A (A within)							
Francis Garthorne	L	1697	1677	1723	R	waved shareform	–
	L	–	–	–	–	–	FG
G A & Co							
George Ashforth & Co	S	1773	1774	1822	R	square	–
G B							
George Boothby	L	1720	1722	1752	R	ovate rectangle	bird
	L	1739	–	–	S	oval	–
	L	1720	–	–	–	–	BO
George Bulman	Nc	–	1724	1743	R	rectangle	–
	Nc	–	–	–	S	rectangle	–
	Nc	–	–	–	G	rectangle	–
George Baskerville	L	1738	1745	1814	R	circle	–
	L	1745	–	–	R	rectangle	–
	L	1755	–	–	R	oval	–
	L	1780	–	–	R	oval	pellet
George Burrows I	L	1769	1781	1823	R	rectangle	–
George Brasier	L	1785	1789	1800	R	oval	–
	L	1787	–	–	R	rectangle	–
Gustavus Byrne	Db	1791	1793	1807	S	rectangle	–
George Beckwith	L	1804	–	1805	R	rectangle	–
George Burrows II	L	1819	1823	1824	R	bifoil	pellet
	L	1821	–	–	R	rectangle	pellet
G B **T B**							
George II & T. Burrows	L	–	1795	1803	R	square	(doubtful ascription)

Maker's initial(s) & maker(s)	Town of registration	Date of mark registration	Earliest example	Latest example	Letter style G Gothic R Roman S Script	Punch shape	Additional features/notes
G $^{\text{T}}_{\text{M}}$ B George Baskerville & T. Morley	L	1775	1775	–	R	oval	–
G C George Cooper	A	1728	–	1730	R	bifoil	–
George Campar	L	1749	1730	1757	S	tridentate arcade	pellet
George Cowles	L	1777	1778	1802	R	rectangle	–
G. Cooper	S	1788	–	–	R	bevelform	pellet
George Clements	L	1825	–	1838	R	ovoid	–
G C & Co G. Cooper & Co	S	–	1818	1819	R	arched rectangle	crescent
G C **I C** George & John Cowie	L	1822	–	1838	R	square	–
G D George Day	L	1809	–	1812	R	oval	–
	L	1814	–	–	R	rectangle	–
G E Griffith Edwards	L	1733	–	1735	R	cambered hatchment	2 florets, 4 pellets
	L	1739	–	–	S	profiloid	2 pellets
G E D Dougal Ged	Ed	1734	1740	1759	R	rectangle	–
G E **& Co** George Eadon & Co (*or* Eadon, Kibble & Weaver)	S	1795	1796	1813	R	square	–
G E **& S** George Edwards & Sons	L	–	1860	1927	R	square	–
G F George Fenwick	Ed	–	1806	1823	R	rectangle	–
George Ferris	Ex	–	1815	1838	R	bifoil	–
George Fox	L	–	1861	1906	R	quatrefoil	–
G F P George Frederick Pinnell	L	1830	1830	1849	R	rectangle	2 pellets

Maker's initial(s) & maker(s)	Town of registration	Date of mark registration	Earliest example	Latest example	Letter style G Gothic R Roman S Script	Punch shape	Additional features/notes
G G							
George Giles	L	1762	1783	1797	R	bifoil	–
George Gray	L	1782	1788	1800	R	rectangle	–
	L	–	–	–	R	oval	–
George Glenny	L	1815	–	1818	–	[no shape]	incuse
G G & Co							
A. Goodman Gainsford & Co	S	1797	1799	1834	R	rectangle	–
	S	1800	–	–	–	–	A G & Co
G H							
George Hindmarsh	L	1731	1731	1754	R	ovoid	–
	L	1739	–	–	R	bevelform	–
George Hunter I	L	1748	1735	1764	R	rectangle	–
	L	1765	–	–	R	oval	–
	L	1767	–	–	R	bifoil	–
George Hill	Db	1759	1765	1766	R	rectangle	–
George Hunter II	L	1817	–	1831	R	bifoil	–
G. Hawksley & Co	S	1858	–	1859	R	rectangle	–
	S	1856	–	–	–	–	GH CH
G H **C H**							
G. Hawksley & Co	S	1856	–	1859	R	bevelled square	–
	S	1858	–	–	–	–	GH
G^W_CH							
George Heming & William Chawner I	L	1774	1776	1781	R	baluster	pellet
	L	1781	–	–	–	–	GH WC
	L	1781	–	–	–	–	–
G H **W C**							
George Hemming & William Chawner I	L	1781	1776	1781	R	square	2 pellets
	L	1774	–	–	–	–	G^W_CH
	L	1781	–	–	–	–	–
G I							
Edward Gibson	L	1697	1702	1705	R	heart	2 mullets, crescent
Richard Gines	L	1698	1693	1725	R	rectangle	–
	L	1714	–	–	G	tridentate escutcheon	–
	L	1720	–	–	–	–	RG

Maker's initial(s) & maker(s)	Town of registration	Date of mark registration	Earliest example	Latest example	Letter style G Gothic R Roman S Script	Punch shape	Additional features/notes
Glover Johnson	L	1720	1713	1726	R	quatrefoil	2 fleurs de lis
	L	1712	–	–	–	–	IO
George Greenhill Jones	L	1726	1724	1754	R	trifid rectangle	crown, floret
	L	1739	–	–	S	bifoil	–
	L	1719	–	–	–	–	IO
George Ibbot	L	1753	1759	1760	S	rectangle	pellet
	L	1759	–	–	–	–	IBBOT
George Ivory	L	–	1844	1876	R	hatchment	–
Gi							
William Gibson	L	1697	1698	1705	G	octagon	double thread octagon
John Gibbons	L	1700	1703	1729	R	acorn	mullet
	L	1724	–	–	–	–	IG
Edward Gibbon	L	1719	1723	1730	R	globate oval	mullet, pellet
	L	1723	–	–	–	–	EG
G J							
George Jamieson	A (*also* Ed & L)	–	1841	1867	R	rectangle	–
G K							
George Knight	L	1818	1818	1825	R	rectangle	pellet
George King	L	1819	–	1825	R	bifoil	–
G & K							
Gillsland & Ker	Ed	1763	1764	1768	S	rectangle	–
G L							
George Lyng	Db	1706	1699	–	R	oval	–
George Lowe	Ch	1791	1796	1841	R	rectangle	–
	Ch	–	–	–	R	bifoil	pellet
	L	1791	–	–	R	rectangle	–
G. S. Lewis	Nc	–	1807	–	R	lobate rectangle	–
G L J W							
George Lewis & John Walker	Nc	–	1794	1822	R	quatrefoil	–
G L N							
James Glen	Gl	1743	1743	1752	R	rectangle	–
	Gl	1743	–	–	–	–	IG
G M							
George Methuen	L	1743	1744	1771	S	trifid invectoid	mullet
George Morris	L	1750	1752	1753	R	ovoid	pellet
	L	1751	–	–	S	domate rectangle	2 pellets, swan
George Murray	Nc	–	1805	–	R	oval	–

Maker's initial(s) & maker(s)	Town of registration	Date of mark registration	Earliest example	Latest example	Letter style G Gothic R Roman S Script	Punch shape	Additional features/notes
G MH **(MH conjoined)**							
G. McHattie	Ed	–	1806	1827	R	rectangle	–
G N							
Gawen Nash	L	1724	1726	1737	R	ovoid	–
	L	1726	–	–	R	trefoil	dog, pellet
	L	1739	–	–	S	bevelform	–
George Natter	L	1773	–	1801	R	concave archform	–
	L	1772	–	–	R	oval	pellet, thread oval
	L	1773	–	–	R	rectangle	–
George Nangle	L	1797	1800	1807	R	oval	–
	L	1818	–	–	R	rectangle	–
G N **R H**							
Nathan & Hayes	Ch (*also* B)	–	1890	1916	R	tridentate escutcheon	–
G O							
John Goode	L	1701	1702	1719	R	trifid biloboid	crown
James Goodwin	L	1710	1712	1729	R	bifoil	–
	L	1710	–	–	R	trefoil	crown
	L	1721	–	–	–	–	IG
James Gould	L	1722	1722	1748	R	heart	pellet, mullet
	L	1722	–	–	–	–	IG (monogram)
	L	1739	–	–	–	–	IG
Meschach Godwin	L	1723	1723	1725	R	globate biloboid	floret
	L	1723	–	–	–	–	MG
William Gould	L	1734	1732	1767	R	oval	–
	L	1732	–	–	–	–	WG
G P							
George Purse	L	–	1817	1823	R	bifoil	–
G R							
Henry Green	L	1700	1701	1717	R	lobate triad	2 pellets, crescent
	L	1720	–	–	–	–	HG
George Robertson	A	1708	–	1725	R	rectangle	–
Gundry Roode	L	1721	1711	1735	R	heart	–
	L	1737	–	–	R	heart	mullet
	L	–	–	–	R	trefoil	mullet
	L	1710	–	–	–	–	RO
Richard Green	L	1726	1703	1730	R	heart	fleur de lis
	L	1703	–	–	–	–	R within G
	L	1723	–	–	–	–	others similar

Maker's initial(s) & maker(s)	Town of registration	Date of mark registration	Earliest example	Latest example	Letter style G Gothic R Roman S Script	Punch shape	Additional features/notes
George Ridout	L	1743	–	1744	R	rectangle	pellet
George Reid	L	1811	–	1829	R	ovoid	–
Gr							
Nathaniel Greene	L	1699	–	1706	G	ogee triad	fleur de lis
David Green	L	1701	1718	1728	G	trifid biloboid	crown
	L	1720	–	–	–	–	DG
GR (R within)							
Richard Green	L	1703	1703	1730	R	ogee cuspoid	–
	L	1723	–	–	–	–	others similar
	L	1726	–	–	–	–	RG
G R **E B**							
G. Roberts & E. Briggs	L	–	1835	1903	R	quatrefoil	–
	L	1859	–	–	–	–	R & B
G S							
Gilbert Shepherd	L	1631	1657	1663	R	loboid	crozier, 2 pellets
George Scott II	Ed	1697	1701	1703	R	heart	–
George Squire	L	1720	–	1726	R	ogee triad	3 pellets
	L	1720	–	–	–	–	SQ
Gabriel Sleath	L	1720	1709	1752	R	ogee triad	fleur de lis
	L	1739	–	–	S	oval	–
	L	1707	–	–	–	–	SL
George Smith I	L	1732	1739	1777	R	rectangle	pellet
	L	1739	–	–	S	square	pellet
George Smith II	L	1767	1765	1819	R	rectangle	thread rectangle
	L	1771	–	–	R	rectangle	–
	L	–	–	–	R	oval	pellet
George Seatoun	L	–	1769	1780	R	oval	–
George Smith III	L	1774	1781	1783	S	concave rectangle	–
George Smith IV	L	1799	–	–	R	delphate rectangle	–
	L	1803	–	–	R	rectangle	pellet
	L	1812	–	–	R	rectangle	–
G & S Co **Ltd**							
Goldsmiths & Silversmiths Co Ltd	L	–	1893	1950	R	trefoil	–
	S	–	1901	1948	–	–	–
	B	–	1889	1934	–	–	–

Maker's initial(s) & maker(s)	Town of registration	Date of mark registration	Earliest example	Latest example	Letter style G Gothic R Roman S Script	Punch shape	Additional features/notes
G^F_CS							
Gabriel Sleath & Francis Crump	L	1753	1753	1754	R	octagon	pellet
G^S_SS							
George I & Samuel III Smith	L	1750	1751	1752	R	quatrefoil	pellet
G S T H							
George Smith II & Thomas Hayter	L	1792	1791	1818	R	square	–
G S W F							
George Smith III & William Fearn	L	1786	1786	1832	R	square	–
G T							
George Turner	Ex	–	1810	1834	R	rectangle	–
G. Thompson	Gl	1833	1829	1837	R	rectangle	2 pellets
G U							
Nathaniel Gulliver	L	1722	1722	1727	R	lozenge	–
	L	1722	–	–	–	–	NG
George Unite	B	1832	1830	1910	R	rectangle	–
	S	1861	–	–	R	tridentate escutcheon	–
G W							
George Weeks	L	1735	1734	1737	R	ovate rectangle	crown
George Wickes	L	1735	1719	1757	R	crested rectangle	crown, pellet
	L	1739	–	–	G	trifid biloboid	PoW feathers, pellet
	L	1722	–	–	–	–	GW (W within)
	L	1722	–	–	–	–	WI
George Walker	Ch	–	1768	1794	R	rectangle	–
George Wintle	L	1787	1791	1826	S	oval	–
	L	1791	–	–	R	oval	–
	L	1813	–	–	R	rectangle	–
George West	Db	1793	1794	1833	R	oval	thread oval
George Wheatley	Db	–	1794	1797	R	rectangle	–
Gervase Wheeler	B	1831	1831	1841	R	rectangle	–
G W (W within)							
George Wickes	L	1722	1719	1757	R	octagon	–
	L	1722	–	–	–	–	WI
	L	1735	–	–	–	–	GW

Maker's initial(s) & maker(s)	Town of registration	Date of mark registration	Earliest example	Latest example	Letter style G Gothic R Roman S Script	Punch shape	Additional features/notes
Gy & Co							
Gray & Co	Ch	1900	1912	1926	–	–	–
H & Co Ltd							
Heming & Co Ltd	L	–	1904	1972	R	trefoil	–
H A							
Pierre Harache I	L	1697	1684	1704	R	profiloid	crown, 2 balusters
George Havers	L	1697	–	1699	R	circle	4 annulets
Benjamin Harris	L	1697	–	1699	R	trifid loboid	crown
Pierre Harache II	L	1698	–	1705	R	trifid triad	crown, 2 mullets, 6 pellets, crescent
	L	1698	–	–	R	trifid loboid	crown, 9 pellets, 3 fleurs de lis
	L	1698	–	–	R	trifid triad	crown, 2 balusters, crescent
Paul Hanet	L	1716	1718	1738	R	bevelled hatchment	fleur de lis, mullet
	L	1717	–	–	–	–	incuse
	L	1721	–	–	–	–	PH
Edward Hall	L	1721	–	1722	R	rectangle	–
	L	1721	–	–	–	–	EH
Henry Atkin	S	1841	1841	–	R	rectangle	pellet
Atkin Bros & Co	S	1853	1859	1959	R	rectangle	–
	S	1853	–	–	R	rectangle	pellet
Archer, Machin & Marsh	S	1854	1858	1924	R	rectangle	–
Henry Archer & Co	S	1855	1846	1896	R	rectangle	–
	S	1855	–	–	R	2 ovals	–
Ha							
John Harris I	L	1717	*	*	R	ogee triad	3 pellets
John Harvey I	L	1739	1740	1745	R	tabled rectangle	crown
	L	1738	–	–	–	–	IH
H & A							
Horton & Allday	B	–	1887	1908	–	–	–
A^H E							
Hennell & Anthony Elson	L	1971	–	–	R	fleur de lis	pellet

Maker's initial(s) & maker(s)	Town of registration	Date of mark registration	Earliest example	Latest example	Letter style G Gothic R Roman S Script	Punch shape	Additional features/notes
H B							
Harry Beathune	Ed	1704	1716	1726	R	bifoil	–
Henry Brind	L	1742	1742	1763	R	rounded rectangle	–
Henry Bayley (*or* Bailey)	L	1750	1757	1769	R	tridentate rectangle	crown, pellet
	L	–	–	–	S	profiloid	pellet
Hester Bateman	L	1761	1763	1795	S	woolsack	others similar
	L	1771	–	–	S	rounded rectangle	others similar
	L	1776	–	–	S	woolsack	–
	L	1778	–	–	S	rounded rectangle	–
	L	1787	–	–	R	rectangle	–
H B & H							
Harrison Bros & Howson	S	1849	1849	1945	R	tridentate escutcheon	–
	S	1849	–	–	–	–	HH
H C							
Henry Clarke I	L	1723	1711	1722	R	tridentate chinoid	–
	L	–	–	–	R	tridentate triad	pellet
	L	1709	–	–	–	–	CL
Henry Cory	L	1754	1759	1767	R	rectangle	pellet
Henry Cowper	L	1782	1788	1790	R	rectangle	–
	L	1782	–	–	S	rectangle	–
Henry Chawner	L	1786	1778	1809	R	oval	–
	L	1787	–	–	R	rectangle	–
H C I E							
Henry Chawner & John Emes	L	1796	1796	1797	R	oval	–
H D							
Henry Hutton	L	1754	1757	1763	S	waveform	–
Henry Daniel	L	1778	–	–	R	rectangle	pellet
James Henry Daniel	L	1820	1826	1829	R	rectangle	–
	L	1823	–	–	–	–	IHD
H E							
Henry Ellis	Ex	–	1849	1851	S	rectangle	–

Maker's initial(s) & maker(s)	Town of registration	Date of mark registration	Earliest example	Latest example	Letter style G Gothic R Roman S Script	Punch shape	Additional features/notes
H E & Co Hawkesworth, Eyre & Co Ltd	S	1833	1834	1931	R	quatrefoil	–
	S	1867	–	–	–	–	CH JE
	S	1869	–	–	–	–	JKB TH GW
	S	–	–	–	–	–	JKB
	B	–	1933	1937	–	–	–
	L	–	1858	1925	–	–	–
HᴬₚE Hugh Arnett & Edward Pocock	L	1720	1719	1734	R	quatrefoil	–
	L	1720	–	–	–	–	A R P O
H E W E Henrietta & William Eastwick	L	1802	1801	–	R	square	–
H F Henry Flavelle	Db	1837	1825	1851	R	rectangle	–
F H H Hennell, Frazer & Haws	L	1967	1870	1893	R	[stepform]	pellet
	L	1972	–	–	R	[fleur de lis]	pellet
H G Henry Greene	L	1720	1701	1717	R	trigonate triad	2 pellets
	L	1700	–	–	–	–	GR
Hugh Gordon	Ed	1727	1731	1756	R	bifoil	–
Henry Greenway	L	1775	1775	1798	R	rectangle	pellet
Henry Green	L	1786	1794	1797	R	rectangle	–
H H Henry Hebert	L	1734	1733	1745	R	rectangle	pellet
	L	1735	–	–	R	trifid rectangle	3 crowns, pellet
	L	1739	–	–	S	cambered cleftform	crown, fleur de lis
	L	1739	–	–	S	ovate rectangle	crown
Henry Hallsworth	L	–	1763	1804	G	delphate rectangle	–
Hyam Hyams	L	1821	1821	1879	R	rectangle	pellet
Henry Hyde	L	1834	–	1839	R	rectangle	pellet
Harrison Bros & Howson	S	1849	1849	1945	R	rectangle	pellet
	S	1849	–	–	–	–	HB &H

Maker's initial(s) & maker(s)	Town of registration	Date of mark registration	Earliest example	Latest example	Letter style G Gothic R Roman S Script	Punch shape	Additional features/notes
Henry Holland	L	–	1854	1881	R	bifoil	–
HH (conjoined)							
Henry Hayens	L	1749	1748	1769	R	reelform	–
H H & J E B							
Walker & Hall	S	1868	1892	1968	R	rectangle	–
	L	–	1887	1941	–	–	–
	B	–	1883	1938	–	–	–
	Ch	–	1906	1938	–	–	–
	S	1862	–	–	–	–	W & H
H & H							
Howard & Hawksworth	S	1835	1833	1852	R	rectangle	–
Hopkins & Hopkins	Db	1883	–	1904	R	rectangle	–
H I							
Samuel Hitchcock	L	1713	1715	1729	R	waved triad	fleur de lis
	L	1720	–	–	–	–	SH
Hi							
Robert Hill	L	1717	–	1719	G	circle	shield, 3 pellets
	L	1730	–	–	–	–	RH
H & I							
Hamilton & Inches	Ed	1880	1873	1956	R	rectangle	–
	Ed	1899	–	–	S	rectangle	–
H L							
Henry Lambert & Co	L	–	1902	1915	R	escutcheon	–
H L H L							
Henry Lias Jr & Son	L	1867	1850	1876	R	quatrefoil	–
H M							
Henry Matthews	Db	1706	1704	1706	R	oval	bird, pellet
Henry Morris	L	1720	1739	1758	R	rectangle	–
	L	1739	–	–	S	rectangle	–
	L	1744	–	–	S	profiloid	pellet
	L	1749	–	–	R	profiloid	pellet
	L	–	–	–	G	bifoil	–
	L	1718	–	–	–	–	MO
	L	–	–	–	–	–	HM (conjoined)
Henry Miller I	L	1720	–	1721	R	waveform	pellet
	L	1714	–	–	–	–	MI
Henry Miller II	L	1733	1732	1753	R	rectangle	–

Maker's initial(s) & maker(s)	Town of registration	Date of mark registration	Earliest example	Latest example	Letter style G Gothic R Roman S Script	Punch shape	Additional features/notes
Hugh Mills	L	1739	1741	1751	R	rectangle	–
	L	1746	–	–	S	profiloid	–
	L	–	–	–	G	bifoil	–
	L	–	–	–	–	–	HM (conjoined)
Henry Matthews	B	–	1896	1929	R	2 rectangles	–
HM (conjoined)							
Henry Morris	L	–	1739	1758	R	rectangle	–
	L	1718	–	–	–	–	MO
	L	1720	–	–	–	–	HM
Hugh Mills	L	–	1741	1751	R	rectangle	–
	L	1739	–	–	–	–	HM
H N							
Henry Nutting	L	1796	1796	1824	R	rectangle	–
Hannah Northcote	L	1798	1779	1819	R	rectangle	–
H N **R H**							
Henry Nutting & Robert Hennell II	L	1808	1808	1809	R	bevelled square	–
H O							
Samuel Hood	L	1697	1685	1701	R	oval	fleur de lis, 3 pellets
	L	1697	–	–	–	–	Ho
Thomas Holland I	L	1707	1707	1715	R	circle	crown
Edward Holaday	L	1709	1710	1718	R	rectangle	–
John Holland I	L	1711	1712	1743	R	ovate globoid	2 fleurs de lis
	L	1720	–	–	–	–	IH
Sarah Holaday	L	1719	1721	1729	R	lozenge	mullet, fleur de lis
	L	1725	–	–	–	–	SH
Ho							
Samuel Hood	L	1697	1685	1701	G	octagon	–
	L	1697	–	–	–	–	HO
Richard Hobbs	Nc	–	1702	1744	R	grooved hatchment	mullet
HO (monogram)							
John Hodson	L	1697	1697	–	R	trifid loboid	–
H P							
Harvey Price	L	1727	1726	1749	R	globate invectoid	stag's head
Hugh Penman	Ed	1734	1734	–	R	rectangle	–
Humphrey Payne	L	1739	1701	1739	R	quatrefoil	heart, pellet, mullet
	L	–	–	–	S	quatrefoil	4 trefoils, 2 pellets
	L	1701	–	–	–	–	Pa

Maker's initial(s) & maker(s)	Town of registration	Date of mark registration	Earliest example	Latest example	Letter style G Gothic R Roman S Script	Punch shape	Additional features/notes
H P & C							
H. Prince & Co	Y	1795	1795	1806	R	square	–
	Y	–	–	–	–	–	HP &Co
	Y	–	–	–	–	–	HP &C (HP conjoined)
H P & Co							
H. Prince & Co	Y	1795	1795	1806	R	square	HP &C
	Y	–	–	–	–	–	HP &C (HP conjoined)
H P & C (HP conjoined)							
H. Prince & Co	Y	1795	1795	1806	R	rectangle	–
	Y	–	–	–	–	–	HP &C
	Y	–	–	–	–	–	HP &Co
H & P							
J. Hampston & J. Prince	Y	–	1777	1808	R	rectangle	pellet $I^I_P H$
	Y	–	–	–	–	–	IH IP
	Y	–	–	–	–	–	JH JP
H & R Ltd							
Hunt & Roskell Ltd	L	1897	1846	1915	R	globate rectangle	crown
	L	1901	–	–	R	rectangle	crown abandoned
	L	1842	–	–	–	–	ISH
	L	1865	–	–	–	–	IH RR
	L	1882	–	–	–	–	RR AR IMH
	L	1889	–	–	–	–	$H^A H^B W$
	L	1895	–	–	–	–	$A^A H^B B$
H S							
Richard Hutchinson I of Colchester	L	1699	1703	1719	S	oval	hatch & thread oval

Maker's initial(s) & maker(s)	Town of registration	Date of mark registration	Earliest example	Latest example	Letter style G Gothic R Roman S Script	Punch shape	Additional features/notes
Hugh Spring	L	1722	1721	–	R	domate rectangle	mullet
	L	1721	–	–	–	–	SP
Henry Stratford	S	1879	1879	1918	R	rectangle	pellet
	L	–	1893	1901	R	rectangle	pellet
H & T							
J. Hilliard & J. Thomason	B	1853	1850	1898	R	bevelform	–
	B	–	–	–	R	rectangle	–
	Ch	–	1898	1899	–	–	–
H T							
T L							
Henry Tudor & Thomas Leader	S	1773	1773	1795	R	square	2 pellets
HU							
Rene Hudell	L	1718	–	1720	R	globate globoid	hat, crescent
Samuel Hutton	L	1725	1726	1736	R	hatchment	pellet
	L	1724	–	–	–	–	SH
H V							
Alexander Hudson	L	1701	–	1708	R	waved triad	fleur de lis
	L	1704	–	–	R	waved square	–
Henry Vincent	L	1783	–	1798	R	rectangle	–
H W							
Henry Wilkinson & Co	L	–	1860	1910	R	oval	–
	S	1831	–	–	–	–	HW &Co
	B	–	–	–	–	–	HW Ld
Lee & Wigful	S	1879	1872	1928	R	rectangle	pellet
	B	–	1872	–	–	–	–
H W							
& Co							
Henry Wilkinson & Co	S	1831	1815	1889	R	quatrefoil	–
	S	1831	–	–	–	–	HW
	S	1852	–	–	–	–	NEILL
	L	–	1860	1910	–	–	HW
	B	–	1901	1922	–	–	HW Ld
H W Ld							
H. Williamson Ltd	B	–	1901	1922	R	bevelform	–
I A							
Charles Jackson	L	1714	1713	1728	R	globate globoid	2 pellets
	L	–	–	–	R	arched shareform	mullet, 2 pellets, billet
	L	1720	–	–	–	–	CI
John Albright	L	1720	1717	1724	R	rectangle	–
	L	1718	–	–	–	–	AL

Maker's initial(s) & maker(s)	Town of registration	Date of mark registration	Earliest example	Latest example	Letter style G Gothic R Roman S Script	Punch shape	Additional features/notes
John Alcock	L	1725	1719	–	G	rectangle	–
John Alderhead	L	1750	–	1752	R	bevelform	floret
Jonathan Allein	L	1771	1770	1798	S	rectangle	pellet
	L	–	–	–	–	–	JA
John Arnell	L	1773	1772	1774	R	rectangle	pellet
Joseph Abraham	L	1796	–	1804	R	rectangle	–
Joseph Ash I	L	1801	1805	1809	R	ovoid	pellet
	L	1810	–	–	–	–	others similar
Joseph Ash II	L	1811	1811	1812	R	ovoid	–
Ia							
Henry Jay	L	–	1714	1721	G	ogee triad	mullet, pellet
I A							
MF (conjoined)							
Joseph Allen & Mordecai Fox	L	1730	–	1732	R	lobate triad	–
	L	1739	–	–	S	chamfered loboid	MF (separate)
I A C							
James Anthony Calame	L	–	1764	1774	R	trifid rectangle	crown
	L	1764	–	–	–	–	AC
I B							
Johan Got-help-Bilsings	Gl	1717	1717	1731	R	rectangle	–
John Burdon	Ex	–	1719	1739	R	circle	crown, pellet
	Ex	–	–	–	S	cambered rectangle	crown
John Barnard I	L	1720	1699	1713	R	heart	–
	L	1697	–	–	–	–	Ba
	L	1720	–	–	–	–	BA
John Bignell	L	1720	1720	1732	R	oval	–
	L	1718	–	–	–	–	BI
John Bache	L	1720	1701	1725	R	quatrefoil	mullet, fleur de lis, pellet
	L	1700	–	–	–	–	BA
Joseph Bird	L	1724	1697	1723	R	tabled coneform	3 pellets
	L	–	–	–	R	concave escutcheon	pellet
	L	–	–	–	R	tabled coneform	–
	L	1697	–	–	–	–	Bi
	L	1697	–	–	–	–	BI
John Barbe	L	1735	1737	1766	R	arched cleftform	fleur de lis
	L	1739	–	–	S	ovate plinthform	crown, pellet
	L	1739	–	–	S	ovoid	–
John Berthelot	L	1738	1747	1787	R	concave rectangle	–
	L	1739	–	–	S	rectangle	–
	L	–	–	–	R	cinquefoil	pellet

Maker's initial(s) & maker(s)	Town of registration	Date of mark registration	Earliest example	Latest example	Letter style G Gothic R Roman S Script	Punch shape	Additional features/notes
Joseph Barbut (or Barbit)	L	1739	1706	1720	S	profiloid	floret
	L	–	–	–	R	profiloid	crown, mullet
	L	1703	–	–	–	–	BA
James Barker	L	1746	–	1766	R	bifoil	pellet
	L	1746	–	–	R	rectangle	pellet
John Bayley	L	1751	–	1753	S	concave rectangle	–
Joseph Bell II	L	1756	1762	1764	R	rectangle	pellet
	L	–	–	–	–	–	I BELL
John Bucket (or Buket)	L	1760	–	1764	S	profiloid	–
	L	–	–	–	R	ovoid	2 pellets
John Bassingwhite	L	1770	1769	1802	R	rectangle	pellet
John Baker II	L	1770	1770	1772	R	ovoid	–
	L	1770	–	–	–	–	JB
John Baxter	L	1770	–	1773	R	rectangle	–
John Bourn(e)	L	1774	–	1791	R	oval	–
	L	1774	–	–	R	rectangle	–
	L	1774	–	–	R	rectangle	pellet
Joseph Bradley	L	1776	–	1784	R	oval	pellet
John Beldon	L	1784	1794	1800	R	bevelform	pellet
	L	–	–	–	R	oval	–
John Blake	L	1788	1797	1804	R	rectangle	–
J. Brady	Db	–	1797	1803	R	rectangle	–
John Booth	L	1813	1814	1817	R	rectangle	pellet
James Barratt	L	1801	1805	1821	R	rounded rectangle	pellet
John Brough	L	1813	–	1814	R	rectangle	pellet
	L	1803	–	–	–	–	JB
Joseph Biggs	L	1816	1817	1818	R	rectangle	pellet
John Bettridge	B	1817	1817	1834	R	oval	–
John Baddeley	L	1818	–	1820	R	rectangle	pellet
J. Buckton	Db	–	1818	1837	R	rectangle	–
John Bridge	L	1823	1798	1833	R	rectangle	pellet
	L	1823	–	–	R	domate rectangle	crown, pellet
John Brydie	L	1823	–	1826	R	rectangle	pellet
IBBOT							
George Ibbot	L	1759	1759	1760	R	rectangle	–
	L	1753	–	–	–	–	GI
I BELL							
Joseph Bell II	L	–	1762	1764	R	rectangle	pellet
	L	1756	–	–	–	–	IB
I B							
E B							
James & Elizabeth Bland	L	1794	1794	1800	R	square	–

Maker's initial(s) & maker(s)	Town of registration	Date of mark registration	Earliest example	Latest example	Letter style G Gothic R Roman S Script	Punch shape	Additional features/notes
I B							
I S							
James Sutton & James Bult	L	–	1766	1784	R	square	–
	L	1782	–	–	–	–	IS IB
I C							
John Cuthbert I	Db	1670	1685	1729	R	hatchment	pellet, gibbet
	Db	1702	–	–	R	ovoid	–
John Cuthbert II	Db	1702	1725	1729	R	oval	–
James Clarke	Ed	1710	1722	1742	R	rectangle	–
John Clifton I	Db	1719	1714	1722	R	circle	lion rampant
Isaac Cornafleau	L	–	1719	1723	R	crested coneform	crown, mullet
	L	–	–	–	–	–	CO
John Clifton II	Db	–	1719	1726	R	escutcheon	4 mullets, arrow
John Carman I	L	1720	–	–	R	quatrefoil	mullet, pellet
	L	1716	–	–	–	–	CA
Jonah Clifton	L	1720	1703	1725	R	crested biloboid	crown, floret
	L	1725	–	–	R	trifid triad	crown, floret, fleur de lis
	L	1703	–	–	–	–	CL
Joseph Clare I	L	1720	1714	1737	R	heart	pellet
	L	1713	–	–	–	–	CL
	L	1721	–	–	–	–	+C
John Chartier	L	1723	1699	1714	R	domate rectangle	fleur de lis
	L	–	–	–	–	–	CH
Isaac Callard	L	1726	1732	1769	R	waved cuspoid	2 mullets, pellet
	L	1739	–	–	S	globate triad	pellet, kidney
	L	1747	–	–	S	lobate loboid	2 mullets, pellet
	L	1726	–	–	–	–	CA
Isaac Cookson	Nc	1728	1722	1772	R	trefoil	annulet, pellet
	Nc	–	–	–	R	trefoil	annulet
	Nc	–	–	–	S	trefoil	annulet, 2 pellets
	Nc	–	–	–	S	oval	–
John Chapman I	L	1730	1727	1738	R	ovate rectangle	crown, pellet
John Clayton	L	1736	1744	1745	G	profiloid	–
John Cafe	L	1740	1742	1762	R	ovoid	pellet
	L	1742	–	–	G	trefoil	floret, 2 pellets
John Christie	Db	–	1748	1760	R	oval	–
John Carman II	L	1748	1749	1756	S	profiloid	pellet
	L	1756	–	–	R	bifoil	pellet

Maker's initial(s) & maker(s)	Town of registration	Date of mark registration	Earliest example	Latest example	Letter style G Gothic R Roman S Script	Punch shape	Additional features/notes
Joseph Cullen	Db	1753	–	1770	R	rectangle	–
James Crawford	Nc	–	1763	1771	R	chevroned square	cup
Joseph Clare II	L	1763	–	1768	R	rectangle	–
	L	1767	–	–	–	–	CLARE
John Craig	Db	1769	1771	1790	R	rectangle	pellet
John Carter II	L	1776	1776	1784	R	rectangle	pellet
	L	1776	–	–	R	rectangle	–
Joseph Creswick	S	1777	1776	1819	R	rectangle	–
John Cook	Nc	–	1811	–	R	ovoid	pellet
Joseph Cradock	L	1825	1825	1829	R	rectangle	–
	L	1827	–	–	R	oval	–
IC							
Joseph Clare I	L	1721	1714	1737	R	heart	pellet
	L	1713	–	–	–	–	CL
	L	1720	–	–	–	–	IC
IC (monogram)							
James Coburn	Ed	1669	1687	1702	R	escutcheon	–
ICF							
John Cope Folkard	L	1819	1820	1822	R	rectangle	2 pellets
IC TH							
John Crouch & Thomas Hannam	L	–	1763	1809	R	cleft square	2 pellets
IC WR							
Joseph Cradock & William K. Reid	L	1812	1812	1825	R	quatrefoil	–
ID							
Josiah Daniel	L	1724	1715	1719	R	rectangle	–
	L	1715	–	–	–	–	DA
Isaac D'Olier	Db	1731	1741	1767	R	[no shape]	crown, incuse
	Db	–	–	–	R	dextroid	–
Isaac Duke	L	1743	1744	1746	S	trifid triad	crown, mullet
Jabez Daniell	L	1749	1749	1783	S	profiloid	–
John Delmestre	L	1755	1754	1774	R	trigon	–
	L	–	–	–	R	ovoid	mullet
John Dawson	Db	1764	1751	1753	R	trefoil	mullet
John Denwall	L	1768	1766	1774	R	bifoil	pellet
John Denziloe	L	1774	1765	1802	G	rectangle	–
James Dempster	Ed	1775	1777	1805	R	rectangle	–
John Dutton	L	1776	1761	–	R	rectangle	pellet
John Deacon	L	1776	1762	1776	R	rectangle	–
James Darquits II	L	1787	–	1802	R	rectangle	pellet

Maker's initial(s) & maker(s)	Town of registration	Date of mark registration	Earliest example	Latest example	Letter style G Gothic R Roman S Script	Punch shape	Additional features/notes
Joseph Dodds	L	1789	1797	1800	R	rectangle	pellet
John Dalrymple	Db	–	1790	–	R	oval	pellet
James Douglas of Aberdeen	A	–	1791	1806	R	rectangle	–
	A	–	–	–	R	ovoid	–
	A	–	–	–	R	rectangle	pellet
	Ed	1785	–	–	–	–	JD
John Douglas	L	1788	–	1817	R	–	cameo
	L	1804	–	–	R	rectangle	–
I D **A D** John & Archibald Douglas	L	1821	1822	1824	R	square	2 pellets
I I D M Jabez Daniell & James Mince	L	1766	1767	1771	R	cruciform	pellet
I T D D Thomas & Jabez Daniell	L	–	1771	1777	R	cruciform	pellet
I E Samuel Jefferys	L	1697	–	1731	R	hatchment	crown, pellet
John Elston I	Ex	–	1701	1728	R	ogee hatchment	2 pellets
	Ex	–	–	–	–	–	JE
	Ex	–	–	–	–	–	EI
John Eckfourd I	L	–	1703	1719	R	rectangle	–
	L	1698	–	–	–	–	EC
Edward Jennings	L	1720	1723	1730	R	oval	–
	L	1710	–	–	–	–	Ie
	L	1720	–	–	–	–	EI
John East	L	1721	1697	1725	R	heart	lozenge, fleur de lis
	L	1697	–	–	–	–	EA
John Edwards II	L	1724	*	*	R	globate rectangle	floret
	L	1739	–	–	S	globate rectangle	mullet, 2 pellets
	L	1753	–	–	R	globate rectangle	mullet, pellet
	L	1724	–	–	–	–	ED
John Eckfourd II	L	1725	1724	1747	R	kidney	mullet
	L	1739	–	–	S	tridentate escutcheon	–
	L	1725	–	–	–	–	EC
John Elston II	Ex	–	1726	1747	S	escutcheon	battlement
John Ebbs	Db	1766	1815	1820	R	rectangle	pellet
John Edwards III	L	1788	1790	1809	R	rectangle	pellet
James England	Db	1791	1796	1819	R	rectangle	–

Maker's initial(s) & maker(s)	Town of registration	Date of mark registration	Earliest example	Latest example	Letter style G Gothic R Roman S Script	Punch shape	Additional features/notes
Ie							
Thomas Jenkins	L	1697	1671	1717	R	quatrefoil	2 pellets
Edward Jennings	L	1710	1723	1730	R	globate rectangle	heart
	L	1720	–	–	–	–	EI
	L	1720	–	–	–	–	IE
William Jelf	L	–	1717	1720	R	oval	–
	L	1720	–	–	–	–	WI
I E & Co							
James Ellis & Co	S	1793	1818	1824	R	billet	–
	S	–	–	–	–	–	JE & Co
I E **A H**							
James Ede & Alexander Hewat	L	1808	1808	1810	R	square	–
I E **E E**							
John III & Edward I Edwards	L	1811	–	1815	R	square	–
I E T							
John Edward Terrey	L	1816	1815	1847	R	rectangle	–
I F							
Jonathan French	Nc	1703	1705	1728	G	oval	–
	Nc	–	–	–	R	rectangle	–
John Falconer	Gl	1709	1707	–	R	rectangle	–
John Farnell	L	1720	1715	1727	R	heart	pellet, thread heart
	L	1714	–	–	–	–	Fa
	L	1719	–	–	–	–	FA
James Fraillon	L	1723	1702	1727	R	globate loboid	mullet, pellet
	L	1711	–	–	–	–	Fr
John Fossey	L	1733	1737	1743	R	octagon	2 pellets
	L	1739	–	–	G	waved rectangle	–
	L	–	–	–	R	ovoid	pellet
John Fray	L	1748	1749	1753	R	rectangle	pellet
John Fountain	L	1792	1792	1805	R	rectangle	–
	L	1797	–	–	R	rectangle	pellet
James Fry	Db	–	1819	1823	R	rectangle	–
John Foligno	L	–	1820	1868	R	bifoil	–
John Fry II	L	1826	1830	1835	R	rectangle	–
James Franklin	L	–	1829	1849	R	bifoil	–
James Fray	Db	1829	1818	1841	R	rectangle	–

Maker's initial(s) & maker(s)	Town of registration	Date of mark registration	Earliest example	Latest example	Letter style G Gothic R Roman S Script	Punch shape	Additional features/notes
John Figg	L	1834	1836	1881	R	bifoil	–
	L	1838	–	–	–	–	–
J. Francis	Db	1840	1836	1840	R	rectangle	pellet
I F & Co Fenton, Allanson & Co	S	1816	–	1824	R	rectangle	–
I F **I B** John Fountain & John Beadnell	L	1793	1793	–	R	square	2 pellets
I F P **C & Co** Creswick & Co	S	1858	–	1865	R	quatrefoil	–
	S	1863	–	–	–	–	C & Co
I G James Goodwin	L	1721	1712	1729	S	rectangle	pellet, Roman G
	L	1710	–	–	–	–	GO
John Gibbons	L	1724	1703	1729	R	concave rectangle	pellet
	L	–	–	–	R	rectangle	2 pellets
	L	1700	–	–	–	–	Gi
John Gorsuch	L	1726	–	1733	R	cambered square	mitre, pellet
John Gamon	L	1727	1723	1739	R	heart	pellet
	L	1739	–	–	G	oval	–
John Gorham	L	1728	1748	1759	R	rectangle	pellet
	L	1739	–	–	S	profiloid	–
	L	1739	–	–	S	profiloid	pellet
	L	1757	–	–	G	bifoil	pellet
	L	–	–	–	S	–	mullet
James Gould	L	1739	1722	1748	G	trefoil	mullet
	L	1743	–	–	G	profiloid	–
	L	–	–	–	R	octagon	crown
	L	1722	–	–	–	–	GO
	L	1722	–	–	–	–	IG (monogram)
James Glen	Gl	1743	1743	1752	R	rectangle	–
	Gl	1743	–	–	–	–	GLN
James Gilsland	Ed	1748	1752	1777	R	arched escutcheon	–
James Gordon	A	1766	1766	–	R	rectangle	–
James Graham	Db	–	1769	1770	R	oval	–
I G (monogram) James Gould	L	1722	1722	1748	R	heart	–
	L	–	–	–	R	globate rectangle	crown
	L	1722	–	–	–	–	GO
	L	1739	–	–	–	–	IG

Maker's initial(s) & maker(s)	Town of registration	Date of mark registration	Earliest example	Latest example	Letter style G Gothic R Roman S Script	Punch shape	Additional features/notes
IG & Co							
John Green & Co	S	1792	1782	1819	R	rectangle	–
John Green, Roberts, Mosley & Co	S	1793	1796	1798	R	rectangle	–
I G							
C L							
J Gibson & Langman	L	–	1883	1900	R	ogee escutcheon	(also B, S & Db)
I H							
John Humphrys	Db	1685	1693	1696	R	heart	pellet
John Hamilton	Db	1709	1708	1745	R	trifid rectangle	crown, pellet
John Holland I	L	1720	1712	1743	R	globate globoid	3 pellets
	L	1711	–	–	–	–	HO
Jean Harache	L	1726	–	–	R	trifid loboid	crown, lion rampant
John Harvey I	L	1738	1740	1745	R	crested rectangle	crown
	L	1739	–	–	S	domate rectangle	crown
	L	1745	–	–	S	globate rectangle	crown
	L	1746	–	–	S	profiloid	mullet, pellet
	L	1750	–	–	S	rectangle	
	L	1739	–	–	–	–	Ha
John Holland II	L	1739	1739	1751	S	oval	
John Hyatt	L	1742	1761	1763	R	waved rectangle	pellet
Joseph Heriot	L	1756	1775	1791	R	rectangle	pellet
John Horsley	L	–	1760	1762	R	rectangle	pellet
John Harris II	L	1761	*	*	R	rectangle	pellet
	L	1761	–	–	–	–	incuse
James Hyde	L	1777	1793	1796	R	rectangle	pellet
	L	1778	–	–	S	oval	–
	L	1786	–	–	R	oval	pellet
John Hutson	L	1784	1786	1812	R	rectangle	–
John Harris III	L	1786	1786	–	R	rectangle	–
Joseph Hardy	L	1799	1797	1828	R	rectangle	–
John Hawkins	L	1802	–	1827	R	rectangle	–
	L	1821	–	–	R	rectangle	pellet
Jonathan Hayne	L	1808	1817	1835	S	rectangle	–
	L	1821					
John Houle	L	1811	1810	1820	R	rectangle	–
John Harris IV	L	1818	*	*	R	rectangle	–
	L	1820	–	–	R	bifoil	–
	L	1822	–	–	R	ovoid	–
	L	1825	–	–	R	woolsack	pellet
John Harris V	L	1831	*	*	R	oval	–
	L	1839	–	–	R	rectangle	–

Maker's initial(s) & maker(s)	Town of registration	Date of mark registration	Earliest example	Latest example	Letter style G Gothic R Roman S Script	Punch shape	Additional features/notes
John Harrison & Co	S	1866	1853	1882	R	rectangle	pellet
	S	1833	–	–	–	–	JH & Co
I H **Co** John Hoyland & Co	S	1773	1774	1778	R	ovoid	–
	S	1773	–	–	–	–	IH & Co
I H & Co John Hoyland & Co	S	1773	1774	1778	R	rectangle	IH
	S	1773	–	–	–	–	Co
I H D James Henry Daniel	L	1823	1826	1829	R	rectangle	–
	L	1825	–	–	R	rectangle	pellets
	L	1820	–	–	–	–	HD
I H **I P** J. Hampston & J. Prince	Y	–	1777	1808	R	square	2 pellets
	Y	–	–	–	–	–	H & P
	Y	–	–	–	–	–	I$_P^I$H
	Y	–	–	–	–	–	JH JP
I$_P^I$H J. Hampston & J. Prince	Y	–	1777	1808	R	quatrefoil	pellet
	Y	–	–	–	R	octagon	pellet
	Y	–	–	–	–	–	H & P
	Y	–	–	–	–	–	IH IP
	Y	–	–	–	–	–	JH JP
I H **R R** Hunt & Roskell (John Hunt & Robert Roskell)	L	1865	1842	1915	R	trifid biloboid	crown
	L	1842	–	–	–	–	ISH
	L	1865	–	–	–	–	IH RR
	L	1882	–	–	–	–	RR AR IMH
	L	1889	–	–	–	–	H^{A}H^{B}W
	L	1895	–	–	–	–	A^{A}H^{B}B
	L	1897	–	–	–	–	H & R Ltd

Maker's initial(s) & maker(s)	Town of registration	Date of mark registration	Earliest example	Latest example	Letter style G Gothic R Roman S Script	Punch shape	Additional features/notes
I I							
John Jones I	L	1723	1724	1736	R	rectangle	pellet
	L	1729	–	–	R	crested rectangle	crown, 2 pellets
	L	1733	–	–	S	rectangle	
	L	1739	–	–	S	bevelled biloboid	crown
	L	1723	–	–	–	–	IO
James Jenkins	L	1731	1731	–	S	domate rectangle	fleur de lis
	L	1739	–	–	R	ovate rectangle	crown, pellet
John Jacob	L	1734	1734	1764	R	ovate globoid	crown, pellet, mullet
	L	1739	–	–	S	cambered globoid	crown, mullet
Joseph Jackson	Db	1775	1774	1805	R	rectangle	pellet
	Db	–	–	–	R	oval	–
I & I W & Co							
Waterhouse, Hodson & Co (I. & I. Waterhouse & Co)	S	1822	1824	1835	R	rectangle	–
I J							
John Jones III	L	1824	1824	–	R	rectangle	–
I J K							
John James Keith	L	1824	1827	1853	R	rectangle	2 pellets
I K							
James Kelly	Db	1672	–	1679	R	heart	3 pellets, floret
James Kirkup	Nc	1713	1728	1758	R	rectangle	pellet
	Nc	–	–	–	R	concave bipod	pellet
	Nc	–	–	–	–	–	Ki
Jeremiah King	L	1723	1726	1766	R	globate rectangle	crown
	L	1736	–	–	R	globate rectangle	bird
	L	1739	–	–	–	–	I KING
	L	1723	–	–	–	–	KI
James Ker	Ed	1723	1723	1745	R	arched escutcheon	pellet
John Kincaid	Ed	1726	–	1746	R	ogee chinoid	pellet
John Kincaid	L	1743	1744	1746	R	trifid arcade	crown, pellet
	L	1745	–	–	–	–	others similar
John Kirkup	Nc	1753	1741	1773	S	rectangle	–
	Nc	1753	–	–	R	bifoil	pellet
John King	L	1775	1775	1796	R	rectangle	pellet
John Kelly	Db	1776	1782	1785	R	rectangle	–
John Kidder	L	1780	1775	1792	R	rectangle	–
James Keating	Db	1795	1788	1812	R	rectangle	pellet

Maker's initial(s) & maker(s)	Town of registration	Date of mark registration	Earliest example	Latest example	Letter style G Gothic R Roman S Script	Punch shape	Additional features/notes
I KAY & Co							
John Kay & Co	S	1795	–	1809	R	bevelform	–
I K I W & Co							
Kirkby, Waterhouse & Co	S	1793	1811	1823	R	rectangle	3 pellets
	S	1818	–	–	R	rectangle	pellet
	S	1793	–	–	–	–	IKIW & Co
	S	1793	–	–	–	–	KW & Co
I K & S							
John Knowles & Son	S	1860	1861	1862	R	square	–
I K T G							
John Kentesber & Thomas Grove	L	1757	1757	–	R	square	–
I L							
John Lawe	Ed	1661	1684	1688	R	ogee escutcheon	pellet
John Luke II	Gl	1699	1704	1707	R	heart	pellet
John Lingard	L	1720	1721	1726	R	quatrefoil	2 pellets
	L	1718	–	–	–	–	LI
	L	1719	–	–	–	–	Li
John Ludlow	L	1720	1716	–	R	ogee shareform	3 pellets, annulet, fleur de lis
	L	1720	–	–	R	ogee cuspoid	3 pellets
	L	1713	–	–	–	–	LV
Isaac Liger	L	1720	1709	1729	R	trifid cuspoid	plant
	L	1704	–	–	–	–	LI
Jane Lambe	L	–	1720	1727	R	lozenge	lamb
	L	–	–	–	–	–	LA
John Luff	L	1724	1727	1747	R	loboid	pellet, baluster
	L	1739	–	–	S	globate woolsack	trefoil, pellet
	L	–	–	–	R	loboid	mullet
	L	1724	–	–	–	–	I LUFF
James Bartholomew Langlois	L	–	1732	1738	R	waved rectangle	pellet
	L	1738	–	–	–	–	IL.G
John Lampfert	L	1748	1755	1778	S	cleft rectangle	pellet
	L	1749	–	–	S	rectangle	pellet
John Laughlin I	Db	1751	1741	1758	R	rectangle	mullet
	Db	–	–	–	R	oval	–

Maker's initial(s) & maker(s)	Town of registration	Date of mark registration	Earliest example	Latest example	Letter style G Gothic R Roman S Script	Punch shape	Additional features/notes
John Langlands I	Nc	1754	1741	1803	R	domate rectangle	annulet, pellet
	Nc	–	–	–	S	profiloid	annulet, 2 pellets
	Nc	–	–	–	R	rectangle	–
	Nc	–	–	–	R	rectangle	pellet
Joseph Lejeune	L	1760	1773	1791	–	–	incuse
	L	1778	–	–	–	–	ILI
John Lloyd	Db	1768	1771	1782	S	oval	–
John Lautier	L	1773	1773	1789	R	rectangle	pellet
John Lambe	L	1774	1773	1801	R	oval	pellet
	L	1785	–	–	R	rectangle	pellet
John Locker	Db	1775	1769	1772	R	oval	pellet
Joseph Lock	L	1778	–	1779	G	rectangle	–
	L	1775	–	–	–	–	JL
John Leslie	A	1782	1782	1802	R	rectangle	–
	A	–	–	–	R	rectangle	pellet
John Laughlin II	Db	–	1783	1795	S	oval	–
	Db	–	–	–	R	rectangle	pellet
John Law	S	1790	1807	1825	R	rectangle	pellet
John Langlands II	Nc	–	1793	1807	R	oval	–
John Lias	L	1799	1806	1817	R	rectangle	–
	L	1802	–	–	R	rectangle	pellet
Josiah Low	Db	1819	1837	1842	R	rectangle	–
I L & Co							
John Love & Co	S	1783	1784	1819	R	rectangle	–
I L B							
James Le Bass	Db	1810	1803	1846	R	rectangle	2 pellets
	Db	1819	–	–	R	rectangle	–
I L G							
James Bartholomew Langlois	L	1738	1732	1738	G	trifid cuspoid	3 pellets, floret, animal, fleur de lis
	L	–	–	–	–	–	IL
I L **H L**							
John & Henry Lias	L	1818	1816	1849	R	cavetto square	–
I L **H L** **C L**							
John Henry & Charles Lias	L	1823	1823	1840	R	bevelform	–

Maker's initial(s) & maker(s)	Town of registration	Date of mark registration	Earliest example	Latest example	Letter style G Gothic R Roman S Script	Punch shape	Additional features/notes
I L I							
Joseph Lejeune	L	1778	1773	1791	–	–	incuse
	L	1760	–	–	–	–	IL
I L							
I G							
John Langlands & John Goodriche	Nc	–	1754	1781	S	quatrefoil	2 pellets
I L or **IL IR**							
I R							
John Langlands & John Robertson	Nc	–	1778	1808	R	domate square	annulet, 2 pellets
	Nc	–	–	–	R	square	2 pellets
	Nc	–	–	–	R	square	–
	L	1780	–	–	R	square	–
	Nc	–	–	–	–	–	L & R
	L	1780	–	–	–	–	IL IR
I L							
S							
John Langlands II & John Sebille	L	1766	1763	1775	R	cruciform	pellet
	L	1770	–	–	R	quatrefoil	pellet
I LUFF							
John Luff	L	1724	1727	1747	R	rectangle	–
	L	1724	–	–	–	–	IL
I M							
James Mitchelson	Ed	1706	1710	1728	R	ogee escutcheon	–
John Millington	L	1720	1721	1722	R	lobate globoid	2 pellets, mullet
	L	1728	–	–	R	crested rectangle	crown
	L	1718	–	–	–	–	MI
James Morson	L	1720	1744	1758	R	heart (inverted)	swan
	L	1716	–	–	–	–	MO
Jacob Margas	L	–	1705	1725	R	globate rectangle	crown, pellet
	L	1706	–	–	–	–	MA
James Manners	L	1726	1734	1739	–	incuse	floret
	L	1734	–	–	R	globate rectangle	floret, pellet
	L	1739	–	–	S	globate rectangle	floret, pellet
John Moore	Db	1728	1728	1758	R	rectangle	–
	Db	–	–	–	S	rectangle	–
	Db	–	–	–	–	–	IM monogram
John Main	Ed	1729	1726	1742	R	ogee escutcheon	–
James Maitland	L	–	1730	1731	R	profiloid	grasshopper, fish

Maker's initial(s) & maker(s)	Town of registration	Date of mark registration	Earliest example	Latest example	Letter style G Gothic R Roman S Script	Punch shape	Additional features/notes
Jessie McFarlan	L	1739	–	1756	S	lozenge	2 pellets
James Morison	L	1740	1744	1759	S	lobate invectoid	–
Jacob Marsh	L	1744	1743	1773	R	serrated rectangle	mullet
James McKenzie	Ed	1747	1749	1750	R	waved rectangle	–
John Muns	L	1753	1753	1765	R	rectangle	pellet
John Moore	L	1758	1756	1822	S	profiloid	mullet
	L	1778	–	–	R	rectangle	pellet
J. Mappin	S	1775	–	1778	R	rectangle	–
John Merry	L	1782	1790	1809	R	rectangle	–
	L	1789	–	–	R	rectangle	pellet
John Mitchison	Nc	–	1784	1790	R	rectangle	pellet
James Mince	L	1790	1790	1802	R	oval	–
John Mewburn	L	1793	1794	1826	R	rectangle	–
	L	–	–	–	R	ovate rectangle	crown
I M (monogram)							
John Moore	Db	1728	1728	1758	S	hatchment	–
	Db	–	–	–	–	–	IM
I M & Co							
J. Mappin & Co	S	1775	1775	–	R	billet	pellet
IMD (MD conjoined)							
John McDonald	Ed	–	1800	1809	R	rectangle	–
I M / D I							
John Moliere & Dyall Jones	L	1767	–	1768	R	square	–
I I S M H							
John Mortimer & John Samuel Hunt	L	1839	1841	1945	–	–	crown
I M / W H							
James Mince & William Hodgkins II	L	1780	1780	–	R	square	–
I N							
John Newton	L	1726	1726	1749	R	heart	thread heart, pellet
	L	1739	–	–	S	profiloid	–
Joseph Nixon	Db	1759	1775	1803	S	rectangle	–
Joseph Nowill	S	1783	1825	1831	R	rectangle	–
	S	1813	–	–	–	–	JN
John Nicklin	Db	–	1814	1833	R	rectangle	pellet

Maker's initial(s) & maker(s)	Town of registration	Date of mark registration	Earliest example	Latest example	Letter style G Gothic R Roman S Script	Punch shape	Additional features/notes
I N E							
John Neville	L	1745	1745	–	S	ovate rectangle	crown
I O							
John Oliver	Y	1676	–	–	R	circle	crown, pellet
Lawrence Jones	L	1697	1692	1723	S	cambered shareform	crown
	L	–	–	–	S	ovate triad	crown, mullet
Glover Johnson	L	1712	1713	1726	R	heart	–
	L	1720	–	–	–	–	GI
George Greenhill Jones	L	1719	1724	1754	R	trifid rectangle	crown, floret
	L	1726	–	–	–	–	GI
John Jones I	L	1723	1724	1736	R	oval	–
	L	–	–	–	R	domate rectangle	fleur de lis
	L	1723	–	–	–	–	II
Simon Jouet	L	–	1726	1756	R	circle	–
	L	1725	–	–	–	–	SI
	L	1739	–	–	–	–	SJ
John Orme II	L	1796	1797	–	R	rectangle	–
I P							
James Plummer	Y	1619	1636	1653	R	trifid triad	–
John Plummer	Y	1648	1653	1673	R	tridentate chinoid	–
	Y	–	–	–	R	tridentate chinoid	2 pellets
	Y	–	–	–	R	quatrefoil	–
John Phillips	Db	1679	1696	1703	R	heart	mullet
	Db	–	–	–	R	profiloid	crown, pellet
John Pero	L	1732	–	1738	R	trifid cuspoid	crown, pellet, fleur de lis
	L	1739	–	–	G	ovate triad	crown, mullet
	L	1717	–	–	–	–	PE
John Pollock	L	1734	1738	1755	R	bifoil	pellet
	L	1739	–	–	S	heart	–
Isabel Pero	L	1741	1741	1742	G	ovate archform	crown
John Priest (or Preist)	L	1748	1748	1759	R	waved rectangle	pellet
John Payne	L	1751	1750	1776	S	cleft rectangle	pellet
	L	–	–	–	S	profiloid	pellet
	L	–	–	–	S	waved rectangle	2 pellets
John Pittar	Db	1756	1748	1804	R	oval	pellet
	Db	–	–	–	R	oval	mullet
	Db	–	–	–	–	–	JP
John Perry	L	1757	1756	1759	R	trefoil	mullet, pellet
	L	–	–	–	R	rectangle	pellet
James Phipps I	L	1767	1767	1776	R	rectangle	–
	L	1772	–	–	R	rectangle	pellet
Joseph Preedy	L	1777	1773	1819	R	rectangle	–
	L	1800	–	–	R	rectangle	mullet

Maker's initial(s) & maker(s)	Town of registration	Date of mark registration	Earliest example	Latest example	Letter style G Gothic R Roman S Script	Punch shape	Additional features/notes
John Priestman	L	1786	–	1793	R	rectangle	–
John Parker II	L	–	1802	1804	R	oval	pellet
Joseph Pritchard	L	1825	1825	–	R	rectangle	–
Isaac Parkin	Ex	1835	1824	1829	R	rectangle	–
IP (monogram)							
James Penman	Ed	1673	1685	1705	S	heart	–
I P & Co							
John Parsons & Co	S	1783	1783	1804	R	rectangle	–
	S	–	–	–	R	rectangle	pellet
I P **E W**							
John Parker I & Edward Wakelin	L	–	1760	1784	R	trifid square	fleur de lis, 2 pellets
	L	–	–	–	–	–	P & W
I P **G P**							
Josiah & George Piercy	L	1812	1812	1817	R	square	2 pellets
I P **I P**							
Jonathan I & Jonathan II Perkins	L	1795	–	1797	R	square	2 pellets
I Q							
John Quantock	L	–	1750	1764	R	rectangle	pellet
	L	1754	–	–	S	rectangle	–
I R							
John Ramsey	Nc	1698	1700	1708	R	circle	crescent, pellet, dotted circle
	Nc	–	–	–	–	–	Ra
Edward Ironside	L	1702	1702	–	R	trifid triad	mullet, pellet
	L	1702	–	–	–	–	Ir
John Robinson I	L	1723	–	1728	R	globate globoid	mullet, fleur de lis
	L	1723	–	–	–	–	RO
Isaac Ribouleau	L	1724	1724	1730	R	globate rectangle	crescent
	L	1724	–	–	–	–	RI
John Rollo	Ed	1731	–	1732	R	rectangle	–
John Robinson II	L	1738	1749	1767	R	arched shareform	star, pellet
	L	1739	–	–	S	arched triloboid	star
	L	–	–	–	R	globate rectangle	floret, pellet
John Roker	L	1743	1740	–	S	trifid rectangle	crown
John Rowe	L	1749	1749	1779	R	rectangle	pellet
John Richardson II	L	1752	1759	1762	S	ovate rectangle	crown

Maker's initial(s) & maker(s)	Town of registration	Date of mark registration	Earliest example	Latest example	Letter style G Gothic R Roman S Script	Punch shape	Additional features/notes
John Rich	L	1765	1789	1810	S	ovoid	–
	L	–	–	–	S	bevelform	–
	L	–	–	–	S	profiloid	–
John Rowbotham of Sheffield	L	1768	–	–	S	rectangle	pellet
John Romer	L	1771	1756	1792	R	quatrefoil	–
John Robins	L	1774	1776	1821	R	rectangle	pellet
	L	–	–	–	S	rectangle	–
James Ruell	L	1795	1802	1806	R	rectangle	–
John Robertson	Nc	–	1795	1801	R	rectangle	pellet
	Nc	–	–	–	S	rectangle	–
John Reily	L	1801	1791	1829	R	rectangle	–
	L	1823	–	–	R	quatrefoil	–
Joseph Rogers & Sons	S	1812	1812	1937	R	rectangle	pellet
J. Read	Db	1827	–	1831	R	rectangle	pellet

Ir

Edward Ironside	L	1702	1702	–	G	octagon	–
	L	–	–	–	–	–	IR

I R Co   I R Co

John Rowbotham & Co	S	1774	1775	1807	R	billet	pellet
	S	1774	–	–	R	bevelled square	–

I R & Co

John Roberts & Co	S	–	1775	1826	R	rectangle	pellet

I R D D

John Robertson & David Darling	Nc	–	1795	1801	R	square	2 pellets
	Nc	–	–	–	–	–	R & D

I R I W

John Robertson & John Walton	Nc	–	1793	1819	R	square	–

I S

John Seatoun	Ed	1685	–	1712	R	ogee escutcheon	2 crescents
Joyce Issod	L	–	1697	–	R	lozenge	crown, 3 pellets
Joseph Smith I	L	1720	1728	1742	R	bifoil	–
	L	1723	–	–	R	bifoil	pellet
	L	1728	–	–	R	ovoid	pellet
	L	1707	–	–	–	–	SM
James Smith I	L	1720	1718	1746	R	globate rectangle	mullet
	L	1718	–	–	–	–	SM

Maker's initial(s) & maker(s)	Town of registration	Date of mark registration	Earliest example	Latest example	Letter style G Gothic R Roman S Script	Punch shape	Additional features/notes
Joseph Steward I	L	1720	–	1739	R	tridentate plinthform	–
	L	1739	–	–	S	oval	–
	L	1719	–	–	–	–	ST
James Seabrook	L	1720	1711	1720	R	bifoil	pellet
	L	1714	–	–	–	–	Se
John Sanders I	L	1720	1717	1746	R	circle	pellet, 2 trefoils
	L	1717	–	–	–	–	SA
John Hugh Le Sage	L	1772	1719	1749	R	trifid triad	crown, goblet, pellet
	L	1739	–	–	S	ovate globoid	crown, pellet, floret
	L	1739	–	–	S	rectangle	–
	L	–	–	–	S	profiloid	crown
	L	1718	–	–	–	–	SA
James Stone	L	1726	–	1749	R	globate rectangle	mullet
Joseph Sanders	L	1730	1730	1747	S	rectangle	–
	L	1739	–	–	R	oval	thread oval
James Shruder	L	1737	1737	1746	R	ogee triad	pellet
	L	1739	–	–	S	ogee triad	pellet
	L	1739	–	–	S	ogee triad	–
John Swift	L	1739	1729	1778	S	oval	–
	L	1770	–	–	S	bifoil	–
	L	–	–	–	R	oval	pellet, dotted oval
	L	–	–	–	R	cleft cleftform	pellet
John Schuppe	L	1753	1754	1768	S	rectangle	–
Joseph Steward II	L	1755	–	1760	R	2 circles	–
	L	1768	–	–	R	ovoid	–
	L	1770	–	–	R	oval	pellet
	L	1773	–	–	R	rectangle	pellet
James Stamp	L	1774	1777	1782	R	rectangle	pellet
	L	1777	–	–	R	cleft cleftform	pellet
John Smith	S	1775	–	1780	R	rectangle	–
John Scofield	L	1778	1770	1809	R	bifoil	pellet
	L	–	–	–	–	–	JS
James Sutton	L	1780	1780	1781	R	oval	pellet
J. Staniforth & Co	S	1783	1811	1828	R	rectangle	pellet
John Steward	L	1786	1795	1796	R	rectangle	pellet
	L	1784	–	–	S	rectangle	–
	L	1786	–	–	–	–	–
Joseph Scammell	L	1788	1790	1794	S	rectangle	–
John Stoyte	Db	1789	1793	1805	R	rectangle	pellet
John Shaw	B	–	1790	1829	R	rectangle	–
James Scott	Db	1800	1800	1834	R	rectangle	–
	Db	–	–	–	R	rectangle	pellet

Maker's initial(s) & maker(s)	Town of registration	Date of mark registration	Earliest example	Latest example	Letter style G Gothic R Roman S Script	Punch shape	Additional features/notes
Isaac Simmons	S	–	1839	1840	R	rectangle	–
I S (monogram) James Sympsone	Ed	1687	1702	1709	R	oval	chain oval
	Ed	–	–	–	R	lozenge	2 pellets, 2 annulets
	Ed	–	–	–	R	circle	2 mullets, 2 curves
I S H Hunt & Roskell (John Samuel Hunt)	L	1842	1844	1870	R	trifid biloboid	crown
	L	1865	–	–	–	–	IH RR
	L	1882	–	–	–	–	RR AR IMH
	L	1889	–	–	–	–	H^{A}H^{B}W
	L	1895	–	–	–	–	A^{A}H^{B}B
	L	1897	–	–	–	–	H&R Ltd
I$^{HS}_{C}$ John Hyatt & Charles Semore	L	1757	1757	1761	R	quatrefoil	annulet
I S I B James Sutton & James Bult	L	1782	1766	1784	R	rectangle	–
	L	–	–	–	–	–	IB IS
I S T S J. & T. Settle & Gunn & Co	S	1825	1825	1826	R	square	–
I S W H John Settle & Henry Wilkinson	S	–	1829	1831	R	quatrefoil	–
I$_{Z}$S Thomas Issod	L	1697	1694	1697	R	hatchment	3 pellets
I T John Thomason (or Thompson)	Y	1633	1635	1679	R	ogee escutcheon	–
	Y	–	–	–	R	hatchment	pellet, floret

Maker's initial(s) & maker(s)	Town of registration	Date of mark registration	Earliest example	Latest example	Letter style G Gothic R Roman S Script	Punch shape	Additional features/notes
John Tuite	L	1721–5	1714	1759	R	concave loboid	ewer
	L	–	–	–	S	octagon	ewer
John Taylor	Db	1729	1724	1734	R	trigonate rectangle	crown, pellet
	Db	–	–	–	R	oval	–
James Timberlake	L	1743	–	1759	R	–	+, pellet
	L	1755	–	–	R	oval	pellet
James Tookey	L	1750	1761	1766	R	rectangle	pellet
Job Tripp	L	1754	1754	–	S	quatrefoil	–
	L	1757	–	–	R	rectangle	pellet
John Tayleur	L	1775	1788	1790	R	rectangle	pellet
	L	1776	–	–	R	rectangle	–
Joseph Taylor	B	–	1777	1845	R	oval	–
	B	–	–	–	R	rectangle	–
James Tibbits	S	1778	1775	1776	R	rectangle	pellet
	S	1778	–	–	–	–	JT
John Tweedy	L	1783	1792	1793	R	rectangle	pellet
John Troby	L	1787	1797	1801	R	rectangle	–
	L	1803	–	–	R	rectangle	pellet
John Toleken	Co	–	1795	1836	R	rectangle	–
	Co	–	–	–	–	–	IT TOLEKEN
John Teare	Db	1796	1819	1843	R	ogival escutcheon	–
John Turner	B	–	1801	1803	R	rectangle	–
James Turner	L	1804	–	1808	R	rectangle	pellet
John Terry	L	1818	–	1825	R	rectangle	pellet
Joseph Taylor	L	–	1832	1847	R	bifoil	pellet
John Tapley	L	1833	–	1848	R	rectangle	pellet
	L	1836	–	–	R	bifoil	pellet
	L	1840	–	–	R	quatrefoil	–
I & T S							
John & Thomas Settle	S	1815	1816	1828	R	rectangle	pellet
	S	1815	–	–	–	–	T & I S
ITY & Co **I T Y** **& Co**							
John T. Young & Co	S	1788	1778	1822	R	rectangle	–
I V							
William Juson	L	1704	–	1708	R	concave chinoid	pellet
	L	–	–	–	R	domate shareform	animal head, pellet
I W							
Joseph Walker I	Db	1690	1693	1725	S	tridentate escutcheon	–
	Db	–	–	–	–	–	IW (monogram)
Joseph Walker II	Db	1710	1717	1740	S	tridentate escutcheon	–
	Db	1710	–	–	–	–	IW (monogram)

Maker's initial(s) & maker(s)	Town of registration	Date of mark registration	Earliest example	Latest example	Letter style G Gothic R Roman S Script	Punch shape	Additional features/notes
John Williamson	Db	1716	1734	1737	R	crested rectangle	pellet, PoW feathers
John Wisdome	L	1720	1713	1719	R	crested rectangle	floret
	L	1704	–	–	–	–	WI
James Wilks	L	1722	1724	1748	R	rectangle	–
	L	1739	–	–	G	ovoid	–
	L	1742	–	–	S	oval	2 pellets
	L	1722	–	–	–	–	WI
John White	L	1725	1722	1736	R	waved rectangle	–
	L	1739	–	–	S	profiloid	mullet
	L	1719	–	–	–	–	Wh
	L	–	–	–	–	–	WH
James Williams	Ex	1717	1724	1732	R	grooved hatchment	crown, mullet
James Weems	Ed	1738	1743	1763	R	rectangle	–
John Welsh	Ed	1742	1762	1769	G	trifid triad	–
James Welsh	Ed	1746	1746	1774	R	arched rectangle	human figure
John Wirgman	L	1751	1744	1754	S	rectangle	pellet
James Waters	L	1769	1769	1774	S	serrated circle	2 pellets
	L	1775	–	–	R	oval	–
John Wren II	L	1777	1785	1802	S	rectangle	pellet
Joseph Walley	Ch	–	1780	1786	R	oval	pellet
John Wall	L	1783	–	1790	R	oval	–
John Whittingham	L	1788	1790	1797	R	oval	pellet
	L	1788	–	–	R	rectangle	pellet
	L	1788	–	–	R	bevelform	pellet
John Watson	S	1795	1778	1844	R	rectangle	pellet
John West	Db	1796	1767	1800	R	rectangle	–
	Db	1796	–	–	–	–	JW
John Walton	Nc	–	1802	1860	R	rectangle	–
John Wakefield	L	1806	1809	1836	R	rectangle	–
	L	1818	–	–	R	rectangle	pellet
Joseph Wilson	L	–	1807	1844	R	rectangle	–
James Wintle	L	1821	1815	1838	R	rectangle	pellet
	L	1812	–	–	–	–	JW
John James Whiting	L	1833	1833	1860	S	rectangle	–
I W (monogram)							
Joseph Walker II	Db	1710	1717	1740	S	square	–
	Db	1710	–	–	–	–	IW
I W & Co							
John Winter & Co	S	1773	1773	1814	R	rectangle	–
I W B							
John William Blake	L	1823	1823	–	R	rectangle	–

Maker's initial(s) & maker(s)	Town of registration	Date of mark registration	Earliest example	Latest example	Letter style G Gothic R Roman S Script	Punch shape	Additional features/notes
I W **R G** John Wakelin & Robert Garrard I	L	1792	1792	1819	R	square	2 pellets
I W S Joseph William Story	L	1803	1807	1811	R	rectangle	–
I_WW_ES Joseph William Story & William Elliott	L	1809	1809	1815	R	rectangle	–
I W **W M** John Wrangham & William Moulson	L	1822	1823	1839	R	rectangle	–
I W **W T** John Wakelin & William Taylor	L	1776	1776	1801	R	trifid escutcheon	fleur de lis, 2 pellets
	L	1777	–	–	R	bevelform	fleur de lis, 2 pellets
I Y James Young	L	1760	1769	1792	R	rectangle	pellet
I Y **O I** James Young & Orlando Jackson	L	1774	1773	1774	R	rectangle	2 pellets
I Z John Ziegler	Ed	1798	1806	1807	R	rectangle	–
	Ed	–	–	–	S	bevelform	–
J A Jonathan Alleine	L	–	1770	1798	R	rectangle	–
	L	1771	–	–	–	–	IA
James Atkins	L	1795	1800	1812	R	oval	pellet
James Aldridge	L	1798	1801	1809	R	rectangle	–
Joseph Angel I	L	1811	1813	*	R	rectangle	–
	L	1824	–	–	R	rectangle	pellet
Joseph Angel II	L	–	1841	1858	R	bifoil	pellet
John Andrews II	L	1818	1808	–	R	cleftform	–

Maker's initial(s) & maker(s)	Town of registration	Date of mark registration	Earliest example	Latest example	Letter style G Gothic R Roman S Script	Punch shape	Additional features/notes
Ja							
John Jackson I	L	1697	1688	1708	G	hatchment	2 pellets, fleur de lis, dotted hatchment
	L	1697	–	–	G	waved triad	fleur de lis
J_FA							
John A. Fetter	GL	–	1902	–	R	trefoil	thread trefoil
J_&A **G&A**							
John & George Angel	L	1840	–	–	R	quatrefoil	–
J A **I A**							
Joseph II & John Angel	L	1831	1839	1866	R	quatrefoil	2 pellets, mullet
J A **J S**							
J. Aldwincle & J. Slater	L	–	1879	1894	R	quatrefoil	(also Holland, Aldwincle & Slater)
JB							
John Baker II	L	1770	1770	1772	R	woolsack	–
	L	1770	–	–	–	–	IB
John Brough	L	1803	–	1814	R	bifoil	–
	L	1807	–	–	R	rectangle	pellet
	L	1813	–	–	–	–	IB
James Barber	Y	–	1805	1857	R	bifoil	–
James Beebe	L	1811	1803	1833	R	ovoid	–
	L	1826	–	–	R	bifoil	–
Joseph Bell III	L	1818	*	*	R	oval	–
James Britton	L	1820	1823	1835	R	rectangle	–
Joseph Josiah Burtt	L	1828	1838	1848	R	rectangle	–
John Biggin	S	1855	–	1864	R	lozenge	–
	S	1855	–	–	G	rectangle	–
Jocelyn Burton	L	–	–	1975	–	bevelform	–
J B **& Co**							
James Barber & Co	Y	–	1818	1824	R	square	–

Maker's initial(s) & maker(s)	Town of registration	Date of mark registration	Earliest example	Latest example	Letter style G Gothic R Roman S Script	Punch shape	Additional features/notes
J B C John Boddington Carrington	L	–	1882	1959	R	arched shareform	2 pellets, thread profile
	L	–	–	–	–	–	C & Co
	L	–	–	–	–	–	JBC &S L
J B C & S L Carrington & Co	L	–	1882	1959	R	tridentate cuspoid	–
	L	–	–	–	–	–	JBC
	L	–	–	–	–	–	C&Co
J B E B Thomas Bradbury & Sons	S	1832	1867	1928	R	quatrefoil	–
	S	1867	–	–	–	–	JB TB
	L	–	–	–	–	–	TB
	S	–	–	–	–	–	TB&S
	S	–	–	–	–	–	TB &S
J B G C W N James Barber, George Cattle & William North	Y	–	1825	1833	R	quadriform	–
	Y	–	–	–	R	domate quadriform	3 pellets, dome
	Y	–	–	–	–	–	BC &N
	L	–	–	1835	–	–	–
J B H James Barclay Hennell	L	1877	1877	1885	R	rectangle	–
J B T B Thomas Bradbury & Sons	S	1867	–	–	R	quatrefoil	–
	S	1863	–	–	–	–	JB EB TB
	L	–	–	–	–	–	TB & S
	S	1832	–	–	–	–	TB
	S	1858	–	–	–	–	&S

Maker's initial(s) & maker(s)	Town of registration	Date of mark registration	Earliest example	Latest example	Letter style G Gothic R Roman S Script	Punch shape	Additional features/notes
J B **W N** James Barber & William North	Y	–	1836	1847	R	square	–
J B **W W** James Barber & William Whitwell	Y	–	1812	1841	R	square	–
J C Joseph Collier of Plymouth	Ex	1713	1726	1737	G	lobate biloboid	–
	Ex	–	–	–	G	globate biloboid	mullet
John Carnaby	Nc	1717	1719	1724	G	trifid rectangle	crown
	Nc	1717	–	–	–	–	Ca
John Crouch II	L	1808	1807	1825	R	octagon	–
John Cowie	L	1813	1813	1819	R	rectangle	–
John Croakley	Ch	–	1828	1834	R	rectangle	–
J & C Jones & Crompton	B	–	1900	1913	–	[in shield]	–
J C E James Charles Edington	L	1828	1828	1864	R	rectangle	2 pellets
J C **N C** T., J. & N. Creswick	S	1853	1811	1865	R	quatrefoil	–
	S	1819	–	–	–	–	TJ & NC
	S	1832	–	–	–	–	TI NC
	S	1852	–	–	–	–	T_CJ & _CN
J D James Douglas of Aberdeen	Ed	1785	1791	1806	R	rectangle	–
	A	–	–	–	–	–	ID
John Daly	Db	1786	–	1798	S	oval	–
James Downie	Gl	1812	–	1820	R	rectangle	pellet
John Durandeau	L	1824	–	1826	R	rectangle	–
J D & S James Dixon & Sons	S (*also* L & B)	1867	1850	1944	R	ogee escutcheon	–

Maker's initial(s) & maker(s)	Town of registration	Date of mark registration	Earliest example	Latest example	Letter style G Gothic R Roman S Script	Punch shape	Additional features/notes
J D **& S**							
James Deakin & Sons	S	1878	1880	1932	R	ogival escutcheon	–
	B	–	1893	1903			
		–	1894	1926	–	–	J D WD
	Ch						
	S	–	–	–	–	–	–
J D **W D**							
James Deakin & Sons	S	1878	1880	1932	R	escutcheon	–
	B	–	1893	1903			
	Ch	–	1894	1926			
	S	–	–	–	–	–	JD & S
J E							
John Elston I	Ex	–	1701	1728	S	escutcheon	battlement
	Ex	–	–	–	–	–	El
	Ex	–	–	–	–	–	IE
John Elston II	Ex	1723	1726	1747	S	escutcheon	battlement
John Emes	L	1798	1797	1820	R	bifoil	pellet
	L	1798	–	–	R	quatrefoil	pellet
Joseph Emanuel	L	1820	–	1829	R	rectangle	–
	L	1833	–	–	R	rectangle	pellet
J E & Co							
James Ellis & Co	S	1793	1818	1824	R	rectangle	–
	S	–	–	–	–	–	IE & Co
J$_G$E$_W$M							
Mappin & Webb	L	–	1861	1966	R	trefoil	–
	S	–	–	–	–	–	J$_G$N$_W$M
	S	–	–	–	–	–	M & W
J F F **& F F**							
Fenton Bros Ltd	S	1868	1857	1932	R	tridentate escutcheon	–
J G							
John Gilbert	S	1841	1845	1877	R	rectangle	pellet
	S	1841	–	–	R	rectangle	–
	B						
J H							
James Hewitt	Ed	1750	1779	1791	S	rectangle	–
James Holt	Ex	–	1768	1798	S	rectangle	–

Maker's initial(s) & maker(s)	Town of registration	Date of mark registration	Earliest example	Latest example	Letter style G Gothic R Roman S Script	Punch shape	Additional features/notes
Joseph Hicks	Ex	–	1784	1830	R	rectangle	–
	Ex	–	–	–	R	bipod	–
	Ex	–	–	–	R	bifoil	–
J. Hay	Ed	–	1816	1856	R	rectangle	–
John Harris VI	L	1818	*	*	R	rectangle	–
James Hobbs	L	–	1821	1835	S	rectangle	–
J H & Co							
James Howden & Co	Ed	–	1829	1846	R	rectangle	–
John Harrison & Co	S	1833	1853	1882	R	rectangle	–
	S	1866	–	–	–	–	IH
Joseph Haywood & Co	Gl (*also* S)	–	1893	–	R	rectangle	–
J H							
J P							
J. Hampston & J. Prince	Y	–	1777	1808	R	square	pellet
	Y	–	–	–	–	–	IH IP
	Y	–	–	–	–	–	I$_P^I$H
	Y	–	–	–	–	–	H & P
J J							
James Jones	Db	1784	–	1791	R	rectangle	fleur de lis
	Db	–	–	–	R	rectangle	–
Joseph Johnson	Db	1804	1808	1855	S	rectangle	–
	Db	–	–	–	G	ogee escutcheon	–
J K							
John Kentesber	L	–	1755	1786	R	rectangle	–
John Keene	Db	1789	1787	1807	R	ovoid	pellet
John Kearns	Db	1797	1800	1802	R	kidney	–
J K & Co							
Kirkby, Waterhouse & Hodgson	S	1808	–	1811	R	rectangle	–
J K & Co							
J. Kirkby, Gregory & Co	S	1822	–	1823	R	square	pellet

Maker's initial(s) & maker(s)	Town of registration	Date of mark registration	Earliest example	Latest example	Letter style G Gothic R Roman S Script	Punch shape	Additional features/notes
J K B Hawksworth, Eyre & Co Ltd	S	–	1834	1931	R	rectangle	2 pellets
	S	1833	–	–	–	–	H E & Co
	S	1867	–	–	–	–	C H J E
	S	1869	–	–	–	–	JKB TH GW
	B	–	1933	1937			–
	L	–	1858	1925			–
J K B **T H** **G W**	*as* **JKB**						
J L Joseph Lock	L	1775	–	1779	R	rectangle	pellet
	L	1778	–	–	–	–	IL
J. Langdon	Ex	–	1808	1813	R	rectangle	pellet
John Linnit	L	1815	1824	1831	R	rectangle	–
	L	1821	–	–	R	bevelform	pellet
	L	1824	–	–	R	profiloid	pellet
John Lowe	Ch	–	1856	1880	R	rectangle	pellet
J M Jonathan Millidge	Ed	–	1807	1833	R	rectangle	–
James Moore	Db	1818	1812	1836	R	rectangle	pellet
Joseph Mappin & Son	S	1833	1821	1833	R	ovoid	–
John Mitchell	G	1834	1826	1853	R	rectangle	–
	G	–	–	–	R	rectangle	2 pellets
J. Mahoney	Db	1845	1835	1847	R	rectangle	pellet
Joseph Mayer	Ch	–	1846	1873	R	rectangle	–
J. Murray	G	–	1854	1867	R	rectangle	–
J M B J. Millward Banks & Co	L (*also* B, S & Ch)	–	1890	1912	R	rectangle	2 pellets
J Mc John McKay	Ed	1793	1773	1866	R	rectangle	–
	Ed	–	–	–	R	rectangle	pellet
J M J^R J. Muir Jr	Gl	–	1837	–	R	rectangle	–
J M & S J. Muirhead & Sons	Gl	–	1865	1881	R	rectangle	–

Maker's initial(s) & maker(s)	Town of registration	Date of mark registration	Earliest example	Latest example	Letter style G Gothic R Roman S Script	Punch shape	Additional features/notes
J N							
Joseph Nowill	S	1813	1825	1831	R	rectangle	–
	S	1783	–	–	–	–	IN
James Nasmith	Ed	–	1831	1853	R	ogee escutcheon	–
	Ed	–	–	–	–	–	JN & Co
J N & Co							
James Nasmith & Co	Ed	–	1831	1853	R	rectangle	–
	Ed	–	–	–	–	–	JN
J N M							
John Newton Mappin	L	1882	–	–	R	oval	also other shapes
J$_G$N$_W$M							
John Newton Mappin & George Webb	L	1866	1861	1966	–	–	–
	S	1860	1857	1959	–	–	M&W
	B	–	1912	1966	–	–	–
J O							
John Osborne	Db	–	1789	1796	S	oval	–
John (or James) Osmont	Ex	1835	1827	1855	R	bifoil	–
	Ex	–	–	–	R	rectangle	pellet
	Ex	–	–	–	R	rectangle	–
J P							
John Pittar	Db	1756	1748	1804	R	rectangle	pellet
	Db	–	–	–	–	–	IP
John Power	Db	–	1787	1814	R	rectangle	–
J R							
John Ramsey II	Nc	–	1720	1732	G	rectangle	–
Josephus Read	L	1816	–	1829	R	rectangle	–
John Russell	Gl	1845	1848	1872	R	oval	–
J. Reid	Gl	–	1864	1883	R	oval	–
John Round & Son	S	1867	1868	1937	R	oval	thread oval
	S	1867	–	–	–	–	JR ER
James Ramsey of Dundee	Db	1912	1913	1918	R	lozenge	–
	L	–	1923	1937	–	–	–
	B	–	1936	1937	–	–	–
	S	–	1911	–	–	–	–
J R **E R**							
John Round & Son	S	1867	1868	1937	R	tridentate escutcheon	–
	S	1867	–	–	–	–	JR

Maker's initial(s) & maker(s)	Town of registration	Date of mark registration	Earliest example	Latest example	Letter style G Gothic R Roman S Script	Punch shape	Additional features/notes
J S							
James Strang	Ex	1705	1726	1748	S	rectangle	pellet
John Shields	Db	1762	1782	1794	R	rectangle	pellet
John Scofield	L	1778	1770	1809	R	cleft cleftform	mullet
	L	1778	–	–	–	–	IS
Josiah Snatt	L	1798	1799	1817	R	rectangle	–
John Shea	L	1807	1807	–	R	rectangle	pellet
John Sutters	Ch	–	1815	1889	R	ogival escutcheon	–
John Stone	Ex	1841	1840	1861	R	bifoil	pellet
	Ex	–	–	–	R	rectangle	pellet
John Smythe & Sons	Db	–	1845	1929	R	ogee escutcheon	–
	Db	–	–	–	R	oval	thread oval, pellet
J & S							
Jones & Son	L	–	1933	1937	R	ovoid	–
J S **A S**							
Joseph II & Albert Savory	L	1835	1834	1867	R	square	–
J T							
James Tibbits	S	1778	1775	1776	R	rectangle	pellet
	S	1778	–	–	–	–	IT
James Thompson	S	1868	–	1877	G	rectangle	pellet
	S	1868	–	–	R	rectangle	pellet
J W							
Joseph Wyatt	L	1789	1790	1791	R	rectangle	pellet
John West	Db	1796	1767	1800	R	rectangle	–
	Db	1796	–	–	–	–	IW
Joseph Willmore	B	–	1790	1846	R	rectangle	pellet
	B	–	–	–	R	spiked ovoid	–
James Wintle	L	1812	1815	1838	R	rectangle	pellet
	L	1818	–	–	R	oval	pellet
	L	1821	–	–	–	–	IW
Jacob Wintle	L	–	1846	1853	S	rectangle	–
James Weir	Gl	–	1895	1898	R	rectangle	pellet
J W **& Co**							
J. Whipple & Co	Ex	–	1865	1880	R	quatrefoil	–

Maker's initial(s) & maker(s)	Town of registration	Date of mark registration	Earliest example	Latest example	Letter style G Gothic R Roman S Script	Punch shape	Additional features/notes
J W D J. W. Dobson	L	–	1882	–	R	ogee escutcheon	–
	L	–	–	–	–	–	P D H / C D W
J W **E H** John Waterhouse, E. Hatfield & Co	S	1836	1840	1845	R	square	2 pellets
J W **F C W** J. Wakeley & F. C. Wheeler Ltd	L	–	1884	1966	R	trefoil	–
	Db	–	1897	1919	–	–	–
	Ch	–	–	1953	–	–	–
	Ed	–	–	1969	–	–	–
	L	–	–	–	–	–	W & W
	Db	–	–	–	–	–	W & W
J & W M James & William Marshall	Ed	–	1816	1857	R	rectangle	–
J. & W. Mitchell	Gl	1834	1836	1855	R	rectangle	–
	Ed	–	1841	–	–	–	–
K A Charles Frederick Kandler I	L	–	1694	1777	R	stepped hatchment	mitre, pellet
	L	1751	–	–	S	profiloid	fleur de lis
	L	1727	–	–	–	–	CK
	L	1735	–	–	–	–	FK
K & D Ker & Dempster	Ed	–	1747	1766	R	rectangle	–
K E William Keatt	L	1697	1694	1706	R	hatchment	2 mullets
	L	1697	–	–	–	–	Ke
Thomas Kedden	L	1700	1704	1715	R	lobate triad	–
John Keigwin	L	1710	1710	1711	R	lobate biloboid	crown, pellet
Robert Kempton	L	1710	1712	1713	R	globate globoid	2 mullets
Ke William Keatt	L	1697	1694	1706	R	hatchment	6 pellets
	L	1697	–	–	R	ogee hatchment	2 pellets, mullet
	L	1697	–	–	–	–	KE

Maker's initial(s) & maker(s)	Town of registration	Date of mark registration	Earliest example	Latest example	Letter style G Gothic R Roman S Script	Punch shape	Additional features/notes
Robert Keble	L	1707	1712	1713	G	ogee escutcheon	–
	L	1710	–	–	R	oval	dotted oval
	L	1711	–	–	R	oval	thread oval
Launcelot Keatt	L	1709	1709	1717	R	domate loboid	2 pellets
K E R							
William Ker	Ed	–	1758	1770	R	billet	–
K I							
Jonathan Kirke	L	1697	1683	1697	R	ogee triad	crown, crescent
Jerimiah King	L	1723	1726	1766	R	globate triloboid	crown
	L	1723	–	–	–	–	IK
	L	1739	–	–	–	–	I KING
Ki							
James Kirkup	Nc	1713	1728	1758	R	spikeform	–
	Nc	–	–	–	R	domate loboid	2 pellets, mullet
	Nc	–	–	–	–	–	IK
K M							
Kenneth McKenzie	Ed	1714	1718	1723	R	oval	–
K W & Co							
Kirkby, Waterhouse & Co	S	1793	1811	1823	R	rectangle	–
	S	1793	–	–	–	–	IKIW & Co
K & W							
Kitchen & Walker	S	1835	1835	–	R	rectangle	–
L & Co							
John Lawrence & Co	B	1813	1818	1831	R	rectangle	–
Liberty & Co Ltd (?)	B	1899	1898	1938	R	3 lozenges (overlapping)	–
L & SONS							
Lister & Sons	Nc	–	1863	–	R	rectangle	–
L A							
John Laughton I	L	1697	1699	1701	R	cleft hatchment	2 volutes
Jonathan Lambe	L	1699	1699	1727	R	ogee invectoid	–
John Ladyman	L	1699	1700	1714	S	crested triad	crown, pellet
John Langwith	Y	1699	1703	1714	R	cleft escutcheon	–
Paul de Lamerie	L	1713	1712	1751	R	crested globoid	crown, mullet, fleur de lis
	L	1733	–	–	–	–	PL
George Lambe	L	1713	1713	1723	R	profiloid	lamb, annulet
Thomas Langford	L	1715	1715	–	R	domate rectangle	dog
Jane Lambe	L	–	1720	1727	R	lozenge	lamb
	L	–	–	–	–	–	IL

Maker's initial(s) & maker(s)	Town of registration	Date of mark registration	Earliest example	Latest example	Letter style G Gothic R Roman S Script	Punch shape	Additional features/notes
La							
Dennis Langton	L	1716	–	1734	G	oval	–
	L	1729	–	–	–	–	DL
L A C							
Crichton Bros	L	–	1892	1939	R	rectangle	–
LAW							
William Law	Db	–	1789	1822	R	[no shape]	–
	Db	1774	–	–	–	–	WL
Thomas Law	S	–	1774	1819	R	rectangle	–
	S	1773	–	–	–	–	TL
	S	1773	–	–	–	–	T LAW
Langley Archer West	Db	1900	–	–	R	trefoil	–
	Db	1902	–	–	–	–	W&S
L B							
Louis Black	L	1756	1759	1764	R	profiloid	–
Levesley Bros	S	1863	1901	1916	R	lobate biloboid	–
	S	1863	–	–	R	ovoid	–
L C							
Louis Cuny	L	1732	1697	1729	R	tridentate rectangle	crown, fleur de lis
	L	1703	–	–	–	–	CV
Louisa Perina Courtauld	L	–	1765	1767	R	lozenge	–
L & C							
William Lea & Co	B	1811	1813	1827	R	rectangle	–
Lea & Clark	B	1824	1819	1826	R	rectangle	–
L C **G C**							
Louisa Perina Courtauld & George Cowles	L	1773	1765	1777	R	grooved square	–
L C **S C**							
Louisa Perina Courtauld & Samuel Courtauld II	L	1777	–	–	R	square	–
L D							
Louis Dupont	L	1736	1736	1747	R	hexagon	2 pellets, mullet
	L	1739	–	–	S	ovate ovoid	crown
Louis Delisle	L	1775	–	–	S	profiloid	pellet

Maker's initial(s) & maker(s)	Town of registration	Date of mark registration	Earliest example	Latest example	Letter style G Gothic R Roman S Script	Punch shape	Additional features/notes
L E							
Timothy Ley	L	1697	1691	1733	R	circle	2 mullets, 7 pellets
	L	–	–	–	–	–	TL
George Lewis	L	1699	1698	1704	R	trifid rectangle	crown
John Leach	L	1699	1699	1707	R	spiked rectangle	–
Samuel Lee	L	1701	1698	1712	G	tridentate escutcheon	crown
	L	1720	–	–	–	–	SL
Le							
Ralph Leeke	L	1699	1698	1701	G	ogee triad	fleur de lis
	L	–	–	–	R	trifid escutcheon	crown
Petley Ley	L	1715	1718	1720	G	octagon	bird, mullet, 2 thread octagons
Let							
John Letablere	Db	1737	1743	1751	R	rectangle	–
L F N							
Luke F. Newland	G Ed	1816	1817	1821	R	rectangle	2 pellets
L H							
Louis (or Lewis) Hamon	L	1736	1747	1750	R	profiloid	bird holding twig
	L	1738	–	–	R	octagon	bird, pellet
	L	1739	–	–	S	lobate rectangle	bird, pellet
	L	1752	–	–	G	bifoil	pellet
L^F_BH							
Lewis Herne & Francis Butty	L	1757	1757	1764	R	quatrefoil	mullet
L I							
Isaac Liger	L	1704	1709	1729	R	cambered reelform	floral spray
	L	1720	–	–	–	–	IL
John Lingard	L	1718	1721	1726	R	rectangle	–
	L	1719	–	–	R	ogee globoid	pellet
	L	1719	–	–	–	–	Li
	L	1720	–	–	–	–	IL
Lawrence Johnson	L	1751	1751	–	R	quatrefoil	pellet
	L	1752	–	–	R	rectangle	pellet
Li							
John Lingard	L	1719	1721	1726	G	ogee triad	pellet
	L	1719	–	–	R	ogee globoid	pellet
	L	1718	–	–	–	–	LI
	L	1720	–	–	–	–	IL

Maker's initial(s) & maker(s)	Town of registration	Date of mark registration	Earliest example	Latest example	Letter style G Gothic R Roman S Script	Punch shape	Additional features/notes
L L							
Louis Laroche	L	1725	1731	1739	R	profiloid	crown, bird in flight
	L	1739	–	–	S	octagon	crown, mullet, pellet
L M							
Lewis Mettayer	L	1720	1708	1717	R	bevelform	–
	L	–	–	–	R	domate loboid	pellet
	L	1700	–	–	–	–	ME
L N							
Lawrence Nowlan	Db	1814	1817	1840	R	rectangle	–
L O							
Nathaniel Lock	L	1697	1699	1716	R	oval	–
	L	1699	–	–	R	spiked chinoid	key, baluster
	L	1699	–	–	R	ogee cycloid	key
Seth Lofthouse	L	1699	1697	1719	G	ogee hatchment	mullet
Robert Lovell	L	1703	–	1710	R	escutcheon	2 mullets
William Looker	L	1713	1713	1724	R	cleft cleftform	2 pellets
	L	1720	–	–	–	–	WL
Matthew E. Lofthouse	L	–	1708	1730	R	trifid rectangle	plant
	L	1705	–	–	–	–	LO (monogram)
	L	1721	–	–	–	–	ML (conjoined)
Lewis Ourry (*or* Ouvry)	L	1740	1741	1743	S	domate biloboid	crown
LO (monogram)							
Matthew E. Lofthouse	L	1705	1708	1730	S	circle	–
	L	–	–	–	R	trifid rectangle	plant
	L	1721	–	–	–	–	ML (conjoined)
LOW							
Robert Lowe	Ed	1742	1742	1756	R	invected rectangle	–
L P							
Lewis Pantin I	L	1734	1733	1745	R	rectangle	–
	L	1739	–	–	S	globate rectangle	peacock
L P & Co							
Luke Proctor & Co	S	1785	1785	1792	R	square	pellet
L & R							
Lothian & Robertson	Ed	–	1751	1761	R	rectangle	–
John Langlands & John Robertson	Nc	–	1778	1808	R	rectangle	–
	Nc	–	–	–	–	–	IL IR

Maker's initial(s) & maker(s)	Town of registration	Date of mark registration	Earliest example	Latest example	Letter style G Gothic R Roman S Script	Punch shape	Additional features/notes
L S Lewis Samuel of Liverpool	L	1830	1830	1834	R	rectangle	–
	L	1835	–	–	R	rectangle	2 pellets
L U Leonard Urquhart	Ed	–	1825	1844	R	rectangle	–
Lu William Lukin I	L	1699	1699	1736	G	ogee triad	pellet
	L	1725	–	–	–	–	WL
L V John Ludlow	L	1713	–	1716	R	ogee cuspoid	pellet
	L	1720	–	–	–	–	IL
L V & W Ledsam, Vale & Wheeler	B	1825	1825	1830	R	rectangle	–
M A William Mathew I	L	1697	1697	1706	R	oval	thread oval, crown
	L	1700	–	–	R	globate triad	stag's head, mullet
	L	–	–	–	R	waved loboid	–
Willoughby Masham	L	1701	1701	1704	R	oval	bird
Jonathan Madden	L	1702	1702	1708	R	cleft hatchment	2 mullets, fleur de lis
	L	1720	–	–	R	lobate hatchment	3 mullets
Jacob Margas	L	1706	1705	1725	R	trifid spikeform	crown, mullet
	L	–	–	–	R	ovate loboid	crown, crescent
	L	–	–	–	R	ovate loboid	crown, fleur de lis
	L	–	–	–	–	–	IM
Isaac Malyn	L	1710	1710	–	R	bifoil	–
William Mathew II	L	1712	–	1735	R	cleft triad	3 florets, 2 mullets, Roman W
	L	1720	–	–	–	–	WM
Thomas Mann	L	1713	1715	1742	R	ogee triad	mullet
	L	1720	–	–	–	–	TM
Samuel Margas	L	1715	1705	1717	R	trigonate cuspoid	crown, fleur de lis
	L	1721	–	–	–	–	SM
Mary Ashworth of Durham	Nc	–	1794	1800	R	rectangle	–

Maker's initial(s) & maker(s)	Town of registration	Date of mark registration	Earliest example	Latest example	Letter style G Gothic R Roman S Script	Punch shape	Additional features/notes
Ma							
Thomas Mason	L	1716	1717	1749	R	cleft triad	mullet
	L	1720	–	–	–	–	TM
M & A							
Muirhead & Arthur	Gl	–	1846	–	R	rectangle	–
M B							
Michael Boult	L	1720	1714	1718	R	trefoil	anchor
	L	1713	–	–	–	–	BO
Mark Bock	L	1761	1792	1806	R	bifoil	pellet
	L	1764	–	–	R	rectangle	pellet
	L	–	–	–	R	oval	–
Margaret Binley	L	1764	–	–	R	cleft cleftform	pellet
Benjamin Montague (*or* Mountigue)	L	1772	1781	1789	R	rectangle	–
	L	1771	–	–	–	–	BM
Moser Brent	L	1775	1791	1817	R	rectangle	–
Matthew Boulton	B	1790	1776	1809	R	rectangle	2 suns
Michael Barnett	L	1781	1791	1820	R	rectangle	–
Matthew Boulton & Plate Co	B	1820	–	1833	R	rectangle	–
Mappin Bros	S	1859	1889	1954	R	rectangle	–
	S	1859	–	–	G	rectangle	–
	S	1856	–	–	–	–	M&B CM EM JM FC CH WG JLL EM WG M Mn JM JLL Bros Bros
M Bros							
Mappin Bros	S	1894	1889	1954	R	lozenge	*as above*
Mn Bros							
Mappin Bros	S	1894	1889	1954	R	lozenge	*as above*
M & B							
Mappin Bros	S	1856	1889	1954	G	rectangle	*as above*
MB (conjoined)							
Marmaduke Best	Y	1657	1663	1702	R	engrailed biloboid	–
M B Co							
Mammat Buxton & Co	S	1865	–	1899	R	3 squares	–
MB IF							
Matthew Boulton & John Fothergill	B	1773	1769	1781	R	2 rectangles	–
	Ch	1769	–	–	–	–	B & F

Maker's initial(s) & maker(s)	Town of registration	Date of mark registration	Earliest example	Latest example	Letter style G Gothic R Roman S Script	Punch shape	Additional features/notes
M C							
Matthew Cooper I	L	1720	1703	–	R	bifoil	–
	L	1702	–	–	–	–	CO
Matthew Cooper II	L	1725	–	1731	R	rectangle	–
	L	1725	–	–	–	–	CO
Matthew Craw	Ed	–	1802	1816	R	oval	–
Mary Ann Crosswell	L	1805	–	1810	R	rectangle	–
Morris Cadman	L	1810	–	1829	R	rectangle	–
Mary Chawner	L	1834	1834	1840	R	rectangle	–
M & C							
Milne & Campbell	Ed	–	1764	1848	S	rectangle	–
	Gl	–	–	–	R	rectangle	–
Mackay & Chisholme	Ed	–	1835	1941	R	waved rectangle	–
M C **G A**							
Mary Chawner & George William Adams	L	–	1840	–	R	quatrefoil	–
M D							
Marmaduke Daintry	L	1737	1741	1751	R	trifid rectangle	crown
	L	1739	–	–	G	rectangle	–
	L	1747	–	–	S	domate rectangle	crown
M E							
Lewis Mettayer	L	1700	1708	1717	R	trifid rectangle	baluster, 2 sickles
	L	1720	–	–	–	–	LM
Me							
Thomas Merry	L	1701	1711	1716	R	rectangle	–
	L	1711	–	–	R	waved rectangle	–
M E **M E**							
Morris & Michael Emanuel	L	1825	–	1829	R	square	–
M F							
Magdalen Feline	L	1753	1753	1766	S	lozenge	2 pellets
	L	1757	–	–	S	lozenge	pellet
M F **& Co**							
Fenton, Creswick & Co	S	–	1776	1792	R	square	–
	S	1773	–	–	–	–	MF RC
	S	1773	–	–	–	–	MF& Co

Maker's initial(s) & maker(s)	Town of registration	Date of mark registration	Earliest example	Latest example	Letter style G Gothic R Roman S Script	Punch shape	Additional features/notes
M F & Co							
Fenton, Creswick & Co *or* M. Fenton & Co *or* Fenton, Creswick, Oaks & Co	S	1773	1776	1792	R	heart	–
	S	1773	–	–	–	–	MF RC
	S	1773	–	–	–	–	MF &Co
M F R C							
Fenton, Creswick & Co *or* M. Fenton & Co	S	1773	1776	1792	R	square	–
	S	1773	–	–	–	–	MF& Co
	S	–	–	–	–	–	MF &Co
M G							
Meschach Godwin	L	1723	1723	1725	R	globate bipod	floret
	L	1723	–	–	–	–	GO
M H							
Michael Hewitson	Db	1727	1725	1728	R	rectangle	–
Michael Homer	Db	–	1752	1794	R	rectangle	–
Metcalf Hopgood	L	1835	1833	1846	R	quatrefoil	–
M H & Co							
Martin Hall & Co Richard Martin & Ebenezer Hall	S	1854	1848	1945	R	ogival chinoid	–
	S (*also* L & B)	1854	–	–	–	–	RM EH
M H I R							
Mary Hyde & John Reily	L	1799	1799	–	R	square	–
M I							
William Middleton	L	1700	1698	–	R	tridentate hatchment	3 pellets
Henry Miller I	L	1714	–	1721	R	trifid triad	4 pellets
	L	1720	–	–	R	oval	pellet
	L	1720	–	–	–	–	HM
John Millington	L	1718	1721	1722	R	ogee triad	3 pellets
	L	1720	–	–	–	–	IM

Maker's initial(s) & maker(s)	Town of registration	Date of mark registration	Earliest example	Latest example	Letter style G Gothic R Roman S Script	Punch shape	Additional features/notes
M K							
Michael Keating	Db	1765	1768	1799	R	rectangle	–
	Db	–	–	–	R	concave rectangle	–
	Db	–	–	–	R	biloboid	pellet
MK (conjoined)							
Colin McKenzie	Ed	1695	1698	1719	R	heart	mullet
M L							
Mary Lofthouse	L	1731	–	1732	R	lozenge	pellet, 2 mullets
Matthew Linwood	B	–	1801	1821	R	rectangle	–
Matthew Linwood & Son	B	1813	–	–	R	oval	–
ML (conjoined)							
Matthew E. Lofthouse	L	1721	1708	1730	R	circle	2 mullets
	L	1705	–	–	–	–	LO (monogram)
	L	–	–	–	–	–	LO
M O							
James Morson	L	1716	1744	1758	R	trefoil	swan
	L	1720	–	–	–	–	IM
Thomas Morse	L	1718	1721	1723	R	globate rectangle	dog
	L	1718	–	–	–	–	TM
Henry Morris	L	1718	1739	1758	R	oval	–
	L	1720	–	–	–	–	HM
	L	–	–	–	–	–	HM (conjoined)
MO (monogram)							
Andrew Moore	L	1700	1650	1696	R	stepped reelform	–
M P							
Mary Piers	L	1758	1758	–	R	rectangle	pellet
Michael Plummer	L	1791	1791	1797	R	rectangle	pellet
M R							
Mary Rood(e)	L	1721	1722	1725	R	lozenge	2 pellets
	L	1721	–	–	–	–	RO
M R **C R**							
Mary Ann & Charles Reily	L	1826	1826	1837	R	quatrefoil	–
M$_S$R							
Mary & Richard II Sibley	L	1836	1836	1837	R	heart	–
M & R							
Mitchell & Russell	Ed	1813	–	1818	R	bevelform	–

Maker's initial(s) & maker(s)	Town of registration	Date of mark registration	Earliest example	Latest example	Letter style G Gothic R Roman S Script	Punch shape	Additional features/notes
M S Mary Sumner	L	1807	–	1808	R	oval	–
Michael Starkey	L	1809	1809	1834	R	oval	pellet
	L	1822	–	–	R	bevelform	pellet
M & S Marshall & Sons	Ed	–	1823	1887	R	rectangle	–
M S **E S** Mary & Eliza Sumner	L	1809	1809	1813	R	circle	–
	L	1810	–	–	R	square	–
M T Mehatabell Turton	L	1798	–	1804	R	rectangle	–
Mu Henry Muston	Ex	–	1701	1721	R	ogival loboid	pellet, crescent
M W Matthew West I	Db	1769	1772	1826	R	rectangle	–
MW (monogram) Matthew Walker	Db	1716	1717	1730	S	rectangle	–
M W & Co Mappin (John Newton) & Webb (George)	S	1860	1857	1966	G	profiloid	–
	L	1866	1861	1966	–	–	$J_G N_W M$ M & W
	B	–	1912	1966	–	–	–
M & W Mappin (John Newton) & Webb (George)	S	1860	1857	1966	G	rectangle	–
	L	1866	1861	1966	–	–	MW&Co $J_G N_W M$
	B	–	1819	1966	–	–	–
M Y Mungo Yorstoun	Ed	1702	1710	1719	R	heart	–
	Ed	1702	–	–	R	rectangle	pellet
N S. D. Neill Ltd of Belfast	Db (*also* S)	1906	1902	1930	R	domate loboid	crown, hatched surround
N A Bowles Nash	L	1721	1721	1725	R	heart	fleur de lis BN
	L	1721	–	–	–	–	

Maker's initial(s) & maker(s)	Town of registration	Date of mark registration	Earliest example	Latest example	Letter style G Gothic R Roman S Script	Punch shape	Additional features/notes
NA (monogram)							
Francis Nelme	L	1723	1725	1739	S	waveform	–
	L	1739	–	–	–	–	FN
N C							
Nicholaus Clauson	L	1720	1713	1719	R	domate rectangle	crown
	L	1709	–	–	–	–	CL
Nicholas Cunliffe	Ch	–	1798	1815	R	oval	–
T., J. & N. Creswick	S	1832	1811	1865	R	rectangle	–
	S	1819	–	–	–	–	TJ & NC
	S	1852	–	–	–	–	T J C & N
	S	1853	–	–	–	–	JC NC
N D							
Nicholas Dumee	L	1776	1776	1777	R	ovoid	pellet
Ne							
Anthony Nelme	L	–	1683	1738	R	rectangle	or J. Newton.
	L	1697	–	–	–	–	ANe (AN conjoined)
NEILL							
Henry Wilkinson & Co	S	1852	–	–	R	oval	–
	S	1831	–	–	–	–	HW & Co
N G							
Nathaniel Gulliver	L	1722	1722	1727	R	lozenge	pellet
	L	1722	–	–	–	–	GU
N G Co							
Northern Goldsmiths Co	L	–	1934	1938	–	–	–
N H							
Nicholas Hearnden	L	–	1772	1811	R	rectangle	–
Naphtali Hart	L	1812	1809	1825	R	rectangle	–
N M							
Nathan Murray II	Db	1758	1765	1803	R	rectangle	–
Nathaniel Mills	B	1825	1826	1874	R	rectangle	–
	B	1825	–	–	R	rectangle	pellet
N S							
Nicholas Sprimont	L	1743	1741	1743	S	profiloid	mullet, pellet
Nathaniel Smith	S	1756	1780	1819	R	rectangle	–
	S	1780	–	–	–	–	NS & Co
N S & Co							
Nathaniel Smith & Co	S	1780	1780	1819	R	rectangle	–
	S	1756	–	–	–	–	NS

Maker's initial(s) & maker(s)	Town of registration	Date of mark registration	Earliest example	Latest example	Letter style G Gothic R Roman S Script	Punch shape	Additional features/notes
O & B Ollivant & Botsford	L	–	1909	1936	R	[shield]	–
	S	–	–	1931	–	–	–
	B	–	–	1937	–	–	–
O I Orlando Jackson	L	–	1771	1800	R	profiloid	pellet
	L	–	–	–	–	–	OJ
O J Orlando Jackson	L	–	1771	1800	R	rectangle	pellet OI
O R Omar Ramsden	L	1918	1909	1939	R	rectangle	–
O R A C Omar Ramsden & Alwyn Carr	L	1898	1900	1926	R	square	–
O V Charles Overing	L	1697	1697	1717	G	ogee hatchment	2 pellets, fleur de lis
O Y Phillip Oyles	L	1699	–	1699	R	waveform	–
P Peter Pemberton	Ch	1677	1677	1706	S	invected quadriform	–
	Ch	1677	–	–	–	–	PP
	Ch	1677	–	–	–	–	Pe
Benjamin Pyne	L	–	1682	1727	R	trifid triad	crown
	L	1697	–	–	–	–	PY
	L	1697	–	–	–	–	Py
P A Thomas Parr I	L	1697	1697	1718	R	delphate bipod	–
	L	1717	–	–	R	octafoil	–
Simon Pantin I	L	1701	1702	1732	R	globate coniform	peacock
	L	1717	–	–	R	globate reelform	peacock
	L	1720	–	–	–	–	SP
Mark Paillet	L	–	1703	–	R	trifid rectangle	crown, floret
Peter Archambo I	L	1722	1721	1758	R	trifid cleftform	crown
	L	1739	–	–	S	bifoil	pellet
	L	1721	–	–	–	–	AR
Peter Arthur	Gl	1808	1822	1850	R	rectangle	–
	Gl	1808	–	–	R	rectangle	pellet

Maker's initial(s) & maker(s)	Town of registration	Date of mark registration	Earliest example	Latest example	Letter style G Gothic R Roman S Script	Punch shape	Additional features/notes
Pa							
Humphrey Payne	L	1701	1701	1739	R	globate triad	egg in cup, pellet
	L	1701	–	–	G	globate rectangle	hen & chickens
	L	1739	–	–	–	–	HP
William Paradise	L	1718	1719	1723	R	quatrefoil	bird of paradise
	L	1720	–	–	–	–	WP
P A J^R							
Peter Aitken Jr	Gl	1845	1849	1860	R	rectangle	–
P ^P_M A							
Peter Archambo II & Peter Meure	L	1750	1741	1757	R	quatrefoil	mullet
P B							
Peter Bennett	L	1732	1739	1761	R	trifid rectangle	crown
	L	1739	–	–	S	ovoid	
Philip Bruguier	L	1739	1751	1756	R	cambered square	crown, fleur de lis
	L	1739	–	–	S	ovate ovoid	crown, pellet
P B **A B**							
Peter & Ann Bateman	L	1791	1781	1818	R	square	–
P B **A B** **W B**							
Peter Ann & William I Bateman	L	1800	1791	1823	R	quadriform	–
P B **I B**							
Peter & Jonathan Bateman	L	1790	1790	1790	R	square	–
P B **W B**							
Peter & William I Bateman	L	1805	1789	1830	R	square	–
P C							
Paul Crespin	L	–	1721	1766	R	globate hatchment	crown, pellet, mullet
	L	1739	–	–	S	bifoil	–
	L	1757	–	–	R	oval	pellet
	L	–	–	–	–	–	CR
Paul Callard	L	1752	1760	1767	S	lobate triad	2 mullets, fleur de lis
	L	1759	–	–	R	rectangle	–

Maker's initial(s) & maker(s)	Town of registration	Date of mark registration	Earliest example	Latest example	Letter style G Gothic R Roman S Script	Punch shape	Additional features/notes
Peter Carter	L	1783	1786	1790	R	rectangle	–
P C & S Cunningham & Simpson	Ed	–	1806	1815	R	square	–
	Ed	–	–	–	–	–	PC & S
PC & S Cunningham & Simpson	Ed	–	1806	1815	R	rectangle	–
	Ed	–	–	–	–	–	PC & S
P^WC / G William Gwillim & Peter Castle	L	1744	1744	1745	R	quatrefoil	pellet
P D Peter Desvignes	L	1771	1774	1780	R	rectangle	pellet
P E William Penstone I	L	1697	1699	1715	R	circle	dotted circle, mullet, pellet
Robert Peake	L	1697	1697	1719	R	ogee hatchment	2 pellets
	L	1697	–	–	R	hatchment	3 pellets
Henry Penstone	L	1697	1718	1722	R	ogee chinoid	3 pellets
William Petley	L	1699	1719	1732	S	circle	2 thread circles, crown, 4 pellets
	L	1717	–	–	R	arched loboid	pellet, crown, bird
	L	1720	–	–	–	–	WP
Peter Elliott of Dartmouth	Ex	1703	1703	1738	R	rectangle	–
William Pearson	L	1704	1719	1720	R	rectangle	–
	L	1710	–	–	R	quatrefoil	2 mullets
	L	1710	–	–	R	octagon	bird, pellet, mullet
	L	1717	–	–	R	domate triad	bird, fleur de lis, 2 pellets
	L	1721	–	–	–	–	WP
Edmund Pearce	L	1705	1705	1722	R	domate rectangle	mullet
	L	1720	–	–	–	–	EP
John Pero	L	1717	–	1738	R	ogee triad	mullet, floret
	L	1732	–	–	–	–	IP
Philip Elston	Ex	1723	1707	1748	R	oval	–
	Ex	–	–	–	S	oval	–
Philip Elliott	Ex	–	1725	1729	R	oval	–

Maker's initial(s) & maker(s)	Town of registration	Date of mark registration	Earliest example	Latest example	Letter style G Gothic R Roman S Script	Punch shape	Additional features/notes
Pe							
Edward Peacock	L	1710	–	1724	G	lobate triad	pellet
Peter Pemberton	Ch	1677	1677	1706	S	rectangle	–
	Ch	1677	–	–	–	–	PP
	Ch	1677	–	–	–	–	P
P F							
Philip Freeman	L	1772	1772	1781	R	oval	–
P G							
Patrick Graeme	Ed	1725	–	1729	R	bifoil	–
Philip(s) Garden	L	1738	1741	1756	R	ovate rectangle	crown
	L	1739	–	–	S	globate rectangle	mullet
	L	1744	–	–	R	arched escutcheon	pear, pellet
	L	1748	–	–	S	bevelform	–
	L	1751	–	–	R	invected archform	–
	L	1756	–	–	R	rectangle	pellet
Peter Gillois	L	1782	1754	1783	R	rectangle	pellet
	L	1754	–	–	–	–	P^{I}G
Philip Grierson	Gl	1810	1820	1844	R	rectangle	–
P G D & Sn							
P. G. Dodd & Son	L	–	1937	–	–	[shield]	star
P H							
Phillip Phillis	L	1720	1720	–	R	oval	mullet
	L	1720	–	–	–	–	PP
Paul Hanet	L	1721	1718	1738	R	trifid rectangle	fleur de lis
	L	1716	–	–	–	–	HA
P H A							
Asprey & Co Ltd	L	–	1911	1927	–	–	–
	B	–	1903	1939	–	–	–
	S	–	1911	1965	–	–	–
	Ch	–	1930	1939	–	–	–
P$_C^{D}_H$^{W}							
Dobson & Sons	L	–	1882	–	R	quatrefoil	–
	L	–	–	–	–	–	JWD
P I							
Matthew Pickering	L	1703	–	1705	R	delphate triad	fleur de lis
Peze (Alexis) Pilleau	L	–	1725	1755	R	profiloid	fleur de lis
	L	–	–	–	–	–	PP
P^{I}G							
Peter Gillois	L	1754	1754	1783	R	globate chinoid	crown, pellet, inverted crown
	L	1782	–	–	–	–	PG

Maker's initial(s) & maker(s)	Town of registration	Date of mark registration	Earliest example	Latest example	Letter style G Gothic R Roman S Script	Punch shape	Additional features/notes
P K							
Philip Kinnersley	Db	1716	1717	1733	R	domate rectangle	mullet
P L							
Pierre Platel	L	1699	1699	1718	R	tabled globoid	crown, mullet, fleur de lis
Paul de Lamerie	L	1733	1712	1751	R	globate globoid	crown, mullet, pellet, fleur de lis
	L	1739	–	–	S	globate globoid	crown, 2 pellets
	L	1713	–	–	–	–	LA
Francis Plymley	L	1715	1716	1719	R	oval	–
Patrick Leonard	S	1835	–	1838	R	rectangle	–
	Ch	–	1842	1847	R	rectangle	–
P M							
Peter Moss	L	1728	–	1747	R	rectangle	–
Peter Mathie	Ed	1774	1783	1795	R	rectangle	pellet
Patrick Moore	Db	–	1812	1832	R	oval	–
	Db	–	–	–	R	rectangle	–
PM (monogram)							
Patrick Murray	Ed	1701	1704	1718	R	oval	–
P & M							
Parkin & Marshall	S	1866	–	–	R	rectangle	–
	S	1866	–	–	–	–	WP
P N							
Philip Norman	L	–	1768	1772	R	rectangle	pellet
P O							
John Porter	L	–	1701	1705	R	invected archform	crown, bird
	L	1695	–	–	–	–	Po
Po							
John Porter	L	1695	1701	1705	R	oval	–
	L	–	–	–	R	oval	2 pellets, thread oval
	L	–	–	–	–	–	PO
P P							
Peter Pemberton	Ch	1677	1677	1706	R	ovate rectangle	crown
	Ch	1677	–	–	R	trifid invectoid	crown
	Ch	1677	–	–	R	tridentate chinoid	–
	Ch	1677	–	–	R	square	crown, pellet
	Ch	1677	–	–	–	–	Pe
	Ch	1677	–	–	–	–	P
Phillip Phillis	L	1720	1720	–	R	circle	pellet, 3 florets
	L	1720	–	–	–	–	PH

Maker's initial(s) & maker(s)	Town of registration	Date of mark registration	Earliest example	Latest example	Letter style G Gothic R Roman S Script	Punch shape	Additional features/notes
Philip Platel	L	1737	1737	–	R	profiloid	pellet, scrolls
Peze (Alexis) Pilleau	L	1739	1725	1755	S	globate ovoid	mullet
	L	–	–	–	R	profiloid	fleur de lis, pellet
	L	–	–	–	–	–	PI
Peter Podio	L	1790	1789	1804	R	rectangle	pellet
P R							
Philip Rollos II	L	1720	1705	1716	R	tridentate triad	fleur de lis, mullet
	L	1705	–	–	–	–	RO
Philip Roker II	L	1720	*	*	R	crested loboid	crown
	L	1739	–	–	S	ovate bipod	crown
	L	–	–	–	R	ogee escutcheon	pellet
	L	–	–	–	–	–	P ROKER
	L	1720	–	–	–	–	RO
	L	–	–	–	–	–	PR (R small)
Philip Robinson	L	1723	–	1723	R	lanceolate cuspoid	2 mullets, pellet
	L	1714	–	–	–	–	Ro
Patrick Robertson	Ed	1751	1766	1789	R	rectangle	–
Philip Roker III	L	1776	*	*	R	bifoil	pellet
Philip Rundell	L	1819	1818	1824	R	rectangle	–
	L	1819	–	–	R	rectangle	pellet
P R (R small)							
Edmund Proc(k)ter	L	1700	–	1705	R	invected triad	crown, 2 pellets
Philip Roker II	L	–	*	*	R	rectangle	–
	L	1720	–	–	–	–	PR
P ROKER							
Philip Roker II	L	–	*	*	R	rectangle	–
	L	1720	–	–	–	–	PR
	L	1720	–	–	–	–	RO
P S							
Pentecost Symonds of Plymouth	Ex	1706	1706	1753	S	cleft bevelled square	
	Ex	–	–	–	–	–	SY
	Ex	–	–	–	–	–	Sy
Paul Storr	L	1793	1792	1845	R	rectangle	pellet
	L	1793	–	–	R	bifoil	–
	L	1794	–	–	R	bifoil	pellet
Peter Sutherland	Ed	–	1836	1847	R	rectangle	–

Maker's initial(s) & maker(s)	Town of registration	Date of mark registration	Earliest example	Latest example	Letter style G Gothic R Roman S Script	Punch shape	Additional features/notes
P & S							
Robert Pinckney & Robert Scott	Nc	–	1779	1790	R	rectangle	–
	Nc	–	–	–	–	–	RP RS
P T							
Philip Tough	Db	1705	1708	1714	R	lanceolate rectangle	crown, pellet
Peter Taylor	L	1740	1743	1756	R	trefoil	cup, pellet
P W							
Peter Werritzer	L	1750	1741	1768	R	domate rectangle	mullet
	L	–	–	–	S	waved rectangle	pellet
Peter Walsh	Db	–	1831	1844	R	rectangle	–
P. Weeks (?)	Db	–	1835	1836	R	rectangle	–
P & W							
John Parker & Edward Wakelin	L	–	1760	1784	R	trifid rectangle	fleur de lis
	L	–	–	–	–	–	IP EW
P Y							
Benjamin Pyne	L	1697	1682	1727	R	profiloid	crown, floret
	L	1697	–	–	–	–	Py
	L	–	–	–	–	–	P
Py							
Benjamin Pyne	L	1697	1682	1727	G	oval	thread oval, dotted oval
	L	1697	–	–	–	–	PY
	L	–	–	–	–	–	P
R A							
Andrew Raven	L	1697	1698	1706	R	ogee shareform	2 pellets, raven
	L	1697	–	–	–	–	Ra
	L	–	–	–	–	–	AR
Richard Raine	L	1712	1712	1713	R	globate hatchment	pellet, 2 mullets
Robert Abercromby	L	1731	1731	1754	R	chevroned rectangle	crown, pellet
	L	1739	–	–	S	bifoil	pellet
	L	1740	–	–	–	–	Ab
Ra							
Andrew Raven	L	1697	1698	1706	R	ogee shareform	mullet
	L	1697	–	–	–	–	RA
	L	–	–	–	–	–	AR
John Ramsey	Nc	1698	1700	1708	R	hatchment	2 mullets
	Nc	1698	–	–	–	–	IR
John Rand	L	1704	1703	1711	G	cinquefoil	2 pellets

Maker's initial(s) & maker(s)	Town of registration	Date of mark registration	Earliest example	Latest example	Letter style G Gothic R Roman S Script	Punch shape	Additional features/notes
RA Cox (RA monogram)							
Robert Albin Cox	L	1758	1749	1759	R	rectangle	–
	L	1752	–	–	–	–	RC
R$^{\mathbf{G}}_{\mathbf{H}}$A							
Robert Abercromby & George Hindmarsh	L	1731	1730	–	R	octagon	3 pellets
R A **W S**							
Richard William Atkins & William Nathaniel Somersall	L	1824	1826	1836	R	square	–
R B							
Robert Beckwith	Y	1546	–	1573	R	lobate triad	–
Robert Bruce	Ed	1687	–	1695	R	lobate shareform	chine
Richard Bayley	L	1720	1710	1750	R	octagon	pellet
	L	1739	–	–	S	quatrefoil	–
	L	–	–	–	R	octagon	–
	L	–	–	–	R	domate rectangle	pellet
	L	1708	–	–	–	–	BA
Richard Burcombe	L	1724	–	1731	R	rectangle	pellet
	L	1735	–	–	S	rectangle	–
Richard Beale	L	1733	1730	1749	R	lobate hatchment	3 pellets
	L	1739	–	–	S	crested rectangle	crown
	L	1746	–	–	R	rectangle	–
	L	–	–	–	R	rectangle	pellet
Richard Bell	L	1734	–	1737	R	rectangle	–
Robert Brown	L	1736	1735	1743	R	rectangle	–
	L	1739	–	–	S	quatrefoil	2 mullets
Ralph Bielby	Nc	–	1757	1758	S	domate rectangle	annulet
Richard Binley	L	1760	1793	1794	R	cleft rectangle	pellet
Robert Breading	Db	1782	1782	1816	R	rectangle	–
Robert Boulger	Ch	–	1787	1802	R	rectangle	–
Roger Biggs	L	1791	–	1793	R	rectangle	pellet
Robert Barker	L	1793	–	1794	R	bifoil	pellet
Richard Buckton	L	1806	–	1807	R	rectangle	–
Richard Britton	L	1812	1817	1830	R	rectangle	–
	L	–	–	–	R	rectangle	pellet
R & B							
G. Roberts & E. Briggs	S	1859	1835	1903	R	rectangle	–
	L	–	–	–	–	–	GR EB

Maker's initial(s) & maker(s)	Town of registration	Date of mark registration	Earliest example	Latest example	Letter style G Gothic R Roman S Script	Punch shape	Additional features/notes
S. Roberts & C. Belk	S	1864	1865	1975	R	rectangle	–
	S	1864	–	–	R	3 bevelled squares	–
	S	1867	–	–	–	–	SR CB
	S	1879	–	–	–	–	CB EP
R B & R Rundell, Bridge & Rundell	L	1804	1810	1828	R	domate rectangle	crown
R C Robert Calderwood	Db	1727	1728	1729	R	oval	–
	Db	1727	–	–	R	concave archform	fleur de lis
Robert Albin Cox	L	1752	1749	1759	R	rectangle	pellet
	L	1759	–	–	S	rectangle	–
	L	–	–	–	G	bifoil	–
	L	–	–	–	R	rectangle	pellet
	L	–	–	–	S	bifoil	–
	L	1758	–	–	–	–	RA Cox (RA monogram)
Robert Clark	Ed	1763	1765	1766	R	rectangle	–
Robert Cruickshank	L	c1773	1782	1804	R	rectangle	–
Richard Crossley	L	1782	1782	1812	R	rectangle	–
Richard Cooke	L	1799	1798	1811	R	quatrefoil	pellet
Randall Chatterton	L	1825	1825	1843	R	rectangle	–
R C & Co Roberts, Cadman & Co	S	1786	1792	1826	R	rectangle	pellet
	S	1786	–	–	–	–	SR GC & Co
R C **D S** **R S** Richard Carter, Daniel Smith & Robert Sharp	L	1778	1777	1788	R	quadriform	–
R C **G S** Richard Crossley & George Smith IV	L	1807	1806	1815	R	square	–
R C **J B** Robert Cattle & J. Barber	Y	–	1807	1814	R	bevelled square	–

Maker's initial(s) & maker(s)	Town of registration	Date of mark registration	Earliest example	Latest example	Letter style G Gothic R Roman S Script	Punch shape	Additional features/notes
R D R. Duncan of Carlisle	Nc	–	1833	1834	R	oval	–
R & D John Robertson & David Darling	Nc	–	1795	1801	R	rectangle	–
	Nc	–	–	–	–	–	IR DD
Roberts & Doré	L	–	–	1971	–	–	–
R E Joshua Readshaw	L	1697	1698	1709	R	lobate chinoid	3 fleurs de lis, pellet
Richard Edwards	L	1723	1716	1717	R	trifid rectangle	crown
	L	1716	–	–	–	–	Ed
Richard Evans of Shrewsbury	L	1779	–	–	R	rectangle	–
	B	1787	–	–	R	rectangle	–
Robert Garrard II	L	1818	1825	1880	G	rectangle	RE
	L	1822	–	–	–	–	RG
Re John Read	L	1704	1704	1711	G	invected triad	crown, fleur de lis
R E A John Robinson, Samuel S. Edkins & Thomas Aston	B	1834	1827	1847	R	rectangle	2 pellets
R E E B Rebecca Emes & Edward Barnard I	L	1808	1804	1859	R	quatrefoil	–
R E W E Rebecca & William Emes	L	1808	1804	1838	S	quatrefoil	2 pellets
R F Ralph Frith	L	1728	1728	–	R	rectangle	pellet
	L	1728	–	–	–	–	FR
Richard Ferris	Ex	–	1794	1822	R	rectangle	–
R G Robert Gylmyn	Y	1550	1562	1605	R	delphate archform	–

Maker's initial(s) & maker(s)	Town of registration	Date of mark registration	Earliest example	Latest example	Letter style G Gothic R Roman S Script	Punch shape	Additional features/notes
Robert Goble	Co	–	1696	–	R	cleft escutcheon	–
	Co	–	–	–	R	ogee triad	3 pellets, mullet
	Co	–	–	–	R	domate triad	2 pellets
	Co	–	–	–	R	domate cleftform	mullet
	Co	–	–	–	R	quatrefoil	2 mullets
	Co	–	–	–	R	domate archform	mullet
	Co	–	–	–	R	engrailed invectoid	–
	Co	–	–	–	R	rectangle	–
	Co	–	–	–	R	ogee bipod	–
Richard Gines	L	1720	1693	1725	R	waved triad	2 mullets
	L	1698	–	–	–	–	GI
Richard Green	L	1726	1703	1730	R	heart	fleur de lis
	L	1703	–	–	–	–	GR (R within)
Richard Gosling	L	1733	1734	1760	R	globate rectangle	crown, pellet
	L	1739	–	–	S	globate ovoid	crown
	L	–	–	–	S	globate biloboid	pellet
Robert Gordon	Ed	1741	1743	1762	S	ovate loboid	crown
Richard Goldwire of Oxford	L	1753	–	1761	R	rectangle	–
	L	1763	–	–	R	profiloid	fleur de lis, pellet
Richard Gardner	L	–	1770	1785	R	bifoil	–
Robert Gray	G	1776	1776	1846	R	rectangle	–
	G	–	–	–	R	profiloid	–
Robert Green	Ch	–	1790	1803	R	rectangle	–
Robert Gaze	L	1795	1794	1804	R	rectangle	–
Richard Gregory & Co	S	1797	–	1819	R	rectangle	–
Robert Garrard I	L	1802	1807	1828	R	rectangle	pellet
Robert Gainsford	S	1808	1808	1840	R	ogee escutcheon	–
	S	1808	–	–	R	rectangle	–
Robert Garrard II	L	1822	1825	1880	S	globate rectangle	crown
	L	1818	–	–	–	–	RE
Richard Garde of Cork	Db	–	1825	1830	R	rectangle	pellet
R G H R. G. Hennell	L	–	c1880	–	R	rectangle	–
R G & S Robert Gray & Sons of Glasgow	Gl	1819	1804	1847	R	square	–
	Gl	1819	–	–	R	rectangle	–
	Ed	–	–	–	–	–	RG &S

Maker's initial(s) & maker(s)	Town of registration	Date of mark registration	Earliest example	Latest example	Letter style G Gothic R Roman S Script	Punch shape	Additional features/notes
R^T_CG							
Richard Gurney & Thomas Cooke II	L	1727	1727	1768	R	quatrefoil	pellet
Richard Gurney & Co	L	1739	1736	1761	S	quatrefoil	–
R H							
Robert Harrington	Y	1616	1625	1638	R	invected triad	drop
Charles Rhoades	Y	1677	1678	1707	R	quatrefoil	–
	Y	1677	–	–	–	–	CR
Richard Hutchinson II of Colchester	L	1727	*	*	R	profiloid	fleur de lis, 2 pellets
Robert Hill	L	1730	1719	–	R	circle	mullet
	L	1740	–	–	S	circle	2 pellets
	L	1717	–	–	–	–	Hi
Richard Hussey	L	–	1758	–	R	rectangle	pellet
Robert Hennell I	L	1772	1772	*	R	oval	–
	L	1773	–	–	R	oval	pellet
Richard Hoskins of Bristol	L	1791	–	1798	R	rectangle	–
Robert Hennell II	L	1809	–	–	R	ovoid	–
	L	1820	–	–	R	rectangle	–
	L	1826	–	–	R	rectangle	–
Robert Hennell III	L	1834	1835	1859	R	rectangle	pellet
Robert Harper	L	–	1844	1882	R	bifoil	–
William Hutton & Sons	S	1866	1874	1956	R	oval	–
	S	1836	1838	1956	–	–	WH
	L	–	1881	1956	–	–	SHLd &
Robert Hennell IV	L	1869	1856	1872	R	rectangle	–
	L	1869	–	–	R	ovoid	–
	L	1870	–	–	R	rectangle	–
R & H							
Roberts & Hall	S	1847	1849	1853	R	rectangle	–
R H **D H**							
Robert I & David II Hennell	L	1795	1763	1810	R	square	–
	L	1763	–	–	–	–	D^R_HH
R H **D H** **S H**							
Robert I, David II & Samuel Hennell	L	1802	1801	1802	R	bevelled quadriform	–

Maker's initial(s) & maker(s)	Town of registration	Date of mark registration	Earliest example	Latest example	Letter style G Gothic R Roman S Script	Punch shape	Additional features/notes
R H							
S H							
Robert I & Samuel Hennell	L	1802	1795	1812	R	bevelled square	–
R I							
Robert Inglis	Ed	1686	1692	1719	R	heart	pellet, ogee
Richard Joyes II	Gy	–	1695	1725	R	multifoil	pellet
	Gy	–	–	–	R	rectangle	–
Christopher Riley	L	1697	1694	–	R	ogee triad	2 fleurs de lis, 4 pellets
Isaac Ribouleau	L	1724	1724	1730	R	globate rectangle	crescent
	L	1724	–	–	–	–	IR
Robert Innes	L	1743	1743	1756	R	rectangle	pellet
	L						
Robert Jones I	L	1774	1773	1791	R	bifoil	pellet
	L	1778	–	–	R	rectangle	pellet
Robert Jones	Ch	–	1788	1807	R	rectangle	pellet
	Ch	–	–	–	R	ovoid	pellet
Ri							
Edmond Richards	Ex	–	1694	1736	S	circle	–
Richard Richardson I	Ch	–	1701	*	R	square	–
	Ch	–	–	–	R	ogee chinoid	–
	Ch	–	–	–	R	ovoid	–
	Ch	–	–	–	–	–	RR
	Ch	–	–	–	–	–	RR (monogram)
R I							
I S							
Robert Jones I & John Scofield	L	1776	1771	1777	R	square	2 pellets
	L	–	–	–	R	square	–
R K							
Rowland Kirby	Y	1666	1671	1684	R	hexagon	2 pellets
Richard Kersill	L	1744	1744	1746	R	rectangle	pellet
R. Kippax	S	1774	1775	1802	R	rectangle	pellet
	S	1774	–	–	–	–	RK &Co
Robert Keay I	P	1791	1799	1839	R	rectangle	–
Robert Keay II	P	1825	1825	–	R	oval	–
R K							
& Co							
R. Kippax & Co	S	1774	1775	1802	R	square	pellet
	S	1774	–	–	–	–	RK
R L							
Robert Luke	Gl	1721	1725	1752	R	rectangle	–

Maker's initial(s) & maker(s)	Town of registration	Date of mark registration	Earliest example	Latest example	Letter style G Gothic R Roman S Script	Punch shape	Additional features/notes
Robert Lucas	L	1727	1727	1740	R	oval	pellet, 2 mullets
	L	1739	–	–	S	rectangle	–
R L **I D** Richard Lockwood & John Douglas	L	1800	–	1802	R	square	–
R M Robert Makepeace I	Nc	1718	1722	1779	G	rectangle	–
	Nc	–	–	–	R	rectangle	pellet
Ralph Maidman	L	1731	1729	1734	R	oval	crown, pellet
Richard Mills	L	1755	1755	1776	R	rectangle	pellet
	L	1758	–	–	R	bifoil	pellet
	L	1767	–	–	S	rectangle	–
Richard Meach	L	1765	1771	1783	R	rectangle	pellet
	L	1774	–	–	R	rectangle	–
Richard Morton & Co	S	1773	1773	1819	R	rectangle	pellet
	S	1773	–	–	R	oval	pellet
	S	–	–	–	–	–	RM &Co
Robert Makepeace II	L	1795	1795	1810	R	rectangle	–
Robert Metham	L	1808	–	1810	R	rectangle	pellet
R M **& Co** Richard Morton & Co	S	1773	1773	1819	R	square	–
	S	1773	–	–	–	–	RM
R M **B S** Richard Morson & Benjamin Stephenson	L	1762	1773	1774	R	square	–
R M **E H** Martin Hall & Co	L	–	1848	1945	R	quatrefoil	–
	S	1854	–	–	R	quatrefoil	–
	S	–	–	–	–	lozenge	–
	S	1854	–	–	–	–	MH &Co
R M **R C** Robert Makepeace I & Richard Carter	L	1777	1766	1778	R	square	–
R M **T M** Robert II & Thomas II Makepeace	L	1794	1793	1794	R	square	–

Maker's initial(s) & maker(s)	Town of registration	Date of mark registration	Earliest example	Latest example	Letter style G Gothic R Roman S Script	Punch shape	Additional features/notes
R O							
Hugh Roberts	L	1697	1697	1700	R	heart	–
Alexander Roode	L	1697	1702	1718	R	arched cuspoid	2 trilobes, 2 pellets
Philip Rollos I	L	1697	1699	1714	R	circle	6 pellets
Philip Roker I	L	–	1697	–	R	heart	3 trefoils
	L	1697	–	–	–	–	Ro
Philip Rollos II	L	1705	1705	1716	R	octagon	anchor
	L	1720	–	–	–	–	PR
Ebenezer Roe	L	1709	1709	1716	R	trefoil	deer
James Rood(e)	L	1710	1710	1720	R	bifoil	–
Gundry Roode	L	1710	1711	1735	R	heart	mullet
	L	1721	–	–	–	–	GR
Nathaniel Roe	L	–	1716	–	R	stepped triad	stag's head
Philip Roker II	L	1720	–	1769	R	profiloid	crown, floret
	L	1720	–	–	–	–	PR
Mary Rood(e)	L	1721	1722	1725	R	lozenge	2 pellets
	L	1721	–	–	–	–	MR
John Robinson I	L	1723	–	1728	R	globate globoid	mullet, fleur de lis
	L	1723	–	–	–	–	IR
Ro							
Thomas Robinson	Ch	–	1682	1719	R	ogee triad	–
Philip Roker I	L	1697	1697	*	G	invected triad	pellet
	L	–	–	–	–	–	RO
Philip Robinson	L	1714	–	1723	R	quatrefoil	2 mullets
	L	1723	–	–	–	–	PR
R P							
Richard Pargeter	L	1730	1727	1746	R	rectangle	–
	L	1737	–	–	R	oval	–
	L	1739	–	–	G	rectangle	–
Robert Pertt (*or* Perth)	L	1738	1748	1754	R	rectangle	–
	L	–	–	–	S	rectangle	–
Richard Palmer	L	1759	1761	1765	R	rectangle	pellet
	L	–	–	–	–	–	incuse
	L	1780	–	–	–	cameo	–
	L	1795	–	–	–	cameo	pellet
Robert Peaston	L	1762	1759	1780	R	rectangle	fleur de lis
	L	–	–	–	R	rectangle	mullet
Robert Piercy	L	1775	1762	1782	R	rectangle	–
	L	–	–	–	R	rectangle	pellet
Richard Pearce	L	1812	1812	1824	R	rectangle	–

Maker's initial(s) & maker(s)	Town of registration	Date of mark registration	Earliest example	Latest example	Letter style G Gothic R Roman S Script	Punch shape	Additional features/notes
Robert Peppin	L	1817	1817	1834	R	rectangle	–
	L	1817	–	–	R	rectangle	pellet
	L	1829	–	–	R	oval	–
Richard Pouldon	L	1818	1819	1824	R	rectangle	pellet
R P **G B** Richard Pearce & George Burrows II	L	1826	1826	1851	R	square	2 pellets
R P **R S** Robert Pinckney & Robert Scott	Nc	–	1779	1790	R	square	–
	Nc	–	–	–	–	–	P & S
R R Richard Richardson I	Ch	–	1701	*	R	rectangle	–
	Ch	–	–	–	R	ogee chinoid	pellet
	Ch	–	–	–	R	invected invectoid	–
	Ch	–	–	–	–	–	ℜℜ (conjoined)
	Ch	–	–	–	–	–	Ri
Robert Rew	L	1754	1758	1783	R	rectangle	pellet
Richard Rugg	L	1754	1755	1782	R	rectangle	pellet
	L	1775	–	–	R	bifoil	pellet
Richard Richardson II	Ch	–	1756	1784	R	spikeform	–
	Ch	–	–	–	R	rectangle	–
Robert Rutland	L	1807	1807	1826	R	rectangle	–
	L	1824	–	–	R	oval	–

ℜℜ (conjoined)

Maker's initial(s) & maker(s)	Town of registration	Date of mark registration	Earliest example	Latest example	Letter style G Gothic R Roman S Script	Punch shape	Additional features/notes
Richard Richardson I	Ch	–	1701	*	R	ogee hatchment	–
	Ch	–	–	–	R	circle	–
	Ch	–	–	–	–	–	RR
	Ch	–	–	–	–	–	Ri

Maker's initial(s) & maker(s)	Town of registration	Date of mark registration	Earliest example	Latest example	Letter style G Gothic R Roman S Script	Punch shape	Additional features/notes
R R **A R** **I M H** Hunt & Roskell (Robert Roskell, Allen Roskell & John Mortimer Hunt)	L	1882	1842	1915	R	–	crown
	L	1842	–	–	–	–	ISH
	L	1865	–	–	–	–	IH RR
	L	1889	–	–	–	–	H^{A}H^{B}W
	L	1895	–	–	–	–	A^{A}H^{B}B
	L	1897	–	–	–	–	H & R Ltd
R & RK R. & R. Keay	P	–	1836	–	R	rectangle	–
R S Robert Smith	Db	–	1714	–	R	bifoil	–
Richard Scarlett	L	1720	1723	1732	R	crested triad	crown
	L	1723	–	–	R	ovate triloboid	crown
	L	1719	–	–	–	–	SC
Robert Swanson	L	1743	1743	1769	R	rectangle	–
Robert Salmon	L	1773	1779	1805	R	rectangle	–
R. Sutcliffe & Co	S	1781	1789	1796	R	rectangle	–
Robert Sharp	L	1788	1785	1805	R	rectangle	–
Robert Smith	Db	–	1791	1857	R	ovoid	–
Richard Sibley I	L	1805	1800	1872	R	concave rectangle	pellet
	L	1812	–	–	S	rectangle	–
Richard Sawyer I	Db	1807	1797	–	R	rectangle	–
Richard Sawyer II	Db	1830	–	1846	R	rectangle	pellet
R. Sherwin	Db	1836	–	1850	R	rectangle	–
Robert Stewart	Gl	1842	1842	1876	R	bifoil	–
Robert Scott	Gl	–	1897	–	R	oval	pellet
R & S Roberts & Slater	S	1844	1845	1858	R	rectangle	–
R S **& Co** Robert Sporle & Co	S	1792	–	1794	R	rectangle	–
R T Robert Tyrill	L	1742	–	1743	R	rectangle	pellet
R. Tricket	S	1773	1775	1803	R	rectangle	pellet
	S	1786	–	–	R	ovoid	pellet
	S	1786	–	–	–	–	RT & Co

Maker's initial(s) & maker(s)	Town of registration	Date of mark registration	Earliest example	Latest example	Letter style G Gothic R Roman S Script	Punch shape	Additional features/notes
Richard Tudor	Db	–	1775	1791	R	rectangle	pellet
R T & Co							
R. Tricket & Co	S	1786	1775	1803	R	rectangle	–
	S	1773	–	–	–	–	RT
R$_B$BT							
Bennett Bradshaw & Robert Tyrill	L	1737	1736	1740	R	arched chinoid	pellet
	L	1739	–	–	–	–	B$_R$TB
R U							
John Ruslen	L	1697	1701	1703	R	oval	crown, pellet
	L	1697	–	–	R	circle	crown, pellet
R W							
Robert Williamson	Y	1623	1623	1679	R	hexagon	mullet
	Y	–	–	–	R	heart	mullet
	Y	–	–	–	R	ogee loboid	mullet
Ralph Walley	Ch	–	1682	1692	R	ogee chinoid	–
Richard Watts	L	1720	1710	1720	R	globate triad	pellet, floret
	L	1720	–	–	R	globate rectangle	crown
	L	–	–	–	R	rectangle	–
	L	1710	–	–	–	–	Wa
Robert Williams	L	1726	1724	1728	R	globate rectangle	mitre, pellet
	L	1726	–	–	–	–	WI
Richard Williams	Db	1752	1767	1800	R	rectangle	pellet
Robert Wyke	Db	1784	1781	–	R	oval	thread oval
Robert Williams	Db	1789	1789	1798	R	oval	–
Richard Whitford	Db	1802	1799	1827	R	rectangle	–
R & W							
Robb & Whittet	Ed	–	1839	1876	R	invected escutcheon	–
R W J W J W							
Robert James & Josiah Williams	Ex	–	1847	1852	R	quadriform	–
RWR (conjoined)							
William Robinson	Nc	1666	1656	1698	R	profiloid	crown
	Nc	–	–	–	–	–	WR (conjoined)
R & W S							
R. & W. Sorley	Gl	–	1896	1927	R	rectangle	–

Maker's initial(s) & maker(s)	Town of registration	Date of mark registration	Earliest example	Latest example	Letter style G Gothic R Roman S Script	Punch shape	Additional features/notes
R Z Richard Zouch	L	1735	1734	1740	R	globate rectangle	fleur de lis, pellet
	L	1739	–	–	S	globate rectangle	mullet, pellet
S Alexander Sinclair	Db	1694	1700	1718	R	trifid escutcheon	crown
S A Thomas Sadler	L	1701	1701	1719	R	profiloid	lion erased
	L	1701	–	–	R	invected profiloid	lion erased
	L	–	–	–	–	–	TS
John Sanders I	L	1717	1717	1746	R	globate globoid	2 pellets
	L	1720	–	–	–	–	IS
John Hugh Le Sage	L	1718	1719	1749	R	trifid triad	crown, floret, pellet
	L	1722	–	–	–	–	IS
Stephen Adams I	L	1760	1765	1819	R	rectangle	pellet
Stephen Adams II	L	1792	1811	–	R	rectangle	–
Sa Thomas Sampson	Ex	1706	1707	1728	R	circle	crown
S B Samuel Blachford of Plymouth	Ex	1706	1720	1730	R	trifid biloboid	crown
	Ex	–	–	–	–	–	BL
Sampson Bennet of Falmouth	Ex	1721	1734	1759	R	ovoid	–
Stephen Buckle(s)	Nc	–	1740	1741	R	ovoid	pellet
Susanna Barker	L	1778	1770	1792	R	rectangle	–
	L	1789	–	–	R	rectangle	pellet
Sarah Buttall	L	1754	–	1790	R	lozenge	–
	L	–	–	–	G	rectangle	pellet
	L	–	–	–	R	rectangle	–
S. Bergin	Db	–	1815	1822	R	rectangle	–
Samuel Beere	Db	1818	1821	1829	R	rectangle	–
S B **G G** Barclay & Goodwin	Gl	–	1852	–	R	square	–
S B **I B** Sarah & John William Blake	L	1809	1810	1821	R	square	–
	L	1821	–	–	–	–	–

Maker's initial(s) & maker(s)	Town of registration	Date of mark registration	Earliest example	Latest example	Letter style G Gothic R Roman S Script	Punch shape	Additional features/notes
S C							
William Scarlett	L	1697	1689	1727	R	ogee triad	2 mullets
	L	1720	–	–	–	–	W S
	L	1725	–	–	–	–	WS
Richard Scarlett	L	1719	1723	1732	R	globate rectangle	crown, floret, 2 pellets
	L	1720	–	–	–	–	RS
Samuel Courtauld I	L	1746	1747	1764	R	trefoil	mullet, pellet
	L	1751	–	–	R	ovoid	pellet
Simeon Coley	L	1761	1763	1812	R	rectangle	pellet
	L	1763	–	–	R	rectangle	–
Sebastian Crespel II	L	1826	1825	1854	R	rectangle	–
S C **I C**							
Sebastian I & James Crespel	L	–	1761	1776	R	quadriform	mullet, pellet
S C Y & Co							
S.C. Young & Co	S	1811	1811	1836	R	rectangle	–
S D							
Sandylands Drinkwater	L	1735	–	1740	R	bifoil	mullet
	L	–	–	–	S	profiloid	crown
Samuel Davenport	L	1786	1786	1826	R	rectangle	–
Samuel Dutton	L	1823	–	1824	R	rectangle	–
Stuart Devlin	L	–	1959	1969	–	oval	–
S D **E D**							
Samuel & Edward Davenport	L	1794	1786	1815	R	square	–
S E							
Samuel Eaton	L	1736	–	1764	R	oval	pellet
	L	1759	–	–	R	rectangle	–
	L	–	–	–	R	rectangle	pellet
	L	–	–	–	S	rectangle	–
Se							
James Seabrook	L	1714	1711	1720	G	domate loboid	2 mullets
	L	1720	–	–	–	–	IS
S G							
Samuel Godbehere	L	1784	1785	1789	R	rectangle	pellet

Maker's initial(s) & maker(s)	Town of registration	Date of mark registration	Earliest example	Latest example	Letter style G Gothic R Roman S Script	Punch shape	Additional features/notes
S G **E W** Samuel Godbehere & Edward Wigan	L	1786	1786	1813	R	square	pellet
S G **E W** **I B** Samuel Godbehere, Edward Wigan & James Bult	L	1800	1801	1807	R	quadriform	–
S G **T H** George Smith II & Thomas Hayter	L	1792	1791	1818	R	square	–
S_{**W**}**G** Samuel II & George Whitford	L	1802	1802	1807	R	square	–
S & G Smith & Gamble	Db	1822	1825	1837	R	bifoil	–
	Db	–	–	–	R	rectangle	–
S H Joseph Sheene	L	1697	1676	1705	R	cambered triad	trefoil, pellet
Alice Sheene	L	1700	1703	1714	R	lozenge	fleur de lis, pellet
Samuel Hitchcock	L	1720	1715	1729	R	hatchment	fleur de lis
	L	1730	–	–	R	lobate hatchment	fleur de lis
	L	1713	–	–	–	–	HI
Samuel Hutton	L	1724	1726	1736	R	hatchment	heart, pellet
	L	1740	–	–	G	[stepform]	pellet
	L	1725	–	–	–	–	HU
Sarah Holaday	L	1725	1721	1729	R	lozenge	mullet, fleur de lis
	L	1719	–	–	–	–	HO
William Shaw I	L	1729	1730	1774	R	oval	–
	L	1728	–	–	–	–	WS
Samuel Herbert	L	1747	1750	1775	S	trifid escutcheon	pellet
Solomon Howland	L	1760	1765	1767	R	quatrefoil	pellet
	L	1760	–	–	R	rectangle	–
Samuel Harbert (Harbet?)	L	1771	1789	1793	R	rectangle	–
Solomon Hougham	L	1793	1793	1817	R	rectangle	–
Simon Harris	L	1795	1794	1816	R	bifoil	pellet
	L	1795	–	–	R	rectangle	pellet

Maker's initial(s) & maker(s)	Town of registration	Date of mark registration	Earliest example	Latest example	Letter style G Gothic R Roman S Script	Punch shape	Additional features/notes
Samuel Hennell	L	1811	1790	1821	R	concave rectangle	pellet
Samuel Harwood	S	1835	1835	1839	R	rectangle	–
S h							
Nathaniel Shaw	Nc	–	1715	1741	R	stepped biloboid	billet, 2 pellets
S & H							
Sansom & Harwood	S	1833	1829	–	R	rectangle	–
S H Ld **&**							
William Hutton & Sons Ltd	L	–	1881	1956	S	cambered plinthform	–
	B	–	1899	1927	–	–	–
	S	1836	1838	1956	–	–	WH
	S	1866	–	–	–	–	RH
	Ch	–	–	1911	–	–	–
S H **D C**							
Samuel Hayne & Dudley Cater	L	1836	1837	1861	S	square	–
	L	1837	–	–	R	square	–
S$_B^H$H							
Samuel Herbert & Co	L	1750	–	–	R	cruciform	pellet
S H **I T**							
Samuel Hennell & John Terrey	L	1814	1814	–	R	square	–
S H **S R** **I E D**							
Solomon Hougham, Solomon Royes & John East Dix	L	1817	1817	1818	R	quadriform	4 pellets
S I							
Francis Singleton	L	1697	1698	1702	R	escutcheon	billet
Simon Jouet	L	1725	1726	1756	R	circle	crown
	L	1739	–	–	–	–	SJ
	L	–	–	–	–	–	IO
Samuel James	Nc	–	1759	1769	R	concave ovoid	cup
	Nc	–	–	–	R	rectangle	–
S$_G^{LI}$							
Samuel Laundy & Jeffery Griffith	L	1731	1731	–	R	oval	floret

Maker's initial(s) & maker(s)	Town of registration	Date of mark registration	Earliest example	Latest example	Letter style G Gothic R Roman S Script	Punch shape	Additional features/notes
S J							
Simon Jouet	L	1739	1726	1756	G	ovoid	–
	L	1748	–	–	S	multifoil	–
	L	1725	–	–	–	–	SI
	L	–	–	–	–	–	IO
S J P							
S.J. Phillips Ltd	L	–	1900	1974	S	trefoil	crown
S K							
Samuel Kirkby & Co	S	1784	1799	1806	R	rectangle	pellet
Samuel Knight	L	1816	1816	1817	R	rectangle	–
S L							
Gabriel Sleath	L	1707	1709	1752	R	globate biloboid	sheaf
	L	1707	–	–	R	ogee triad	pellet
	L	1720	–	–	–	–	GS
Samuel Lee	L	1720	1698	1712	R	ogee escutcheon	crown
	L	1701	–	–	–	–	LE
Samuel Laundy	L	1727	1728	1730	R	crested rectangle	crown
	L	1727	–	–	R	oval	3 pellets
Simon Le Sage	L	1754	1753	1760	S	domate triad	cup, pellet, mullet
	L	1754	–	–	S	rectangle	pellet
Simon Lery	Ex	–	1823	1828	R	rectangle	–
S L'B							
Samuel Le Bass	Db	1859	1859	1870	R	rectangle	2 pellets
S M							
John Smithsend	L	1697	–	1698	R	invected square	2 annulets, pellet
John Smith I	L	1697	–	1703	R	ogee triad	bird, mullet
	L	1697	–	–	R	ovate rectangle	crown, floret
Benjamin Smith I	L	1706	–	–	R	circle	M (smaller)
Joseph Smith I	L	1707	1728	1742	R	ogee chinoid	2 pellets
	L	1720	–	–	–	–	IS
James Smith I	L	1718	1718	1746	R	circle	mullet
	L	1720	–	–	–	–	IS
Samuel Smith II	L	1719	*	*	R	trifid triad	2 fleurs de lis
Samuel Margas	L	1721	1705	1717	R	trifid triad	crown, fleur de lis
	L	1715	–	–	–	–	MA
Samuel Meriton I	L	1739	1747	*	R	concave archform	–
	L	1746	–	–	R	ovoid	pellet
Samuel Meriton II	L	1775	1773	1781	R	rectangle	–
Samuel Massey	L	1773	1760	1796	R	rectangle	cameo
	L	1780	–	–	R	rectangle	cameo

Maker's initial(s) & maker(s)	Town of registration	Date of mark registration	Earliest example	Latest example	Letter style G Gothic R Roman S Script	Punch shape	Additional features/notes
Sampson Mordan & Co	L (*also* B & Ch)	–	1855	1937	–	–	–
Sm Samuel Smith I	L	1700	*	*	S	cleft loboid	mitre, pellet, crescent
S N Samuel Neville	Db	1795	1796	1837	R	rectangle	pellet
	Db	–	–	–	R	rectangle	–
Stephen Noad	L	1806	–	1826	R	rectangle	–
S O William Soame	L	1723	–	1762	R	oval	pellet
	L	1723	–	–	–	–	WS
SOBEY William R. Sobey	Ex	–	1831	1855	R	rectangle	–
	Ex	1835	–	–	–	–	WRS
S P William Spackman	L	1714	1717	1726	R	ogee cuspoid	2 annulets, pellet, bird
	L	–	–	–	R	ogee cuspoid	3 pellets, bird
	L	1720	–	–	–	–	WS
Simon Pantin I	L	1720	1702	1732	R	globate concave rectangle	peacock
	L	1701	–	–	–	–	PA
Hugh Spring	L	1721	1721	–	R	domate rectangle	mullet
	L	1722	–	–	–	–	HS
Sarah Parr	L	1728	–	1732	R	lozenge	–
Simon Pantin II	L	1729	–	1732	R	globate rectangle	peacock pellet
Francis Spilsbury I	L	1739	1729	1776	G	heart	mullet
	L	1729	–	–	–	–	FS
Samuel Pemberton	B	1778	1781	1823	R	rectangle	–
	B	–	–	–	R	oval	–
	B	–	–	–	S	rectangle	–
Sydenham William Peppin	L	1816	1815	1817	R	rectangle	–
Sarah Purver	L	1817	1817	1819	R	rectangle	pellet
Sp Thomas Spackman	L	1700	1703	1714	S	cleft triad	2 pellets
	L	1700	–	–	R	cleft chinoid	–
	L	–	–	–	R	cleft chinoid	2 pellets
William Spring	L	1701	1704	1706	R	oval	thread oval, flower stem
	L	1701	–	–	G	oval	2 pellets

Maker's initial(s) & maker(s)	Town of registration	Date of mark registration	Earliest example	Latest example	Letter style G Gothic R Roman S Script	Punch shape	Additional features/notes
S Q							
George Squire	L	1720	–	1726	R	oval	–
	L	1720	–	–	–	–	GS
S R							
Samuel Roby	L	1740	1740	1745	R	rectangle	–
Solomon Royes	L	1820	1820	1821	R	rectangle	–
S R & Co							
Samuel Roberts & Co	S	1773	1773	1837	R	rectangle	pellet
S. Roberts Smith & Co	S	1826	–	1828	R	rectangle	pellet
S R **C B**							
Roberts & Belk	S	1869	1865	1975	R	square	–
	S	1864	–	–	–	–	R & B
	S	1879	–	–	–	–	CB EP
I^S^E^R^D							
Solomon Royes & John East Dix	L	1818	1818	1819	R	square	–
S R **G C & Co**							
Roberts Cadman & Co	S	1786	1792	1826	R	taperform	–
	S	1786	–	–	–	–	RC & Co
S S							
Samuel Smith III	L	1754	–	1755	R	profiloid	pellet
Samuel Siervent	L	1755	–	1762	R	concave archform	pellet
Stephen Smith & Co	L	–	1858	1885	R	oval	–
S & S							
Thomas Simpson & Son	B	1809	1810	1820	R	rectangle	–
James Smith & Son	S	1829	1829	1831	R	rectangle	–
	S	1829	–	–	–	–	₅ SMI ₅ TH
₅ SMI ₅ **TH**							
James Smith & Son .	S	1829	1829	1831	R	3 rectangles	–
	S	1829	–	–	–	–	S & S
S^E^S^D^D							
S. S. & E. Drew	L	–	1891	1926	–	[shield]	–

Maker's initial(s) & maker(s)	Town of registration	Date of mark registration	Earliest example	Latest example	Letter style G Gothic R Roman S Script	Punch shape	Additional features/notes
S T							
Joseph Stokes	L	1697	–	1701	R	heart	–
Joseph Steward I	L	1719	–	1739	R	trifid triad	2 pellets
	L	1720	–	–	–	–	IS
Samuel Taylor	L	1744	1749	1772	S	heart	–
Samuel Thompson	Nc	–	1750	1785	S	rectangle	–
St							
John Martin Stockar	L	1697	1697	1714	R	trigon	3 annulets
	L	1710	–	–	G	bevelled square	thread, bevelled square
Robert Stokes (?)	L	1698	1698	1704	R	domate triad	–
Ambrose Stevenson	L	1707	1708	1720	R	globate circle	mullet, pellet
	L	1720	–	–	–	–	AS
H S & T T							
Smith, Tate, Hoult & Tate	S	–	1811	1828	R	square	–
S & T N & H							
G. Smith, R. Tate, W. Nicholson & E. Holt	S	1810	1810	1826	R	bevelled square	–
St Pe							
John Martin Stockar & Edward Peacock	L	1705	1707	1709	G	tridentate triad	–
S U							
Thomas Sutton	Db	–	1717	1740	R	bifoil	–
	Db	–	–	–	–	–	TS
	Db	1720	–	–	–	–	U S
2 Suns							
Matthew Boulton	S	1784	1776	1832	–	–	2 suns
	B	–	–	–	–	–	MB
S V							
Stephen Venables	L	–	1640	1665	R	trifid triad	–
John Sutton	L	1697	1671	1708	R	oval	thread oval, dotted oval
S V / T V							
Samuel & Thomas Varden	L	1775	1784	1785	R	square	–

Maker's initial(s) & maker(s)	Town of registration	Date of mark registration	Earliest example	Latest example	Letter style G Gothic R Roman S Script	Punch shape	Additional features/notes
S W							
Starling Wilford	L	1720	1722	1734	R	ogee chinoid	–
	L	1729	–	–	R	concave rectangle	–
	L (?)	–	–	–	R	rectangle	7 pellets
	L (?)	–	–	–	R	rectangle	2 pellets
	L	1718	–	–	–	–	WI
Samuel Welder	L	1720	1715	1738	R	bifoil	–
	L (?)	–	–	–	R	rectangle	7 pellets
	L (?)	–	–	–	R	rectangle	2 pellets
	L	–	–	–	–	–	We
Samuel Wastell	L	1722	1702	1722	R	chevroned rectangle	mitre
	L	1701	–	–	–	–	WA
Samuel Wood	L	1733	1725	1774	R	oval	pellet
	L	1739	–	–	S	profiloid	pellet
	L	1754	–	–	R	oval	pellet
	L	–	–	–	R	biloboid	pellet
	L	–	–	–	G	rectangle	–
Samuel Walker	Db	–	1738	1759	R	rectangle	–
Samuel Wight Welles	L	1741	1748	1760	S	circle	pellet
Samuel Wheat	L	1756	1757	1782	R	bifoil	–
	L	1757	–	–	R	biloboid	pellet
	L	–	–	–	G	rectangle	–
Samuel White	L (?)	1764	–	1766	R	rectangle	pellet
	L (?)	1759	–	–	G	rectangle	–
Samuel Whitford I	L	1764	1762	1825	R	rectangle	pellet
Samuel Whitford II	L	1800	1816	1864	R	rectangle	–
	L	1817	–	–	G	rectangle	–
Samuel Wheatley	L	1811	–	1819	R	rectangle	–
S W **& Co**							
Samuel Walker & Co	S	1836	1836	1837	R	rectangle	–
S W **G P**							
Samuel Whitford II & George Pizey	L	1810	1810	–	R	square	–
S W **I E**							
Samuel Wheatley & John Evans I	L	1810	1810	–	R	square	–
S W S							
S. W. Smith & Co of Birmingham	L	–	1893	1919	R	tridentate escutcheon	–
	B	–	–	–	R	tridentate escutcheon	–

Maker's initial(s) & maker(s)	Town of registration	Date of mark registration	Earliest example	Latest example	Letter style G Gothic R Roman S Script	Punch shape	Additional features/notes
S Y							
Pentecost Symonds of Plymouth	Ex	1706	1706	1753	R	tridentate escutcheon	pellet, mullet
	Ex	–	–	–	–	–	PS
	Ex	–	–	–	–	–	Sy
Sy							
Pentecost Symonds of Plymouth	Ex	1706	1706	1753	G	bevelled quadriform	crown, floret
	Ex	–	–	–	G	oval	–
	Ex	–	–	–	G	circle	–
	Ex	–	–	–	–	–	SY
	Ex	–	–	–	–	–	PS
Richard Syng	L	1697	1698	1708	G	trifid triad	bird, fleur de lis
	L	–	–	–	G	oval	bird, fleur de lis
T							
James Taitt	Ed	1704	1729	1741	R	domate cuspoid	pellet
T A							
David Tanqueray	L	1713	1715	1724	R	globate globoid	floret, thistle
	L	–	–	–	–	–	DT
Anne Tanqueray	L	–	1726	1732	R	lozenge	floret, thistle
	L	–	–	–	–	–	AT
Thomas Appleby	Ch	–	1791	1812	R	concave archform	pellet
T B							
Thomas Bolton (*or* Boulton)	Db	1686	1696	1725	S	bevelled square	crown
	Db	–	–	–	–	–	TB (monogram)
	Db	–	–	–	–	–	B
Thomas Burridge	L	1720	1712	1732	R	oval	–
	L	1706	–	–	–	–	Bu
Thomas Bamford I	L	1720	1716	1732	R	ovoid	–
	L	1739	–	–	S	ogee escutcheon	–
	L	1720	–	–	–	–	Ba
Thomas Beezley	L	1755	1754	1755	R	rectangle	pellet
	L	–	–	–	R	delphate bipod	–
Thomas Brough	L	1795	1797	1814	R	rectangle	–
Thomas Wilkes Barker	L	1805	1804	1827	R	rectangle	–
	L	–	–	–	R	rectangle	pellet
	L (?)	–	–	–	R	quatrefoil	pellet
Thomas Biddell	L	1811	–	1813	R	rectangle	thread rectangle, pellet
Thomas Balliston	L	1812	1809	1825	R	rectangle	pellet
Thomas Ballam	L	1820	1823	1824	R	rectangle	pellet
Thomas Burwash	L	1821	–	1822	R	bifoil	pellet

Maker's initial(s) & maker(s)	Town of registration	Date of mark registration	Earliest example	Latest example	Letter style G Gothic RR Roman S Script	Punch shape	Additional features/notes
Thomas Byne	Ex	1855	1839	1849	R	rectangle	–
Thomas Bradbury of Sheffield	L	–	1892	1907	R	tridentate escutcheon	–
	S	–	–	–	–	–	see TB & Sons
TB (monogram)							
Thomas Bolton (or Boulton)	Db	1686	1696	1725	S	waved triad	–
	Db	–	–	–	–	–	TB
	Db	–	–	–	–	–	B
T B & Co							
Thomas Blagden & Co	S	1808	1808	1829	R	rectangle	pellet
T¡B e							
Robert Timbrell & Joseph Bell I	L	–	1710	1715	G	quatrefoil	–
T B & S							
Thomas Bradbury & Sons	S	1832	1839	1944	R	rectangle	–
	S	1858	–	–	–	–	T B & S
	S	1863	–	–	–	–	J B E B
	S	1867	–	–	–	–	J B T B
	L	–	–	–	–	–	T B
T B & S							
Thomas Bradbury & Sons	S	1858	1839	1944	R	tridentate escutcheon	–
	S	1832	–	–	–	–	T B & S
	S	1863	–	–	–	–	J B E B
	S	1867	–	–	–	–	J B T B
	L	–	–	–	–	–	TB
T O B I							
Thomas Bumfriss & Orlando Jackson	L	1766	1766	–	R	rectangle	–
T C							
Thomas Cumming	Gl	1682	1699	1704	R	chevroned engrailoid	inverted taurus
Thomas Cooke I	L	1727	–	–	R	domate rectangle	bird
	L	1713	–	–	–	–	CO

Maker's initial(s) & maker(s)	Town of registration	Date of mark registration	Earliest example	Latest example	Letter style G Gothic R Roman S Script	Punch shape	Additional features/notes
Thomas Chawner	L	1773	1766	1786	R	rectangle	–
	L	1773	–	–	R	rectangle	pellet
	L	1783	–	–	R	rectangle	pellet
C^TH J W	–	–	–	–	–	–	*see* C H J W
T C S Thomas Cox Savory	L	1827	1827	1831	R	rectangle	2 pellets
T C **W C** Thomas & William I Chawner	L	1765	1760	1771	R	square	2 pellets
	L	1763	–	–	–	–	W^T_CC
	L	1764	–	–	–	–	T^C_WW
	L	1768	–	–	–	–	T^W_CC
T^W_CC							
Thomas & William Chawner	L	1768	1760	1771	R	rectangle	–
	L	1763	–	–	–	–	W^T_CC
	L	1764	–	–	–	–	T^C_WW
	L	1765	–	–	–	–	T C W C
T D Tompson Davis	L	1757	1763	1764	R	circle	–
	L	1758	–	–	S	rectangle	–
Thomas Dealtry	L	1765	1771	1814	S	rectangle	–
Thomas Dene	L	1767	1767	1768	R	rectangle	pellet
Thomas Daniell	L	1774	1768	1790	R	rectangle	scroll rectangle
	L	1775	–	–	R	rectangle	–
	L	1782	–	–	R	ovoid	–
Thomas Duffus	Ed	1780	1788	1828	R	rectangle	–
Thomas Dicks	L	1792	1812	1834	R	rectangle	–
	L	1811	–	–	R	rectangle	pellet
	L	1798	–	–	R	oval	pellet
Thomas Davie	Gr	–	1795	1800	R	oval	–
Thomas Death	L	1812	1812	1832	R	rectangle	–
Thomas Paine Dexter	L	1805	1817	1837	R	ovoid	–
Thomas Diller	L	1828	1836	1850	R	bifoil	–

Maker's initial(s) & maker(s)	Town of registration	Date of mark registration	Earliest example	Latest example	Letter style G Gothic R Roman S Script	Punch shape	Additional features/notes
T D **I W** Thomas Daniell & John Wall	L	1781	1781	–	R	square	2 pellets
T D **J D** Thomas & James Dicks	L	1821	1821	–	R	square	–
T D **W W** Thomas Devonshire & William Watkins	L	1756	1757	1760	R	hatchment	pellet
	L	1756	–	–	R	oval	pellet
	L	1756	–	–	–	–	D & W
T E Thomas Tearle	L	1719	1718	1739	R	lozenge	mullet, fleur de lis
	L	1720	–	–	–	–	TT
Thomas England	L	1725	1727	1746	R	trigonate escutcheon	crown, pellet
	L	1739	–	–	S	ovoid	pellet
	L	1725	–	–	–	–	En
Thomas Evans	L	1774	1769	1785	R	rectangle	–
	L	–	–	–	R	rectangle	pellet
Thomas Eustace	Ex	1779	1780	1785	S	profiloid	2 pellets
	Ex	–	–	–	R	rectangle	–
	Ex	–	–	–	S	rectangle	pellet
Thomas Ellis	L	1780	1785	1805	R	bevelform	–
Thomas Edwards	L	1816	–	1827	R	oval	–
	L	1820	–	–	R	bevelform	pellet
T E **R S** Thomas Ellerton & Richard Sibley I	L	1803	–	1804	R	square	2 pellets
T F Thomas Farren	L	1720	1710	1742	R	domate lobus	fleur de lis, mullet
	L	1739	–	–	S	profiloid	–
	L	1707	–	–	–	–	FA
Thomas Folkingham	L	1721	1707	1734	R	kidney	pellet
	L	1707	–	–	–	–	FO
Thomas Fair	L	1768	–	1769	S	rectangle	–
Thomas Foster	L	1769	1768	1770	R	rectangle	pellet
	L	–	–	–	R	ovoid	–
	L	–	–	–	R	bevelform	pellet
	L	–	–	–	–	–	incuse

Maker's initial(s) & maker(s)	Town of registration	Date of mark registration	Earliest example	Latest example	Letter style G Gothic R Roman S Script	Punch shape	Additional features/notes
Thomas Freeth I	L	1773	–	1819	R	biloboid	pellet
Thomas Freeth II	L	1820	–	–	R	rectangle	–
T. Farnett	Db	–	1825	1831	R	rectangle	–
Thomas Freeman	S	1845	–	–	R	rectangle	–
	B	–	1838	–	–	–	–
T G Thomas Gilpin	L	1730	1737	1758	R	concave archform	–
	L	1739	–	–	S	ovate triad	oak twig, pellet
	L	1739	–	–	S	rectangle	pellet
	L	–	–	–	S	trifid triad	crown, mullet
	L	–	–	–	S	stepped rectangle	cup, baluster
Thomas Graham of Bath	L	1792	1792	1801	R	rectangle	–
T G **I G** Thomas & Joseph Guest	L	1805	–	1810	R	square	–
T G **I G** **I C** Thomas & Joseph Guest & Joseph Craddock	L	1806	1806	1810	R	quadriform	–
T G **I W** Thomas Graham & Jacob Willis of Bath	L	1789	1789	1790	R	square	–
T H Thomas Havers	Nw	1674	1675	1691	R	loboid	mullet
	Nw	–	–	–	R	hatchment	mullet
Thomas Hebden	H	1681	–	–	R	cuspoid	4 mullets
Samuel Thorne	L	1697	1704	1705	R	heart	chain, pellet
Thomas Heming	L	1745	1746	1789	S	ovoid	–
	L	–	–	–	S	globate rectangle	crown
Thomas Howell of Bath	L	1784	1788	1815	R	rectangle	–
Thomas Harper I	L	1790	1792	*	R	rectangle	–
	L	1812	–	–	R	rectangle	pellet
Thomas Hobbs	L	1796	1805	1807	R	rectangle	–
Thomas Holland II	L	1798	1799	1827	R	rectangle	–
Thomas Hayter	L	1805	1805	1813	R	oval	–
Thomas Harper II	L	1806	–	1821	R	rectangle	pellet
Thomas Halford	L	1807	1805	1815	R	rectangle	pellet
	L	1812	–	–	R	rectangle	–

Maker's initial(s) & maker(s)	Town of registration	Date of mark registration	Earliest example	Latest example	Letter style G Gothic R Roman S Script	Punch shape	Additional features/notes
TH (monogram) Thomas Hartwell	Db	–	1700	1702	R	engrailed triad	–
T H **G H** Thomas & George Hayter	L	1816	1816	1828	R	square	–
	L	1821	–	–	R	quatrefoil	–
T H **I C** Thomas Hannam & John Crouch II	L	1799	–	1807	R	quatrefoil	–
T H **R M** Thomas Hannam & Richard Mills	L (?)	–	1763	1764	R	quatrefoil	–
	L (?)	–	–	–	R	square	–
T I Thomas Jackson I	L	1736	1737	1746	R	ovoid	cross
	L	1739	–	–	S	ovate rectangle	animal
Thomas Justis	L	1761	–	1766	R	profiloid	pellet
	L	1762	–	–	R	rectangle	pellet
	L	1766	–	–	S	ovoid	–
Thomas Jackson II	L	1769	1766	1810	R	oval	pellet
Thomas Joyce	L	1791	–	–	R	rectangle	–
Ti Robert Timbrell	L	1697	1690	1714	R	cuspoid	2 mullets
T & I S Thomas & John Settle	S	1815	1816	1828	R	rectangle	pellet
	S	1815	–	–	–	–	I & TS
T J Thomas Johnston	Db	1770	1761	1776	R	rectangle	–
Thomas Jones	Db	1771	1776	1788	R	rectangle	–
Thomas Johnson	L	1800	1814	1851	R	rectangle	–
Thomas James	L	1804	1809	1830	R	rectangle	pellet
T J C Thomas & James Creswick	S	1810	1811	1826	S	rectangle	pellet

Maker's initial(s) & maker(s)	Town of registration	Date of mark registration	Earliest example	Latest example	Letter style G Gothic R Roman S Script	Punch shape	Additional features/notes
T$_C$$^J_N$ &							
T. J. & N. Creswick	S	1852	1811	1865	R	quatrefoil	–
	S	1819	–	–	–	–	TJ & NC
	S	1832	–	–	–	–	NC
	S	1853	–	–	–	–	JC NC
TJ & NC							
T. J. & N. Creswick	S	1819	1811	1865	R	rectangle	–
	S	1832	–	–	–	–	NC
	S	1852	–	–	–	–	T$_C$$^J_N$ &
		1853	–	–	–	–	JC NC
	S						
T K							
Thomas Ker	Ed	1694	1696	1715	R	lobate invectoid	2 mullets
	Ed	1694	–	–	R	lobate triad	pellet
T & K							
George Tye & James Kilner	B	1826	1826	–	R	rectangle	–
T L							
Timothy Ley	L	–	1691	1733	R	circle	2 mullets, 7 pellets
	L	1697	–	–	–	–	LE
Thomas Law	S	1773	1774	1819	R	rectangle	–
	S	1773	–	–	S	profiloid	–
	S	1773	–	–	R	–	L LAW
	S	1773	–	–	R	–	LAW
Thomas Langford II	L	–	1775	–	R	oval	–
T LAW							
Thomas Law	S	1773	1774	1819	R	rectangle	pellet
	S	1773	–	–	R	–	TL
	S	1773	–	–	R	–	LAW
	S	1773	–	–	S	–	TL
T L **D L**							
Thomas & Daniel Leader	S	1798	1801	1807	R	square	–
T M							
Thomas Morse	L	1718	1721	1723	R	globate rectangle	dog
	L	1718	–	–	–	–	MO
Thomas Mason	L	1720	1717	1749	R	waved triad	mullet
	L	1733	–	–	R	tridentate triad	3 pellets
	L	1739	–	–	G	ovoid	–
	L	1745	–	–	S	rectangle	–
	L	1716	–	–	–	–	Ma
	L	1740	–	–	–	–	TM (monogram)

Maker's initial(s) & maker(s)	Town of registration	Date of mark registration	Earliest example	Latest example	Letter style G Gothic R Roman S Script	Punch shape	Additional features/notes
Thomas Mann	L	1720	1715	1742	R	rectangle	–
	L	1736	–	–	R	globate rectangle	mullet
	L	1739	–	–	G	rectangle	–
	L	1713	–	–	–	–	MA
Thomas Makepeace	Nc	1728	1732	1738	G	rectangle	–
Thomas Moore II	L	1750	1755	1762	S	rectangle	pellet
Thomas Mangy	Y	1664	1662	1689	R	heart	pellet, bird
	Y	–	–	–	R	heart	mullet
	Y	–	–	–	R	ogee escutcheon	–
	Y	–	–	–	R	rectangle	pellet
Thomas Mallinson	L	1773	1778	1802	R	rectangle	pellet
Thomas Morley	L	1778	–	1779	R	rectangle	pellet
Thomas Meriton	L	1791	1797	1801	R	rectangle	–
Thomas Meade	Db	1835	1832	1834	R	rectangle	–
TM (monogram)							
Thomas Maundy	L	–	1634	1650	R	stepped escutcheon	–
Thomas Mason	L	1740	1717	1749	G	ovoid	–
	L	1716	–	–	–	–	Ma
	L	1720	–	–	–	–	TM
T N							
Thomas Nash I	L	1759	1768	1774	S	rectangle	–
	L	1767	–	–	R	bifoil	pellet
	L	–	–	–	R	rectangle	–
Thomas Northcote	L	1776	1777	1819	R	rectangle	fleur de lis
	L	1779	–	–	R	rectangle	pellet
	L	1782	–	–	R	rectangle	–
Thomas Newby	L	1816	–	1817	R	oval	–
Thomas Newbold	B	1820	1820	1828	R	rectangle	–
T N **G B**							
Thomas Northcote & George Bourne	L	1794	1794	–	R	square	–
T O							
William Toone	L	1725	1725	1729	R	circle	2 pellets
	L	1725	–	–	–	–	WT
Thomas Ollivant of Manchester	L	1789	1784	1806	R	rectangle	–
TOLEKEN							
John Toleken	Co	–	1795	1836	R	rectangle	–
	Co	–	–	–	–	–	IT
T P							
Thomas Partis I	Nc	–	1720	1734	R	rectangle	–

Maker's initial(s) & maker(s)	Town of registration	Date of mark registration	Earliest example	Latest example	Letter style G Gothic R Roman S Script	Punch shape	Additional features/notes
Thomas Parr II	L	1733	1741	1754	R	oval	–
	L	1739	–	–	S	oval	pellet
	L	1739	–	–	S	quatrefoil	–
Thomas Powell	L	1756	1758	1787	S	ovoid	pellet
Thomas Pitts I	L	–	1761	1789	R	rectangle	pellet
T. Pierpoint	Ch	–	1784	1787	R	rectangle	–
Thomas Pemberton & Son	B	–	1796	1838	R	rectangle	–
T & P John Taylor & John Perry	B	1832	1829	1849	R	rectangle	–
T P **A H** Thomas Pratt & Arthur Humphreys	L	1780	1780	1783	R	quatrefoil	–
	L	1780	–	–	–	–	TP AH
T P A H Thomas Pratt & Arthur Humphreys	L	1780	1780	1783	R	rectangle	–
	L	1780	–	–	–	–	TP AH
T P **E R** Thomas Phipps & Edward Robinson II	L	–	1777	1820	R	quatrefoil	2 pellets
T P **E R** **J P** Thomas Phipps, Edward Robinson & James Phipps II	L	–	1786	1815	R	quatrefoil	–
T P **I P** Thomas Phipps & James Phipps II	L	1816	1815	1820	R	quatrefoil	–
T P **R P** Thomas & Richard Payne	L	1777	1777	1778	R	square	–
T P & S Thomas Pratt & Sons	B	–	1864	1875	R	rectangle	–
T R George Trowbridge	Ex	1710	1711	1717	R	quatrefoil	coronet
	Ex	–	–	–	R	circle	coronet

Maker's initial(s) & maker(s)	Town of registration	Date of mark registration	Earliest example	Latest example	Letter style G Gothic R Roman S Script	Punch shape	Additional features/notes
William Truss of Reading	L	–	1710	1725	R	octagon	2 pellets
	L	1721	–	–	R	rectangle	–
	L	1721	–	–	–	–	WT
Thomas Rush	L	1724	1725	1760	R	ovoid	pellet
	L	1731	–	–	R	oval	–
	L	1739	–	–	S	ovoid	acorn
	L	1739	–	–	S	rectangle	–
Thomas Rowe	L	1753	–	1754	R	cleftform	pellet
Timothy Renou	L	1792	1792	1803	R	rectangle	–
	L	1800	–	–	R	bevelform	–
	L	1800	–	–	R	rectangle	–
Thomas Robins	L	1801	1794	1830	S	bifoil	–
Thomas Robinson I	L	1802	1805	1828	R	rectangle	pellet
	L	1813	–	–	R	rectangle	–
Thomas Richards	L	1812	1812	1813	R	rectangle	–
Thomas Ross	L	1819	–	1824	R	bifoil	–
	L	1821	–	–	S	rectangle	–
	L	1825	–	–	S	invected rectangle	–
Tr							
Anthony Tripe	Ex	1712	1695	1731	S	circle	crown
	Ex	–	–	–	–	–	AT (monogram)
Benjamin Traherne	L	1697	–	1700	S	ogee triad	pellet
T R & S							
Thomas Rylands & Sons	B	1830	1830	1834	R	rectangle	–
T S							
Thomas Sadler	L	–	1701	1719	R	trifid triad	fleur de lis, pellet
	L	1701	–	–	–	–	SA
Thomas Sampson	Ex	1706	1707	1728	S	arched biloboid	–
	Ex	–	–	–	–	–	Sa
Thomas Sutton	Db	–	1717	1740	R	trigonate rectangle	crown, pellet
	Db	1720	–	–	–	–	U S
	Db	–	–	–	–	–	SU
Thomas Slade	Db	–	1724	1725	R	oval	–
Thomas Smith I	L	1750	1752	1788	R	heart	–
Thomas Shepherd	L	1769	1770	1809	R	rectangle	–
	L	1769	–	–	R	rectangle	pellet
	L	1785	–	–	R	bevelform	–
Thomas Sharratt	L	1772	1774	1778	R	rectangle	–
Thomas Satchwell	L	1773	1769	1799	R	rectangle	pellet
Thomas Shaw	L	1785	1770	1830	S	rectangle	–

Maker's initial(s) & maker(s)	Town of registration	Date of mark registration	Earliest example	Latest example	Letter style G Gothic R Roman S Script	Punch shape	Additional features/notes
Thomas Streetin	L	1794	1789	1810	R	rectangle	–
	L	1798	–	–	R	oval	–
	L	1820	–	–	R	rectangle	pellet
Thomas Shaw	B	1822	1820	1839	R	rectangle	pellet
Thomas Spicer of Coventry	B	1830	1831	1836	R	rectangle	pellet
Thomas Sewill	Nc	–	1846	1880	R	rectangle	–
T T							
Thomas Tearle	L	1720	1718	1739	R	cambered rectangle	mullet
	L	1739	–	–	S	globate biloboid	crown, pellet
	L	1719	–	–	–	–	TE
Thomas Tookey	L	1773	1778	1780	R	rectangle	pellet
	L	1775	–	–	R	rectangle	–
	L	1779	–	–	S	oval	–
Thomas Tudor	Db	1797	1815	1816	R	bevelform	–
Thomas Townsend	Db	1797	–	1805	R	oval	pellet
Thomas Turner	S	1853	–	1890	R	rectangle	pellet
T & T							
Thropp & Taylor	B	1810	1810	1827	R	billet	–
Tu							
Francis Turner	L	1709	1718	1734	G	quatrefoil	2 mullets, 2 pellets
	L	1721	–	–	R	hatchment	pellet
	L	1720	–	–	–	–	FT
Edward Turner	L	1720	1720	1726	R	cuspoid	pellet
T W							
William Twell	L	1709	1717	1718	R	quatrefoil	–
Thomas Walker	Db	1714	1715	1728	R	woolsack	crown, pellet
	Db	–	–	–	R	ovate rectangle	crown, pellet
Thomas Wright	L	1721	1750	1756	R	oval	pellet
Thomas Williamson	Db	1726	1730	1751	R	trifid cleftform	crown, pellet
Thomas Whipham	L	1737	1737	1776	R	globate rectangle	mullet, pellet
	L	1739	–	–	S	invected rectangle	–
	L	–	–	–	S	rectangle	–
Thomas Wynne of Bath	L	1754	1753	1783	R	rectangle	pellet
Thomas Wallis I	L	1758	1766	1767	R	tetragon	pellet
Thomas Wigan of Bristol	L	1763	–	1801	S	rectangle	–
Thomas Willmore	B	1773	1790	1828	R	rectangle	pellet
	B	–	–	–	R	oval	pellet
	L	1790	–	–	R	rectangle	–
T. Willmore & Alston	B	–	1777	1802	R	rectangle	–
Thomas Wallis II	L	1778	1783	1809	R	rectangle	–
	L	1792	–	–	S	rectangle	–

Maker's initial(s) & maker(s)	Town of registration	Date of mark registration	Earliest example	Latest example	Letter style G Gothic R Roman S Script	Punch shape	Additional features/notes
Thomas Watson	L	1784	1785	1790	R	rectangle	–
Thomas Watson	Nc	–	1785	1842	R	rectangle	–
	Nc	–	–	–	R	rectangle	pellet
	Nc	–	–	–	R	oval	–
	Nc	–	–	–	S	ovoid	–
Thomas Willats	L	1809	1809	1810	R	rectangle	pellet
Thomas Wimbush	L	1828	1828	1833	R	rectangle	–
TW (monogram) Thomas Waite	Y	1613	1630	1655	R	profiloid	–
T & W Carden Terry & John Williams	Co	–	1795	1819	R	rectangle	–
	Co	–	–	–	–	–	C & T I W C T I W
	Db	–	–	–	–	–	CT IW
Tudor & Whitford	Db	–	1806	1807	R	rectangle	–
T C W Thomas Whipham & Charles Wright	L	1757	1757	1781	R	circle	thread circle, pellet
T W D Thomas William Dee	B	–	1864	1890	–	–	–
T W H H Thomas Wimbush & Henry Hyde	L	1834	1833	–	R	quatrefoil	–
T W J H Thomas Wallis II & Jonathan Hayne	L	1810	1813	1820	R	square	2 pellets
T W W W Thomas Whipham & William Williams I	L	1740	1739	1742	R	quatrefoil	pellet
TWY+ Edward Twycross	Db	1831	1828	1832	R	rectangle	–

Maker's initial(s) & maker(s)	Town of registration	Date of mark registration	Earliest example	Latest example	Letter style G Gothic R Roman S Script	Punch shape	Additional features/notes
U & H							
Duncan Urquhart & Naphtali Hart	L (?)	–	1789	1812	R	rectangle	–
	L	1791	–	–	–	–	DU NH
George Unite & J. Hilliard	B	1825	1826	1842	R	rectangle	–
U							
S							
Thomas Sutton	Db	1720	1717	1740	R	ovoid	–
	Db	–	–	–	–	–	SU
	Db	–	–	–	–	–	TS
U W							
& Co							
Underwood, Wilkinson & Co	S	1826	–	1827	R	rectangle	–
V I							
Edward Vincent	L	–	1713	1740	R	oval	mullet
	L	–	–	–	–	–	EV
W A							
Joseph Ward	L	1697	1697	1722	R	trifid triad	anchor
	L	–	–	–	–	–	Wa
Samuel Wastell	L	1701	1702	1722	R	domate rectangle	bird, pellet
	L	1701	–	–	R	globate ovoid	mitre, pellet
	L	1722	–	–	–	–	SW
William Archdall	Db	1704	1712	1729	S	oval	–
	Db	–	–	–	R	oval	–
Thomas Wall	L	1708	1723	1728	R	oval	crown, bird, 2 pellets
William Aytoun	Ed	1718	1729	1749	R	bifoil	–
William Atkinson	L	1725	1726	1729	R	profiloid	cup
	L	1725	–	–	–	–	AT
William Alexander	L	1743	1752	1759	R	tridentate arcade	–
	L	–	–	–	R	rectangle	pellet
William Abdy I	L	1763	1762	1797	R	rhombus	–
	L	1767	–	–	R	concave rectangle	–
	L	1779	–	–	–	–	incuse
	L	1784	–	–	R	rectangle	–
	L	–	–	–	R	rectangle	pellet
	L	–	–	–	R	waved invectoid	–
William Abdy II	L	1790	1791	1809	R	rectangle	pellet
	L	1822	–	–	R	rectangle	–
William Allen III	L	1798	1799	1805	S	oval	–

Maker's initial(s) & maker(s)	Town of registration	Date of mark registration	Earliest example	Latest example	Letter style G Gothic R Roman S Script	Punch shape	Additional features/notes
Wa							
Joseph Ward	L	–	1697	1722	R	rectangle	–
	L	1697	–	–	–	–	WA
Benjamin Watts	L	1698	1704	1718	R	invected triad	stag's head
	L	1720	–	–	–	–	BW
White Walsh	L	1698	1698	–	R	invected triad	crown
Richard Watts	L	1710	1710	1720	R	domate triad	mullet, fleur de lis
	L	1710	–	–	R	invected biloboid	–
	L	1720	–	–	–	–	RW
W A & Co							
William Allanson & Co	S	1832	–	1836	R	rectangle	–
W B							
William Busfield	Y	1679	1677	1705	R	octafoil	–
	Y	–	–	–	R	multifoil	lozenge
	Y	–	–	–	R	multifoil	–
	Y	–	–	–	–	–	WB (conjoined)
	Y	–	–	–	–	–	Bu
William Bellassyse	L	1723	1722	1723	R	profiloid	mitre
	L	1717	–	–	–	–	BE
William Beilby	Nc	–	1733	1765	S	domate rectangle	annulet
William Bagnall	L	1744	1749	1754	R	ovoid	pellet
	L	1744	–	–	R	ovoid	–
Walter Brind	L	1749	1746	1789	R	ovoid	pellet
	L	1751	–	–	R	rectangle	pellet
	L	1757	–	–	R	invected rectangle	–
	L	1781	–	–	R	rectangle	–
	L	–	–	–	R	ovoid	–
William Bell	L	1759	–	–	R	lanceolate rectangle	bell, pellet
	L	1772	–	–	R	bevelform	–
	L	1763	–	–	–	–	incuse bell, pellet
William Bayley I	L	1759	–	–	R	bevelform	pellet
William Bayley II	L	1770	1781	1806	R	bevelform	–
William Barrett I	L	1771	1788	1791	R	rectangle	–
Wilkes Booth	L	1787	1792	1812	R	rectangle	others similar
William Bond	Db	1791	1777	1809	S	rectangle	pellet
William Bennett	L	1796	1792	1827	R	rectangle	–
	L	1808	–	–	R	rectangle	pellet
William Bruce	L	1811	1813	1818	R	rectangle	pellet
William Burwash	L	1802	1803	1821	R	bifoil	pellet
	L	1813	–	–	S	rectangle	–
	L	–	–	–	S	profiloid	pellet
	L	–	–	–	S	–	incuse pellet
William Bateman I	L	1815	1816	1838	R	delphate bipod	pellet

Maker's initial(s) & maker(s)	Town of registration	Date of mark registration	Earliest example	Latest example	Letter style G Gothic R Roman S Script	Punch shape	Additional features/notes
William Bellchambers	L	–	1820	1839	R	rectangle	–
William Barrett II	L	1812	1814	1825	R	rectangle	–
William Brown	L	1823	1826	1837	R	bifoil	pellet
William Bateman II	L	1827	1827	1835	R	reelform	–
WB (conjoined)							
William Busfield	Y	1679	1677	1705	R	trifid escutcheon	2 pellets
	Y	–	–	–	–	–	WB
	Y	–	–	–	–	–	Bu
W B & Co							
W. Birks & Co	S	1773	–	1779	R	square	–
W B & Co							
William Blackwell & Co	S	1816	1823	1824	R	rectangle	–
W B D B							
William Bateman II & Daniel Ball	L	1839	1839	1841	R	quatrefoil	–
W B J							
Walter & John II Barnard	L	–	1877	1896	R	stepped heart	–
W B J B							
Wilkes & John Booth	L	1810	1810	–	R	square	–
W B R S							
William Burwash & Richard Sibley I	L	1805	1805	1840	R	square	2 pellets
W C							
William Clarke	Co	–	1710	1719	S	rectangle	–
	Co	–	–	–	S	bifoil	–
William Cripps	L	1743	1744	1777	R	ogee archform	pellet
	L	1746	–	–	R	bevelform	pellet
	L	1751	–	–	R	rectangle	pellet
William Caldecott	L	1756	1756	1777	R	bifoil	–
William Cafe	L	1757	1740	1771	G	trefoil	mullet
William Cattell	L	1771	1773	1778	R	rectangle	–
William Constable	Du	–	1806	1809	R	rectangle	–
W. Cummins	Db	–	1813	1828	R	rectangle	–
William Chawner II	L	1815	1813	1833	R	rectangle	–
	L	1820	–	–	R	rectangle	pellet
	L	1820	–	–	R	bevelform	–
	L	–	–	–	R	globate rectangle	pellet

Maker's initial(s) & maker(s)	Town of registration	Date of mark registration	Earliest example	Latest example	Letter style G Gothic R Roman S Script	Punch shape	Additional features/notes
William Crouch	Ed	–	1832	1863	R	ogee escutcheon	–
William Cooper	L	–	1839	1851	R	rectangle	–
William Coghill	Gl	–	1866	–	R	rectangle	pellet
W. Comyns	L	–	1887	1915	R	oval	–
	B	–	–	1907	–	–	–
William Comyns & Sons Ltd	L	–	1887	1915	R	ogival escutcheon	pellet
	L	–	–	–	R	oval	pellet
W & Co							
George Waterhouse & Co	S	1842	1842	1847	R	rectangle	–
	S	1842	–	–	–	–	W & S
W C **P C**							
W & P Cunningham	Ed	–	1784	1826	R	square	pellet
	Ed	–	–	–	–	–	W& P C
	Ed	–	–	–	–	–	W P C
	Gl	–	1821	1824	–	–	–
W T C							
Thomas & William I Chawner	L	1763	1760	1771	R	cruciform	pellet
	L	1764	–	–	–	–	T C W
	L	1765	–	–	–	–	T C / W C
	L	1768	–	–	–	–	T W C
W D							
William Darker	L	1720	1719	1733	R	trifid biloboid	trefoil
	L	1731	–	–	R	trefoil	floret
	L	1719	–	–	–	–	DA
William Dalton	Nc	1725	1724	1767	R	rectangle	–
	Nc	–	–	–	S	rectangle	–
William Davie	Ed	1740	1745	1789	R	rectangle	–
	Ed	1740	–	–	S	rectangle	–
William Dempster	Ed	1742	1741	1770	R	rectangle	mullet
William Doyle	Db	1795	1796	1813	R	ovoid	pellet
W D D							
William & John Deane	L	1759	1762	1764	R	oval	–
	L	1762	–	–	–	–	W D I
W E							
Matthew West	L	1697	1716	1793	R	ogee chinoid	4 pellets, mullet

Maker's initial(s) & maker(s)	Town of registration	Date of mark registration	Earliest example	Latest example	Letter style G Gothic R Roman S Script	Punch shape	Additional features/notes
William J. Edwards	L	1778	–	1786	R	rectangle	pellet
	L	–	–	–	R	rectangle	–
	L	–	–	–	R	oval	–
William Eley I	L	1778	1774	1838	R	rectangle	–
	L	1794	–	–	R	waved oval	–
William Ellerby	L	1802	–	1812	R	rectangle	pellet
	L	1802	–	–	R	rectangle	–
	L	1810	–	–	R	oval	pellet
William Elliott	L	1813	1823	1851	R	rectangle	pellet
William Eaton	L	1813	1813	1864	R	rectangle	pellet
	L	1813	–	–	R	rectangle	–
	L	1828	–	–	R	quatrefoil	–
We							
Samuel Welder	L	1714	1715	1738	R	heart	–
	L	1717	–	–	R	heart	3 pellets
	L	–	–	–	R	heart	2 pellets, trefoil
	L	1720	–	–	–	–	SW
W E **C E** **H E**							
William II, Charles & Henry Eley	L	1824	1824	–	R	quadriform	–
W E H							
William Hall	L	–	1795	1828	R	rectangle	–
	L	1795	–	–	–	–	WH
W E **W F**							
William Eley I & William Fearn	L	1797	1789	1836	R	square	–
W E **W F** **W C**							
William Eley I, William Fearn & William Chawner II	L	1808	1806	1826	R	quadriform	–
W & E T							
William & Edward Turnpenny	B	1844	1845	1847	R	rectangle	–
W F							
William Fawdery	L	–	1700	1726	R	ovate ovoid	crown
	L	1697	–	–	–	–	FA
	L	1720	–	–	–	–	F

Maker's initial(s) & maker(s)	Town of registration	Date of mark registration	Earliest example	Latest example	Letter style G Gothic R Roman S Script	Punch shape	Additional features/notes
William Fordham	L	–	1726	1731	R	ovoid	pellet
	L	1707	–	–	–	–	FO
William Fearn	L	1769	1771	1800	R	rectangle	pellet
	L	1774	–	–	R	rectangle	–
William Lewis Foster	L	1775	1774	–	R	rectangle	pellet
	L	–	–	–	R	rhombus	–
William Frisbee	L	1792	1795	1822	R	rectangle	pellet
	L	1798	–	–	R	bifoil	–
	L	1801	–	–	R	cleftform	–
William Fountain	L	1794	1793	1828	R	bifoil	–
	L	1798	–	–	S	rectangle	–
	L	1821	–	–	R	rectangle	–
William Fell	L	1818	–	1826	R	bevelform	–
W & F Jonathan Wright & George Fairburn	S	1809	1809	1812	R	rectangle	–
W F **A F** Fordham & Faulkener	S	1890	1896	1915	R	square	2 pellets
	L	–	1896	–	–	–	–
W F **D P** William Fountain & Daniel Pontifex	L	1791	1788	1798	R	square	–
W F **I F** William & John Fisher	L	1793	–	1811	R	square	pellet
W F **P S** William Frisbee & Paul Storr	L	1792	1791	1792	R	square	–
	L	1792	–	–	–	–	2 pellets
W G William Ged	Ed	1706	1707	1718	R	waved biloboid	–
William Gould	L	1732	1732	1767	R	globate loboid	candlestick, mullet
	L	1739	–	–	R	biloboid	–
	L	1739	–	–	G	[stepform]	candlestick
	L	1753	–	–	S	profiloid	pellet
	L	1734	–	–	–	–	GO
William Garrard	L	1735	1737	1745	R	oval	–
	L	1739	–	–	G	rectangle	–
	L	1749	–	–	R	rectangle	–
William Gilchrist	Ed	1736	1751	1755	R	oval	–

Maker's initial(s) & maker(s)	Town of registration	Date of mark registration	Earliest example	Latest example	Letter style G Gothic R Roman S Script	Punch shape	Additional features/notes
William Gwillim	L	1740	1740	1743	R	ovoid	–
William Grundy	L	1743	1733	1777	S	profiloid	pellet
	L	1748	–	–	–	–	–
	L	1777	–	–	S	rectangle	–
William Gallimore & Sons	S	1867	1894	1895	R	hatchment	pellet
	S	1867	–	–	R	tridentate escutcheon	–
W G							
J L							
W. Gibson & J. Langman	L	–	1886	1899	–	–	–
	B	–	1883	–	–	–	–
	S	–	1884	1893	R	tridentate escutcheon	–
	Db	–	–	1900	–	–	–
WG JLL							
Mappin Bros	S	1889	1889	1954	R	2 rectangles	–
	S	1856	–	–	–	–	MB
							M&B
							FC CH
							FC
							CH
							M
							Bros
							Mn Bros
							EM
							JM
J^W_LG$_L$							
Mappin Bros	S	1893	1889	1954	R	bevelled quadriform	–
	S	1856	–	–	–	–	*as above*
W H							
John White	L	–	1722	1736	R	ogival loboid	2 mullets
	L	1719	–	–	–	–	Wh
	L	1725	–	–	–	–	IW
William Hunter I	L	1755	1755	*	S	profiloid	–
	L	1756	–	–	R	rectangle	–
William Homer	Db	1758	1764	1770	S	profiloid	–
William Hughes	Db	1767	1760	1781	R	trifid rectangle	crown, pellet
William Holmes	L	1776	1767	1814	R	oval	–
	L	1792	–	–	R	rectangle	–
William Hall	L	1795	1795	1828	R	rectangle	–
	L	1795	–	–	–	–	WEH
William Hunter II	L	–	1828	1838	R	rectangle	–

Maker's initial(s) & maker(s)	Town of registration	Date of mark registration	Earliest example	Latest example	Letter style G Gothic R Roman S Script	Punch shape	Additional features/notes
William Hewitt	L	1829	1836	1846	R	rectangle	pellet
	L	1834	–	–	R	oval	–
	L	1843	–	–	G	oval	–
William Hutton	S	1836	1838	1956	R	rectangle	–
	S	1857	–	–	R	oval	–
	(*also* L, B & Ch)						
William Hutton & Sons Ltd	S	1836	1838	1956	–	–	–
	S	1866	–	–	–	–	RH
	L	–	–	–	–	–	SHLd &
William Hattersley	L	–	1840	1864	R	rectangle	pellet
Wh							
John White	L	1719	1722	1736	R	ogival chinoid	2 mullets
	L	1725	–	–	–	–	IW
	L	–	–	–	–	–	WH
William Whitfield	Nc	1720	1720	1746	G	oval	–
	Nc	1720	–	–	–	–	WW
W H **I R**							
W. Hancock & J. Rowbotham	S	1773	1773	–	R	square	2 pellets
	B	1773	1773	–	R	square	2 pellets
	S	1773	–	–	–	–	I$^{W}_{R}$H & Co
I$^{W}_{R}$H & Co							
W. Hancock & J. Rowbotham	S	1773	1773	–	R	[stepform]	–
	S	1773	–	–	–	–	W H / I R
	B	1773	–	–	–	–	W H / I R
W H **N D**							
William Holmes & Nicholas Dumee	L	1773	1773	1774	R	bevelled square	2 pellets
W & H							
Walker & Hall	S	1862	1892	1968	R	rectangle	–
	S	–	–	–	R	concave archform	–
	S	–	–	–	R	[flag]	–
	S	1868	–	–	–	–	HH& JEB
	L	–	1887	1941	–	–	–
	B	–	1883	1938	–	–	–
	Ch	–	1906	1938	–	–	–

Maker's initial(s) & maker(s)	Town of registration	Date of mark registration	Earliest example	Latest example	Letter style G Gothic R Roman S Script	Punch shape	Additional features/notes
W I							
David Willaume I	L	1697	1698	1744	R	lobate triad	2 mullets, fleur de lis
	L	1720	–	–	–	–	DW
Edward Wimans	L	1697	1697	1704	R	octagon	6 annulets
Mrs Edward Wimans	L	–	–	–	R	lozenge	2 pellets
Richard Wilcock of Plymouth	Ex	–	1707	1717	R	circle	crown
	Ex	1704	–	–	–	–	Wi
John Wisdome	L	1704	1713	1719	R	waved cuspoid	fleur de lis
	L	1720	–	–	–	–	IW
Richard Williams	L	1712	1713	1714	R	trifid biloboid	fleur de lis
Starling Wilford	L	1718	1722	1734	R	rectangle	–
	L	1720	–	–	–	–	SW
William Jelf	L	1720	1717	1720	R	rectangle	–
	L	–	–	–	–	–	Ie
George Wickes	L	1722	1719	1757	R	domate ovoid	fleur de lis, pellet
	L	1722	–	–	–	–	G enclosing W
	L	1735	–	–	–	–	GW
James Wilks	L	1722	1724	1748	R	rectangle	–
	L	1722	–	–	–	–	IW
Robert Williams	L	1726	1724	1728	R	globate rectangle	mitre
	L	1726	–	–	–	–	RW
David Willaume II	L	1728	1725	1743	R	rectangle	–
	L	1728	–	–	–	–	DW
William Jamieson of Aberdeen	Ed	1729	1729	–	R	bifoil	–
William Justis (*or* Justus)	L	1739	1729	1762	G	[grooved rectangle]	–
	L	–	–	–	R	oval	–
	L	–	–	–	R	rectangle	–
	L	–	–	–	R	reelform	pellet
John Williams	Co	–	1791	1795	R	invected rectangle	–
Wi							
Richard Wilcock of Plymouth	Ex	1704	1707	1717	R	trifid cuspoid	mullet, 2 pellets, plant
	Ex	–	–	–	–	–	WI
Zachariah Williams of Plymouth	Ex	1720	1717	1721	S	ogee loboid	–
W J							
William Johnson	L	1822	1826	1832	R	rectangle	–
Walter Jordan	L	1834	1833	–	R	rectangle	pellet

Maker's initial(s) & maker(s)	Town of registration	Date of mark registration	Earliest example	Latest example	Letter style G Gothic R Roman S Script	Punch shape	Additional features/notes
W B J M S R D W. J. M. & S. Barnard & R. Dubock (Edward Barnard & Sons Ltd)	L	–	1840	1974	R	ovate cuspoid	–
	B	–	1919	–	–	–	–
W K William Kidney	L	1734	1735	1742	R	ogee archform	–
	L	1739	–	–	S	rectangle	–
	L	1739	–	–	G	concave archform	–
William Kersill	L	1749	1749	1765	R	rectangle	–
	L	1757	–	–	R	profiloid	pellet
William Kinman	L	1759	–	1771	R	profiloid	pellet
William King	L	1761	1760	1771	R	globate rectangle	mullet, pellet
	L	1761	–	–	–	–	incuse
William Kingdon	L	1811	1811	1841	R	rectangle	pellet
William Knight II	L	1816	1815	1837	R	rectangle	–
William King	L	1826	1829	1834	R	rectangle	–
W & K William Wardell & Peter Kempson	B	1813	–	1819	R	rectangle	–
W K & Co Walker Knowles & Co	S	1840	1819	1854	R	square	–
W K R William Ker Reid	L	1828	1826	1882	R	bifoil	2 pellets
	L	1825	–	–	–	–	WR
W K S K William II & Samuel Knight	L	1810	1809	1815	R	square	–
W L William Looker	L	1720	1713	1724	R	domate rectangle	crown, pellet
	L	–	–	–	R	trifid biloboid	trefoil
	L	1713	–	–	–	–	LO
William Lukin I	L	1725	1699	1736	R	invected shareform	pellet
	L	1699	–	–	–	–	Lu
William Law	Db	1774	1789	1822	R	rectangle	–
William Laver	L	1789	1791	1792	R	rectangle	pellet
William Lister	Nc	–	1826	1834	R	rectangle	–

Maker's initial(s) & maker(s)	Town of registration	Date of mark registration	Earliest example	Latest example	Letter style G Gothic R Roman S Script	Punch shape	Additional features/notes
W & L							
Winder & Lamb	Db	–	1861	1883	R	rectangle	–
W M							
William Matthew II	L	1720	–	1735	R	ogee triad	crown, mullet
	L	1712	–	–	–	–	MA
William Morgan	Db	1806	1818	1834	R	rectangle	–
William Mill	M	1811	–	–	R	rectangle	–
William Marshall	Ed	–	1821	1883	R	rectangle	–
William Mann	L	–	1840	1858	R	rectangle	pellet
W M (monogram)							
William Mackenzie	L	1748	1749	1750	S	oval	–
W **M**							
William Maundy	L	–	1630	1634	R	delphate escutcheon	–
W N							
William Nowlan	Db	1827	1811	1832	R	rectangle	pellet
William Nelson	Db	–	1828	–	R	rectangle	pellet
W O							
Edward Wood	L	1722	1723	1759	R	circle	mullet, pellet, arrow
	L	1722	–	–	–	–	EW
W P							
William Petley	L	1720	1719	1732	R	ovate rectangle	crown, mullet
	L	1699	–	–	–	–	PE
William Paradise	L	1720	1719	1723	R	waved triad	mullet
	L	1718	–	–	–	–	Pa
William Pearson	L	1721	1719	1720	R	octagon	bird, pellet, mullet
	L	1704	–	–	–	–	PE
William Partis	Nc	1731	1736	1757	S	rectangle	–
	Nc	1731	–	–	–	–	WP (conjoined)
William Parry	Ex	–	1743	1779	R	rectangle	–
	Ex	–	–	–	R	woolsack	–
William Peaston	L	1746	1739	1774	R	heart	–
William Plummer	L	1755	1755	1791	R	cleftform	pellet
William Pickett	L	1769	–	–	R	rectangle	pellet
William Pitts	L	1781	1782	1817	R	oval	–
William Pugh	B	–	1790	1816	R	rectangle	–
	Ch	–	–	–	R	rectangle	–
William Parker	L	1798	1800	1805	R	rectangle	–
	L	1803	–	–	R	rectangle	pellet
William Purse	L	–	1803	1817	R	rectangle	pellet

Maker's initial(s) & maker(s)	Town of registration	Date of mark registration	Earliest example	Latest example	Letter style G Gothic R Roman S Script	Punch shape	Additional features/notes
William Phillips of Handsworth	B	1832	1832	1835	R	rectangle	–
William Pope	Ex	–	1833	1853	R	rectangle	pellet
Parkin & Marshall	S	1866	1865	–	R	rectangle	–
	S	1866	–	–	–	–	P & M
WP (conjoined)							
William Partis	Nc	1731	1736	1757	R	dextroid	–
	Nc	1731	–	–	–	–	WP
W P **B S**							
William Parker & Benjamin Simpson	L	1799	1799	1800	R	quatrefoil	–
W P C							
W & P Cunningham	Ed	–	1784	1826	R	rectangle	–
	Ed	–	–	–	–	–	W& PC
	Ed	–	–	–	–	–	WC PC
	Gl	–	1821	1824	–	–	–
W & **P C**							
W. & P. Cunningham	Ed	–	1784	1826	R	square	–
	Ed	–	–	–	–	–	WPC
	Ed	–	–	–	–	–	WC PC
	Gl	–	1821	1824	–	–	–
W P **I P**							
William Pitts & Joseph Preedy	L	1791	1799	1820	R	oval	2 pellets
W P **J P**							
William & James Priest	L	1768	1762	1772	R	square	cross
W P **R P**							
William & Robert Peaston	L	–	1753	1759	R	bevelled square	pellet, 4 scrolls
	L	1756	–	–	–	–	W^{Rp}_P
W^R$_P$P							
William & Robert Peaston	L	1756	1753	1759	R	quatrefoil	pellet
	L	–	–	–	–	–	WP RP

Maker's initial(s) & maker(s)	Town of registration	Date of mark registration	Earliest example	Latest example	Letter style G Gothic R Roman S Script	Punch shape	Additional features/notes
W R							
William Robertson	L	1753	1756	1762	S	quatrefoil	–
	L	1755	–	–	S	rectangle	–
William Reynolds	Co	1758	1757	1764	R	rectangle	–
	Co	–	–	–	–	–	WR (conjoined)
William Robertson	Ed	1789	1791	1795	R	rectangle	–
William Ker Reid	L	1825	1826	1882	R	bifoil	pellet
	L	1828	–	–	–	–	WKR
William Russell	Gl	1827	–	1836	R	rectangle	–
WR (conjoined)							
William Robinson	Nc	1666	1656	1698	R	waved escutcheon	–
	Nc	–	–	–	R	crested triad	crown
	Nc	–	–	–	R	heart	4 scrolls
	Nc	–	–	–	R	heart	–
	Nc	–	–	–	–	–	RWR (conjoined)
William Richardson	Ch	–	1721	1751	R	rectangle	–
William Reynolds	Co	1758	1757	1764	S	rectangle	–
	Co	–	–	–	S	ogee escutcheon	–
	Co	–	–	–	S	profiloid	–
	Co	–	–	–	–	–	WR
W R S							
William R. Sobey	Ex	1835	1831	1855	R	trefoil	–
	Ex	–	–	–	–	–	SOBEY
William Robert Smiley	L	–	1841	1865	R	rectangle	–
	L	–	–	–	–	–	W$_S$R
W$_S$R							
William Robert Smiley	L	–	1841	1865	R	trefoil	–
	L	–	–	–	–	–	WRS
W S							
Walter Scott	Ed	1701	–	1707	R	cambered shareform	–
William Spackman	L	1720	1717	1726	R	cleft cuspoid	2 pellets, mullet
	L	1714	–	–	–	–	SP
William Soame	L	1723	–	1762	R	oval	pellet
	L	1739	–	–	R	ovoid	pellet
	L	1739	–	–	S	octagon	–
William Scarlett	L	1725	1689	1727	R	ogee hatchment	–
	L	1697	–	–	–	–	SC
	L	1720	–	–	–	–	W S
William Shaw I	L	1728	1730	1774	R	tabled rectangle	mitre
	L	1739	–	–	S	domate rectangle	mitre
	L	1745	–	–	R	waved archform	pellet
	L	1729	–	–	–	–	SH

Maker's initial(s) & maker(s)	Town of registration	Date of mark registration	Earliest example	Latest example	Letter style G Gothic R Roman S Script	Punch shape	Additional features/notes
William Solomon	L	1747	–	1758	R	bifoil	pellet
	L	1747	–	–	R	domate biloboid	fleur de lis
William Sheen (or Skeen)	L	1755	1755	1799	R	rectangle	–
	L	1775	–	–	R	ovoid	–
William Sample	L	1755	1756	1774	R	rectangle	–
William Smith I	L	1758	–	–	R	rectangle	–
	L	1762	–	–	R	rectangle	pellet
William Sudell	L	1767	–	1778	R	rectangle	pellet
	L	1774	–	–	R	rectangle	–
William Simons	L	1776	1777	1806	R	rectangle	–
	L	1776	–	–	R	rectangle	pellet
William Smith II	L	1777	1777	1780	R	rectangle	–
William Sherwin	Db	1779	1805	1834	R	rectangle	–
William Sutton	L	1784	1782	1801	R	rectangle	pellet
William Sumner I	L	1782	1777	1814	G	rectangle	–
	L	1784	–	–	R	oval	–
	L	–	–	–	R	oval	pellet
	L	–	–	–	R	rectangle	pellet
William Sumner II	L	1787	1788	1811	R	rectangle	pellet
William Stroud	L	1788	1788	1812	R	rectangle	–
	L	1821	–	–	G	rectangle	–
William Seaman	L	1804	1789	1813	R	oval	pellet
	L	–	–	–	R	oval	–
William James Southey	L	1810	1812	1824	R	rectangle	–
	L	1821	–	–	R	rectangle	pellet
William Sharp	L	1817	1819	1826	R	rectangle	–
	L	1824	–	–	R	rectangle	pellet
William Sansom	S	1835	–	1837	R	rectangle	–
William Smiley	L	–	1855	1888	R	rectangle	–
W. Smith of Liverpool	Ch	–	1870	1887	R	bevelform	–
W **S**							
William Scarlett	L	1720	1689	1727	R	stepped cuspoid	–
	L	1722	–	–	–	–	–
	L	1697	–	–	–	–	SC
	L	1725	–	–	–	–	WS
W & S							
George Waterhouse & Co	S	1842	1842	1847	R	rectangle	–
	S	1842	–	–	–	–	W & Co
Wilson & Sharp Ltd	B	–	1935	–	–	–	–
	Ed	–	1902	1908	–	–	–
	Gl	–	1866	–	–	–	–

Maker's initial(s) & maker(s)	Town of registration	Date of mark registration	Earliest example	Latest example	Letter style G Gothic R Roman S Script	Punch shape	Additional features/notes
West & Son	Db	1877	1884	1972	R	tridentate escutcheon	–
	Db	1902	–	–	R	trefoil	–
	Db	1900	–	–	–	–	LAW
	L	–	1894	–	–	–	–
W S **G S** William & George Sissons	S	1858	1858	1926	R	quatrefoil	–
	L	–	1871	1907	–	–	–
W S **H S** William & Henry Stratford	S	1855	1853	1877	R	square	–
W S **I M** William Stalker & John Mitchison	Nc	1774	1773	1792	R	square	2 pellets
W S **R C** William Sumner & Richard Crossley	L	1775	1774	1814	R	square	–
W W S P William Shaw II & William Priest	L	1749	1746	1769	R	cruciform	pellet
W T William Truss of Reading	L	1721	1710	1725	R	rectangle	–
	L	–	–	–	R	octagon	2 pellets
	L	1721	–	–	–	–	TR
William Toone	L	1725	1725	1729	R	quatrefoil	2 mullets
	L	1725	–	–	–	–	To
William Townsend	Db	1736	1734	1753	R	biloboid	–
	Db	–	–	–	R	rectangle	pellet
William Taylor	Ed	1753	1757	1766	R	rectangle	–
William Turner	L	1754	1755	1768	S	rectangle	pellet
	L	1764	–	–	S	lobate biloboid	mullet
William Tuite	L	–	1759	1771	R	oval	–
	L	–	–	–	R	kidney	pellet
	L	–	–	–	R	oval	pellet
	L	–	–	–	R	pentagon	pellet
William Tant	L	1762	1763	1779	S	waved rectangle	–
	L	1783	–	–	R	oval	–

Maker's initial(s) & maker(s)	Town of registration	Date of mark registration	Earliest example	Latest example	Letter style G Gothic R Roman S Script	Punch shape	Additional features/notes
William Turton	L	1773	1774	1788	R	ovoid	–
	L	1780	–	–	R	rectangle	pellet
	L	–	–	–	R	ovoid	pellet
Walter Tweedie	L	1775	1765	1825	R	rectangle	pellet
	L	1779	–	–	R	rectangle	–
	L	1781	–	–	S	rectangle	pellet
	L	1781	–	–	S	rectangle	mullet
William Thompson	Db	1795	–	1797	R	rectangle	pellet
William Bamforth Troby	L	1812	1822	1830	R	rectangle	–
William Traies	L	1822	1821	1846	R	rectangle	pellet
	L	1824	–	–	R	oval	pellet
William Theobalds	L	1829	1829	1840	R	rectangle	pellet
	L	1835	–	–	R	rectangle	–
W T & Co							
William Tucker, James Fenton & Co	S	1796	1796	1815	R	oval	–
W T **I T**							
W. & J. Taylor	Ed	–	1771	1777	R	square	–
W T **L B**							
William Theobalds & Lockington Bunn	L	1835	1835	–	R	square	–
W T **R A**							
William Theobalds & Robert Atkinson	L	1838	1838	1840	R	square	–
W U							
William Ure	Ed	1715	1717	1730	R	oval	–
	Ed	–	–	–	–	–	WV
W V							
William Ure	Ed	1715	1717	1730	R	oval	–
	Ed	–	–	–	–	–	WU
William Vincent	L	–	1766	1817	R	rectangle	–
W I V **L**							
John Henry Vere & William Lutwyche	L	–	1761	1768	R	quatrefoil	–
W W							
William Whitfield	Nc	1720	1720	1746	G	rectangle	–
	Nc	–	–	–	R	rectangle	–
	Nc	–	–	–	–	–	Wh

Maker's initial(s) & maker(s)	Town of registration	Date of mark registration	Earliest example	Latest example	Letter style G Gothic R Roman S Script	Punch shape	Additional features/notes
William Williamson	Db	1726	1728	1782	R	globate biloboid	floret
	Db	–	–	–	R	domate biloboid	floret
William Woodward	L	1731	1742	1747	R	cavetto square	2 mullets, pellet
	L	1743	–	–	S	rectangle	pellet
William Williams I	L	1740	1743	1758	R	oval	–
	L	1742	–	–	R	oval	2 pellets, floret
William Walsh	Db	1745	1740	1753	R	profiloid	–
William Wooller	L	1750	–	1764	R	ovoid	pellet
William Withers	L	1762	1762	1764	R	oval	–
William Worthington	L	1771	1762	1772	R	rectangle	pellet
	L	1772	–	–	R	rectangle	–
William Ward	Db	1774	1782	1807	R	rectangle	pellet
William Welch of Plymouth	Ex	–	1799	1837	R	rectangle	–
	Ex	–	–	–	G	rectangle	–
William Weston	L	1810	1810	–	R	rectangle	pellet
	L	1822	–	–	R	oval	pellet
W&W J. Wakeley & F. C. Wheeler Ltd	L	–	1884	1969	S	trefoil	also DB
	L (*also* Ch & Ed)	–	–	–	–	–	F J C W W
W W F D William Thomas Wright & Frederick Davies	L	1864	1870	1891	R	quatrefoil	2 pellets
W W H W. W. Harrison & Co	S	1856	1862	1900	R	rectangle	–
	S	1861	–	–	R	3 circles	–
	S	1857	–	–	–	–	WWH&Co
	S	1866	–	–	–	–	W H W
W H W W. W. Harrison & Co	S	1866	1862	1900	R	trefoil	–
	S	1856	–	–	–	–	WWH
	S	1857	–	–	–	–	WWH & Co
W W H & Co W. W. Harrison & Co	S	1857	1862	1900	G	–	–
	S	1856	–	–	–	–	WWH
	S	1866	–	–	–	–	W H W

Maker's initial(s) & maker(s)	Town of registration	Date of mark registration	Earliest example	Latest example	Letter style G Gothic R Roman S Script	Punch shape	Additional features/notes
W & W **J H** White, Henderson & Co	S	1866	1871	1878	R	quatrefoil	2 pellets
W W **T J** White & Johnstone	S	1859	1862	1863	R	tridentate hatchment	3 pellets
WW&TB William Watson & Thomas Bradbury	S	–	1790	1825	R	rectangle	–
J W **J W** Robert James & Josiah Williams	Ex	–	1847	1852	R	quadriform	–
YG&H Young, Greaves & Hoyland	S	1779	1780	1786	R	rectangle	pellet
Y O Edward Yorke	L	1705	1709	1731	G	domate triad	2 mullets
	L	1730	–	–	–	–	EY
Y&W John Yapp & John Woodward	B	1845	1845	1854	R	rectangle	–
	L	1845	–	1847	–	–	–

* Date separation between generations is uncertain.
(?) Identity of maker or mark is uncertain.
[flag] Square brackets indicate shape not included in punch shape charts on pages 14 and 15.

L London
A Aberdeen
B Birmingham
Ch Chester
Co Cork
Db Dublin
Du Dundee

Ed Edinburgh
Ex Exeter
Gl Glasgow
Gr Greenock
Gy Galway
H Hull
M Montrose

Nc Newcastle
Nw Norwich
P Perth
S Sheffield
Y York

Maker's name	Town of registration	Earliest mark registration	Earliest example	Latest example	Maker's mark/notes
Alexander, William	L	1743	1752	1759	WA
Allan, Coline	A	1748	1748	1750	CA
Allanson, William, & Co	S	1832	–	1836	WA & Co
Alleine, Jonathan	L	1771	1770	1798	JA IA
Allen, Joseph, & Fox, Mordecai	L	1730	–	1732	IA IA MF MF
Allen, Thomas	L	1697	1694	1719	AL
Allen, William III	L	1798	1799	1805	WA
Allen & Darwin	S	1887	1895	1920	–
Allison, Andrew	Gl	–	1836	–	AA
Andrews, John II	L	1818	1808	–	JA
Andrews, William	L	1697	1697	1713	AN (N smaller)
Angel, George	L	–	1841	1892	GA
Angel, John	L	–	1855	–	(no personal mark)
Angel, John Charles (worked only with uncle Joseph Angel)	L	1832	–	–	–
Angel, John & George	L	–	1840	1847	–
Angel, Joseph I	L	1811	1813	*	JA
Angel, Joseph II	L	–	1841	1858	JA
Angel, Joseph III	L	–	*	*	–
Angel, Joseph II & Joseph III	L	–	1841	1846	–
Angel, Joseph & John	L	1831	1839	1866	JA IA
Annesley, Arthur	L	1758	1758	1760	AA
Anthony, Edward	Ex	1612	1610	1667	E A
Appleby, Thomas	Ch	–	1791	1812	TA
Appleton & Smith see Smith & Appleton					
Archambo, Peter I	L	1721	1721	1758	AR PA
Archambo, Peter II, & Meure, Peter	L	1750	1741	1757	P PA M
Archbold, Francis	L	1697	1699	1714	AR
Archdall, William	Db	1704	1712	1729	WA
Archer, Andrew	L	1703	1703	1719	A AR
Archer, Hy, & Co	S	1855	1846	1896	HA
Archer, Machin & Marsh	S	1854	1858	1924	HA

Maker's name	Town of registration	Earliest mark registration	Earliest example	Latest example	Maker's mark/notes
Abdy, William I	L	1763	1762	1797	WA
Abdy, William II	L	1790	1791	1809	WA
Abercromby, Robert	L	1731	1731	1754	Ab RA
Abercromby, Robert, & Hindmarsh, George	L	1731	1730	–	R GA H
Abraham, Joseph	L	1796	–	1804	IA
Adam, Charles	L	1703	1698	1719	AD
Adams, George W.	L	1840	1840	1892	GA
Adams, Stephen I	L	1760	1765	1819	SA
Adams, Stephen II	L	1813	1811	–	SA
Adie Bros Ltd.	B	–	1902	1963	–
Ainsworth, Taylor & Co	B	–	c1900	–	AT & Co
Aitken, Peter II	Gl	1845	1849	1860	PAJ R
Aitken Bros Ltd,	B	–	1893	1931	–
Aitken, William	S	–	1915	1933	–
	Ch	–	1899	1901	–
Alanson, Matthew	Db	–	1736	–	–
Albright, John	L	1718	1717	1724	AL IA
Alchorn, Charles	L	1729	1730	1738	CA
Alcock, G.	Db	–	1841	1842	GA
Alcock, John	L	1725	1719	–	IA
Alderhead, John	L	1750	–	1752	IA
Aldridge, Charles	L	1786	1787	1809	CA
Aldridge, Charles, & Green, Henry	L	1775	1767	1788	C HA G
Aldridge, Edward I	L	1724	1734	1772	EA
Aldridge, Edward I, & Stamper, John	L	1753	1753	1759	E IA S
Aldridge, James	L	1798	1801	1809	JA
Aldwincle, J., & Slater, J. (of Holland, Aldwincle & Slater)	L	–	1879	1894	JA JS

Maker's name	Town of registration	Earliest mark registration	Earliest example	Latest example	Maker's mark/notes
Armstead, Henry Hugh (born 1828)	–	–	1854	1871	–
Army & Navy Co-operative Society Ltd	L	–	1892	1928	BMW
Arnell, John	L	1773	1772	1774	IA
Arnett, Hugh, & Pocock, Edward	L	1720	1719	1734	A^R_OP H^A_PE
Arnold & Lewis of Manchester	L	–	1911	–	A & L
Arthur & Co Ltd	B	–	1910	–	–
Arthur, Peter	Gl	1808	1822	1850	PA
Artificers Guild Ltd	L	–	1924	1932	–
Arts & Crafts Movement see Guild of Handicrafts					
Ash, Joseph I	L	1801	1805	1809	IA
Ash, Joseph II	L	1811	1811	1812	IA
Ash, Thomas	L	1697	1702	1714	AS ASH
Ashbee, Charles Robert (1863–1942)	L	1896	1887	1900	CRA from 1888)
	L	1898	1905	1908	GofH$_L$ D
Ashberry, Philip & Sons	S	1830	–	1872	–
Ashforth, George, & Co	S	1773	1774	1822	GA &Co
Ashforth & Harthorne	S	1826	1824	1831	AH
Ashworth, Mary, of Durham	Nc	–	1794	1800	MA
Asman, Frederick C., & Co	S	–	1904	–	–
Asprey & Co Ltd	L	–	1911	1972	PHA
	B	–	1903	1939	-
	S	–	1911	1965	–
	Ch	–	1930	1939	–
Aston, Thomas & Son	B	1858	1858	–	A & S
Atkin Bros	S	1853	1859	1859	HA
Atkin, Henry	S	1841	1841	–	HA
Atkin & Oxley	S	1824	1828	1839	A & O
Atkin, James	L	1795	1800	1812	JA
Atkins, Richard William	L	–	1815	–	RA see WS
Atkins, Richard William, & Somersall, William Nathaniel	L	1824	1826	1836	RA WS
Atkinson, William	L	1725	1726	1729	AT WA
Attenborough, Richard see Jay, Richard Attenborough	S	–	–	–	–
Audrey, John	Ex	–	1701	1705	Au
Aytoun, William	Ed	1718	1729	1749	WA
Backe, John	L	1700	1701	1725	BA IB
Bacon, F.C.	L	–	1904	–	–
Baddeley, John	L	1818	–	1820	IB
Bagnall, William	L	1744	1749	1754	WB
Bailey, Henry	L	1750	1760	1769	HB
Bainbridge, William I	L	1697	1698	1711	BA (A smaller)
Baker Bros	Ch	–	1902	1926	BB (?)
Baker, John II	L	1770	1770	1772	IB JB
Ballam, Thomas	L	1820	1823	1824	TB
Balliston, Thomas	L	1812	1809	1825	TB
Bamford, Thomas I	L	1720	1716	1732	Ba TB
Banks, J. Millward, & Co see Millward Banks, J., & Co	Ch	–	–	–	–
Barbe, John	L	1735	1737	1766	IB
Barber, James	Y	–	1805	1857	JB
Barber, James & Co	Y	–	1818	1824	JB &Co JB
Barber, James; Cattle, George, & North, William	Y	–	1825	1833	BC GC &N WN
Barber, James, & North, William	Y	–	1836	1847	JB WN
Barber, James, & Whitwell, William	Y	–	1812	1841	JB WW
Barbut (or Barbit), Joseph	L	1703	1706	1720	BA IB
Barclay & Goodwin	Gl	–	1852	–	SB GG
Barkentin, Jes (of Barkentin & Krall) see Krall, Carl Christof	L	–	1871	1880	–

Maker's name	Town of registration	Earliest mark registration	Earliest example	Latest example	Maker's mark/notes
Barkentin & Krall	L	–	1894	1915	CK (Carl Krall)
Barker Bros & Sons Ltd	B	–	1897	1938	–
	Ch	–	1907	1946	–
Barker, Christopher & Thomas W.	L	1800	1800	1804	CB TB
Barker, Ellis & Co Ltd	B	–	1965	–	–
Barker, James	L	1746	–	1766	IB
Barker, Robert	L	1793	–	1794	RB
Barker, Susanna	L	1778	1770	1792	SB
Barker, Thomas Wilkes	L	1805	1804	1827	TB
Barnard, Edward & Sons Ltd	L	–	1897	1974	$\begin{smallmatrix}W&&J\\&B&\\M&&S\\R&&D\end{smallmatrix}$
Barnard, Edward I, Edward II, John & William	L	1829	1828	1895	$\begin{smallmatrix}E&&E\\&B&\\J&&W\end{smallmatrix}$
Barnard, Edward & John	L	–	1851	1869	E&B EB J B JB
Barnard, E., J. & W.	L	–	1835	1871	$\begin{smallmatrix}E&&J\\&\&B&\\&&W\end{smallmatrix}$
Barnard, John I	L	1697	1699	1713	Ba IB BA
Barnard, Michael & Stanley, & Joynes, George W.	L	–	1930	–	–
Barnard, Walter & John II	L	–	1877	1896	WBJ
Barnard, W., J., M. & S., & Duback, R.	L	–	1897	1974	$\begin{smallmatrix}W&&J\\&B&\\M&&S\\R&&D\end{smallmatrix}$
Barnett, Edward	L	1715	1711	1717	BA
Barnett, Michael	L	1781	1791	1820	MB
Barraclough, Z. & Sons Ltd	S	–	1898	1906	–
	Ch	–	1931	1937	–
Barrett, A.J. (Designer for Hunt & Roskell)	L	–	1862	–	–
Barrett, A. & Sons	L	–	1896	1908	–
	B	–	1895	–	–
Barrett, Edward	Db	1702	1700	1738	EB
Barrett, Edward	L	–	1714	1723	BA
Barrett, James	L	1801	1805	1821	IB
Barrett, William I	L	1771	1788	1791	WB
Barrett, William II	L	1821	1814	1825	WB
Bartleman, J. & Son	Ed	–	1908	–	–
Barton, Edward	L	1822	1821	1832	EB
Baskerville, George	L	1738	1745	1814	GB
Baskerville, George, & Morley, Thomas	L	1775	1775	–	$G\begin{smallmatrix}T\\M\end{smallmatrix}B$
Bassingwhite, John	L	1770	1769	1802	IB
Baston, Henry John, & Albert, Edward	L	–	1903	1927	–
Bateman, Hester	L	1761	1763	1795	HB
Bateman, Peter & Ann	L	1791	1781	1818	PB AB
Bateman, Peter, Ann & William I	L	1800	1791	1823	PB AB WB
Bateman, Peter & Jonathan	L	1790	1790	1790	PB IB
Bateman, Peter & William I	L	1805	1789	1830	PB WB
Bateman, William I	L	1815	1816	1838	WB
Bateman, William II	L	1827	1827	1835	WB
Bateman, William II, & Ball, Daniel	L	1839	1839	1841	WB DB
Bates, Daniel	L	1778	1777	–	DB
Batson *see* Baston					
Batt, John	S	1880	1881	1884	–
Batt, W. & Sons	S	1881	–	–	–
Batty, Francis I	Nc	1674	–	1703	Ba
Batty, Francis II	Nc	1708	1712	1736	Ba FB
Batty, Howard & Hawksworth	S	1815	1811	1829	BH &H
Baxter, John, of Banbury	L	1770	1770	1773	IB
Bayley (or Bailey), Henry	L	1750	1757	1769	HB
Bayley, John	L	1751	–	1753	IB
Bayley, Richard	L	1708	1710	1750	BA RB
Bayley, William I	L	1759	–	–	WB
Bayley, William II	L	1770	1781	1806	WB
Beale, George	L	1699	1714	1729	Be BE

Maker's name	Town of registration	Earliest mark registration	Earliest example	Latest example	Maker's mark/notes
Beale, Richard	L	1733	1730	1749	RB
Beathune, Harry	Ed	1704	1716	1726	HB
Beckwith, George	L	1804	–	1805	GB
Beckwith, Robert	Y	1546	–	1573	RB
Beebe, James	L	1811	1803	1833	JB
Beere, Samuel	Db	1818	1821	1829	SB
Beezley, Thomas	L	1755	1754	1755	TB
Beilby, Ralph	Nc	–	1757	1758	RB
Beilby, William	Nc	–	1733	1765	WB
Beldon, John	L	1784	1794	1800	IB
Bell, David	L	1756	1756	1778	DB
Bell, Joseph I	L	1716	1716	–	BE
Bell, Joseph II	L	1756	1762	1764	IB IBELL
Bell, Joseph III	L	1818	*	*	JB
Bell, Richard	L	1734	–	1737	RB
Bell, William	L	1759	–	1763	WB
Bellassyse, William	L	1717	1722	1723	BE WB
Bellchambers, William	L	–	1820	1839	WB
Bennett, Edward I	L	1727	1731	1750	EB
Bennett, Peter	L	1732	1739	1761	PB
Bennett, Sampson, of Falmouth	Ex	1721	1734	1759	SB
Bennett, William	L	1796	1792	1827	WB
Bennett, Sir John, Ltd	L	–	1937	–	–
Benney, Gerald	L	–	1956	1974	AGB
Benson, Alfred, & Arthur, Henry see Hunt & Roskell	L	1895	–	1901	A^{A}H^{B}B
Benson, Alfred, & Wintle, H.H. see Hunt & Roskell	L	1889	1889	1895	H^{A}H^{B}W
Benson, J.W., Ltd see Hunt & Roskell	L	–	1877	1892	–
Benson, W.A.S. (1854–1924)	L	–	1880	–	–
Bentley, Benjamin	L	1698	1710	1716	BE BB
Bergin, S.	Db	–	1815	1822	SB
Berresford, J.S.	L	–	1887	1889	–
Berthelot, John	L	1738	1747	1787	IB
Beschefer, James	L	1704	–	1706	BE
Best, Marmaduke	Y	1657	1663	1702	MB
Betagh, William	Db	1751	–	1775	–
Betjamen, G. & Sons	L	–	1879	1889	–
Bettridge, John	B	1817	1817	1834	IB
Bevault, Thomas	L	1712	–	1714	Be
Biddell, Thomas	L	1811	–	1813	TB
Bigge, Richard	L	1700	–	1702	BI
Biggin, G.H.	S	–	1898	1899	–
Biggin, John	S	1855	–	1864	JB
Biggin, Samuel & Son	S	–	1894	–	–
Biggs, Joseph	L	1816	1817	1818	IB
Biggs, Roger	L	1791	–	1793	RB
Bignell, John	L	1718	1720	1732	BI IB
Billingsley, Francis	L	1697	–	1698	Bi
Bilton, Eli	Nc	1683	1683	1711	Bi EB
Bingham, J.E.	B	–	1898	–	–
	S	–	1876	1891	–
see Walker & Hall					
Binley, Margaret	L	1764	–	–	MB
Binley, Richard	L	1760	1793	1794	RB
Birch, C.B.	–	–	1880	1891	–
see Hunt & Roskell and Hancocks					
Birch, Derek	B	–	1971	–	–
Bird, Joseph	L	1697	1697	1723	Bi BI IB
Birks, W., & Co.	S	1773	–	1779	WB &Co
Birks, Henry, & Co	B	–	1908	–	–
Biron & Gaydon Ltd	L	–	1935	–	–
Black, Louis	L	1756	1759	1764	LB
Blackbeard, Francis	L	1824	1824	–	FB
Blackford, Samuel, of Plymouth	Ex	1706	1720	1730	BL SB
Blackford, Anthony	L	1702	1703	1704	BL
Blackmore & Sons Ltd	L	–	1918	1938	–
	B	–	1917	1932	–
	Ch	–	1912	1939	–
Blackwell, William, & Co	S	1816	1823	1824	WB & Co
Blagdon, Thomas, & Co	S	1808	1808	1829	TB &Co
Blair, Charles	Ed	1707	1709	1724	CB
Blake, John	L	1788	1797	1804	IB
Blake, John William	L	1823	1823	–	IWB
Blake, Sarah & John William	L	1809	1810	1821	SB IB
Blakeley, Benjamin	L	1715	1716	1725	BL BB

Maker's name	Town of registration	Earliest mark registration	Earliest example	Latest example	Maker's mark/notes
Blanckensee & Sons Ltd	B	–	1917	1922	–
	Ch	–	1934	–	–
Bland, Cornelius	L	1772	1788	1800	CB
Bland, James & Elizabeth	L	1794	1794	1800	IB EB
Boardman & Glossop & Co Ltd	B	–	1927	1937	–
	S	–	1879	1920	–
Bock, Mark	L	1761	1792	1806	MB
Boddington, John	L	1697	1697	1713	BO
Bodenick, Jacob	L	–	1680	–	–
Bolton (or Boulton), Thomas	Db	1686	1696	1725	B TB TB monogram
Bond, William	Db	1791	1777	1809	WB
Boosey, C.	L	–	1889	–	–
Booth, John	L	1813	1814	1817	IB
Booth, Wilkes	L	1787	1792	1810	WB
Booth, Wilkes & John	L	1810	1810	–	WB JB
Boothby, George	L	1720	1722	1752	BO GB
Borthwick, John	Ed	1681	1681	1696	B
Boulger, Robert	Ch	–	1787	1802	RB
Boult, Michael	L	1713	1714	1718	BO MB
Boulton, Matthew (1728–1809)	B	1790	1776	1809	MB
Boulton, Matthew Robinson see Boulton Plate Co	B	–	–	–	–
Boulton Plate Co	B	1809	1811	1833	MB
Boulton, Matthew, & Fothergill, John	B	1773	1769	1781	MB IF
	Ch	–	1768	–	B&F (separate crowns)
Bourn(e), John	L	1774	–	1791	IB
Boxwell, Ambrose	Db	1768	1767	1788	AB
Boyton, Charles	L	1825	1826	1933	CB
Boyton, Charles, & Sons Ltd	L	–	1906	1932	–
Bradbury, Thomas, & Sons	S	1832	1839	1944	TB&S JB JB TB EB TB &S
	L	–	1892	1907	TB &S
Bradley, Jonathan	L	1697	1696	1697	BR
Bradley, Joseph	L	1776	–	1784	IB
Bradley, Samuel	L	–	1791	–	SB
Bradshaw, Bennett, & Tyrill, Robert	L	1737	1737	1740	R$_B^B$T B$_R^T$B
Brady, J.	Db	–	1797	1803	IB
Braford, Benjamin	L	1697	1697	1698	BR
Bragg, T. & J.	B	–	1876	–	–
Brasier, George	L	1785	1789	1800	GB
Brasted, Frederick	L	–	1864	1887	–
Breading, Robert	Db	1782	1782	1816	RB
Brent, Moses	L	1775	1791	1817	MB
Brewis & Co	S	–	1909	–	–
Brewood, Benjamin I	L	1729	–	–	BB
Brewood, Benjamin II	L	1755	1758	1767	BB
Briddon Bros	S	1863	1863	–	BB
Bridge, John (of Rundell, Bridge & Rundell)	L	1823	1798	1833	IB
Bridge, John Gawler see Rundell & Bridge	L	–	–	–	–
Bridgeman, Thomas	Ex	1686	1696	1725	B TB TB monogram
Brind, Henry	L	1742	1742	1763	HB
Brind, Walter	L	1749	1746	1789	WB
Britton, James	L	1820	1823	1835	JB
Britton, Richard	L	1812	1817	1830	RB
Broak, John	L	1699	1699	1711	Br
Brogden, John	L	–	1851	–	–
Brokesby, Abel	L	1727	1727	1728	AB
Brook & Son	S	–	1906	1934	B & S
	Ed	–	1888	1937	B & S
Brough, John	L	1803	–	1814	IB JB
Brough, Thomas	L	1795	1797	1814	TB
Brown, Alexander	Db	1726	1727	1736	AB
Brown, Alfred see Hunt & Roskell	L	–	–	–	–
Brown, Edward Charles	L	–	1867	1882	E$_B$C
Brown, Howard J., of Norwich	L	–	1952	–	–
Brown, Mathias	Db	–	1752	–	–
Brown, Robert	L	1736	1735	1743	RB

Maker's name	Town of registration	Earliest mark registration	Earliest example	Latest example	Maker's mark/notes
Brown, Thomas *see* Hunt & Roskell	L	–	–	–	–
Brown, William, of Coventry	L	1822	1826	1837	WB
Brown & Clarke	B	–	1854	–	–
Brownett, Jane	L	–	1885	1895	–
Bruce, Robert	Ed	1687	–	1695	RB
Bruce, William	L	1811	1813	1818	WB
Bruguier, Philip	L	1739	1751	1756	PB
Brush, Philip	L	1707	–	1710	Br
Brydie, John	L	1823	–	1826	IB
Brydon, Thomas	L	1697	1696	1697	Br BR
Bu(c)kett, John	L	1760	–	1764	IB
Buckle(s), Stephen	Nc	–	1740	1741	SB
Buckton, J.	Db	–	1818	1837	IB
Buckton, Richard	L	1806	–	1807	RB
Bull, F.D.	L	–	1881	–	–
Bulman, George	Nc	–	1724	1743	GB
Bumfries, Thomas, & Jackson, Orlando	L	1766	1766	–	T^O_IB
Burridge, R.W.	L	–	1914	1960	–
	S	–	1911	1975	–
Burbury, J.	S	–	1830	–	–
Burcombe, Richard	L	1724	–	1731	RB
Burdon, John	Ex	–	1719	1739	IB
Burrell, Edwin	S	–	1892	–	–
Burridge, J.	L	–	1720	–	IB
Burridge, Thomas	L	1706	1712	1732	Bu TB
Burrows, Alice & George II	L	1801	1801	1837	AB GB
Burrows, George I	L	1769	1781	1823	GB
Burrows, George II	L	1819	1823	1824	GB
Burrows, George II, & Pearce, Richard	L	1826	1826	1851	RP GB
Burrows, George II & T.	L	–	1795	1803	GB TB
Burrows, C.T. & Sons	B	–	1931	–	–
Burton, Jocelyn	L	–	1975	–	JB
Burtt, Joseph Josiah	L	1828	1838	1848	JB
Burwash, Thomas	L	1821	–	1822	TB
Burwash, William	L	1802	1803	1821	WB
Burwash, William, & Sibley, Richard I	L	1805	1805	1840	WB RS

Maker's name	Town of registration	Earliest mark registration	Earliest example	Latest example	Maker's mark/notes
Busfield, William	Y	1679	1677	1705	Bu WB WB conjoined
Buteux, Abraham	L	1721	1722	1731	BV AB
Buteux, Elizabeth (*later* Elizabeth Godfrey)	L	1731	1731	1732	EB
Butler, George, & Co Ltd	S	–	1895	–	–
Buttall, Sarah	L	1754	–	1790	SB
Butty, Francis, & Dumee, Nicholas	L	1761	1765	1772	FB ND
Byrne, Gustavus	Db	1791	1793	1807	GB
Byrne, Thomas	Ex	1855	1839	1849	TB
Cachart, Elias *see* Catchart					
Cadman, Morris	L	1810	–	1829	MC
Cafe, John	L	1740	1742	1762	IC
Cafe, William	L	1757	1740	1771	WC
Calame, James Anthony	L	1764	1764	1774	AC IAC
Caldecott, William	L	1756	1756	1777	WC
Calderwood, Robert	Db	1727	1728	1729	RC
Callard, Isaac	L	1726	1732	1769	CA IC
Callard, Paul	L	1752	1760	1767	PC
Callow	L	–	1913	–	–
Cameron, Alexander, of Dundee	Du	–	1797	1833	AC CAM ERON DUN DEE
Campbell, Colin	Ed	1711	1711	1722	CC
Camper (*or* Campar), George	L	1749	1730	1757	GC
Canner, Christopher I	L	1697	–	1698	CA (A within)
Canner, Christopher II	L	1716	1718	1723	Ca (a within) ƆC
Capper, Edward	L	1792	–	1820	EC
Carman, John I	L	1716	–	1720	CA IC
Carman, John II	L	1748	1749	1756	IC
Carnaby, John	Nc	1717	1719	1724	Ca (a within) JC

Maker's name	Town of registration	Earliest mark registration	Earliest example	Latest example	Maker's mark/notes
Carr, Alwyn	L	–	1903	1930	–
Carrington & Co Ltd	L	–	1882	1959	C&Co JBC & S L
Carrington, John Boddington	L	–	1882	1959	JBC
Carter, G.A. see Hunt & Roskell	–	–	c1880	c1890	–
Carter, John I	L	1697	–	1741	CA
Carter, John II	L	1776	1776	1784	IC
Carter, Peter	L	1783	1786	1790	PC
Carter, Richard; Smith, Daniel, & Sharp, Robert	L	1778	1777	1788	RC DS RS
Cartwright, Benjamin I	L	1739	–	1740	BC
Cartwright, Benjamin II	L	1754	–	1770	BC
Cartwright, Woodward & Co	B	–	1846	1867	–
Catchart, Elias	L	1742	1740	1765	EC
Catchpole & Williams	L	–	1902	1934	–
Cattell, William	L	1771	1773	1778	WC
Cattle, Robert, & Barber, J.	Y	–	1807	1814	RC JB
Chadwick, James	L	1697	1697	1702	CH
Chapman, John I	L	1730	1727	1738	IC
Chapple & Mantell	L	–	1884	–	–
Charnelhouse, William	L	1703	1706	1711	CH
Chartier, Daniel	L	1740	1739	–	DC
Chartier, John	L	1723	1699	1714	CH IC
Chatterley, John B., & Sons	B	–	1965	–	–
Chatterton, Randall	L	1825	1825	1843	RC
Chawner, Henry	L	1786	1778	1809	HC
Chawner, Henry, & Emes, John	L	1796	1796	1797	HC IE
Chawner, Mary	L	1834	1834	1840	MC
Chawner, Mary, & Adams, George William	L	–	1840	–	MC GA
Chawner, Thomas	L	1773	1766	1786	TC
Chawner, Thomas & William I	L	1763	1760	1771	W$^{T}_{C}$ T$^{W}_{C}$ TC WC C$^{C}_{W}$ WC
Chawner, William II	L	1815	1813	1833	WC
Chawner & Co	–	1834	1881	–	–
Cheese, Clement	L	1823	1826	1828	CC
Cheshire, C.H.	B	–	1875	1888	–
	Ch	–	1876	1924	–
Chester, W. & H.	L	–	1874	–	–
Chesterman, Charles I	L	1741	1752	1792	CC
Chesterman, Charles II	L	1801	1811	1828	CC
Chesterman, Ann	L	1775	–	1776	AC
Christie, John	D	–	1748	1761	IC
Clare, Joseph I	L	1713	1714	1737	IC IC CL
Clare, Joseph II	L	1763	–	1768	IC CL ARE
Clark, Alfred	L	–	1810	–	–
Clark, Charles	L	1739	–	1768	CC
Clark, Francis	B	1826	1830	1848	FC
Clark, John	Ed	1751	1755	1765	CLARK
Clark, Robert	Ed	1763	1765	1766	RC
Clark, John Edward, & Smith, Edward	B	–	1825	–	–
Clark, Alexander, Manufacturing Co Ltd	L	–	1903	1926	–
	B	–	1917	1938	–
	S	–	1896	1924	–
	Ch	–	1906	–	–
Clarke, Henry I	L	1709	1711	1722	CL HC
Clarke, James	Ed	1710	1722	1742	IC
Clarke, John II	L	–	1809	–	–
Clarke, William	Co	–	1710	1719	WC
Clausen, Nicholaus	L	1709	1713	1719	CL NC
Clayton, John	L	1736	1744	1745	IC
Clements, Eric see Wakeley & Wheeler	L	–	1960	1962	–
Clements, George	L	1825	–	1838	GC
Clifton, John I	Db	1719	1714	1722	IC

Maker's name	Town of registration	Earliest mark registration	Earliest example	Latest example	Maker's mark/notes
Clifton, John II	Db	–	1719	1726	IC
Clifton, Jonah	L	1703	1703	1725	CL IC
Coates, Alexander, & French, Edward	L	1734	1734	–	AC EF
Cobb, Frank, & Co	S	–	1929	1935	–
Cockburn, James	Ed	1669	1687	1702	IC monogram
Cocks & Bettridge	B	1813	1814	1823	C&B
Coghill, William	Gl	–	1866	–	WC
Coker, Ebenezer	L	1738	1748	1775	EC
Coker, Ebenezer, & Hannam, Thomas	L	1759	1759	–	EC TH
Cole, John	L	1697	1697	1706	CO
Coleman, John	L	–	1777	–	–
Coleman, Stephen	L	1697	1681	1701	CO
Coles, Lawrence	L	1697	1674	1709	CO
Coley, Simeon	L	1761	1763	1812	SC
Collier, Joseph, of Plymouth	Ex	1713	1726	1737	JC
Collingwood & Co	L	–	1900	1931	–
Collins, D.G.	S	–	1908	–	–
Collins, J.	L	1754	–	–	IC
Collis, G.R., & Co	B	1837	1842	1846	–
Comyns, Charles & Richard	L	–	1918	1926	C&R C
Comyns, William & Sons Ltd	L	–	1887	1915	WC
(also B)					
Comyns, Richard	L	–	1926	1972	–
Comyns, R. & W.	L	–	1924	–	–
Conen, Edward	L	1724	1724	–	EC
Connel, C.L.	B	–	1913	1926	–
	L	–	1902	–	CLC
Connell, W.G.	L	–	1901	–	–
Constable, William	Du	–	1806	1809	WC
Cook, John	Nc	–	1811	–	IC
Cooke, Elizabeth	L	1764	1763	1772	EC
Cooke, Richard	L	1799	1798	1811	RC
Cooke, Thomas I	L	1713	–	–	TC CO
Cooke, Thomas II	L	1727	–	–	TC
Cooke, Thomas II, & Gurney, Richard	L	1727	1727	1768	$R^T_C G$
Cookson, Isaac	Nc	1728	1722	1772	IC
Cooper, Benjamin I	L	1724	–	1759	BC
Cooper, Benjamin II	L	1764	1767	1785	BC
Cooper, Edward	L	1775	–	1776	EC
Cooper, George	A	1728	–	1730	GC
Cooper, G., & Co	S	–	1818	1819	GC&Co
Cooper, H.J.	B	–	1902	–	–
Cooper, Matthew I	L	1702	1703	1731	CO MC
Cooper, Matthew II	L	1725	–	1731	CO MC
Cooper, Robert	L	1697	1682	1716	CO
Cooper, William	L	–	1839	1851	WC (probably)
Cooper Bros & Sons Ltd	L	–	1889	1973	$J^T W^C C$
(also B)					
Cope, Erasmus	Db	1707	1717	1736	EC
Corbett, Thomas	L	1699	–	1703	CO
Cornasseau, Isaac (or Cornafleur)	L	–	1719	1723	CO IC
Cornock, Edward	L	1707	1707	1733	CO EC
Corporon, John	L	1717	1717	–	CO
Corry, Henry	L	1754	1759	1767	HC
Cory, John	L	1697	1698	1704	CO
Cotterill, Edmund	L	–	1843	1858	–
Courtauld, Augustine	L	1708	1710	1743	CO AC
Courtauld, Louisa Perina	L	–	1765	1767	LC
Courtauld, Louisa Perina, & Cowles, George	L	1773	1765	1777	LC GC
Courtauld, Louisa Perina & Samuel II	L	1777	–	–	LC SC
Courtauld, Samuel I	L	1746	1747	1764	SC
Courthorpe, Edward	L	1697	–	1701	CO
Courthorpe, Frederick	L	1884	–	1886	–
Cowie, George & John	L	1822	–	1838	GC IC
Cowie, John	L	1813	1813	1819	JC
Cowles, George	L	1777	1778	1802	GC
Cowper, Henry	L	1782	1788	1790	HC
Cox, George	L	1698	1698	1715	CO
Cox, Robert Albin	L	1752	1749	1759	RC
Craddock, Joseph	L	1825	1825	1829	IC

Maker's name	Town of registration	Earliest mark registration	Earliest example	Latest example	Maker's mark/notes
Craddock, Joseph, & Reid, William K.	L	1812	1812	1825	IC WR
Craig, Anne, & Neville, John	L	1740	1740	1742	AC IN
Craig, John	Db	1769	1771	1790	IC
Craw, Matthew	Ed	–	1802	1816	MC
Crawford, David	Nc	–	1763	1784	DC
Crawford, James	Nc	–	1763	1771	IC
Crespel, Sebastian II	L	1826	1825	1854	SC
Crespel, Sebastian I & James	L	–	1761	1776	SC IC
Crespel & Parker	L	–	1871	–	–
Crespin, Paul	L	1740	1721	1766	CR PC
Creswick, Joseph	S	1777	1776	1819	IC
Creswick, Thomas & James	S	1810	1811	1826	TJC
Creswick, T., J. & N.	S	1819	1811	1865	T C J & N TJ&NC JC NC
Creswick & Co	S	1858	–	1865	IFP C&Co C&Co
Crichton, L. Alexander	L	–	1882	1939	LAC
Crichton, J.	Ed	–	1874	1879	JC J CRICHTON
Crichton & Co	Ed	–	1891	1896	JC&Co
Cripps, William	L	1743	1744	1777	WC
Crisford & Norris	B	–	1902	1916	–
Croakley, John, of Liverpool	Ch	–	1828	1834	JC
Crofton, Edward	Db	1827	1815	1831	EC
Crossley, Richard	L	1782	1782	1812	RC
Crossley, Richard, & Smith, George IV	L	1807	1806	1815	RC GS
Croswell, Mary Ann	L	1805	–	1810	MC
	L	1816	–	–	–
Crouch, John II	L	1808	1807	1825	JC
Crouch, John I & Hannam, Thomas	L	–	1763	1809	IC TH
Crouch, William	Ed	–	1832	1863	WC
Cruickshank, Robert	L	c1773	1782	1804	RC
Crump, Francis	L	1741	1742	1790	FC
Crutchfield, Jonathan	L	1697	–	1704	CR(R smaller)
Cullen, Joseph	Db	1753	–	1770	IC
Cumming, Thomas	Gl	1682	1699	1704	TC
Cummins, C. I	Db	–	1836	*	CC
Cummins, C. II	Db	–	1848	1863	CC
Cummins, W.	Db	–	1813	1828	WC
Cunliffe, Nicholas	Ch	–	1798	1815	NC
Cunningham, Daniel (Peter)	L	1717	1720	1720	CV DC
Cunningham, W. & P.	Ed	–	1784	1826	WPC W& PC WC PC
	Gl	–	1821	1824	–
Cunningham & Simpson	Ed	–	1806	1815	PC &S PC&S
Cuny, Louis	L	1703	1697	1729	CV LC
Curry, Henry William	L	–	1868	1885	–
Cuthbert, John I	Db	1670	1685	*	IC
Cuthbert, John II	Db	1702	1725	1729	IC
Daintry, Marmaduke	L	1737	1741	1751	MD
Dalrymple, John	Db	–	1790	–	ID
Dalton, Isaac	L	1711	1706	1719	DA
Dalton, William	Nc	1725	1724	1767	WD
Daly, John	Db	1786	–	1798	JD
Daniel, Henry	Db	1778	–	–	HD
Daniel, Jabez	L	1749	1749	1783	ID
Daniel, Jabez, & Mince, James	L	1766	1767	1771	$I_M D$
Daniel, James Henry	L	1820	1826	1829	IHD HD
Daniel, Josiah	L	1715	1715	1724	DA ID
Daniel, Thomas	L	1774	1768	1790	TD
Daniel, Thomas & Jabez	L	–	1771	1777	$I_D^T D$
Daniel, Thomas, & Wall, John	L	1781	1781	–	TD IW
Daniel & Arter	B	–	1912	1934	D&A
	S	–	1892	1900	–
Darker, William	L	1719	1719	1733	DA WD
Darling, David	Nc	–	1802	1804	DD
Darquits, James II	L	1787	–	1802	ID
Darvill, Edward	L	1757	–	1773	ED

Maker's name	Town of registration	Earliest mark registration	Earliest example	Latest example	Maker's mark/notes
Davenport, Burrage	L	–	1768	1784	BD
Davenport, Isaac	L	1697	1697	1720	DA
Davenport, Samuel	L	1786	1786	1826	SD
Davenport, Samuel & Edward	L	1794	1786	1815	SDED
David, Fleurant	L	–	1724	1725	DA FD
Davie, Thomas	Gr	–	1795	1800	TD
Davie, William	Ed	1740	1745	1789	WD
Davis, Benjamin	L	1823	–	1826	BD
Davis, Tompson	L	1757	1763	1764	TD
Dawson, John	Db	1764	1751	1753	ID
Dawson, Nelson	L	–	1891	1896	–
Dawson, Stewart, & CoB Ltd		–	1912	1913	–
Day, George	L	1809	–	1812	GD
Deacon, John	L	1776	1762	1776	ID
Deakin & Francis	B	–	1886	1956	–
Deakin, James & Sons Ltd	S	1878	1880	1932	JD &S JD WD
	B	–	1893	1903	–
	Ch	–	1894	1926	–
Dealtry, Thomas	L	1765	1771	1814	TD
Deane, William & John	L	1759	1762	1764	W^{D}I WDDJ
Death, Thomas	L	1812	1812	1832	TD
Dee, Henry William (of H.W. & L. Dee)	L	–	1867	1877	–
Dee, Louis (of H.W. & L. Dee)	L	–	1878	1884	–
Dee, H.W. & L.	L	–	1870	1883	–
Dee, Thomas William	L	–	1864	1890	TWD (?)
De Lamerie, Paul	L	1713	1712	1751	LA PL
Delisle, Louis	L	1775	–	–	LD
Dell, Samuel	L	1697	1698	1703	DE
Delmester, John	L	1755	1754	1774	ID
Demster, James	Ed	1775	1777	1805	ID
Demster, William	Ed	1742	1741	1770	WD
Dene, Thomas	L	1767	1767	1768	TD
Denney, Daniel	L	1786	1786	–	DD
Denny, William	L	1697	1700	1705	DE
Denny, William, & Backe, John	L	1697	1698	1699	DE^E_AB
Denwall, John	L	1768	1766	1774	ID
Denziloe, John	L	1774	1765	1802	ID
Denziloe, Francis	L	–	1786	1794	–
Derry & Jones	B	–	1862	–	–
Desvignes, Peter	L	1771	1774	1780	PD
Devlin, Stuart	L	–	1959	1969	SD (?)
Devonshire, Thomas, & Watkins, William	L	1756	1757	1760	TD WW
Dexter, Benjamin Reece	L	1835	1835	1838	BD
Dexter, Thomas Paine	L	1805	1817	1837	TD
Dicken, Arthur	L	1720	–	1723	Di
Dicks, Thomas	L	1792	1812	1834	TD
Dicks, Thomas & James	L	1821	1821	–	TDJD
Dickson, Charles	Ed	1719	1721	1748	CD
	Du	1722	–	–	CD
Diggle, John	L	1697	–	1702	DI
Dighton, Isaac	L	1697	1697	1705	DI
Diller, Thomas	L	1828	1836	1850	TD
Dimmer & Son	Ch	–	1938	–	–
Dingley Bros	B	–	1937	–	–
Dixon, Arthur (1856–1929)	B	–	1895	1898	–
Dixon, James & Sons	S (also L & B)	1867	1850	1952	JD&S
Dobson, Edward; Pryor, William, & Williams, James	L	1755	1754	1755	DPW
Dobson & Sons	L	–	1882	–	PD^H C^{D}W JWD
Dobson, T.W.	L	–	1889	1902	–
Dobson, T.W. & H.H.	L	–	1878	1881	–
Dobson, P.H. & C.W.	L	–	1908	–	–
Dodd, P.G. & Son	L	–	1937	–	PGD&Sn
Dodds, Joseph	L	1789	1797	1800	ID
D'Olier, Isaac	Db	1731	1741	1767	ID
Donald, John (born 1928)	–	–	1959	1963	–
Douglas, Archibald	L	1826	1826	1833	AD
Douglas, Francis	L	1837	1837	1861	FD
Douglas, James, of Aberdeen	Ed	1785	1791	1806	ID JD

Maker's name	Town of registration	Earliest mark registration	Earliest example	Latest example	Maker's mark/notes
Douglas, John	L	1788	–	1817	ID
Douglas, John & Archibald	L	1821	1822	1824	ID AD
Dowdall, Edward	Db	–	1715	–	ED
Downes, John	L	1697	1697	1707	Do
Downie, James	Gl	1812	–	1820	JD
Doyle, William	Db	1795	1796	1813	WD
Dresser, Christopher	–	–	1879	1881	–
Drew, S., S. & E.	L	–	1891	1926	$S_E S_D D$
Drinkwater, Sandilands	L	1735	–	1740	SD
Drury, Dru II	L	1767	–	–	DD
Dudley, James	L	–	1894	1897	–
Duffus, Thomas	Ed	1780	1788	1828	TD
Duke, Isaac	L	1743	1744	1746	ID
Dumee, Nicholas	L	1776	1776	1777	ND
Duncan, R., of Carlisle	Nc	–	1833	1834	RD
Dupont, Louis (*or* Lewis)	L	1736	1736	1747	LD
Durandeau, John	L	1824	–	1826	JD
Durbin, Leslie G.	L	–	1946	1963	–
Durousseau, Matthieu	L	1705	–	–	DV
Dutton, Henry	L	1754	1757	1763	HD
Dutton, John	L	1776	–	1761	ID
Dutton, Samuel	L	1823	–	1824	SD
Dyson, Abraham	S	1835	–	1836	AD
Eadon, Kibbles & Weaver (*or* Eadon, G., & Co)	S	1795	1796	1813	GE &Co
Eady, Messrs	L	–	1858	1862	EE JE
East, John	L	1697	1697	1725	EA IE
Easterbrook, William	L	–	1824	1835	–
Eastwick, Henrietta & William	L	1802	1801	–	HE WE
Eaton, Elizabeth	L	–	1829	1857	EE
Eaton, Elizabeth & John	L	–	1859	1863	–
Eaton, Robert	L	–	1800	–	–
Eaton, Samuel	L	1736	–	1764	SE
Eaton, William	L	1813	1813	1864	WE
Ebbs, John	Db	1766	1815	1820	IE
Eckfourd, John I	L	1698	1703	1719	EC IE
Eckfourd, John II	L	1725	1724	1747	EC IE
Ede, James, & Hewat, Alexander	L	1808	1808	1810	IE AH
Edgar, James	L	–	1697	1698	ED
Edington, James Charles	L	1828	1828	1864	JCE
Edmonston, Alexander	Ed	1779	1795	1805	AE
Edwards, Charles	L	–	1880	1919	CE (?)
Edwards, Edward	L	1697	–	–	EE
Edwards, Edward I	L	1816	1816	1818	EE
Edwards, Edward II	L	1828	1828	1857	EE
Edwards, George & Sons (*also* B, S, Ed & Gl)	L	–	1860	1927	CE &S
Edwards, Griffith	L	1733	–	1735	GE
Edwards, John I	L	1697	1701	*	ED
Edwards, John II	L	1724	–	1744	IE ED
Edwards, John III	L	1788	1790	1809	IE
Edwards, John III & Edward I	L	1811	–	1815	IE EE
Edwards, Richard	L	1716	1716	1717	Ed RE
Edwards, Thomas	L	1816	–	1827	TE
Edwards, William J.	L	1778	–	1786	WE
Egan, Daniel	Db	1800	1789	1816	DE
Egan, William, of Cork	Db	–	1924	1966	–
Elder & Co	Ed	–	1831	1865	E&Co
Eley, Charles	L	1825	1824	1828	CE
Eley, Thomas	L	–	1819	1850	TE
Eley, William I	L	1778	1774	1838	WE
Eley, William II, Charles & Henry	L	1824	1824	–	WE CE HE
Eley, William I, & Fearn, William	L	1797	1789	1836	WE WF
Eley, William I; Fearn, William, & Chawner, William II	L	1808	1806	1829	WE WF WC
Elkington, Frederick	B (*also* L)	–	1869	1888	FE
Elkington, George Richard	L	–	1866	–	–

Maker's name	Town of registration	Earliest mark registration	Earliest example	Latest example	Maker's mark/notes
Elkington & Co Ltd	B	–	1844	1970	E&Co / E&Co Ld
	(also L, S & Db)				
Elkington, Mason & Co	B	1843	1844	1862	EM&Co
	S	1859	–	–	–
Ellerby, William	L	1802	–	1812	WE
Ellerton, Thomas, & Sibley, Richard I	L	1803	–	1804	TE RS
Elliott, Peter, of Dartmouth	Ex	1703	1703	1738	PE
Elliott, Philip	Ex	–	1725	1729	PE
Elliott, William	L	1813	1823	1851	WE
Ellis, Henry	Ex	–	1847	1851	HE
Ellis, Isaac & Sons	S	–	1895	–	–
Ellis, James, & Co	S	1793	1818	1824	IE&Co
Ellis, Thomas	L	1780	1785	1805	TE
Elson, Anthony	L	–	1973	–	AGE
Elston, John I	Ex	–	1701	1728	EI JE IE
Elston, John II	Ex	–	1726	1747	IE
Elston, Philip	Ex	1723	1707	1748	PE
Emanuel, Joseph	L	1820	–	1829	JE
Emanuel, Lawrence	B	–	1888	1923	–
Emanuel, Morris & Michael	L	1825	–	1829	ME ME
Emes, John	L	1798	1797	1820	JE
Emes, Rebecca & William	L	1808	1804	1838	RE WE
Emes, Rebecca, & Barnard, Edward I	L	1808	1804	1859	RE EB
England, James	Db	1791	1796	1819	IE
England, Thomas	L	1725	1727	1746	En TE
England, William, & Vaen, John	L	1714	1714	–	EN VA
Eustace, Thomas	Ex	1779	1780	1785	TE
Evans, John	L	–	1842	1859	–
Evans, John II	L	–	1837	–	–
Evans, Richard, of Shrewsbury	L	1779	–	–	RE
	(also B)				
Evans, Thomas	L	1774	1769	1785	TE
Ewesdin, Thomas	L	1713	1717	1725	EW
Fainell, Joseph see John Farnell					
Fair, Thomas	L	1768	–	1769	TF
Falconer, John	Gl	1709	1707	–	IF
Farnell, John	L	1714	1715	1727	Fa FA IF
Farnett, T.	Db	–	1825	1831	TF
Farrell, Edward	L	1813	1814	1845	EF
Farren Thomas (or Farrar Farrer)	L	1707	1710	1742	FA TF
Fattorini & Sons	Ch	–	1909	1916	F&S
	(also B)				
Favell, Charles, & Co	S	1887	1870	1894	–
Fawdery, Hester	L	1727	1727	–	F
Fawdery, John I	L	1697	1698	1734	FA
Fawdery, William	L	1697	1700	1726	F FA WF
Fawler, Thomas	L	1707	1707	1709	Fa
Fearn, William	L	1769	1771	1800	WF
Feline, Edward	L	1720	1721	1750	Fe EF
Feline, Magdalin	L	1753	1753	1766	MF
Fell, William	L	1818	–	1826	WF
Fenton, Allanson & Co	S	1816	–	1824	IF&Co
Fenton, Creswick & Co	S	1773	1776	1792	MF MF RC &Co MF& Co
Fenton, Creswick Oaks & Co	S	1773	1776	1792	as above
Fenton, Matthew, & Co	S	1773	1776	1792	as above
Fenton, Danby & Webster	S	1823	–	1825	FW &D
Fenton Bros Ltd	S	1868	1857	1932	JFF &FF
Fenton, Russell & Co Ltd	S	–	1931	–	FR&CoLtd
	(also B)				
Fenwick, George	Ed	–	1806	1823	GF
Ferguson & MacBean	Ed	–	1891	–	F&M
Fernell, Edward	L	1780	1779	1802	EF
Ferris, George	Ex	–	1815	1838	GF
Ferris, Richard	Ex	–	1794	1822	RF
Fetter, John A.	Gl	–	1902	–	J F A
Field, Alexander	L	1780	1790	1808	AF
Field, Joshua	L	1701	–	1716	FI
Fielding, Owen, of Plymouth Dock	Ex	–	1824	–	–
Figg, John	L	1834	1836	1881	IF
Finlay & Field	Gl	–	1848	–	F&F

Maker's name	Town of registration	Earliest mark registration	Earliest example	Latest example	Maker's mark/notes
Finlay, Edgar, & Taylor, Hugh	L (also B)	–	1884	1892	–
Finnigans Ltd of Manchester	L (also B & Db)	–	1903	1936	–
Fisher, William & John	L	1793	–	1811	WF IF
Flavell, Charles (of Creswick & Co)	S	1863	1870	1874	–
Flavelle, Henry	Db	1837	1825	1851	HF
Fleming, William	L	1697	1701	1728	FL
Fletcher, Bernard	L	1725	–	1727	BF
Fletcher, Charles William	L	–	1910	1932	–
Fletcher, Edith	L	–	1729	1730	EF
Flight, John	L	1710	1702	–	FL
Fogelberg, Andrew	L	–	1770	1811	AF
Fogelberg, Andrew, & Gilbert, Stephen	L	1780	1778	1792	AF SG
Folkard, John Cope	L	1819	1820	1822	ICF
Folkingham, Thomas	L	1707	1707	1734	FO TF
Foote, Thomas	Ex	–	1701	1703	FO
Forbes, Alexander	Ed (also A)	1692	1703	1728	AF
Fordham, William	L	1707	1726	1731	FO WF
Fordham & Faulkner	S (also L)	1890	1896	1915	WF AF
Forsyth, R.W., Ltd	Gl	–	1912	1915	–
Fossey, John	L	1733	1737	1743	IF
Foster, Thomas	L	1769	1768	1770	TF
Foster, William Lewis	L	1775	1774	–	WF
Fountain, John	L	1792	1792	1805	IF
Fountain, John, & Beardnell, John	L	1793	1793	–	IF IB
Fountain, William	L	1794	1793	1828	WF
Fountain, William, & Pontifex, Daniel	L	1791	1788	1798	WF DP
Fox, Charles I	L	1804	–	1808	CF
Fox, Charles II	L	1822	1822	1861	CF
Fox, Charles T. & George	L	–	1841	1906	$C_G T_F F$
Fox, C.	Db	–	1747	1774	CF
Fox, George	L	–	1861	1906	GF

Maker's name	Town of registration	Earliest mark registration	Earliest example	Latest example	Maker's mark/notes
Fox, R.F. see C.T. & G. Fox	L	–	1911	1916	–
Fraillon, James	L	1711	1702	1727	Fr IF
Francis, J.	Db	1840	1836	1840	IF
Francis, William	L	1697	–	1709	FR
Franklin, James	L	–	1829	1849	IF
Fraser, John	L	–	1836	1837	–
Fray, Dennis	Db	–	1785	–	–
Fray, James	Db	1829	1818	1841	IF
Fray, John	L	1748	1749	1753	IF
Frazer, J., & Haws, E. see Hennell, Frazer & Haws	L	–	1870	1893	$F^H H$
Freeman, Philip	L	1772	1772	1781	PF
Freeman, Thomas	S (also B)	1845	1838	–	TF
Freeth, Charles	B	–	1775	1798	CF
Freeth, Thomas I	L	1773	–	1819	TF
Freeth, Thomas II	L	1820	–	–	TF
French, Jonathan	Nc	1703	1705	1728	IF
Frisbee, William	L	1792	1795	1822	WF
Frisbee, William, & Storr, Paul	L	1792	1791	1792	WF PS
Frith, Ralph	L	1728	1728	–	FR RF
Fry, Charles & John II	L	1822	–	1823	CF IF
Fry, James	Db	–	1819	1823	IF
Fry, John II	L	1826	1830	1835	IF
Fuller, Crispin	L	1792	1793	1835	CF
Gainsford, Robert	S	1808	1808	1840	RG
Gairdner, Alexander	Ed	1754	1762	1799	AG
Gallimore, William & Sons	S	1867	1894	1895	WG
Gamble, William	L	1697	1698	1721	GA
Gamon, Dinah	L	1740	1740	1742	DG
Gamon, John	L	1727	1723	1739	IG
Garde, Richard of Cork	Db	–	1825	1830	RG
Garden, Phil Phil(l)ip(s)	L	1738	1741	1756	PG
Gardner, Richard	L	–	1770	1785	RG
Garland, James William	L	1826	–	1827	–

Maker's name	Town of registration	Earliest mark registration	Earliest example	Latest example	Maker's mark/notes
Garnier, Daniel	L	1697	1697	1698	GA
Garrard, James I (of R. & S. Garrard & Co)	L	–	1876	*	–
Garrard, James II (of R. & S. Garrard & Co)	L	–	*	1899	–
Garrard, Robert I (partner John Wakelin 1792)	L	1802	1807	1828	RG
Garrard, Robert II	L	1818	1825	1880	RE
Garrard, R. & S., & Co	L	–	1843	1960	–
Garrard, Sebastian see R. & S. Garrard & Co	L	–	1901	1938	–
Garrard, William	L	1735	1737	1745	WG
Garrard & Co Ltd (also B & S)	L	–	1953	1974	G & Co Ltd
Garthorne, Francis	L	1697	1677	1723	GA (A within) FG
Garthorne, George (?)	L	1697	1681	1709	GA
Gaunt, J.R., Ltd	B	–	1973	–	JRG
Gaze, Robert	L	1795	1794	1804	RG
Ged, Douglas	Ed	1734	1740	1759	GED
Ged, William	Ed	1706	1707	1718	WG
Gerard, Francis	Db	1704	1712	1715	FG
Gibbon, Edward	L	1719	1723	1730	Gi EG
Gibbons, Charles	L	1732	–	1734	CG
Gibbons, John	L	1700	1703	1729	Gi IG
Gibson, Charles	L	1828	1828	–	CG
Gibson, Edward	L	1697	1702	1705	GI
Gibson, William	L	1697	1698	1705	Gi
Gibson & Co Ltd	S	–	1912	1913	–
Gibson W., & Langman, J. (also B, S & Db)	L	–	1883	1900	WG JL
Gignac, Benjamin	L	1745	1745	1776	BG
Gilbert, John (also S)	B	1841	1845	1877	JG
Gilbert, Stephen see Andrew Fogelberg	L	–	–	–	–
Gilchrist, William	Ed	1736	1751	1755	WG
Giles, George	L	1762	1783	1797	GG
Gillois, Peter (Pierre)	L	1754	1754	1783	PG P I G
Gilsland, James	Ed	1748	1752	1777	IG
Gilsland & Ker	Ed	1763	1764	1768	G&K
Gilpin, Thomas	L	1730	1737	1758	TG
Gines, Richard	L	1698	1693	1725	GI RG
Gladwin Ltd	S	–	1926	1939	–
Glaser, Thomas	L	–	1892	1894	–
Glen, James	Gl	1743	1743	1752	IG GLN
Glenny, George	L	1815	–	1818	GG
Gloster, Joseph, Ltd	B	–	1902	1967	–
Goble, Robert	Co	–	1696	–	RG
Goble, Robert Jr	Co	–	–	–	RG
Godbehere, Samuel	L	1784	1785	1789	SG
Godbehere, Samuel, & Wigan, Edward	L	1786	1786	1813	SG EW
Godbehere, Samuel; Wigan, Edward, & Bult, James	L	1800	1799	1814	SG EW IB (or Godbehere & Co)
Godfrey, Benjamin	L	1732	1730	1768	BG
Godfrey, Elizabeth (formerly Elizabeth Buteux)	L	1741	1741	1765	EG
Godwin, Meshach	L	1723	1723	1725	GO MG
Goldsmiths Alliance Ltd	L	–	1866	1887	–
Goldsmiths & Silversmiths Co Ltd (also B & S)	L	–	1889	1950	G&SCo Ltd
Goldstein, Martin	L	–	1880	1884	–
Goldwire, Richard, of Oxford	L	1753	–	1761	RG
Goode, John	L	1701	1702	1719	GO
Goodman, Alexander, & Co	S	1800	1799	1834	AG&Co
Goodman, Gainsford & Fairbairn	S	1797	1799	1834	GG&Co
Goodman, James	L	–	1701	–	–
Goodwin, Charles	L	1799	–	1836	CG
Goodwin, Elizabeth	L	1729	1729	1730	EG
Goodwin, James	L	1710	1712	1729	GO IG

Maker's name	Town of registration	Earliest mark registration	Earliest example	Latest example	Maker's mark/notes
Gordon, Charles	L	1828	1837	1840	CG
Gordon, Hugh	Ed	1727	1731	1756	HG
Gordon, James	A	1766	1766	–	IG
Gordon, Robert	Ed	1741	1743	1762	RG
Gorham, John	L	1728	1748	1759	IG
Gorham Manufacturing Co	B	–	1913	–	–
Gorsuch, John	L	1726	–	1733	IG
Gosling, Richard	L	1733	1734	1760	RG
Got–helf–Bilsings, Johan	Gl	1717	1717	1731	IB
Gough, William	B	1840	1851	1868	–
Gould, James	L	1722	1722	1748	IG IG monogram
Gould, William	L	1732	1732	1767	GO WG
Gowland & Grant of Sunderland	B	–	1934	–	–
Graeme, Patrick	Ed	1725	–	1729	PG
Graham, Adam	Gl (also Ed)	1763	1784	1789	AG
Graham, James	Db	–	1769	1770	IG
Graham, Thomas, of Bath	L	1792	1792	1801	TG
Graham, Thomas, & Willis, Jacob, of Bath	L	1789	1789	1790	TG IW
Gray, George	L	1782	1788	1800	GG
Gray, Robert	Gl	1776	1776	1846	RG
Gray, Robert & Son	Gl (also Ed)	1819	1804	1847	RG&S RG &S
Gray (or Grey) & Co	Ch	1900	1912	1926	Gy&C
Greaves, H.	L	–	1899	1909	–
Greaves & Hoyland	S	–	1781	–	–
Green, Charles S., & Co Ltd	B	–	1911	1940	–
Green, David	L	1701	1718	1728	Gr DG
Green, Henry	L	1786	1794	1797	HG
Green, John, & Co	S	1792	1782	1819	IG&Co
Green, John; Roberts, Mosley & Co	S	1793	1796	1798	IG&Co
Green, Nathaniel	L	1699	–	1706	Gr
Green, Richard	L	1703	1703	1730	GR (R within) RG
Green, Robert	Ch	–	1790	1803	RG
Greenberg, I.S., & Co	B	–	1904	–	–
Greene, Henry	L	1700	1701	1717	GR HG
Greenway, Henry	L	1775	1775	1798	HG
Greenwood, William & Sons	B	–	1937	–	–
Gregory, Richard & Co	S	1797	–	1819	RG
Grierson, Philip	Gl	1810	1820	1844	PG
Grundy, William	L	1743	1733	1777	WG
Guest, Thomas & Joseph	L	1805	–	1810	TG IG
Guest, Thomas & Joseph, & Craddock, Joseph	L	1802	1806	1810	TG IG IC
Guild of Handicrafts (1887–1908; Ltd 1898)	L	1898	1905	1908	GofH$_L$ D
Gulliver, Nathaniel	L	1722	1722	1727	GU NG
Gurney, Richard, & Co	L	1739	1736	1761	$R^T_C G$
Gurney, Richard, & Cooke, Thomas II	L	1727	1727	1768	$R^T_C G$
Gylmyn, Robert	Y	1550	1562	1605	RG
Gwillim, William	L	1740	1740	1743	WG
Gwillim, William, & Castle, Peter	L	1744	1744	1745	$P^W_G C$
Haddaway, W.S.	L	–	1904	–	–
Hadfield, Aaron see Hatfield	S	–	–	–	–
Haines, Christopher	Db	1784	1770	1811	CH
Halford, Thomas	L	1807	1805	1815	TH
Hall, Edward	L	1721	–	1722	HA EH
Hall, William	L	1795	1795	1828	WH WEH (?)
Hallmark Replicas Ltd	L	–	1973	1974	–
Hallsworth, Henry	L	–	1763	1804	HH
Halstaff & Hannaford	L	–	1853	1870	–
Hamilton, John	Db	1709	1708	1745	IH
Hamilton, Crichton & Co	Ed	–	1876	1879	–

Maker's name	Town of registration	Earliest mark registration	Earliest example	Latest example	Maker's mark/notes
Hamilton & Inches	Ed	1880	1873	1956	H&I
Hammond, Creake & Co	S	–	1907	–	–
Hamon, Lewis (or Louis)	L	1736	1747	1750	LH
Hampston, J., & Prince, J.	Y	–	1777	1808	H&P IH IP I$_P$H JH JP
Hancock, Charles Frederick	L	1850	1854	1912	CFH
Hancock, W., & Rowbotham, J.	S (also B)	1773	1773	–	WH IR I W$_R$H &Co
Hands & Son	L	–	1825	1881	DH CH
Hanet, Paul	L	1716	1718	1738	HA PH
Hannam, Thomas, & Crouch, John II	L	1799	–	1807	TH IC
Hannam, Thomas, & Mills, Richard	L	–	1763	1764	TH RM
Harache, Jean	L	1726	–	–	IH
Harache, Pierre I	L	1697	1684	1704	HA
Harache, Pierre II	L	1698	–	1705	HA
Harbert, Samuel	L	1771	1789	1793	SH
Hardman, John, & Powell, William II	B	–	1858	1877	JH&Co (also J. Hardman & Co)
Hardy, Joseph	L	1799	1797	1828	IH
Harper, Joseph	L	–	1894	1897	–
Harper, Robert & Son	L	–	1844	1882	RH
Harper, Thomas I	L	1790	1792	*	TH
Harper, Thomas II	L	1806	*	1821	TH
Harrington, Christopher	Y (also L)	1595	1597	1663	CH
Harrington, Robert	Y	1616	1625	1638	RH
Harris, Benjamin	L	1697	–	1699	HA
Harris, Charles Stuart	L	–	1863	1936	C$_H$S (also Harris & Son Ltd)
Harris, John I	L	1717	*	*	Ha
Harris, John II	L	1761	*	*	IH
Harris, John III	L	1786	*	*	IH
Harris, John IV	L	1818	*	*	IH
Harris, John V	L	1831	*	*	IH
Harris, John VI	L	–	*	*	JH
Harris, Simon	L	1795	1794	1816	SH
Harrison, C.F.	L	–	1865	–	CFH (or C.F. Hancock)
Harrison, John, & Co	S	1833	1853	1882	JH&Co
Harrison, W.W., & Co	S	1856	1862	1900	WWH W$_H$W WWH&Co
Harrison Bros & Howson	S (also L)	1849	1849	1945	HH WH &H
Harrods Ltd	L (also S)	–	1914	1938	–
Hart, Naphtali	L	1812	1809	1825	NH
Hart & Dumee see Dumee & Hart					
Hartley, Elizabeth	L	1748	1748	1751	EH
Hartwell, Thomas	Db	–	1700	1702	TH monogram
Harvey, John I	L	1738	1740	1745	Ha IH
Harwood, Samuel	S	1835	1835	1839	SH
Haseler, Edward John, & Noble	L (also B & Ch)	–	1888	1920	EJH CB (?)
Haseler, William Hair	L	–	1896	1937	–
Hatfield, Aaron	S	1823	1820	1850	AH
Hatfield, Charles	L	1727	1723	1738	CH
Hattersley, William	L	–	1840	1864	WH
Havers, George	L	1697	–	1699	HA
Havers, Thomas	Nw	1674	1675	1691	TH
Haviland–Nye, A.	L	–	1965	1980	H^{A}N
Hawkins, John	L	1802	–	1827	IH
Hawksley, G. & J.W., Ltd	S	1856	–	1859	GH CH
Hawksworth, Eyre, & Co Ltd	S	1833	1833	1937	HE CH &Co JE JKB JKB TH GW

Maker's name	Town of registration	Earliest mark registration	Earliest example	Latest example	Maker's mark/notes
Hay, J.	Ed	–	1816	1856	JH
Hayens, Henry	L	1749	1748	1769	HH conjoined
Hayne, Jonathan	L	1808	1817	1835	IH
Hayne, Samuel, & Cater, Dudley	L	1836	1837	1861	SH DC
Hayter, Thomas	L	1805	1805	1813	TH
Hayter, Thomas & George	L	1816	1816	1828	TH GH
Haywood, Joseph, & Co	S (also Gl)	1880	–	1893	JH&Co
Hearnden, Nicholas	L	–	1772	1811	NH
Heaslewood, Arthur	Nw	1661	1661	1670	AH
Heath, George	L	–	1889	–	–
Heath, J.T., & Middleton, J.H.	L (also B)	–	1885	1906	–
Hebert, Henry	L	1734	1733	1745	HH
Heming, Joseph, & Co	L	–	1904	1972	H&Co Ltd
Heming, Thomas	L	1745	1746	1789	TH
Heming, George, & Chawner, William	L	1774	1776	1781	GH WC G^W_CH
Henderson, Alexander	Ed	1792	1792	1812	AH
Hennell, David I	L	1736	1736	1762	HD
Hennell, David II	L	1795	–	–	(no individual mark)
Hennell, James Barclay	L	1877	1877	1885	JBH
Hennell, Robert I	L	1772	1772	*	RH
Hennell, Robert II	L	1809	–	–	RH
Hennell, Robert III	L	1834	1835	1859	RH
Hennell, Robert IV	L	1869	1856	1872	RH
Hennell, R.G.	L	–	1860	–	RGH
Hennell, Robert I & David II	L	1763	1763	1810	RH DH D^R_HH
Hennell, Robert I, & David II & Samuel	L	1795	1801	1802	RH DH SH
Hennell, Robert I, & Samuel	L	1802	1795	1812	RH SH
Hennell, Samuel	L	1811	1790	1821	SH
Hennell, Samuel, & Terrey, John	L	1814	1814	–	SH IT
Hennell & Elson, Anthony	L	1719	–	–	A^H_E
Hennell, Frazer & Haws	L	1967	1870	1893	F^H_H
Herbert, Samuel	L	1747	1750	1775	SH
Heredities Ltd	S	–	1970	–	–
Heriot, Joseph	L	1756	1775	1791	IH
Herne, Lewis, & Butty, Francis	L	1757	1757	1764	L^F_BH
Hewat, Alexander	L	1810	1810	–	AH
Hewitt, James	Ed	1750	1779	1791	JH
Hewitt, William	L	1829	1836	1846	WH
Hewitson, Michael	Db	1727	1725	1728	MH
Hickleton & Sydal	L	–	1929	–	–
Hickleton & Phillips	L	–	1936	–	–
Hicks, Joseph	Ex	–	1784	1830	JH
Higgins, Francis	L	1817	1818	1940	FH
Hill, Caleb	L	1728	1730	1733	CH
Hill, George	Db	1759	1765	1766	GH
Hill, Robert	L	1717	–	1719	Hi RH
Hillan, Christian	L	1736	1739	1741	CH
Hilliard, J., & Thomason, J.	B (also Ch)	1853	1850	1899	H & T
Hindmarsh, George	L	1731	1731	1754	GH
Hitchcock, Samuel	L	1713	1715	1729	HI SH
Hobbs, James	L	–	1821	1835	JH (doubtful attribution)
Hobbs, Richard	Nc	–	1702	1744	Ho
Hobbs, Thomas	L	1796	1805	1807	TH
Hobson, Henry & Sons	S	–	1898	–	–
Hockly, Daniel	L	1810	1810	1818	DH
Hockly, Daniel, & Bosworth, Thomas	L	1815	1815	–	DH TB
Hodd, Richard & Son (also R. & R. Hodd)	L	–	1871	1890	–
Hodson, John I	L	1697	1697	–	HO monogram
Holaday, Edward	L	1709	1710	1718	HO
Holaday, Sarah	L	1719	1721	1729	HO SH
Holland, Henry	L	–	1854	1881	HH

Maker's name	Town of registration	Earliest mark registration	Earliest example	Latest example	Maker's mark/notes
Holland, John I	L	1711	1712	1743	HO IH
Holland, John II	L	1739	1739	1751	IH
Holland, Aldwincle & Slater (*also* Aldwincle & Slater)	L	–	1879	1912	JA JS
Holland, P., & Gibson, G.E.	L	–	1875	–	–
Holland, Thomas I	L	1707	1707	1715	HO
Holland, Thomas II	L	1798	1799	1827	TH
Holmes, William	L	1776	1767	1814	WH
Holmes, William, & Dumee, Nicholas	L	1773	1773	1774	WH ND
Holt, James	Ex	–	1768	1798	JH
Holy, Daniel, & Co	S	1776	1776	1825	DH DH&Co
Homer, Michael	Db	–	1752	1794	MH
Homer, William	Db	1758	1764	1770	WH
Hood, Samuel	L	1697	1685	1701	HO Ho
Hopgood, Metcalf	L	1835	1833	1846	MH
Hopkins & Hopkins	Db	1883	–	1904	H&H
Horsley, John	L	–	1760	1762	IH
Horton & Allday	B	–	1887	1908	H&A (?)
Hoskins, Richard, of Bristol	L	1791	–	1798	RH
Hougham, Charles	L	1769	1776	1813	CH
Hougham, Solomon	L	1793	1793	1817	SH
Hougham, Solomon; Royes, Solomon, & Dix, John East	L	1817	1817	1818	SH SR IED
Houle, D. & C.	L	–	1844	1885	–
Houle, John	L	1811	1810	1820	IH
Howard, Francis	S	–	1971		–
Howard & Hawksworth	S	1835	1833	1852	H&H
Howden, Francis	Ed	1781	1785	1820	FH
Howden, James, & Co	Ed	–	1829	1846	JH&Co
Howell, S.	L	–	1802	1813	–
Howell, Thomas, of Bath	L	1784	1788	1815	TH
Howell & James Ltd	S	1886	–	1888	–
Howland, Solomon	L	1760	1765	1767	SH
Hoyland, John, & Co	S	1773	1774	1778	IH Co IH&Co
Hudell, Rene	L	1718	–	1720	HU

Maker's name	Town of registration	Earliest mark registration	Earliest example	Latest example	Maker's mark/notes
Hudson, Alexander	L	1701	–	1708	HV
Hughes, William	Db	1767	1760	1781	WH
Hukin & Heath (*also* B & S)	L	–	1881	1934	–
Humphry, John	Db	1685	1693	1696	IH
Hunt, John (1811–1879) Partner Hunt & Roskell; son of John Samuel Hunt	L	–	–	–	–
Hunt, John Mortimer (1844–1897) Partner Hunt & Roskell; son of John Hunt	L	–	–	–	–
Hunt, John Samuel (1785–1865) Partner Hunt & Roskell; father of John Hunt	L	1844	1844	1870	ISH
Hunt & Roskell (1842–1897)	L	1842	1846	1915	ISH (John Samuel Hunt)
	L	1865	–	–	IH RR (John Hunt) (Robert Roskell)
	L	1882	–	–	RR AR IMH (Robert Roskell) (Allen Roskell) (John Mortimer Hunt)
	L	1889	–	–	$H^A H^B W$ (Alfred Benson) (H.H. Wintle)
	L	1895	–	–	$A^A H^B B$ (Alfred Benson) (Arthur Henry Benson)
Hunt & Roskell Ltd	L	1897	–	–	H&RLtd

Maker's name	Town of registration	Earliest mark registration	Earliest example	Latest example	Maker's mark/notes
Hunter, George I	L	1748	1735	1764	GH
Hunter, George II	L	1817	–	1831	GH
Hunter, William I	L	1755	*	*	WH
Hunter, William II	L	–	1828	1838	WH
Hussey, Richard	L	–	1758	–	RH
Hutchinson, Richard I, of Colchester	L	1699	1703	1719	HS
Hutchinson, Richard II, of Colchester	L	1727	–	–	RH
Hutson, John	L	1784	1786	1812	IH
Hutton, Edward	L	–	1855	1896	EH
Hutton, Samuel	L	1724	1726	1736	HU SH
Hutton, William	S (also B, L & Ch)	1836	1838	1956	WH
Hutton, William & Sons Ltd	S (also B, L & Ch)	1857	1874	1956	WH RH H&SLd
Hyams, Hyam	L	–	1821	1879	HH
Hyatt, John	L	1742	1761	1763	IH
Hyatt, John, & Semore, Charles	L	1757	1757	1761	IHS C
Hyde, Henry	L	1834	–	1839	HH
Hyde, James	L	1777	1793	1796	IH
Hyde, Mary, & Reily, John	L	1799	1799	–	MH IR
Ibbot, George	L	1753	1759	1760	GI IBBOT
Inglis, Robert	Ed	1686	1692	1719	RI
Innes, Robert	L	1743	1743	1756	RI
Ironside, Edward	L	1702	1702	–	Ir IR
Issod, Joyce	L	–	1697	–	IS
Issod, Thomas	L	1697	1694	1697	I Z S
Ivory, Alfred	L	–	1867	1869	Z
Ivory, George	L	1845	1844	1876	GI
Jackson, Charles	L	1714	1713	1728	CI IA
Jackson, Elizabeth	L	1748	1748	1750	EJ
Jackson, George Maudsley	L	–	1883	1899	–
Jackson, G.W.	L	–	1892	–	–
Jackson, John I	L	1697	1688	1708	Ja
Jackson, John II	L	–	1764	–	II
Jackson, John III	L	1792	–	–	II
Jackson, Joseph	Db	1775	1774	1805	II
Jackson, Orlando	L	–	1771	1800	OI OJ
Jackson, Thomas I	L	1736	1737	1746	TI
Jackson, Thomas II	L	1769	1766	1810	TI
Jackson & Deere	L	–	1893	–	–
Jackson, G.M., & Fullerton, D.L.	L	–	1888	1926	–
Jacob, John	L	1734	1734	1764	II
Jacob, Samuel	L	–	1894	1910	–
Jacobson, S.	L	–	1899	–	–
Jacobson, J., & Yardley, J.	L	–	1780	–	–
James, Samuel	Nc	–	1759	1769	SI
James, Thomas	L	1804	1809	1830	TJ
Jamieson, George	A (also L & Ed)	–	1841	1867	GJ
Jamieson, William, of Aberdeen	Ed	1729	1729	–	WI
Jay, Edward	L	1757	1775	1795	EJ EI
Jay, Henry	L	–	1714	1721	Ia
Jay, Richard Attenborough, & Co Ltd	S (also Ch)	–	1904	1934	–
Jays of Brighton	B	–	1911	–	–
Jefferys, Samuel	L	1697	–	1731	IE
Jelf, William	L	1720	1717	1720	Ie WI
Jenkins, James	L	1731	1731	–	II
Jenkins, Thomas	L	1697	1671	1717	Ie
Jenkins & Timm	S	1857	1894	1929	F&E T Co
Jenner & Knewstub	L	–	1864	1879	–
Jennings, Edward	L	1710	1723	1730	Ie IE EI
Jessop, Matthew John	L	–	1885	–	–
Johnson, Edmond I, Ltd	Db	1825	1833	1853	EJ
Johnson, Edmond II, Ltd	Db (also L & S)	1881	1925	1927	EJ EJ monogram E JOHNSON
Johnson, Glover	L	1712	1713	1726	IO GI
Johnson, Joseph	Db	1804	1808	1855	JJ

Maker's name	Town of registration	Earliest mark registration	Earliest example	Latest example	Maker's mark/notes
Johnson, Lawrence	L	1751	1751	–	LI
Johnson, Durban & Co Ltd	B	–	1898	–	–
Johnson, Thomas	L	1800	1814	1851	TJ
Johnson, William	L	1822	1826	1832	WJ
Johnson, Walker & Tolhurst	L	–	1889	1914	–
Johnson, Alexander	L	1733	1748	1771	AJ
Johnston, Thomas	Db	1770	1761	1776	TJ
Jones, A. Edward (1879–1954)	B	–	–	–	AEJ
Jones, A. Edward, Ltd (founded 1902; continued by son Kenneth Crisp Jones)	B	–	1904	1936	AEJ
Jones, Elizabeth	L	1783	1784	1795	EI
Jones, George Greenhill	L	1719	1724	1754	IO GI
Jones, James	Db	1784	–	1791	JJ
Jones, John I		1723	1724	1736	IO II
Jones, John II	L	1763	–	–	JJ
Jones, John III	L	1824	1824	–	IJ
Jones, Kenneth Crisp (son and successor of A. Edward Jones)	B	–	–	–	–
Jones, Lawrence	L	1697	1692	1723	IO
Jones, Robert	Ch	–	1788	1807	RI
Jones, Robert I	L	1774	1773	1791	RI
Jones, Robert II	L	1796	–	–	RI
Jones, Robert I, & Schofield, John	L	1776	1771	1777	RI IS
Jones, Thomas	Db	1771	1776	1788	TJ
Jones & Crompton	B	–	1900	1913	J&C
Jones & Son	L	–	1933	1937	J&S
Jordan, Walter	L	1834	1833	–	WJ
Joseph B.H., & Co	Ch	–	1882	–	–
Jouet, Simon	L	1725	1726	1756	IO SI SJ
Joyce, Thomas	L	1791	–	1795	TI
Joyes, Richard	Gy	–	1695	1725	RI
Juson, William	L	1704	–	1708	IV
Justus (or Justis), Thomas	L	1761	–	1766	TI
Justus (or Justis), William	L	1739	1729	1762	WI
Kandler, Charles I (Frederick)	L	1727	1694	1777	KA CK FK
Kandler, Charles II	L	1778	–	–	CK
Kay, John, & Co	S	1795	–	1809	I KAY & Co
Kearns, John	Db	1797	1800	1802	JK
Keating, James	Db	1795	1788	1812	IK
Keating, Michael	Db	1765	1768	1799	MK
Keating, Michael II	Db	1851	–	1854	MK
Keatt, Launcelot	L	1709	1709	1717	Ke
Keatt, William	L	1697	1694	1706	Ke KE
Keay, Robert I	P	1791	1799	–	RK
Keay, Robert II	P	1825	1825	1839	RK
Keay, R. & R.	Ed (also P)	–	1836	1839	R&RK
Keble, Robert	L	1707	1712	1713	Ke
Kedden, Thomas	L	1700	1704	1715	KE
Keeley, S.	B	–	1863	–	–
Keene, John	Db	1789	1787	1807	JK
Keigwin, John	L	1710	1710	1711	KE
Keith, John James	L	1824	1827	1853	IJK
Kelly, James	Db	1672	–	1679	IK
Kelly, John	Db	1776	1782	1785	IK
Kelty, Alexander	Nc	–	1803	–	AK
Kempton, Robert	L	1710	1712	1713	KE
Kentesber, John	L	–	1755	1786	JK
Kentesber, John, & Grove, Thomas	L	1757	1757	–	IK TG
Ker, Daniel	Ed	1764	1767	1773	DK
Ker, James	Ed	1723	1723	1745	IK
Ker, Thomas	Ed	1694	1696	1715	TK
Ker, William	Ed	–	1758	1770	KER
Ker & Dempster	Ed	–	1747	1766	K&D
Kersill, Ann	L	1747	1747	–	AK
Kersill, Richard	L	1744	1744	1746	RK
Kersill, William	L	1749	1749	1765	WK
Kidder, John	L	1780	1775	1792	IK
Kidney, William	L	1734	1735	1742	WK
Killick, Andrew	L	1749	1750	1752	AK
Kilpatrick, T.	L	–	1901	–	–
Kincaid, Alexander	Ed	1692	1700	1734	AK

Maker's name	Town of registration	Earliest mark registration	Earliest example	Latest example	Maker's mark/notes
Kincaid, John	Ed	1726	1744	1746	IK
	L	1743	1744	1746	IK
King, Abstainando	L	1791	1792	1828	AK
King, David	Db	1690	1693	1739	DK
King, George	L	1819	–	1825	GK
King, Jeremiah	L	1723	1726	1766	KI IK
King, John	L	1775	1775	1796	IK
King, William	L	1761	1760	1771	WK
King, William	L	1826	1829	1834	WK
Kingdon, William,	L	1811	1811	1841	WK
Kinman, William	L	1759	–	1771	WK
Kinnersley, Philip	Db	1716	1717	1733	PK
Kippax, R., & Co	S	1774	1775	1802	RK RK&Co
Kirby, Rowland	Y	1666	1671	1684	RK
Kirkby, J., Gregory & Co	S	1822	–	1823	JK &Co
Kirkby, Samuel, & Co	S	1784	1799	1806	SK
Kirkby, Waterhouse & Co	S	1793	1811	1823	KW&Co IKIW&Co I K I W &Co
Kirkby, Waterhouse & Hodgson	S	1808	–	1811	JK&Co
Kirke, Jonathan	L	1697	1683	1697	KI
Kirkup, James	Nc	1713	1728	1758	Ki IK
Kirkup, John	Nc	1753	1741	1773	IK
Kitchen & Walker	S	1835	1835	–	K&W
Kitchen, Walker & Curr	S	1832	–	–	KW &C
Knight, George	L	1818	1818	1825	GK
Knight, Samuel	L	1816	1816	1817	SK
Knight, William I	L	–	–	–	KN
Knight, William II	L	1816	1815	1837	WK
Knight, William II & Samuel	L	1810	1809	1815	WK SK
Knopfell, Frederick	L	1752	1765	1768	FK
Knowles, John & Son	S	1860	1861	1862	IK &S
Krall, Carl Christof	L	–	1894	1915	CK
Lacey & Caine	L	–	1947	–	–
Ladyman, John	L	1699	1700	1714	LA
Laing, J., R. & W.	Gl	–	1908	–	JR&WL
Lamb, Charles	Db	1893	1894	1902	CL

Maker's name	Town of registration	Earliest mark registration	Earliest example	Latest example	Maker's mark/notes
Lambe, Edward I	L	1740	–	1741	EL
Lambe, George	L	1713	1713	1723	LA
Lambe, Jane	L	–	1720	1727	LA IL
Lambe, John	L	1774	1773	1801	IL
Lambe, Jonathan	L	1699	1699	1727	LA
Lambert, George	L	–	1841	1901	–
Lambert, Henry, & Co	L	–	1902	1915	HL
Lambert, Peter, of Berwick	Nc	–	1825	–	PL
Lambert & Rawlings (later Harman & Lambert)	L	–	1841	1852	–
Lampfert, John	L	1748	1755	1778	IL
Landeck, S.B.	S	–	1891	1896	–
Langdon, J.	Ex	–	1808	1813	JL
Langford, John II, & Sebille, John	L	1766	1763	1775	I$_I$ S L
Langford, Thomas I	L	1715	1715	–	LA
Langford, Thomas II	L	–	1775	–	TL
Langlands, Dorothy	Nc	–	1804	1811	DL
Langlands, John I	Nc	1754	1741	*	IL
Langlands, John II	Nc	–	1793	1807	IL
Langlands, John & Goodriche, John	Nc	–	1754	1781	IL IG
Langlands, John, & Robertson, John	Nc	1780	1778	1808	IL IR IL IR L&R
(also L)					
Langlois, James	L	1738	1732	1738	IL IL
Langman & Gibson	L	1881	–	1898	–
Langton, Dennis	L	1716	–	1734	DL La
Langwith, John	Y	1699	1703	1714	LA
Laroche, Louis		1725	1731	1739	LL
Latham, Walter & Sons	S	–	1899	1912	–
Latham & Merton	B	–	1878	–	–
Laughlin, John	Db	1751	1741	1754	IL
Laughton, John	L	1697	1694	1701	LA
Laundy, Samuel	L	1727	1728	1730	SL
Laundy, Samuel, & Griffith, Jeffery	L	1731	1731	–	S^L_GI
Laurence & Allen	B	1801	–	1802	–
Lautier, John	L	1773	1773	1789	IL
Laver, Benjamin	L	1781	1781	1794	BL

Maker's name	Town of registration	Earliest mark registration	Earliest example	Latest example	Maker's mark/notes
Laver, William	L	1789	1791	1792	WL
Law, Andrew	Ed	–	1682	1694	AL
Law, John	S	1790	1807	1825	IL
Law, Thomas	S	1773	1774	1819	TL / T LAW / LAW
Law, William	Db / L	1774	1789	1822	WL / LAW
Lawe, John	Ed	1661	1684	1688	IL
Lawrence, John, & Co	B	1813	1818	1831	L&Co
Lawrence, E. Loyd *see* Hennell	L	1830	–	–	–
Laws, George, & Walker, John	Nc	–	1794	1822	GL / JW
Lea, William, & Co	B	1811	1813	1827	L&C
Lea & Clark	B	1824	1819	1826	L&C
Leach, John	L	1699	1699	1707	LE
Leader, Thomas & Daniel	S	1798	1801	1807	TL / DL
Leake, Francis	L	–	1658	–	FL
Leapidge, Edward	L	1767	1769	1776	EL
Le Bass, James	Db	1824	1803	1846	ILB
Le Bass, Samuel	Db	1859	1859	1870	SL'B
Ledsham, Vale & Wheeler	B	1825	1825	1830	LV&W
Lee, Samuel	L	1701	1698	1712	LE SL
Lee & Wigful Ltd	S (*also* B)	1879	1872	1928	HW
Leeke, Ralph	L	1699	1698	1701	Le
Lees, Edward	L	1803	1803	1807	EL
Lejeune, Joseph	L	1760	1773	1791	IL ILI
Lemaitre, Charles	Db	1735	1733	1736	CL
Leonard, Patrick	S (*also* Ch)	1835	–	1847	PL
Lery, Simon	Ex	–	1823	1828	SL
Le Sage, Augustin	L	–	1761	1779	AL
Le Sage, John Hugh	L	1718	1710	1749	IS SA
Le Sage, Simon	L	1754	1753	1760	SL
Leslie, John, of Aberdeen	A (*also* Gl)	1782	1782	1802	IL
Lestourgeon, Aaron	L	1769	1768	1777	AL
Lestourgeon, William & Aaron	L	1767	–	1769	AWL / L
Letablère, John	Db	1737	1743	1751	Let
Leuchars, William	L	–	1882	1886	–
Levesley Bros	S	1863	1901	1916	LB
Levi & Solomon	B	–	1891	1928	–
Lewis, George	L	1699	1698	1704	LE
Lewis, George Samuel	Nc	–	1807	–	GL
Lewis, J. & Sons	S	–	1899	–	–
Ley, Petley	L	1715	1718	1720	Le
Ley, Timothy	L	1697	1691	1733	LE TL
Lias, Charles	L	1837	1837	1884	CL
Lias, H. & Son	L	1867	1850	1876	HL / HL
Lias, John	L	1799	1806	1817	IL
Lias, John & Henry	L	1818	1816	1849	IL / HL
Lias, John, Henry & Charles	L	1823	1823	1840	IL / HL / CL
Lias & Wakeley	L	–	1882	1884	
Liberty & Co Ltd	B	1899	1898	1938	L&Co
Liger, Isaac	L	1704	1709	1729	LI IL
Lingard, John	L	1718	1721	1726	LI Li IL
Linnit, John	L	1815	1824	1831	JL
Linnit, John & Atkinson, William	L	–	1813	–	–
Linwood, Matthew	B	–	1801	1821	ML
Lister, William	Nc	–	1826	1834	WL
Lister, William & Sons	L	–	1920	–	–
Lister & Sons	Nc	–	1863	–	L&SONS
Livingstone, Edward	Du	–	1809	1840	EL
Lloyd, James	L	–	1805	1819	–
Lloyd, John	Db	1768	1771	1782	IL
Lock, Joseph	L	1775	–	1779	IL JL
Lock, Nathaniel	L	1697	1699	1716	LO
Locker, Christopher	Db	1739	1730	1751	CL
Locker, John	Db	1759	1769	1772	IL
Lockwood, Richard, & Douglas, John	L	1800	–	1802	RL / ID
Lofthouse, Mary	L	1731	–	1732	ML
Lofthouse, Matthew E.	L	1705	1708	1730	LO LO monogram / ML
Lofthouse, Seth	L	1699	1697	1719	LO
London Forgery Group	L	–	1650	–	–

Maker's name	Town of registration	Earliest mark registration	Earliest example	Latest example	Maker's mark/notes
London, William	L	1761	–	–	WL
Looker, William	L	1713	1713	1724	LO WL
Lothian, Edward	Ed	1731	1735	1749	EL
Lothian & Robertson	Ed	–	1751	1761	L&R
Loughlin, John I	Db	1751	1741	1758	IL
Loughlin, John II	Db	–	1783	1795	IL
Love, John, & Co	S	1783	1784	1819	IL&Co
Lovell, Robert	L	1703	–	1710	LO
Low, Josiah	Db	1819	1837	1842	IL
Lowe, Edward	L	1760	1770	1783	EL
Lowe, George	Ch (also L)	1791	1796	1841	GL
Lowe, John	Ch	–	1856	1880	JL
Lowe, Robert	Ed	1742	1742	1756	LOW
Lowenstark, D.	L	–	1863	1865	–
Lucas, Robert	L	1727	1727	1740	RL
Ludlow, John	L	1713	–	1716	LV IL
Luff, John	L	1724	1727	1747	IL I LUFF
Luke, John II	Gl	1699	1704	1707	IL
Luke, Robert	Gl	1721	1725	1752	RL
Lukin, William I	L	1699	1699	1736	WL Lu
Lund, William & Son	L	–	1904	–	–
Lutwyche & Vere see Vere & Lutwyche					
Lyng, George	Db	1706	1699	–	GL
Mabie, Todd & Co Ltd	L	–	1934	–	–
MacDonald, D.	Gl	1828	1819	1841	DMcD
Mackay & Chisholm	Ed	–	1835	1941	M&C
Mackay, Cunningham & Co	Ed	–	1837	1874	–
Mackenzie, Charles	L	1736	–	1773	CM
Mackenzie, William	L	1748	1749	1750	WM monogram
Macrae, Alexander	L	–	1860	1869	–
Macrae, F.B.	L	–	1892	1893	–
Madden, Jonathan	L	1703	1702	1708	MA
Mahoney, J.	Db	1845	1835	1847	JM
Maidman, Ralph	L	1731	1729	1734	RM
Main, John	Ed	1729	1726	1742	IM
Maitland, James	L	–	1730	1731	IM
Makemeid, Christopher	L	1758	–	1772	CM
Makepeace, Robert I	Nc	1718	1722	1779	RM
Makepeace, Robert II	L	1795	1795	1810	RM
Makepeace, Thomas	Nc	1728	1732	1738	TM
Makepeace, Robert I & Carter, Richard	L	1777	1766	1778	RM RC
Makepeace, Robert II & Thomas II	L	1794	1793	1794	RM TM
Mallinson, Thomas	L	1773	1778	1802	TM
Malyn, Isaac	L	1710	1710	–	MA
Mammatt & Sons	S	1865	–	1899	MBCo
Mangy, Thomas	Y	1664	1662	1689	TM
Manjoy, George	L	–	1690	–	MA
Mann, Thomas	L	1713	1715	1742	MA TM
Mann, William	L	–	1840	1858	WM
Mann, William	Ed	–	1825	–	–
Manners, James I	L	1726	1734	1739	IM
Maple & Co Ltd	S	–	1907	1910	–
Mappin, Jonathan	S	1775	1775	–	–
Mappin, John Newton	L	1882	1882	1895	JNM
Mappin, Joseph & Edward	S	1848	–	–	–
Mappin, J., & Co	S	1775	1775	1778	IM&Co
Mappin, Joseph & Sons	S	1833	1821	1833	JM
Mappin, J., Bros	S	1856	–	–	–
	L	1856	1889	1954	MB M&B EM JM CM WG JLL EM JM WG JLL FC CH M Bros Mn Bros
Mappin, John Newton, & Webb, George	L	1866	1857	1966	JNM GW M&W MW&Co
Margas, Jacob	L	1706	1705	1725	MA IM
Margas, Samuel	L	1715	1705	1717	MA SM
Marples & Co	B (also S)	–	1905	1911	–

Maker's name	Town of registration	Earliest mark registration	Earliest example	Latest example	Maker's mark/notes
Marsh, Charles	Db	1816	1817	1833	CM
Marsh, Jacob	L	1744	1743	1773	IM
Marshall, Brian	L	–	1960	1962	–
Marshall, David	Ed	1782	1785	1786	DM
Marshall, James & William	Ed	–	1816	1857	J&WM
Marshall, William	Ed	–	1821	1883	WM
Marshall & Sons	Ed	–	1823	1887	M&S
Marson, Frederick	B	–	1847	1864	–
Martin, Charles	L	1741	1727	1738	CM
Martin, Goldstein	L	–	1880	1884	–
Martin, Hall & Co Ltd	S (also L & B)	1854	1848	1945	RM MH EH &Co
Martin Bros & Co	S	1846	1845	1876	AH
Masham, Willoughby	L	1701	1701	1704	MA
Mason, Thomas	L	1716	1717	1749	Ma TM TM monogram
Massey, Samuel	L	1773	1760	1796	SM
Mathew, William I	L	1697	1697	1706	MA
Mathew, William II	L	1712	–	1735	MA WM
Mathie, Peter	Ed	1774	1783	1795	PM
Matthews, Henry	B	–	1896	1929	HM
Matthews, Henry	Db	1706	1704	1706	HM
Maundy, Thomas	L	–	1634	1650	TM monogram
Maundy, William	L	–	1630	1634	W M
May, Charles	B	–	1885	–	–
Mayer, Joseph	Ch	–	1846	1873	JM
Maxfield J. & J., Ltd	S	–	1902	–	–
Maxfield & Sons	L	–	1894	1895	–
Mayfield, Edward	L	1796	1795	1808	EM
McCrea, Alexander	L	–	1860	1865	–
McCrea, Frederick	L	–	1885	1899	–
McDonald, Angus	Gl	1824	1824	1852	AMcD
McDonald, David	Gl	1828	1819	1841	DMcD
McDonald, John	Ed	–	1800	1809	IMD (MD conjoined)
McFarlan, Jessie	L	1739	–	1756	IM
McHattie, G.	Ed	–	1806	1827	GMH (MH conjoined)
McKay, John	Ed	1793	1773	1866	JMc
McKenzie, Colin	Ed	1695	1698	1719	MK conjoined
McKenzie, James	Ed	1747	1749	1750	IM
McKenzie, Kenneth	Ed	1714	1718	1723	KM
Meach, Richard	L	1765	1771	1783	RM
Meade, Thomas	Db	1835	1832	1834	TM
Medlycott, Edmund	L	1748	1750	1752	EM
Meriton, Samuel I	L	1739	1747	*	SM
Meriton, Samuel II	L	1775	1773	1781	SM
Meriton, Thomas	L	1791	1797	1801	TM
Merry, John	L	1782	1790	1809	IM
Merry, Thomas I	L	1701	1711	1716	Me
Metcalf Hopgood see Hopgood, Metcalf					
Methuen, George	L	1743	1744	1771	GM
Metham, Robert	L	1808	–	1810	RM
Mettayer, Lewis	L	1700	1708	1717	ME LM
Mewburn, Barak	L	1826	–	1830	BM
Mewburn, John	L	1793	1794	1826	IM
Middleton, William	L	1700	1698	–	MI
Miles, R.A.	L	–	1927	1933	–
Mill, William	M	1811	–	1820	WM
Millar, Wilkinson	L	–	1900	1903	–
Miller, Henry I	L	1714	–	1721	MI HM
Miller, Henry II	L	1733	1732	1753	HM
Miller, W., & Co	Ed	–	1893	–	–
Millidge, Jonathan	Ed	–	1807	1833	JM
Millington, John	L	1718	1721	1722	MI IM
Millington, Thomas	B	1836	1826	–	–
Mills, Dorothy	L	1752	1751	1775	DM
Mills, Dorothy, & Sarbitt, Thomas	L	–	1745	1750	DM TS
Mills, George, & Co	B	–	1908	1920	–
Mills, Hugh	L	1739	1741	1751	HM HM conjoined
Mills, Nathaniel	B (also L)	1825	1826	1874	MN
Mills, Richard	L	1755	1755	1776	RM
Milne & Campbell	Ed (also Gl)	–	1764	1848	M&C
Millward Bank, J., & Co	L (also B, S & Ch)	–	1890	1912	JMB

Maker's name	Town of registration	Earliest mark registration	Earliest example	Latest example	Maker's mark/notes
Mince, James	L	1790	1790	1802	IM
Mince, James, & Hodgkins, William II	L	1780	1780	–	IM WH
Mitchell, Alexander	Gl	1822	1833	1838	AM
Mitchell, David	Ed	1700	1720	1739	DM monogram
Mitchell, John	Gl	1834	1826	1853	JM
Mitchell, J. & W.	Gl (also Ed)	1834	1836	1855	J&WM
Mitchell, Robert, & Co	B	–	1811	–	–
Mitchell & Russell	Ed	1813	–	1818	M&R
Mitchellsone, James	Ed	1706	1710	1728	IM
Mitchinson, John	Nc	–	1784	1790	IM
Moliere, John, & Jones, Dyall	L	1767	–	1768	IM DI
Monjoy, Dorothy	Db	–	1725	1730	DM
Moore, Andrew	L	1700	1650	1696	MO monogram
Moore, James	Db	1818	1812	1836	JM
Moore, John	L	1758	1756	1822	IM
Moore, John	Db	1728	1728	1758	IM monogram
Moore, Patrick	Db	–	1812	1832	PM
Moore, Thomas I	L	1723	–	–	MO
Moore, Thomas II	L	1750	1755	1762	TM
Mordan, Sampson & Co	L (also B & Ch)	–	1855	1937	SM
Mordan, Sampson, & Riddle, G.	L	–	1830	–	–
Mordecai, Benjamin	L	1770	1779	1782	BM
Morel, Jean–Valentin	L	–	1849	–	–
Morel & Co	–	–	1851	–	–
Morgan, William	Db	1806	1818	1834	WM
Morison, James	L	1740	1744	1759	IM
Morley, Edward	L	–	1790	1815	EM
Morley, Elizabeth	L	1794	1796	1817	EM
Morley, Thomas	L	1778	–	1779	TM
Morris, George	L	1750	1752	1753	GM
Morris, Henry	L	1718	1739	1758	MO HM HM conjoined
Morse, Thomas	L	1718	1721	1723	MO TM

Maker's name	Town of registration	Earliest mark registration	Earliest example	Latest example	Maker's mark/notes
Morson, James	L	1716	1744	1758	MO IM
Morson, Richard, & Stephenson, Benjamin	L	1762	1773	1774	RM BS
Mortimer, John, & Hunt, John Samuel (formerly Storr & Mortimer; later Hunt & Roskell)	L	1839	1841	1945	$I_S^M H$
Morton, Richard & Co	S	1773	1773	1819	RM &Co
Morton, William & Sons	S	1902	–	–	–
Mosley, R.F., & Co Ltd	S	–	1897	1946	–
Moss, Peter	L	1728	–	1747	PM
Mosse, Barth	Db	1734	–	1735	BM
Moulson, William	L	–	1841	1853	–
Mountigue, Benjamin	L	1771	1781	1789	BM MB
Mowden, David	L	1739	1751	1773	DM
Muir, J. II	Gl	–	1837	–	JMJ^R
Muirhead, J. & Sons	Gl	–	1865	1881	JM&S
Muirhead & Arthur	Gl	–	1846	–	M&A
Mullin, Charles	Db	–	1772	1805	CM
Muns, John	L	1753	1753	1765	IM
Murphy, Arthur	Db	–	1805	–	AM
Murphy, H.G.	L	–	1931	–	–
Murray, Edward	Db	1812	1816	1822	EM
Murray, George	Nc	–	1805	–	GM
Murray, J.	Gl	–	1854	1867	JM
Murray, Nathan II	Db	1758	1765	1803	NM
Murray, Patrick	Ed	1701	1704	1718	PM monogram
Muston, Henry	Ex	–	1701	1721	Mu
Nangle, George	L	1797	1800	1807	GN
Nash, Bowles	L	1721	1721	1725	NA BN
Nash, Gawen	L	1724	1726	1737	GN
Nash, Thomas I	L	1759	1768	1774	TN
Nash, Thomas II	L	1786	–	–	TN
Nasmith, James	Ed	–	1831	1853	JN
Nasmith, James, & Co	Ed	–	1840	–	JN&Co
Nathan & Hayes	Ch (also B)	–	1890	1916	GN RH
Natter, George	L	1773	–	1801	GN

Maker's name	Town of registration	Earliest mark registration	Earliest example	Latest example	Maker's mark/notes
Naylor Bros Ltd	S	–	1840	–	–
	L	–	1916	1976	–
Neale, William & Sons	S	–	1897	–	–
Needham, Charles	S	1810	–	1835	CN
Needham, Veall & Tyzack Ltd	S	–	1922	1928	–
Neill, Stanley, & Co	S	–	1902	–	–
Neill, Sharman D., Ltd	Db	1906	1910	1930	N
	S	–	1902	–	–
Nelme, Anthony	L	1697	1683	1738	Ne ANe (AN monogram)
Nelme, Francis	L	1723	1725	1739	AN monogram FN
Nelson Dawson *see* Dawson, Nelson					
Nelson, William	Db	–	1828	–	WN
Neville, John	L	1745	1745	–	INE
Neville, Samuel	Db	1795	1796	1837	SN
Neville, Thomas	L	–	1774	–	–
Newbold, Thomas	B	1820	1820	1828	TN
Newby, Thomas	L	1816	–	1817	TN
Newland, Luke F.	Gl (*also* Ed)	1816	1817	1821	LFN
Newton, John	L	1726	1726	1749	IN
Nicklin, John	Db	–	1814	1833	IN
Nigretti & Zambra	B	–	1903	–	HCF (?)
Nixon, Charles Edward	S	1880	1897	1905	–
Nixon, Joseph	Db	1759	1775	1803	IN
Noad, Stephen	L	1806	–	1826	SN
Norman, Philip	L	–	1768	1772	PN
Northcote, Hannah	L	1798	1779	1819	HN
Northcote, Thomas	L	1776	1777	1819	TN
Northcote, Thomas, & Bourne, George	L	1794	1794	–	TN GB
Northern Goldsmiths Co	L (*also* B, S, Ch, Ed & Gl)	–	1934	1938	NG Co
Nowill, Joseph	S	1783	1825	1831	IN JN
Nowlan, Lawrence	Db	1814	1817	1840	LN
Nowlan, William	Db	1827	1811	1832	WN
Nutting, Henry	L	1796	1796	1824	HN
Nutting, Henry, & Hennell, Robert II	L	1808	1808	1809	HN RH
Oldfield, Elizabeth	L	1750	1750	1754	EO
Oldfield, R.C.	S	–	1902	–	–
Olivant, Ebenezer	Ed	1737	–	1749	EO
Ollivant, Thomas I	L	1789	1784	1806	TO
Ollivant, Thomas II (?)	L	1830	–	–	TO
Ollivant, Thomas, & Botsford, J.W.	L (*also* B & S)	–	1909	1937	O&B
Oliver, John	Y	1676	–	–	IO
Orme, John II	L	–	1797	–	IO
Osborne, John	Db	–	1789	1796	JO
Osborne, Jonas	Ed (*also* Db)	–	1790	1799	–
Osman, Louis	L	–	1970	–	–
Osmont, John (*or* James)	Ex	1835	1827	1855	JO
Otley, Thomas & Sons	S	1879	–	1890	–
Ourry, Lewis	L	1740	1741	1743	LO
Overing, Charles	L	1697	1697	1717	OV
Oyles, Phillip	L	1699	1699	–	OY
Pages, Francis	L	1729	1730	1754	FP
Paillet, Mark	L	–	1703	–	PA
Palmer, Richard	L	1759	1761	1765	RP
Pantin, Lewis I	L	1734	1733	1745	LP
Pantin, Simon I	L	1701	1702	*	PA SP
Pantin, Simon II	L	1729	–	1732	SP
Paradise, William	L	1718	1719	1723	Pa WP
Pargeter, Richard	L	1730	1727	1746	RP
Parker, John I	L	–	–	–	IP
Parker, John II	L	–	1802	1804	IP
Parker, John III	L	1836	–	–	JP
Parker, William	L	1798	1800	1805	WP
Parker, John I, & Wakelin, Edward	L	–	1760	1784	P&W IP EW
Parker, William, & Simpson, Benjamin	L	1799	1799	1800	WP BS
Parkes, J., & Co	L	–	1927	1932	JP (?)
Parkin, Isaac	Ex	1835	1824	1829	IP
Parkin & Marshall	S	1866	1865	–	P&M WP

Maker's name	Town of registration	Earliest mark registration	Earliest example	Latest example	Maker's mark/notes
Parr, Sarah	L	1728	–	1732	SP
Parr, Thomas I	L	1697	1697	1718	PA
Parr, Thomas II	L	1733	1741	1754	TP
Parry, William	Ex	–	1743	1779	WP
Parsons, A. & F., and A.F., & A.	L	–	1911	1939	AP FP
Parsons, H. & L.	L	–	1960	1971	–
Parsons, John, & Co	S	1783	1783	1804	IP&Co
Partis, Thomas I	Nc	–	1720	1734	TP
Partis, William	Nc	1731	1736	1757	WP WP conjoined
Pasley, Jonathan	Db	–	1758	1759	–
Payne, Humphrey	L	1701	1701	1739	Pa HP
Payne, John	L	1751	1750	1776	IP
Payne, Thomas & Richard	L	1777	1777	1778	TP RP
Payne & Son (Goldsmiths) Ltd	L	–	1966	1972	–
Payne & Son of Oxford	L (also B)	–	1921	1971	–
Peacock, Edward	L	1710	–	1724	Pe EP
Peake, Robert	L	1697	1697	1719	PE
Pearce, Edmund	L	1705	1705	1722	PE EP
Pearce, Richard	L	1812	1812	1824	RP
Pearce, Richard, & Burrows, George II	L	1826	1826	1851	RP GB
Pearce & Sons Ltd of Leeds	L (also S)	–	1902	1936	–
Pearson, William	L	1704	1719	1720	PE WP
Peaston, Robert	L	1762	1759	1780	RP
Peaston, William	L	1746	1739	1774	WP
Peaston, William & Robert	L	1756	1753	1759	WP RP WP RP
Pegler, E.S., of Halifax	–	–	1864	–	–
Pemberton, Benjamin	Ch	–	1723	1753	BP
Pemberton, Peter	Ch	1677	1677	1706	P Pe PP
Pemberton, Samuel	B	1778	1781	1823	SP
Pemberton, Thomas & Son	B	–	1796	1838	TP
Penman, Edward	Ed	1707	1707	1729	EP
Penman, Hugh	Ed	1734	1734	–	HP
Penman, James	Ed	1673	1685	1705	IP monogram
Penstone, Henry	L	1697	1718	1722	PE
Penstone, William I	L	1697	1699	1715	PE
Peppin, Robert	L	1817	1817	1834	RP
Peppin, Sydenham William	L	1816	1815	1817	SP
Perkins, Jonathan I & Jonathan II	L	1795	–	1797	IP IP
Pero, Isabel	L	1741	1741	1742	IP
Pero, John	L	1717	–	1738	PE IP
Perry, John	L	1757	1756	1759	IP
Perth, Robert (or Pertt)	L	1738	1748	1754	RP
Peter, David	Db	1767	1761	1806	DP
Peterson, Abraham	L	1790	1789	1810	AP
Peterson, Abraham, & Podio, Peter	L	1783	1783	1796	AP PP
Petley, William	L	1699	1719	1732	PE WP
Pettifer, David	B	1847	1850	1856	–
Pilleau, Peze (Alexis)	L	1739	1725	1755	PI PP
Pilling, C.C.	L (also S)	–	1900	1912	CCP
Phillips, H.	L	–	1952	–	–
Phillips, John	Db	1679	1696	1703	IP
Phillips, S.J., Ltd	L	–	1900	1974	SJP
Phillips, William, of Handsworth	B	1832	1832	1835	WP
Phillips, W.A.	S	–	1896	–	–
Phillis, Phillip	L	1720	1720	–	PH PP
Phipps, James	L	1767	1767	1776	IP
Phipps, Thomas & James II	L	1816	1815	1820	TP IP
Phipps, Thomas; Robinson, Edward, & Phipps, James II	L	–	1786	1815	TP ER JP
Phipps, Thomas, & Robinson, Edward II	L	–	1777	1820	TP ER
Pickering, Matthew	L	1703	–	1705	PI
Pickett, William	L	1769	–	–	WP
Piercy, Josiah & George	L	1812	1812	1817	IP GP
Piercy, Robert	L	1775	1762	1782	RP
Piers, Daniel	L	1746	1749	1799	DP
Piers, Mary	L	1758	1758	–	MP
Pierpoint, T.	Ch	–	1784	1787	TP

Maker's name	Town of registration	Earliest mark registration	Earliest example	Latest example	Maker's mark/notes
Piesse, A.G.	L	–	1864	–	–
Pinches (Medalists) Ltd	L	–	1972	1976	–
Pinckney, Robert, & Scott, Robert	Nc	–	1779	1790	P&S RP RS
Pinder, John, & Co	S	–	1875	1948	–
Pinnell, George Frederick	L	1830	1830	1849	GFP
Pittar, John	Db	1756	1748	1804	IP JP
Pitts, Thomas I	L	–	1761	1789	TP
Pitts, William	L	1781	1782	1817	WP
Pitts, William, & Preedy, Joseph	L	1791	1799	1820	WP IP
Plante, H.H.	L	–	1912	1969	–
Platel, Philip	L	1737	1737	–	PP
Platel, Pierre	L	1699	1699	1718	PL
Plimpton, Charles	L	1805	1805	–	CP
Plummer, James	Y	1619	1636	1653	IP
Plummer, John	Y	1648	1653	1673	IP
Plummer, Michael	L	1791	1791	1797	MP
Plummer, William	L	1755	1755	1791	WP
Plymley, Francis	L	1715	1716	1719	PL
Pocock, Edward	L	1728	1714	1738	EP
Podio, Peter	L	1790	1789	1804	PP
Pollock, John	L	1734	1738	1755	IP
Pontifex, Daniel	L	1794	1794	1811	DP
Pope, William	Ex	–	1833	1853	WP
Popkins, Daniel	Db	1759	1758	1775	DP
Portal, Abraham	L	1749	1754	1767	AP
Porter, John	L	1698	1701	1705	Po PO
Poston, A.E., & Co Ltd	S (also B)	–	1947	1960	AEP & Co Ltd
Potter, J.H.	S	–	1912	–	–
Poulden, Richard	L	1818	1819	1824	RP
Powell, Francis	L	1818	1817	1823	FP
Powell, Thomas	L	1756	1758	1787	TP
Power, Edward	Db	1816	1817	1835	EP
Power, John	Db	–	1787	1814	JP
Pratt, Thomas & Sons	B	–	1864	1875	TP&S
Pratt, Thomas, & Humphres, Arthur	L	1780	1780	1783	TP AH TP AH
Preedy, Joseph	L	1777	1773	1819	IP
Preston, Benjamin	L	1825	1825	1862	BP
Price, Charles	L	1812	1812	1828	CP
Price, Harvey	L	1727	1726	1749	HP
Priest, John	L	1748	1748	1759	IP
Priest, William & James	L	1768	1762	1772	WP JP
Priestly, Arthur, & Co	S	–	1895	–	–
Priestman, John	L	1786	–	1793	IP
Prince, H., & Co	Y	1795	1795	1806	HP&C HP &C HP conjoined
Pringle, Robert & Sons	L (also Ch)	–	1896	1938	–
Pritchard, Joseph	L	1825	1825	–	IP
Proctor, Edmund	L	1700	–	1705	RP (R smaller)
Proctor, Luke, & Co	S	1785	1785	1792	LP &Co
Pugh, William	B (also Ch)	–	1790	1816	WP
Purdee, E.C.	L	–	1881	1900	e c P
Purse, George	L	–	1817	1823	GP
Purse, William	L	–	1803	1817	WP
Purton, Frances	L	1783	1788	1809	FP
Purton, Frances, & Johnson, Thomas	L	1793	1793	1794	FP TJ
Purver, Sarah	L	1817	1817	1819	SP
Pyne, Benjamin	L	1697	1682	1727	P Py
Quantock, John	L	1754	1750	1764	IQ
Raine, Richard	L	1712	1712	1713	RA
Rait, D. Crighton & Sons	Gl	1832	1830	1897	CDR DCR&S
Ramsay, John	Nc	1698	1700	1708	Ra IR
Ramsay, John II	Nc	–	1720	1732	JR
Ramsey, James, of Dundee	Db (also L, B & S)	1912	1911	1937	JR
Ramsden, Omar (1873–1929)	L	1918	1909	1939	OR
Ramsden, Omar, & Carr, Alwyn	L	1898	1900	1926	OR AC
Rand, John	L	1704	1703	1711	Ra
Randall Chatterton see Chatterton, Randall					

Maker's name	Town of registration	Earliest mark registration	Earliest example	Latest example	Maker's mark/notes
Rattray & Co	B	–	1938	–	–
Raven, Andrew	L	1697	1698	1706	Ra RA AR
Rawlings, Charles	L	1817	1817	1828	CR
Rawlings, John Henry	L	–	1888	1903	–
Rawlings, Charles, & Summers, William	L	1829	1829	1863	CR WS
Read, J.	Db	1827	–	1831	IR
Read, John	L	1704	1704	1711	Re
Read, Josephus	L	1816	–	1829	JR
Readshaw, Joshua	L	1697	1698	1709	RE
Reed, Clement	Y	1698	1695	1698	CR
Reid, Alexander III	Ed	1660	1665	1681	AR AR conjoined
Reid, Christian	Nc	–	1799	1818	CR
Reid, Christian J.	Nc	–	1869	1870	CJR
Reid, Christian Ker & David	Nc (also L)	1815	1799	1829	CR DR
Reid, Christian Ker, David & Christian Bruce	Nc	–	1809	1843	CR DR CR
Reid, David	Nc	–	1846	1867	DR
Reid, Edward	L	–	1768	–	–
Reid, E.K.	L	–	1855	1873	EKR
Reid, George	L	1811	–	1829	GR
Reid, J.	Gl	–	1864	1883	JR
Reid, William Ker	L	1825	1826	1882	WR WKR
Reid & Sons Ltd	L (also B & Ch)	–	1854	1937	–
Reily, Charles	L	–	1820	1823	(no personal mark)
Reily, Charles, & Storer, George	L	1829	1824	1862	CR GS
Reily, John	L	1801	1791	1829	IR
Reily, Mary Ann & Charles	L	1826	1826	1837	MR CR
Renou, Timothy	L	1792	1792	1803	TR
Rew, Robert	L	1754	1758	1783	RR
Reynolds, William	Co	1758	1757	1764	WR WR conjoined
Rhoades, Charles	Y	1677	1678	1707	RH CR

Maker's name	Town of registration	Earliest mark registration	Earliest example	Latest example	Maker's mark/notes
Rhodes, Jehoiada Alsop	S	–	1872	1880	–
Rhodes, Jehoiada Alsop, & Barber	S	–	1874	1881	–
Rhodes, Manoah & Sons Ltd	S (also L)	–	1897	1932	–
Ribouleau, Isaac	L	1724	1724	1730	RI IR
Rich, John	L	1765	1789	1810	IR
Richards, Alexander	Db	–	1737	1765	AR
Richards, Edmond	Ex	–	1694	1736	Ri
Richards, F.C.	B	–	1938	–	–
Richards, G.J.	L	–	1847	1856	–
Richards, G.J., & Brown, E.C.	L	–	1858	1866	–
Richards, Thomas	L	1812	1812	1813	TR
Richardson, John II	L	1752	1759	1762	IR
Richardson, Richard I	Ch	–	1701	*	Ri RR conjoined
Richardson, Richard II	Ch	–	1756	1784	RR
Richardson, Richard	S	–	1896	1905	–
Richardson, William	Ch	–	1721	1751	WR conjoined
Ridout, George	L	1743	–	1744	GR
Riley, Christopher	L	1697	1694	–	RI
Robb & Whittet	Ed	–	1839	1876	R&W
Robert, Hugh	L	1697	1697	1700	RO
Roberts, John, & Co	S	–	1775	1826	IR&Co
Roberts, Samuel, & Co	S	1773	1773	1837	SR&Co
Roberts & Belk	S	1864	1865	1975	R&B SR CB CB EP GR EB
Roberts, G., & Briggs, E.	S (also L)	1859	1835	1903	R&B
Roberts, Cadman & Co	S	1786	1792	1826	RC&Co SR&Co GC&Co
Roberts & Doré Ltd	L	–	1971	–	R&D
Roberts & Hall	S	1847	1849	1853	R&H
Roberts & Slater	S	1844	1845	1858	R&S
Roberts, S., Smith & Co	S	1826	–	1828	SR&Co
Robertson, Ann	Nc	–	1786	1815	AR

Maker's name	Town of registration	Earliest mark registration	Earliest example	Latest example	Maker's mark/notes
Robertson, George	A	1708	–	1725	GR
Robertson, John	Nc (also L)	–	1795	1801	IR
Robertson, Patrick	Ed	1751	1766	1789	PR
Robertson, William	L	1753	1756	1762	WR
Robertson, William	Ed	1789	1791	1795	WR
Robertson, John, & Darling, David	Nc	–	1795	1801	R&D I R DD
Robertson, John, & Walton, John	Nc	–	1793	1819	IR IW
Robins, John	L	1774	1776	1821	IR
Robins, Thomas	L	1801	1794	1830	TR
Robinson, John I	L	1723	–	1728	RO IR
Robinson, Philip	L	1714	–	1723	Ro PR
Robinson, Thomas I	L	1802	1805	1828	TR
Robinson, Thomas II (worked only with S.Harding)	L	1810	–	–	(no personal mark)
Robinson, Thomas	Ch	–	1682	1719	Ro
Robinson, William	Nc	1666	1656	1698	WR conjoined; RWR conjoined
Robinson, John; Edkins, Samuel, & Aston, Thomas	B	1834	1827	1847	REA
Roby, Samuel	L	1740	1740	1745	SR
Rodgers, Joseph & Sons Ltd	S	1812	1848	1937	IR
Roe, Ebenezer	L	1709	1709	1716	RO
Roe, Nathaniel	L	–	1716	–	RO
Roker, John	L	1743	1740	–	IR
Roker, Philip I	L	1697	1697	–	RO Ro
Roker, Philip II	L	1720	*	*	RO PR P ROKER PR (R smaller)
Roker, Philip III	L	1776	*	*	PR
Rollo, John	Ed	1731	–	1732	IR
Rollos, Philip I	L	1697	1699	1714	RO
Rollos, Philip II	L	1705	1705	1716	RO PR
Romer, Emick	L	–	1759	1776	ER
Romer, John	L	1771	1756	1792	IR
Roode, Alexander	L	1697	1702	1718	RO

Maker's name	Town of registration	Earliest mark registration	Earliest example	Latest example	Maker's mark/notes
Roode, Gundry	L	1710	1711	1735	RO GR
Rood(e), James	L	1710	1710	1720	RO
Rood(e), Mary	L	1721	1722	1725	RO MR
Rooke, B. & Son	S	1818	1818	1823	BR
Rosenthal & Jacobs	L	–	1885	1887	–
Roskell, Robert, of Liverpool see Hunt & Roskell					
Roskell, Allen see Hunt & Roskell					
Ross, F.J., & Sons	S	–	1917	–	–
Ross, Thomas	L	1819	–	1824	TR
Round, John & Son Ltd	S (also L)	1867	1868	1937	JR JR ER
Rowbotham, John, & Co	S	1774	1775	1807	IRCo IR Co
Rowe, John	L	1749	1749	1779	IR
Rowe, Thomas	L	1753	–	1754	TR
Royal Irish	Db	–	1966	1967	–
Royes, Solomon	L	1820	1820	1821	SR
Royes, Solomon, & Dix, John East	L	1818	1818	1819	I^{S}E^{R}D
Ruell, James	L	1795	1802	1806	IR
Rugg, Richard	L	1754	1755	1782	RR
Rundell, Edmond Waller see Rundell, Bridge & Rundell					
Rundell, Philip (1743–1827) (founded Rundell & Bridge c.1788)	L	1819	1818	1824	PR
Rundell & Bridge (formed c.1788 by Philip Rundell & John Bridge)	L	–	–	–	–
Rundell, Bridge & Co (formed in 1833)	L	–	–	–	–
Rundell, Bridge & Rundell (formed in 1805)	L	1804	1810	1828	RB&R (much of their work marked PS for Paul Storr)

Maker's name	Town of registration	Earliest mark registration	Earliest example	Latest example	Maker's mark/notes	Maker's name	Town of registration	Earliest mark registration	Earliest example	Latest example	Maker's mark/notes
Rush, Thomas	L	1724	1725	1760	TR	Scarlett, Richard	L	1719	1723	1732	SC RS
Ruslen, John	L	1697	1701	1703	RU	Scarlett, William	L	1697	1689	1727	SC WS W S
Russell, John	Gl	1845	1848	1872	JR						
Russell, Thomas & Co	S	–	1895	–	–	Schuppe, John	L	1753	1754	1768	IS
Russell, William	Gl	1827	–	1836	WR	Schurman, Albartus	L	1756	–	1764	AS
Rutland, Robert	L	1807	1807	1826	RR						
Ryan, Aeneas	Db	1792	1787	1807	AE R (AE conjoined)	Schofield, John	L	1778	1770	1809	IS JS
						Scott, George I	Ed	1677	–	–	GS
Rylands, Thomas & Sons	B	1830	1830	1834	TR&S	Scott, George II	Ed	1697	1701	1703	GS
						Scott, James	Db	1800	1800	1834	IS
Sadler, Thomas	L	1701	1701	1719	SA TS	Scott, Robert	Gl	–	1897	–	RS
Salmon, Robert	L	1773	1779	1805	RS	Scott, Thomas A.	S	–	1901	1909	–
Samuel, Lewis, of Liverpool	L	1830	1830	1834	LS	Scott, Walter	Ed	1701	–	1707	WS
Sampel, William	L	1755	1756	1774	WS	Scott, Digby, & Smith, Benjamin II	L	1802	1802	1808	D & S DS B & S BS
Sampson, Thomas	Ex	1706	1707	1728	Sa TS	Seabrook, James	L	1714	1711	1720	Se IS
Sampson, Mordan & Co *see* Mordan						Seagars, T.E.	L	–	1849	–	–
Sanders, Benjamin	L	1737	1738	1740	BS	Seaman, William	L	1804	1789	1813	WS
Sanders, John	L	1717	1717	1746	SA IS	Seatoun, George	L	–	1769	1780	GS
Sanders, Joseph	L	1730	1730	1747	IS	Seatoun, John	Ed	1685	–	1712	IS
Sanderson, John	S	1880	–	1910	–	Selfridges Ltd	L	–	1908	–	–
						Settle, John & Thomas	S	1815	1816	1828	I&TS T&IS
Sansom, William	S	1835	–	1837	WS	Settle, John & Thomas, & Gunn & Co	S	1825	1825	1826	IS TS
Sansom & Harwood	S	1833	1829	–	S&H						
Sarbitt, Dorothy	L	1753	1753	1754	DS	Settle, John, & Williamson, Henry	S	–	1829	1831	IS HW
Sarbitt, Thomas *see* Mills, Dorothy						Sewill, Thomas	Nc	–	1846	1880	TS
Satchwell, Thomas	L	1773	1769	1799	TS	Sharp, Robert	L	1788	1785	1805	RS
Saunders, Alexander	L	1757	1759	1766	AS	Sharp, William	L	1817	1819	1826	WS
Saunders & Shepherd (*also* B & Ch)	L	–	1889	1925	–	Sharratt, Thomas	L	1772	1774	1778	TS
						Shaw, Edward	B	–	1834	1836	–
						Shaw, John	L	–	1790	1829	IS
Savory, Adey Bellamy	L	1826	1826	1853	ABS	Shaw, Nathaniel	Nc	–	1715	1741	Sh
Savory, Adey Bellamy, Joseph II & Albert	L	1833	1833	1834	AS JS AS	Shaw, Thomas	L	1785	1770	1830	TS
						Shaw, Thomas	B	1822	1820	1839	TS
						Shaw, William I	L	1728	1730	1774	SH WS
Savory, Joseph II & Albert	L	1835	1834	1867	AS JS	Shaw, William II, & Preist (*or* Priest), William	L	1749	1746	1769	W WS P S
Savory, J. & H.	L	–	1886	–	–	Shea, John	L	1807	1807	–	JS
Savory, Thomas Cox	L	1827	1827	1831	TCS	Sheene, Alice	L	1700	1703	1714	SH
Sawyer, J.	Db	–	1856	–	–						
Sawyer, Richard I	Db	1807	1797	–	RS	Sheene, Joseph	L	1697	1698	1705	SH
Sawyer, Richard II	Db	1830	–	1846	RS	Shepherd, Gilbert	L	1631	1657	1663	GS
Scammell, Joseph	L	1788	1790	1794	JS						

Maker's name	Town of registration	Earliest mark registration	Earliest example	Latest example	Maker's mark/notes
Shepherd, Thomas	L	1769	1770	1809	TS
Sherwin, R.	Db	1836	–	1850	RS
Sherwin, William	Db	1779	1805	1834	WS
Sherwood, John & Sons	B	–	1896	1912	JS &S (?)
Shields, John	Db	1762	1782	1794	JS
Shiner, Cyril J.	B	–	1936	1938	–
Shipway, Charles	L	1826	1835	1839	CS
Shruder, James	L	1737	1737	1746	IS
Sibley, Mary & Richard II	L	1836	1836	1837	M$_S$R
Sibley, Richard I	L	1805	1800	1872	RS
Sibray, Hall & Co Ltd	L / S	– / 1878	1887 / 1881	1903 / 1910	FS JH / –
Siervent, Samuel	L	1755	–	1762	SS
Simmons, Isaac	S	–	1839	1840	IS
Simons, William	L	1776	1777	1806	WS
Simpson, Benjamin	L	1800	–	1803	BS
Simpson, Thomas & Son	B	1809	1810	1820	S&S
Sinclair, Alexander	Db	1694	1700	1718	S
Singleton, Francis	L	1697	1698	1702	SI
Sissons, William & George	S (also L)	1858	1867	1926	WS GS
Sheen, William	L	1755	1755	1799	WS
Skinner, Christopher	Db	1736	1737	1768	CS
Skinner & Co	L	–	1909	1912	–
Slade, Thomas	Db	–	1724	1725	TS
Slater, T. & W., & Holland, H.	L	–	1889	1900	–
Sleath, Gabriel	L	1707	1709	1752	SL GS
Sleath, Gabriel, & Crump, Francis	L	1753	1753	1754	G$_C^F$S
Smiley, Samuel	L	–	1866	1878	–
Smiley, Thomas	L	–	1846	1881	–
Smiley, William	L	–	1855	1888	WS
Smiley, William Robert	L	–	1841	1865	WRS W$_S$R
Smith, Alexander	L	–	1873	1891	AS
Smith, Ann, & Appleton, Nathaniel	L	1771	1766	1783	A$_A^N$S
Smith, Benjamin I	L	1706	–	–	SM (M smaller)
Smith, Benjamin II	L	1807	1806	1840	BS

Maker's name	Town of registration	Earliest mark registration	Earliest example	Latest example	Maker's mark/notes
Smith, Benjamin III	L	1818	1821	1846	BS
Smith, Benjamin II & James III	L	1809	1794	1835	BS IS
Smith, Daniel, & Sharp, Robert	L	1768	1757	1789	DS RS D$_S^{RS}$
Smith, Edward	B	1826	1826	1865	ES
Smith, George I	L	1732	1739	1777	GS
Smith, George II	L	1767	1765	1819	GS
Smith, George III	L	1774	1781	1783	GS
Smith, George IV	L	1799	–	–	GS
Smith, George III, & Fearn, William	L	1786	1786	1832	GS WF
Smith, George I & Samuel III	L	1750	1751	1752	G$_S^S$S
Smith, James I	L	1718	1718	1746	SM IS
Smith, James & Son	S	1829	1829	1831	S&S $_S$SMI$_S$ TH
Smith, John	L	1697	–	1703	SM
Smith, John	S	1775	–	1780	IS
Smith, Joseph I	L	1707	1728	1742	SM IS
Smith, Nathaniel, & Co	S	1780	1780	1819	NS&Co
Smith, Nathaniel & George, & Creswick, James	S	–	1798	1801	–
Smith, Robert	Db	–	1714	–	RS
Smith, Robert	Db	–	1791	1857	RS
Smith, Samuel I	L	1700	*	*	Sm
Smith, Samuel II	L	1719	*	*	SM
Smith, Samuel III	L	1754	–	1755	SS
Smith, Stephen & Son	L	–	1858	1885	SS
Smith, Stephen, & Nicholson, William	L	–	1851	1864	
Smith, Nicholson & Co					as above
Smith, S.W., & Co	B (also L)	–	1893	1919	SWS
Smith, Thomas I	L	1750	1752	1788	TS
Smith, Thomas II	L	1772	–	–	–
Smith, W., of Liverpool	Ch	–	1870	1887	WS
Smith, William I	L	1758	–	–	WS
Smith, William II	L	1777	1777	1780	WS
Smith & Gamble	Db	1822	1825	1837	S&G

Maker's name	Town of registration	Earliest mark registration	Earliest example	Latest example	Maker's mark/notes
Smith, George II, & Hayter, Thomas	L	1792	1791	1818	GS TH
Smith, Nicholson & Co see Smith, Stephen					
Smith, Tate, Hoult & Tate	S	–	1811	1828	S T H&T
Smith, G., Tate, R., Nicholson, W., & Holt, E.	S	1810	1810	1826	S T N&H
Smithsend, John	L	1697	–	1698	SM
Smythe, John & Sons	Db	–	1845	1929	JS
Snatt, Josiah	L	1798	1799	1817	JS
Soame (or Soane), William	L	1723	–	1762	SO WS
Sobey, William R.	Ex	1835	1831	1855	WRS SOBEY
Soho Plate Co see Robinson, Edkins, & Aston	B	1834	–	1847	REA
Solomon, William	L	1747	–	1758	WS
Sorley, R. & W.	Gl (also L)	–	1896	1932	R&WS
Southey, William James	L	1810	1812	1824	WS
Spackman, Thomas	L	1700	1703	1714	Sp
Spackman, William	L	1714	1717	1726	SP WS
Sparrow, William Henry	B	–	1905	–	–
Spence, Alex	Ed	1783	1790	1809	AS
Spencer, Edward	L	–	1931	–	–
Spencer, R.	B	–	1911	–	–
Spencer, W.F. (designer for Garrards)	–	–	1849	1860	–
Spicer, Thomas, of Coventry	B	1830	1831	1836	TS
Spilsbury, Francis I	L	1729	1729	*	SP FS
Spilsbury, Francis II	L	1767	1768	1776	FS
Spink, M. & Son	L	–	1801	1896	–
Spooner, Clowes & Co	B	1824	–	1827	–
Sporle, Robert, & Co	S	1792	–	1794	RS &Co
Sprage, Charles	L	1734	–	1736	CS
Sprimont, Nicholas	L	1743	1741	1743	NS
Spring, Hugh	L	1721	1721	–	SP HS
Spring, William	L	1701	1704	1706	Sp

Maker's name	Town of registration	Earliest mark registration	Earliest example	Latest example	Maker's mark/notes
Spurrier & Co	B	–	1889	1892	–
Squire, George	L	1720	–	1726	SQ GS
Stabler, Harold	L	–	1937	–	–
Stalker, William, & Mitchison, John	Nc	1774	1773	1792	WS IM
Stammers, Edward	L	1816	1819	1850	ES
Stamp, Francis	L	1780	1779	1780	FS
Stamp, James	L	1774	1777	1782	IS
Stamp, James, & Baker, John I	L	1764	1768	1782	IS IB
Staniforth, J., & Co	S	1783	1811	1828	IS
Stanley, Anthony	Db	–	1696	1715	AS
Stapleton, Thomas	L	1878	–	1885	–
Starkey, Michael	L	1809	1809	1834	MS
Stephens, Benoni	L	–	1835	1841	–
Stephenson, Benjamin	L	1775	1774	1776	BS
Sterling & Son	S	–	1909	–	–
Stevenson, Ambrose	L	1707	1708	1720	St AS
Steward, John	L	1784	1795	1796	IS
Steward, Joseph I	L	1719	–	1739	ST IS
Steward, Joseph II	L	1755	–	1760	IS
Stewart, R.	Gl	–	1842	1876	RS
Stewart, Robert	S (also L)	–	1904	1933	–
Stockar, John Martin	L	1697	1697	1714	St
Stockar, John Martin, & Peacock, Edward	L	1705	1707	1709	St Pe
Stocker, William	L	–	1878	–	–
Stockwell, E.H.	L	–	1871	1891	–
Stokes, Bartholomew	Db	–	1752	–	BS
Stokes, Joseph	L	1697	–	1701	ST
Stokes, Robert	L	–	1698	1704	St
Stokes & Ireland	B (also Ch)	–	1880	1934	–
Stone, James	L	1726	–	1749	IS
Stone, John	Ex	1841	1840	1861	JS
Stone, R.E.	L	–	1936	–	–
Stonor, Clement	L	–	1683	1689	CS
Storr, Paul (1771–1844) (partner Rundell, Bridge & Rundell 1807–1819)	L	1793	1792	1845	PS

Maker's name	Town of registration	Earliest mark registration	Earliest example	Latest example	Maker's mark/notes
Storr & Co (formed 1807)	L	–	–	–	–
Storr & Mortimer (Paul Storr & John Mortimer) formed 1822; later Mortimer & Hunt (1839)	L	–	–	–	–
Story, Joseph William	L	1803	1807	1811	IWS
Story, Joseph William, & Elliott, William	L	1809	1809	1815	$I_W W_E S$
Stoyte, John	Db	1789	1793	1805	IS
Strachan, Alexander J.	L	1799	1800	1838	AJS
Strang, James	Ex	1705	1726	1748	JS
Stratford, Henry	S	1879	1879	1918	HS
Stratford, Henry, Ltd	L	–	1893	1901	HS
Stratford, William & Henry	S	1855	1853	1877	WS HS
Stratford–on–Avon Applied Art Studios	L	–	1920	–	–
Streeter & Co Ltd	L	–	1899	1906	–
Streetin, Thomas	L	1794	1789	1810	TS
Stroud, William	L	1788	1788	1812	WS
Styles, A.G.	L	–	1953	1968	–
Sudell, William	L	1767	–	1778	WS
Summers, William	L	–	1866	1890	–
Sumner, Mary	L	1807	–	1808	MS
Sumner, Mary & Eliza	L	1809	1809	1810	MS ES
Sumner, William I	L	1782	1777	1814	WS
Sumner, William II	L	1787	1788	1811	WS
Sumner, William I, & Crossley, Richard	L	1775	1774	1814	WS RC
Sutcliffe, R., & Co	S	1781	1789	1796	RS
Sutherland, Millicent	B	–	1914	1915	DSCG
Sutherland, Peter	Ed	–	1836	1847	PS
Sutters, John	Ch	–	1815	1889	JS
Sutton, James	L	1780	1780	1781	IS
Sutton, John	L	1697	1698	1708	SV
Sutton, Thomas	Db	1720	1717	1736	TS SU U_S
Sutton, William	L	1784	1782	1801	WS
Sutton, James, & Bult, James	L	1782	1766	1784	IS IB / IB IS
Swanson, Robert	L	1743	1743	1769	RS
Swift, John	L	1739	1729	1778	IS
Symonds, Pentecost, of Plymouth	Ex	1706	1706	1753	Sy SY PS
Sympsone, James	Ed	1687	1702	1709	IS monogram
Syng, Richard	L	1697	1698	1708	Sy
Tait, Benjamin	Db	1787	1785	1788	BT
Taitt, James	Ed	1704	1729	1741	T
Tanqueray, Ann	L	–	1726	1732	TA AT
Tanqueray, David	L	1713	1715	1724	TA DT
Tant, William	L	1762	1763	1779	WT
Tapley, John	L	1833	–	1848	IT
Tayleur, John	L	1775	1788	1790	IT
Taylor, Abraham	L	1796	1797	1799	AT
Taylor, Alfred	B	–	1854	1863	–
Taylor, James	Gl (also Gr)	1773	–	1780	IT
Taylor, John	Db	1729	1724	1734	IT
Taylor, Joseph	L	–	1832	1847	IT
Taylor, Joseph	B	–	1777	1845	IT
Taylor, Peter	L	1740	1743	1756	PT
Taylor, Phillip	L	–	1751	–	–
Taylor, Samuel	L	1744	1749	1772	ST
Taylor, William	Ed	1753	1757	1766	WT
Taylor, A. & Son	Gl	–	1900	–	AT&S
Taylor, W. & J.	Ed	–	1771	1777	WT I T
Taylor, John, & Perry, John	B	1832	1829	1849	T&P
Taylor & Woodward	L (also B)	–	1810	1820	–
Teare, John	Db	1796	1819	1843	IT
Tearle, Thomas	L	1719	1718	1739	TE (E smaller) TT
Terrey, John Edward	L	1816	1815	1847	IET
Terry, John	L	1818	–	1825	IT
Terry, Carden, & Williams, Jane	Co (also Db)	–	1795	1821	T&W CT IW C&T I&W

Maker's name	Town of registration	Earliest mark registration	Earliest example	Latest example	Maker's mark/notes
Tessiers, Edward, Ltd	L	–	1911	1971	–
Theed, William (partner Rundell, Bridge & Rundell c.1814)					
Theobalds, William	L	1829	1829	1840	WT
Theobalds, William, & Atkinson, Robert	L	1838	1838	1840	WT RA
Theobalds, William, & Bunn, Lockington	L	1835	1835	–	WT LB
Thomas, C.H. & J.W.	L	–	1911	1925	C^{T}H J W
Thomas, David, J.	L	–	1960	–	–
Thomas, Francis Boone, & Co	L	1874	–	1933	–
Thomason, Edward	B	1821	1813	1848	ET
Thomason (or Thompson), John	Y	1633	1635	1679	IT
Thompson, Albert Henry	S	1885	1889	1900	–
Thompson, G.	Gl	1833	1829	1837	GT
Thompson, James	S	1868	–	1877	JT
Thompson, Samuel	Nc	–	1750	1785	ST
Thompson, William	Db	1795	–	1797	WT
Thorne, Samuel	L	1697	1704	1705	TH
Thornhill, Walter, & Co	L	–	1875	1884	FP
Thropp & Taylor	B	1810	1810	1827	T&T
Thurkle, Francis	L	1783	–	1793	FT
Tibbitts, James	S	1778	1775	1776	IT JT
Ticknell, Alexander	Db	1784	–	1797	AT
Timberlake, James	L	1743	–	1759	IT
Timbrell, Robert	L	1697	1690	1714	Ti
Timbrell, Robert, & Bell, Joseph I	L	–	1710	1715	TiB$_e$
Timm, F.E. see Jenkins & Timm	S				
Toleken, John	Co	–	1795	1836	IT TOLEKEN
Tookey, Elizabeth	L	–	1770	–	ET
Tookey, James	L	1750	1761	1766	IT
Tookey, Thomas	L	1773	1778	1780	TT
Toone, William	L	1725	1725	1729	To WT
Tough, Philip	Db	1705	1708	1714	PT
Townsend, Charles	Db	1770	1770	1776	CT
Townsend, Thomas	Db	1797	–	1805	TT
Townsend, William	Db	1736	1734	1753	WT
Traherne, Benjamin	L	1697	–	1700	Tr
Traies, William	L	1822	1821	1846	WT
Tricket, Robert	S	1773	1775	1803	RT RT&Co
Tripe, Anthony	Ex	1712	1695	1731	Tr AT monogram
Tripp, Job	L	1754	1754	–	IT
Troby, John	L	1787	1797	1801	IT
Troby, William Bamforth	L	1812	1822	1830	WT
Trowbridge, George	Ex	1710	1711	1717	TR
Truss, William, of Reading	L	1721	1710	1725	TR WT
Tucker, W., & Co	S	1796	1796	1815	WT&Co
Tudor, Richard	Db	–	1775	1791	RT
Tudor, Thomas	Db	1797	1815	1816	TT
Tudor, Henry, & Leader, Thomas	S	1773	1773	1795	HT TL
Tudor & Whitford	Db	–	1806	1807	T&W
Tuite, Elizabeth	L	1741	–	–	ET
Tuite, John	L	1721–5	1714	1759	IT
Tuite, William	L	–	1759	1771	WT
Tuppy, Abraham	Db	1761	1768	1786	AT
Turner, Francis	L	1709	1718	1734	Tu FT
Turner, George	Ex	–	1810	1834	GT
Turner, James	L	1804	–	1808	IT
Turner, James, & Fox, Charles I	L	1801	1801	–	CJF T
Turner, John	B	–	1801	1803	IT
Turner, Thomas	S	1853	–	1890	TT
Turner, William	L	1754	1755	1768	WT
Turnpenny, William & Edward	B	1844	1845	1847	W&ET
Turton, Mehatabell	L	1798	–	1804	MT
Turton, William	L	1773	1774	1788	WT
Tweedie, John	L	1783	1792	1793	IT
Tweedie, Walter	L	1775	1765	1825	WT
Twell, William	L	1709	1717	1718	TW
Twycross, Edward	Db	1831	1828	1832	TWY
Twycross, John	Db	1803	1819	1824	–

Maker's name	Town of registration	Earliest mark registration	Earliest example	Latest example	Maker's mark/notes
Twycross, John & Son	Db	–	1832	–	–
Tye, George, & Kilner, James	B	1826	1826	–	T&K
Tyrill, Robert	L	1742	–	1743	RT
Underwood, Wilkinson & Co	S	1826	–	1827	UW &Co
Unite, George	B (also S)	1832	1830	1910	GU
Unite & Hilliard	B	1825	1826	1842	U&H
Ure, Archibald	Ed	1715	1725	1739	AU
Ure, William	Ed	1715	1717	1730	WU WV
Urquhart, Leonard	Ed	–	1825	1844	LU
Urquhart, Duncan, & Hart, Naphtali	L	1791	1789	1812	DU U&H NH
Vale Bros & Serman	L (also Ch)	–	1902	–	–
Vander, C.J., Ltd	L (also S)	–	1931	1973	–
Vander, Henry & Arthur	L	–	1907	1924	–
Vander, J.	L	–	1886	1897	–
Varden, Samuel & Thomas	L	1775	1784	1785	SV TV
Vechte, Antoine (designer and maker for Hunt & Roskell)	L	–	1835	1853	–
Venables, Stephen	L	–	1640	1665	SV
Vere, John Henry, & Lutwyche William	L	–	1761	1768	$W_L^I V$
Vickery, James	L	–	1855	–	–
Vickery, J.C.	L (also B & Ch)	–	1904	1925	–
Videau, Ayme	L	1726	1733	1759	AV
Villiers & Jackson	B	–	1953	1957	–
Vincent, Edward	L	1712	1713	1740	VI EV
Vincent, Henry	L	1783	–	1798	HV
Vincent, William	L	–	1766	1817	WV
Viner, Emile Viners Ltd	S	–	1921	1965	EV
Waite, Thomas	Y	1613	1630	1655	TW monogram
Wakefield, John	L	1806	1809	1836	IW
Wakeley, Arthur	L	–	1884	1969	
Wakeley & Wheeler Ltd (also Ed, Ch & Db)	L	–	1884	1969	F JC W W W&W
Wakelin, Edward	L	1747	1741	1762	EW
Wakelin, John, & Garrard, Robert I	L	1792	1792	1819	IW RG
Wakelin, John, & Taylor, William	L	1776	1776	1801	IW WT
Walker, George	Ch	–	1768	1794	GW
Walker, Joseph I	Db	1690	1693	1708	IW
Walker, Joseph II	Db	1710	1717	1740	IW IW monogram
Walker, Mathew	Db	1716	1717	1730	MW
Walker, Samuel	Db	–	1738	1759	SW
Walker, Samuel, & Co	S	1836	1836	1837	SW &Co
Walker, Thomas	Db	1714	1715	1728	TW
Walker & Hall (also B & Ch)	S	1862	1883	1968	W&H HH& JEB
Walker, Knowles & Co	S	1840	1819	1854	WK &Co
Walker, Walter, & Tolhurst, Brownfield	L	–	1889	1904	–
Wall, John	L	1783	–	1790	IW
Wall, Thomas	L	1708	1723	1728	WA
Walley, Joseph	Ch	–	1780	1786	IW
Walley, Ralph	Ch	–	1682	1692	RW
Wallis, Robert	L	–	1837	1850	–
Wallis, Thomas I	L	1758	1766	1767	TW
Wallis, Thomas II	L	1778	1783	1809	TW
Wallis, Thomas II, & Hayne, Jonathan	L	1810	1813	1820	TW JH
Walsh, Peter	Db	–	1831	1844	PW
Walsh, White	L	1698	1698	–	Wa
Walsh, William	Db	1745	1740	1753	WW
Walton, John	Nc	–	1802	1860	IW
Ward, Joseph	L	1697	1697	1722	Wa WA
Ward, Rowland, & Co Ltd	L	–	1889	1920	–
Ward, William	Db	1774	1782	1807	WW

Maker's name	Town of registration	Earliest mark registration	Earliest example	Latest example	Maker's mark/notes
Wardell, William, & Kempson, Peter	B	1813	–	1819	W&K
Warick, James	L	–	1901	1919	–
Warris, George	S	–	1900	–	–
Wastell, Samuel	L	1701	1702	1722	WA SW
Waterhouse, George, & Co	S	1842	1842	1847	W&S W&Co
Waterhouse, John; Hatfield, E., & Co	S	1836	1840	1845	JW EH
Waterhouse, Hodgson & Co	S	1822	1824	1835	I&&CoIW
Waterhouse, I. & I., & Co					as above
Waters, James	L	1769	1769	1774	IW
Watherstone, E.J.	L	–	1704	–	–
Watson, John	S	1795	1778	1844	IW
Watson, Thomas	L	1784	1785	1790	TW
Watson, Thomas	Nc	–	1785	1842	TW
Watson, William, & Bradbury, Thomas	S	–	1790	1825	WW&TB
Watts, Benjamin	L	1698	1704	1718	Wa BW
Watts, Charles	L	1783	–	1803	CW
Watts, Richard	L	1710	1710	1720	Wa RW
Weeks, George	L	1735	1734	1737	GW
Weeks, P.	Db	–	1835	1836	PW
Weems, James	Ed	1738	1743	1763	IW
Weir, James	Gl	–	1895	1898	JW
Weir, T.	Db	1872	–	–	–
Weir & Sons	Db	–	1905	–	–
Welch, Robert	L	–	1954	1966	–
Welch, William, of Plymouth	Ex	–	1799	1837	WW
Welder, Samuel	L	1714	1715	1738	We SW
Wellby, Daniel & John	L	–	1878	1950	D&J W
Welles, Samuel Wight	L	1741	1748	1760	SW
Wells & Lambe	L	–	1863	1864	AB
Welsh, James	Ed	1746	1746	1774	IW
Welsh, John	Ed	1742	1762	1769	IW
Werritzer, Peter	L	1750	1741	1768	PW
West, Benjamin	L	1738	1737	1751	BW
West, George	Db	1793	1794	1833	GW
West, John	Db	1796	1767	1800	IW JW
West, Matthew	L	1697	1716	1793	WE
West, Matthew	Db	1769	1772	1826	MW
West, Langley Archer (West & Son)	Db	1877	1884	1894	LAW W&S
Weston, William	L	1810	1810	–	WW
Westwood, C., & Sons	B	–	1903	–	–
Wheat, Samuel	L	1756	1757	1782	SW
Wheatley, George	Db	–	1794	1797	GW
Wheatley, Samuel	L	1811	–	1819	SW
Wheatley, Samuel, & Evans, John	L	1810	1810	–	SW I E
Wheeler, Gervase	B	1831	1831	1841	GW
Wheeler, Mary, & Cronin, James Bartholomew	B	1842	1844	1845	–
Whipham, Thomas	L	1737	1737	1776	TW
Whipham, Thomas, & Williams, William I	L	1740	1739	1742	T^W_WW
Whipham, Thomas, & Wright, Charles	L	1757	1757	1781	T^C_WW
Whipple, J., & Co	Ex	–	1865	1880	JW &Co
White, Fuller	L	1744	1743	1773	FW
White, John	L	1719	1722	1736	Wh WH IW
White, Samuel	L	1759	–	1766	SW
White, Henderson & Co	S	1866	1871	1878	W & W J H
White & Johnstone	S	1859	1862	1863	WW T J
Whitfield, William	Nc	1720	1720	1746	Wh WW
Whitford, Richard	Db	1802	1799	1827	RW
Whitford, Samuel I	L	1764	1762	1825	SW
Whitford, Samuel II	L	1800	1816	1864	SW
Whitford, George & Samuel II	L	1802	1802	1807	S$_W$G
Whitford, Samuel II, & Pizey, George	L	1810	1810	–	SW GP
Whitehill, Christopher	Y	1676	1684	1693	CW
Whiting, John James	L	1833	1833	1860	IW
Whittingham, John	L	1788	1790	1797	IW
Whyte, David	L	–	1762	1768	DW
Whyte, David, & Holmes, William	L	–	1763	1767	D^W_HW

Maker's name	Town of registration	Earliest mark registration	Earliest example	Latest example	Maker's mark/notes
Wickes, George	L	1722	1719	1757	WI GW GW (W within)
Wigan, Thomas, of Bristol	L	1763	–	1801	TW
Wilcock, Richard, of Plymouth	Ex	1704	1707	1717	Wi WI
Wilford, Starling	L	1718	1722	1734	WI SW
Wilkes, Booth see Booth Wilkes					
Wilkinson, Henry, & Co Ltd	S (also L & B)	1831	1815	1920	HW &Co
Wilkinson, Thomas & Sons	B	–	1867	1902	–
Wilks, Dennis	L	1737	1737	1741	DW
Wilks, James	L	1722	1724	1748	WI IW
Willats, Thomas	L	1809	1809	1810	TW
Willaume, David I	L	1697	1698	1744	WI DW
Willaume, David II	L	1728	1725	1743	WI DW
Williams, James	Ex	1717	1724	1732	IW
Williams, J., & Co	Ex	1857	–	1879	–
Williams, John	Co	–	1791	1795	WI
Williams, James & Josiah	Ex	–	1849	1873	–
Williams, Josiah, & Co	Ex	–	1878	–	–
Williams, Richard	L	1712	1713	1714	WI
Williams, Richard	Db	1752	1767	1800	RW
Williams, Robert	L	1726	1724	1728	WI RW
Williams, Robert	Db	1789	1789	1798	RW
Williams, Robert, James & Josiah	Ex	–	1847	1852	RW JW JW
Williams, William I	L	1740	1743	1758	WW
Williams, Zachariah	Ex	1720	1717	1721	Wi
Williams Brothers see J. & J. and R., J. & J. Williams					
Williams (Birmingham) Ltd	B	–	1902	1918	–
Williamson, H., Ltd	B	–	1901	1922	HWLd
Williamson, John	Db	1716	1734	1737	IW
Williamson, Robert	Y	1623	1623	1679	RW
Williamson, Thomas	Db	1726	1730	1751	TW
Williamson, William	Db	1726	1728	1782	WW
Willis, Mark & Son Ltd	S	1875	1885	1912	–
Willmore, Joseph	B	–	1790	1846	JW
Willmore, Thomas	B	1773	1790	1828	TW
Willmore & Alston	B	–	1777	1802	TW
Wilms, Albert (designer for Elkingtons 1857)	B	–	1851	1894	–
Wilson, Joseph	L	–	1807	1844	IW
Wilson & Sharp Ltd	Ed (also Gl & B)	–	1866	1935	W&S
Wimans, Edward	L	1697	1697	1704	WI
Wimbush, Thomas	L	1828	1828	1833	TW
Wimbush, Thomas, & Hyde, Henry	L	1834	1833	–	TW HH
Winder & Lamb	Db	–	1861	1883	W&L
Winter, John, & Co	S	1773	1773	1814	IW&Co
Winter, Thomas	S	–	1810	–	–
Wintle, James	L	1812	1815	1838	IW JW
Wintle, George	L	1787	1791	1826	GW
Wirgman, John	L	1751	1744	1754	IW
Wisdome, John	L	1704	1713	1719	WI IW
Wish, George	S	1879	1900	1932	–
Wish, Sampson & Co	S	1873	–	1876	–
Withers, William	L	1762	1762	1764	WW
Wood, Edward	L	1722	1723	1759	WO EW
Wood, Samuel	L	1733	1725	1774	SW
Woodward, Charles	L	1741	1742	1776	CW
Woodward, William	L	1731	1742	1747	WW
Wooller, William	L	1750	–	1764	WW
Workman, Edward	Db	1702	1708	1719	EW
Worthington, William	L	1771	1762	1772	WW
Wrangham, John, & Moulson, William	L	1822	1823	1839	I W WM
Wren, John II	L	1777	1785	1802	IW
Wright, Charles	L	1775	1768	1782	CW
Wright, Thomas	L	1721	1750	1756	TW
Wright, William Thomas, & Davies, Frederick	L	1864	1870	1891	WW FD

Maker's name	Town of registration	Earliest mark registration	Earliest example	Latest example	Maker's mark/notes
Wright, Charles, & Whipham, Thomas	L	1757	1757	1781	T^C_WW
Wright, Jonathan, & Fairbairn, George	S	1809	1809	1812	W&F
Wyatt, Joseph	L	1789	1790	1791	JW
Wyke, Robert	Db	1784	1781	–	RW
Wynn, Thomas, of Bath	L	1754	1753	1783	TW
Yapp, John, & Woodward, John	B (also L)	1845	1845	1854	Y&W
Yate, Benjamin	L	–	1624	1634	BY
Yates, William	S	–	1921	1976	–
Yorke, Edward	L	1705	1709	1731	YO EY
Yorstoun, Mungo	Ed	1702	1710	1719	MY
Young, James	L	1760	1769	1792	IY
Young, James, & Jackson, Orlando	L	1774	1773	1774	IY OI
Younge, John T., & Sons	S	1788	1778	1822	ITY &Co ITY&Co
Young, Greaves & Hoyland	S	1779	1780	1786	YG&H
Young, S.C., & Co	S	1811	1811	1836	SCY &Co
Zeigler, Alex	Ed	1782	1768	1827	AZ
Zeigler, John	Ed	1798	1806	1807	IZ
Zimmerman, A. & J.	B	–	1897	1934	A& JZ
Zouch, Richard	L	1735	1734	1740	RZ

* Date separation between generations is uncertain.
(?) Identity of maker or mark is uncertain.

GLOSSARY

Acanthus Formal leaf decoration representing the acanthus plant. Usually embossed.

Adam, Robert (1728–1792) Architect. Originator of the Adam style. Studied classical remains in Italy. Noted for his buildings in London. Published *Works in architecture* in 1779.

Angular Style of silverware popular in the 1860s and 1870s, characterized by exaggerated angles and tapers.

Annulet Small ring or circle.

Anthemion Decoration representing honeysuckle blossom.

Arts and Crafts Movement Formed c.1880 to promote the reform of design, based on the ideas of William Morris.

Ashbee, Charles Robert (1863–1942) Architect. Founded Guild and School of Handicrafts in 1887. Follower of William Morris. Wrote *Modern English Silverwork*, published in 1908.

Assay A test to determine the proportions of different metals in an alloy.

Assay mark Mark stamped after assay to signify satisfactory quality.

Assay Office Place where the assay is made and the mark of origin stamped.

Baluster A pillar, column or stem of varying diameter.

Bateman, Hester (1709–1794) Notable woman silversmith and head of a family of silversmiths. Worked between 1763 and 1795.

Beading Decoration composed of a row of bead shapes.

Benson, W.A.S. (1854–1924) Follower of William Morris. Designer and maker of silverware in the 1880s, when he opened a shop in Bond Street. His style is noted for its simplicity and originality.

Blue john A variegated fluorspar mined in Derbyshire. Used for making ornamental vessels, often with ormolu. Used extensively by Matthew Boulton.

Bombe Slightly bulging, inflated or blown out.

Boulsover, Thomas Invented Old Sheffield plate in 1742.

Boulton, Matthew (1728–1809) English engineer and inventor. Founded Soho Works, Birmingham in 1762. Manufactured much fine silverware in the Adam style. Early partnership with John Fothergill.

Bright cut engraving Fine engraving by bevel cutting to give a sparkle finish.

Cable moulding Moulding or edging in the form of a cable or rope.

Cameo A decoration carved in relief.

Carr, Alwyn Partner of Omar Ramsden, with whom he worked in the early twentieth century, producing wares in *art nouveau* style.

Caryatid A representation of a female figure used in place of a column to support an entablature.

Cast Shaped by using a mould.

Catton, Charles (1756–1819) Designer employed by many manufacturers of silver plate.

Chalice A wine cup used at Communion services.

Chase Surface decoration engraved with the use of a hammer and punch.

Chine A ridge crest.

Chinoiserie Decoration displaying Chinese influence. Particularly popular 1680–1685 and again around 1750 and 1820.

Chippendale Gothic Pierced decoration popular in the Adam period, 1770–1800.

Cinquecento Style of the art of the fifteenth century or Renaissance period.

Collet A decoration in the shape of a ring or collar.

Cut card work Decoration of geometric or foliate shapes cut out and applied to silverware.

Dixon, Arthur (1856–1929) Produced silver with simple, undecorated shaped and hammered surfaces. Founded Birmingham Guild of Handicrafts in 1895.

Dresser, Christopher (1834–1904) Designer noted for his use of functional and plain shapes. Produced numerous designs for silver in the 1870s and 1880s. Published *Grammar of Ornament* in 1857.

Electroplate Copper or other metal plate coated with a covering of silver by a process of electrolysis. Patented by Elkington of Birmingham in 1840.

Embossing Decoration produced by pressing or knocking parts of the surface into relief. Sometimes called *repoussé* work.

Encyclopaedia of Ornament Written by Knight in 1834. An important source of inspiration in ornamental designs and patterns. Subscribed to by several leading silversmiths.

Erased Torn off, so as to leave jagged edges.

Etruscan Pertaining to the Roman finds at Etruria, an ancient state of Italy north of the Tiber. Etruscan shapes form the basis of Adam decoration.

Faceted Composed of small flat surfaces.

Feather edge Edge decoration produced by chased slanted lines.

Finial The terminus of a pinnacle of ornamental handle.

Flat chasing Hammered decoration in low relief.

Flaxman, John (1755–1826) English sculptor. Designer of

silverware for Rundell, Bridge & Rundell including Achilles Shield in 1818.

Fluting Decoration, usually embossed or parallel semi-tubular furrows.

Fothergill, John (c.1700–1782) Partner of Mattheww Boulton.

Frampton, George (1860–1928) English sculptor. Designer and metalworker in beaten silver. Used riveted joints.

Functionalism A style subordinating all features to an object's primary use or function.

Gadroon Decoration composed of short channels or grooves, to form a cable or bead, usually applied in strips or on edges.

Girdle A moulded band round the centre of a vessel to strengthen it or as ornament. Also known as a midband.

Gothic Resembling the architectural style with pointed arches and clustered columns.

Guild and School of Handicrafts Founded in 1887 by C.R. Ashbee to promote his ideas on design.

Hallmarks Authorized marks or symbols on precious metals to guarantee the quality of the metal.

Herculaneum Ancient city of south Italy, buried when Vesuvius erupted in AD 79, and excavated in 1738. The finds later influenced design and decoration.

Hogarth, William (1697–1764) English painter. Engraver on silver plate for master silversmiths.

Incuse Hammered or impressed by stamping.

Jones, Owen (1809–1874) English architect. Influenced silver design in the 1860s. Published *The Polychromatic Ornament of Italy* in 1846 and *Grammar of Ornament* in 1856.

Knop A bulbous part of a stem, baluster or pillar.

Liberty & Co Makers and retailers of silverware etc. Started business as an oriental warehouse in 1875. First to engage designers of the Functionalism and Art Nouveau movements.

Lobed Decorated with lobes or bulges.

Marks, Gilbert (1861–1905) Silversmith noted for his hand-crafted work.

Medallion Medal shape, roundel or cameo incorporated in designs or applied to silverware as decoration. Used extensively in the Adam period. Most famous designer and supplier was James Tassie (1735–1799).

Moorish A style based on North African or Spanish shapes and designs, popular in early Victorian times and later revived.

Morris, William (1834–1896) English poet, artist, designer, printer and social reformer. Published *Designs for Silver* in 1887.

Moulding A decorative strip or shape usually applied to surfaces or edges.

Mullet A five-pointed star.

Naturalism A style in which forms and shapes are designed in imitation of natural forms, popular about 1830 and later revived.

Ogee An S-shaped curve.

Old Sheffield plate A substitute for silver, invented by Thomas Boulsover in 1742, consisting of copper plate fused between thin sheets of silver.

Ormolu A yellowish metal alloy of copper, zinc and sometimes tin.

Oviform Oval or egg-shaped.

Palladian An architectural style featuring pillars and entablature introduced by Andrea Palladio (1518–1580) and later revived.

Pellet A small, rounded boss.

Pistrucci, Benedetto Gem engraver. Designer of important silverware for Rundell, Bridge & Rundell.

Planishing Shaping by hammering with an oval-faced tool.

Pompeii Ancient city of south Italy, buried when Vesuvius erupted in AD 79. Excavations began in the 1750s, the finds later influencing design shapes and forms.

Raising The method of forming a hollow vessel from a flat sheet by hammering.

Ramsden, Omar (1873–1929) Notable maker of art nouveau silver, after about 1900 in partnership with Alwyn Carr.

Reeding Decoration composed of thin parallel ribs.

Reed and Tie Parallel moulding with crossed straps.

Renaissance Rebirth or revival of the arts in the fifteenth century, producing styles that were later revived.

Rococo A style of decoration originating in France, based on endless multiplication of ornamental detail and exaggerated refinement. One of its outstanding masters was Juste-Aurèle Meissonier (1675–1750). Popular for 40 to 50 years after about 1725, with later revivals.

Roman imperial Noble form of classical decoration popular in the Regency period.

Romantic A style associated with exaggerated classical ornamentation.

Roundel A circular or disc-shaped decoration.

Smee, Dr Demonstrated first successful electroplating experiment in 1840. First applied on a commercial scale by Elkington of Birmingham.

Soane, Sir John (1753–1837) English architect. Studied classical remains in Italy and founded museum with his collection.

Storr, Paul (1771–1844) One of the most important English silversmiths, second only to Paul de Lamerie. Apprenticed to Andrew Fogelberg c.1785, and obtained his freedom to trade in 1793.

Stothard, Thomas (1755–1834) English painter, whose designs were used by Paul Storr and others.

Swag A decoration in the form of a festoon or hanging cluster of flowers, leaves or drapes, usually embossed.

Tassie, James (1735–1799) Maker and supplier of medallions or cameos to the metalwork and pottery trades.

Tatham, Charles Heathcote (1772–1842) Architect. Author of *Designs of Ornamental Plate*, published in 1806.

Touch The maker's mark which is impressed with a punch.

Trilobe A three-lobed decoration.

Volute Decoration in the form of a spiral scroll.

Wyatt, Sir Matthew Digby (1820–1877) English architect and designer. Author of *Metalwork and its Artistic Design*, published in 1852, *Industrial Arts of the Nineteenth Century* (1853) and *Art of Illumination* (1860).

BIBLIOGRAPHY

Adam Silver by Robert Rowe, Faber & Faber 1965.

Adam Silver, V & A Museum Publications, H.M.S.O. 1953.

Antique English Silver and Plate by L.G.G. Ramsay, The Connoisseur 1962.

Charles II Domestic Silver, V & A Museum Publications, H.M.S.O. 1949.

Collectors' Terms by Michael Goodwin, Country Life 1967.

A Dictionary of Marks by Margaret Macdonald-Taylor, Connoisseur 1962.

Discovering Hallmarks by John Bly, Shire Publications 1968.

Early Stuart Silver, V & A Museum Publications, H.M.S.O. 1950.

Encyclopaedia of Antiques, Connoisseur 1962.

English Domestic Silver by Charles Oman, A & C Black 1934.

English Silver Drinking Vessels 600–1830 by Douglas Ash, G. Bell & Sons 1964.

English Silver Hallmarks by Judith Banister, W. Foulsham & Co 1970.

English Silversmiths' Work by Charles Oman, H.M.S.O. 1965.

The Great Silver Manufactory by Eric Delieb & Michael Roberts, Studio Vista 1971.

Guide to Marks of Origin on Silver Plate, J.W. Northend 1964.

Guinness Book of Silver by Geoffrey Wills, Guinness Superlatives 1983.

Hallmarks, Assay Offices of Great Britain 1984.

Hallmarks & Date Letters on Gold & Silver, N.A.G. Press 1944.

Hallmarks on Gold & Silver Plate by William Chaffers, Reeves & Turner 1905.

Hester Bateman by David S. Shure, W.H. Allen 1959.

History of Old Sheffield Plate by Frederick Bradbury, J.W. Northend 1912.

Huguenot Silver in England by J.F. Hayward, Faber & Faber 1959.

Investing in Silver by Eric Delieb, Barrie & Rockcliff 1967.

Irish Silver, V & A Museum Publications, H.M.S.O. 1959.

The London Goldsmiths and Their Marks by Sir Charles J. Jackson FSA, Batsford 1949.

The London Goldsmiths 1200–1800 by Sir Ambrose Heal, Cambridge University Press 1935.

London Goldsmiths 1697–1837 by Arthur J. Grimwade, Faber & Faber 1976.

The Marks of the London Goldsmiths & Silversmiths by John P. Fallon, David & Charles 1972.

Mid-Georgian Silver, V & A Museum Publications, H.M.S.O. 1952.

Mid-Victorian Silver, V & A Museum Publications, H.M.S.O. 1950.

Old English Plate by W.J. Cripps, John Murray 1891.

Old Silver Spoons by Norman Gask, Herbert Jenkins 1926.

Paul Storr by N.M. Penzer, B.T. Batsford 1954.

Queen Anne Domestic Silver, V & A Museum Publications, H.M.S.O. 1951.

The Queen's Silver by Arthur J. Grimwade, The Connoisseur 1953.

Regency Silver, V & A Museum Publications, H.M.S.O. 1952.

Royal Plate, V & A Museum Publications, H.M.S.O. 1954.

Sheffield by Mary Walton, The Sheffield Telegraph 1948.

Sheffield Plate by Bertie Wyllie, George Newnes.

Sheffield Plate, V & A Museum Publications, H.M.S.O. 1955.

Silver by Gerald Taylor, Penguin 1956.

Silver by Geoffrey Wills, John Gifford 1969.

Silver Collecting for Amateurs by James Henderson CBE, Frederick Muller 1965.

Victorian Silver by Patricia Wardle, Herbert Jenkins 1963.